What Have We Done?

What Have We Done?

The Foundation for Global Sustainability's State of the Bioregion Report for the Upper Tennessee Valley and the Southern Appalachian Mountains

by

John Nolt
Philosophy Department
University of Tennessee, Knoxville

Athena Lee Bradley

Mike Knapp

Donald Earl Lampard

Jonathan Scherch
College of Social Work
University of Tennessee, Knoxville

The Foundation for Global Sustainability
is a member of Community Shares

Earth Knows Publications
Washburn, Tennessee

Photography Copyright © 1991-1996 by Mignon Naegeli
Design/Production by Maggie Kalen

THIS BOOK WAS PRINTED ON RECYCLED PAPER CONTAINING 30% POST-CONSUMER WASTE

Library of Congress Cataloging-in-Publication Data

Nolt, John Eric
Bradley, Athena Lee
Knapp, Mike
Lampard, Donald Earl
Scherch, Jonathan
    What have we done?

    Bibliography
1. Tennessee River watershed—environmental conditions. 2. Appalachian Region, Southern—environmental conditions
GE155.T3W53 1997 97-60066
ISBN: 0-9644659-2-2

10 9 8 7 6 5 4 3 2 1

CONTENTS

Water in the air

Water that falls in the mountains

Water that falls on fields

Water that falls on asphalt

Flotsam

The old river

Siltation

Toxic sediments

Suffocating waters

Hot water

Surface water pollution

River traffic

Wetlands

Groundwater

Municipal water supplies

The great smoggy mountains

Tropospheric (ground-level) ozone

Stratospheric ozone

Noise

Toxic air, indoors

Toxic air, outdoors

Climate change

What will they breathe?

ACKNOWLEDGEMENTS

The aim of this report is wildly interdisciplinary. No person or group has the qualifications to write such a thing. We, the authors, would not have had the audacity to do it were it not for two circumstances: (1) if we didn't, the stories that are told here in interrelation would be told only piecemeal, so that the big picture could not be generally appreciated, and (2) dozens of generous individuals—each of whom knew something (often many things) that we didn't—offered us their help.

Many people contributed to the research. Among these we want especially to thank Chelsea Reiff, whose month-long internship with FGS provided a wealth of material; Stuart Chapin, who did much of the research for Chapter Five; and Henry Queener and Karen Thomason, who researched Chapter Seven. Many others made important contributions to the research: Aubrey Baldwin, Rachel Ballard, Richard Buckner, Vickie Bott, Roger Clapp, Ginger Lea Clark, Meredith Crosby, Nancy Dumler, Brad Edmonson, Linda Ewald, Robin Hathaway, Wes Heinlein, Dean T. Howell, Marcia Hupfel, Sara Burns Hutchins, Andrew Hutsell, Hugh Irwin, Todd Irwin, Mark Lubkowitz, Brittany Mayfield, Suneel Mendiratta, Richard Tran Mills, Kate Newton, John Reiff, Becky Rountree, Laurie Schwab, Neal Shelton, Bradford Smith, David Tindell, and Kevin Wagoner.

Some top-notch reviewers read all or part of the manuscript. Not all of them agreed with everything they read, but all gave generously of their time and effort. We would especially like to thank Jim Renfro of the National Park Service; Cliff Amundsen, Sherry Cable, Dan Deffenbaugh, Stan Guffey, and Mike McKinney of the University of Tennessee, Knoxville; John Peine of the National Biological Service; Jack Barkenbus, Mary English, Dean Menke, and Catherine Wilt of U.T.s Energy, Environment, and Resources Center; Karen Anderson of the Knoxville Recycling Coalition; and Niki Nicholas and Peggy Shute of TVA. Harry Rothwell meticulously edited nearly the entire manuscript. Others who reviewed or edited portions of the work were Doug Daigle, Bob Grimac, Michelle Hall, Brandon Holton, Cielo Myczack, Wolf Naegeli, Michelle Neal, Brownie Newman, and Stephen Smith.

Maggie Kalen did the layout and design with cool grace under the pressure of severe deadlines. Marcia Wasserman smoothly coordinated publication for Earth Knows. Mignon Naegeli added her wonderfully evocative photography.

Narrow Ridge Earth Literacy Center, through the generosity of McGregor Smith, provided the seed-money for publication.

We would also like to thank George W. Benz for allowing us to see prepublication chapters of Benz and Collins' *Aquatic Fauna in Peril: The Southeastern Perspective*. Finally, we are grateful to the Merck Family Fund for permission to quote from their report "Yearning for Balance, July 1995."

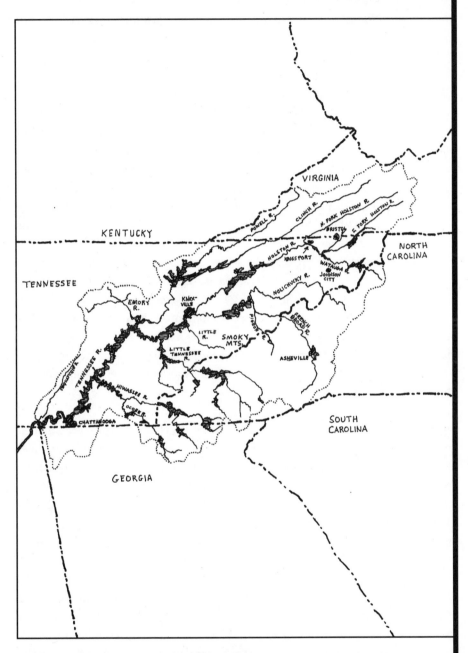

FIGURE 1: The Upper Tennessee Valley and Southern Appalachian Mountains. Dotted lines indicate the boundary of the Upper Tennessee watershed.

...they have trodden my portion under foot, they have made my pleasant portion a desolate wilderness. They have made it desolate and being desolate it mourneth unto me; the whole land is made desolate, because no man layeth it to heart.

—Jeremiah 12:10-11

When the naturalist William Bartram arrived in the Southern Appalachian Mountains just before the American Revolution, he found a pristine land. From the dark cathedral forests, whose ancient trees, wider than a man could reach, rose like pillars to a distant green sunlit canopy, to the wave upon wave of misty blue peaks receding to apparent infinity, this land was wide and pure, both old and young, both rugged and gentle. Its beauty still echoes in the exuberance of his words: *I traveled some miles over a varied situation of ground, exhibiting views of grand forests, dark detached groves, vales and meadows ... flowering plants, and fruitful strawberry beds ... the unparalleled cascade of Falling Creek, rolling and leaping off the rocks ... after this I entered a spacious forest, the land having gradually acquired a more level surface: a pretty grassy vale appears on my right, through which my wandering path led me, close by the banks of a delightful creek, which sometimes falling over steps of rocks, glides gently with serpentine meanders through the meadows. ... the land rises again with sublime magnificence, and I am led over hills and vales, groves and high forests, vocal with the melody of the feathered songsters; the snow-white cascades glittering on the sides of the distant hills.* [1] This is merely a sample. There are pages and pages of it.

But how different this land is today! Slashed by roads and power lines; studded with microwave towers; noisy with the motors of cars, trucks, jet airliners, and chainsaws; water and air polluted, the blue mist of the mountains now often a hazy sulfurous white; suburban sprawl flowing outward from cities small and large; the forests cut and cut again, the big trees all but gone, the solitude unrecoverable; the rivers dammed, tamed, and silting up; the meadows plowed, planted, paved. There are today few other regions in North America where so many assaults on nature intersect as the Upper Tennessee Valley and the Southern Appalachians.

The Cherokees knew the river as "The Long Man," *Yunwi Gunahita*. [2] Borrowing this image, we may picture the upper Tennessee River as a long man whose head is in the mountains of western Virginia and whose feet lie at the bottom of the upper valley near the city of Chattanooga. The Long Man draws in waters from the Cumberlands on the west, the Blue Ridge to the northeast, and the Great Smoky Mountains on the east, conveying them through a great valley of ridged plains southwestward toward northern Alabama. There the middle Tennessee turns west and the lower Tennessee back north, joining the Ohio at Paducah, Kentucky. But these further turnings will not concern us. This study is limited to the watershed of the Tennessee River above Nickajack Dam—a 22,000-square-mile area encompassing East Tennessee, western North Carolina, much of western Virginia, and a bit of northern Georgia (see Figure 1, page 1; a fuller definition is given in Appendix 1).

Today this land is fragmented and transformed by human impositions: dams and powerplants (hydroelectric, coal-fired, and nuclear); Interstates 40, 75, and 81, three of the most traveled highways in the country; the heavily contaminated land and water of the nuclear weapons production facilities and national laboratory at Oak Ridge (which ties with Rocky Flats, Colorado, for third rank among the nation's worst-polluted sites); and the fast-expanding urban sprawl of Chattanooga, Knoxville/Oak Ridge, Pigeon Forge, Asheville, Bristol, Johnson City, and Kingsport. Near these urban hubs, strip development, new roads, and industrial parks multiply and proliferate until it seems that they will swallow up everything.

Through the center of the valley flows the Long Man, the Tennessee River, impounded by the Tennessee Valley Authority (TVA) into four large reservoirs: Fort Loudoun, Watts Bar, Chickamauga, and Nickajack. The river is plugged up, like the circulatory system of a coronary patient, not only by these four dams, but by a total of forty-five dams, most of which lie along its tributaries. A century ago the free-flowing Tennessee harbored the greatest diversity of fresh-water mussels in the world. Today the mussels are rapidly disappearing from its silted, polluted, anoxic waters, many species of fish are going or gone, and unlimited recreational boating and private development along the banks have eroded the wetlands and riparian zones crucial to the stability of the ecological fragments that remain.

Once the river flowed past flourishing farms in rich bottomland. Many of these farms now lie inundated by the deep, permanent flood of the reservoirs. But many more have been claimed by urbanization, suburbanization, and the relentless economics of efficiency. The farms that remain grow hay, cattle, tobacco, and little else; and the valley, once inhabited by some of the sturdiest and most independent farmers on earth, can no longer feed itself, but must depend on a constant influx of tractor-trailers from the Midwest, California, and just about everywhere else.

West of the river, to the Long Man's right, lies the Cumberland Plateau. The pleasantly undulating skyline of the mountaintops is marred by strip mines and clearcuts. Much of this land is owned by coal and timber companies. Near

Chattanooga, the once impressively straight lines of the Plateau's edge are now studded with private residences, conspicuously perched atop the escarpments.

East of the river, to the Long Man's left, the valley rises to scenic hills riven by deep valleys which harbor remnants of the cove hardwood forests, the richest forest ecosystems in eastern North America. But these foothill-and-valley systems are increasingly degraded, especially in Blount and Sevier counties, by the glitter and glitz of tourist traps. Farther east, the slopes mount to the highlands of the Great Smoky Mountains National Park. Acidified soils and streams, ozone-damaged vegetation, traffic snarls, diminished visibility, and overuse threaten this last beleaguered remnant of the wilderness that inspired Bartram's rapture. At the crest of the Park, the unique spruce-fir forests are dying, and the entire Park is under mounting attack by invasive fungi, insects, and weedy plants introduced by human disturbance.

To the north, the Long Man reaches into western Virginia, branching into a multitude of headwaters: the Powell, Clinch, Holston, French Broad, Nolichucky, and Pigeon Rivers. Along the Holston at Kingsport and on the Pigeon at Canton, North Carolina, lie two of the nation's most notorious corporate polluters: Tennessee Eastman and Champion International Corporation. Both, despite genuine improvements (undertaken with much resistance) and extensive image-polishing (undertaken with a will), continue to damage water, land, and people.

To the south and east toward the Long Man's feet, the watershed includes the Hiwassee valley and the mine-ravaged Ocoee valley in northern Georgia and southeastern Tennessee. At Chattanooga the toxic waters of Chattanooga Creek, the region's most polluted stream, run (as do many of the most polluted waters) through the heart of low-income African-American communities.

And beneath the Long Man's feet from out of Mississippi and Alabama, a new wave of deforestation is arising that threatens soon to engulf the entire region. Multinational corporate giants, pitted against one another in a fierce competition for wood, have set their sights on the region's forests, which they plan to export, mostly as chips for paper pulp, down the Tennessee-Tombigbee Waterway to markets as far away as Korea and Japan.

We at the Foundation for Global Sustainability who work to defend and heal this land have long been frustrated at our inability to communicate the depth, breadth, and multiplicity of the assaults we face. Legislators, policymakers, educators, and citizens have a fragmentary awareness of some of the problems, but few have the interest or patience to develop a long-term synoptic ecological understanding. Yet ecological deterioration is systemic; a piecemeal approach misses the interrelations and cumulative impacts that give it urgency. What is needed is a deep, broad, long-term, multidimensional, multidisciplinary understanding—an understanding large enough to match our predicament. This *State of the Bioregion Report* is our contribution toward such an understanding. Over two years in the making, it is the effort of dozens of volunteers to synthesize our own experience, common sense, and the data from hundreds of scientific researchers into a coherent narrative.

Our report is emphatically not just one more bureaucratic or scientific assessment. We have striven for accuracy and accountability (hence the copious notes) and have made ample use of what the bureaucrats and scientists have discovered. But no contributor to this report has made or will make any money from it. As a result, we have not been subject to the pressures to distort or minimize or put the best face on things that inevitably come with a paycheck from an institution with vested interests. This does not, of course, mean that we are unbiased. On the contrary: we are passionately biased—by our love for the wild mountains, lush forests, and shining rivers of Southern Appalachia.

We make no apologies for these biases, for we have done our best to be truthful and not to mislead. But we acknowledge that our biases have focused our interests. Other people will find more salience in other truths.

This is unavoidable. The land we inhabit is infinitely complex, and every description of it—including this one—is finite. Every description, then, is infinitely negligent. All authors, even the most rigorously scientific, select the facts that seem significant to them (or to their discipline—or their bosses) and ignore the rest, and so shape their description with their values. Our discipline is protection and healing of the land, and those aims guide our description.

The description itself takes the form of a bioregional narrative—that is, a synoptic story of a land and its people. The land is the watershed of the Upper Tennessee Valley, which we conceive as a bioregion—a place with a unique ecology and culture. The people—the "we" of the title *What Have We Done?*—are the people, mostly of European descent, who conquered this land in the eighteenth century and who dominate it today. Its former inhabitants, the Cherokees, called this land *Katuah*. We do not yet know it well enough to give it a name of our own.

We have written a bioregional narrative, rather than a scientific report, because we aim not only at truth, but at meaning. Meaning, of course, is a function of what we value. In the public discourse of American culture, value is often reduced to its least common denominator: market value. This we mourn.

Our narrative is shaped by a different value: health. By "health" we mean wholesomeness, healedness, haleness, hallowedness, holiness, the integrity of the whole[3]—health not just of the body, but also of the land, the community, and the spirit; not just for those alive today but for those who will live here when we are gone; not just for human beings but for the entire community of life. Valuing health, we value much: the black bear and the red wolf, the Fraser fir and the Smoky madtom, the Tennessee River and the Cherokee National Forest, the child on our lap and the children to come. Through our narrative we aim to convey not only what is true about these things, but also their meaning when so valued.

We regret that what we report is often disheartening. But to be conscious of wounds is the first step toward shielding and healing them, while to ignore them may be fatal. Some people still insist that there are no serious environmental problems. Others, while acknowledging some general problems, seek in particular instances to reassure us that "the impact is so small it's not worth bothering about" or "it's still not good, but we're doing much better than we were twenty years ago," or "don't worry, we're only cutting twenty percent of the forest here." Taken in isolation, each of the problems represented by such remarks may in fact be insignificant. But the mistake is to take them in isolation. The sum of many individually insignificant acts of greed and negligence is widespread tragedy. But to see the tragedy takes broad vision—and steady resolve to overcome the lethargy of forgetfulness and denial. We must therefore ask much of the reader. Our narrative may cause pain, but (for those who value health) pain has a purpose.

CHAPTER 1

FIGURE 2: Flotsam on Douglas Reservoir.

For the Lord thy God bringeth thee into a good land, a land of brooks of water, of fountains and depths that spring out of valleys and hills.
— Deuteronomy 8:7

Water in the Air

Water comes into the Tennessee Valley by air. The air that brings it flows, when warm, from the tropical waters of the Gulf of Mexico or the Atlantic Ocean (sometimes in violent storms) and, when cold, from the frigid depths of the Canadian arctic. The predominant air flow, however, is from west to east: over the Cumberland plateau, down into the Tennessee Valley, and up again over the Southern Appalachians. The lift of the air as it streams up over the mountains cools it and often condenses its moisture. Then rain falls in the highlands—or, if it is very cold, snow. Hikers on the heath balds at the crest of the Smokies often see sinuous fogs rising up and over the peaks from the west and hear the rush of the air against the silence, eloquent testimony to the forces that shape Southern Appalachian weather.

Because they force the air to rise, condensing the moisture it contains, the Smokies are the wettest part of our bioregion. Some parts of the Smokies are temperate rainforest, with annual rainfalls exceeding a hundred inches per year. But about fifty inches, still an ample amount, is more typical for most of the region.

The rain is not, however, pure. Dotting the Ohio and Cumberland valleys to the northwest and along the Tennessee Valley are the tall stacks of coal-burning power plants—Widows Creek, Kingston, Bull Run, Gallatin, John Sevier, and others. The effluent from these stacks is nearly invisible: not the thick black smoke of early industrialism, but a hot diaphanous billow of oxides of carbon, sulfur, and nitrogen. Moved by the prevailing winds, it trails eastward in the lee of the stacks like the wakes of a flotilla of boats, spreading out in widening plumes. As it approaches the mountains, this polluted air gathers other effluents rising, mostly unseen, from the stacks of thousands of industries, from a multitude of commercial incinerators, and from the exhaust pipes of millions of cars and trucks: oxides, once again, of carbon, sulfur, and nitrogen; hydrocarbons; and, in smaller amounts, a host of such industrial toxics as modern chemistry has devised. The stories of the toxic chemicals, the carbon compounds, and other contaminants will be told mainly in Chapter Two. But the fate of the sulfur and nitrogen oxides lies with the water.

The chemical reactions that seal that fate occur in the clouds. Sulfur dioxide and nitrogen oxides, combining with moisture in the air, form sulfates, nitrates, and dilute sulfuric and nitric acids. Then the moisture cools and condenses to form acid rain, acid ice, acid snow, or acid fog. Dry acidic particles may also settle directly out of the air. All these forms of acidity are known collectively as "acid deposition." Acidity is measured on the pH scale. Lower numbers correspond to greater acidity. Natural precipitation has a pH of 5.0 to 5.6. But the scale is logarithmic, so that a reduction of pH by one unit indicates a tenfold increase in acidity. The average pH of precipitation in the Great Smoky Mountains National Park is 4.4, five to ten times more acidic than natural precipitation.[1] Precipitation with a pH as low as 3.5 has been recorded in recent years.[2] Clouds in the Smoky Mountains have a pH as low as 1.8—considerably more acidic than lemon juice or vinegar.[3]

Water that Falls in the Mountains

When rain falls in the mountains, the acidified water may plummet down mountain streams, to creeks and rivers, or it may disappear underground into the soil and groundwater. In either case, it finds its way eventually to the Tennessee River, which carries it to the Ohio, then the Mississippi, and ultimately the Gulf of Mexico. But the soil at the high elevations of the Smoky Mountains is so saturated with nitrogen deposited by the polluted air that it cannot absorb any more.[4] This means that it no longer has the capacity to neutralize the nitric acid before it runs off into streams or percolates down to the water table. In consequence, rain flushes pulses of acidity into the high streams. Though Southern Appalachian soils have a high sulfate absorption capacity, at the current rate of sulfate influx, that capacity will likely be overrun in a couple of decades. Then mountain soils will stop neutralizing the sulfuric acid as well, and the streams will be laden with still more acid.[5]

The average stream water pH in the most sensitive streams of the Great Smoky Mountains has dropped by almost half a unit over the last twenty years, indicating an approximately threefold increase in acidity. Some of the higher elevation streams have the highest nitrate concentration of any streams draining undisturbed watersheds in the U.S.[6] During heavy rains, stream acidity increases by a factor of ten.[7] Water samples from streams in the Smokies have measured as low as 4.9 to 5.1. If levels fall below 4.7, brook trout may die.[8]

The forests are already dying. Long-time visitors to Mount LeConte, which looms picturesquely above Gatlinburg, recall the red spruce and Fraser fir forest that covered its summit as recently as the 1980s. Now only the bleached skeletons of the trees stand above fields of acid-loving blackberry brambles. And even the blackberry leaves are shriveled and discolored—though as a result of a fungus rust, not of the acid. Over ninety-five percent of the mature trees at the top of Mount LeConte have died. The trees atop Mount Mitchell in North Carolina—at 6,684 feet the highest eminence east of the Mississippi—have been similarly devastated, as have the trees of many other high peaks. These dead forests leave even the most casual viewer with an overwhelming impression of bleakness and disease, yet the official reaction has often been a numbed silence. As Charles Little notes in his book, *The Dying of the Trees*, "These days Mount Mitchell is just barely mentioned in the tourist brochures. A once-popular destination for Blue Ridge vacationers, it is now evidently an embarrassment."[9]

The causes of the die-offs are complex. Infestation by the balsam woolly adelgid (an aphid-like insect resembling a small bit of white fuzz), which was unintentionally imported from Europe, is the immediate cause for the deaths of the Fraser firs. Beginning with the Reagan administration, and continuing even today, there has been strong political pressure to place the blame solely on such "natural" causes.[10] But just as an AIDS victim usually dies, not of AIDS itself, but of secondary infections, so the adelgid may not have been the sole cause of the dying of the fir trees, which may already have been seriously weakened by the effects of the acid.

While the role of acid deposition is controversial for the fir trees, for the red spruce it is well-confirmed. The red spruce are not infected by the adelgid, yet they are dying too. Research has shown that when nitrates and sulfates flow through the soil, they mobilize aluminum, which is naturally present in the soil. Normally, most of the aluminum is bound to other elements in the soil and unavailable to plants. An overdose of free aluminum inhibits root growth and interferes with the spruce tree's ability to absorb calcium and zinc, which are essential nutrients. Red spruce in the Smokies exhibit marked calcium and zinc deficiencies.[11]

Exposure to acid cloudwater also harms plants of many species directly by leaching nutrients from their leaves.[12] Fortunately, as the water moves down the mountain slopes, its acidity decreases and so does the damage. The limestone of the lower elevations and the valley floor is chemically basic, and it (together with the summer respiration of certain algae in the rivers and reservoirs) neutralizes the acid. By the time the water that falls as acid rain in the mountains reaches the

Tennessee River, it is no longer abnormally acidic. Thus the damage done by acid deposition appears to be limited mostly to the highlands. It is, however, spreading downward and outward year by year from the peaks, and the majestic spruce-fir forest of the high Southern Appalachians, the largest remaining forest of its type in the world, may already be damaged beyond recovery.

Water that Falls on Fields

But the rain falls elsewhere too. Some falls on pasture or croplands. The Southern Appalachian hills are much used for grazing, and many pastures extend right down to a river or stream bank. When they do, cattle consume the vegetation along banks, which then crumble and erode, filling the water with muddy silt. Fecal material washed or dropped into the stream contaminates it with viruses and bacteria, making the water unfit for drinking or swimming: swallowing the water may cause gastrointestinal disease; getting it into an open cut can cause infection.

The urine and feces of cattle are high in nitrogen and other nutrients, and these are washed into the streams and rivers. There they are joined by similar nutrients from other sources: leaking septic tanks, urban sanitary sewers or sewage treatment plants, and runoff of fertilizer from agricultural fields and suburban lawns. The combined influx of these nutrients into the waterways is often excessive, sometimes causing extreme growth of algae, which thrive on the nutrients. The algae cloud the water, making it green, and preventing sunlight from penetrating deeply. When they die, some algae release toxins powerful enough to irritate human skin and eyes. More significantly, the decay of dead algae that accumulate on the bottom deprives the water of oxygen. Low oxygen levels, prevalent in many TVA reservoirs, threaten fish and other forms of aquatic life.[13]

The effect of high nutrient runoff is dramatic where clear streams come down from the mountains. The Little River, for example, where it leaves the mountains near Townsend, Tennessee, is, even in the hot summer months, clear as crystal with a sandy and rocky bottom visible six feet below the surface almost as through unsullied air. Trout flit in and out of the shadows of trees near the river bottom. But near Rockford, only a few miles downstream, its summer waters have the appearance of muddy pea soup—the result of runoff of agricultural wastes and fertilizers and leakage from septic tanks—the latter a symptom of Blount County's rapid overdevelopment. By the time the Little River reaches the Tennessee, it is a sad, sluggish, mucky stream—and (to add injury to insult) its thick sediments are laced with carcinogenic PCBs, dumped several decades ago by The Aluminum Corporation of America (ALCOA) and TVA's Singleton Marine Ways facility.[14]

Runoff of nutrients into streams is facilitated by the destruction of their riparian corridors—the borders of vegetation that under natural conditions line a stream or river. Healthy streams in Southern Appalachia do not have bare, mown, or closely-cropped banks; they are lushly overhung by trees and bushes that provide shade and habitat for frogs, turtles, salamanders, herons, and other aquatic creatures. Riparian vegetation filters out contaminants and excessive nutrients before they reach the water, reduces stream-bank erosion, and traps much of the silt carried by surface runoff from fields during heavy rains. It also keeps the water shady and cool, reducing the growth of algae. Healthy streams are normally clear, and they have rocky bottoms rather than the thick oozy bottoms now so common, which are largely the result of disturbance by humans and livestock. While a winding stream through a closely-cropped pasture may be picturesque, it is no more natural or healthy than a typical suburban lawn.

A particularly embarrassing instance of riparian corridor destruction may be seen on the south bank of the Tennessee River just west of the Alcoa highway bridge in Knoxville. There on the agricultural campus of the University of Tennessee (where more enlightened standards ought to prevail), trees and bushes have been removed and fields are plowed almost to the river's edge, producing readily visible gullies and bank erosion.

Turbidity and siltation affect aquatic life. Silt can clog the gills and filter-feeding apparatus of many organisms. Turbidity may block vision and keep animals from finding their food. Many species of fish, insects, and mussels need rocky stream bottoms to reproduce, and many are, as a result, rare, threatened, endangered, or extinct. Most of these species, however, are small and secretive, so that their plight has scarcely been noticed. Their names are largely unfamiliar—Smoky madtom, blackside dace, yellowfin madtom, tippecanoe darter, southern brook lamprey, brook trout, flame chub, blue shiner, splendid darter, Tennessee dace, blotchside logperch, golden topminnow, redband darter, firebelly darter, spotfin chub, slackwater darter, Tuckasegee darter, Barrens topminnow—though one, the snail darter, once achieved a certain notoriety. Their stories will be told more fully in Chapter Three.

These creatures are also assaulted by the chemical-laden run-off from fields, railroad rights of way, or roadsides that have been treated with pesticides and herbicides. Intensely contaminated runoff may kill aquatic life directly; more diluted, it may increase the incidence of cancer and other maladies.

Water that Falls on Asphalt

Because of burgeoning urbanization—particularly around Knoxville, Oak Ridge, Chattanooga, Pigeon Forge, the Tri-Cities, and Asheville—much of the rain that in former years would have watered the woods and fields now falls on asphalt. Of this, a large portion—especially when the asphalt is hot—evaporates back into the air. The remainder mixes with road grit and the toxic effluents of leaky automobiles—antifreeze, brake fluid, gasoline and diesel fuel, grease, windshield washer fluid, transmission fluid, abraded rubber from tires, asbestos from brake linings, and oil—to form a slippery slurry that precipitates automobile accidents like an advancing wave at the forward edge of the rain system. As the rain intensifies, this poisonous slurry washes across the pavement of roads, parking lots, and gas stations. Traveling in iridescent slicks along gutters and curbs, it plummets into a dark underworld of storm sewers, where it is conveyed downward through dark concrete tunnels, from which ultimately it pours out again into a nearby river or stream.

Storm water is untreated. Unlike sanitary sewers, which transport the wastes from indoor drains and toilets (and from businesses and factories) to sewage treatment plants, storm sewers flow directly to the nearest waterway. The chemicals, filth, and trash that people throw, drop or leak onto roads or parking lots are thus transformed directly into water pollution.

So are toxic materials illegally dumped into storm sewers by negligent or unscrupulous businesses. The Norco Metal Finishing Company in Knoxville, for example, has been known to emit toxic chemicals into storm sewers draining directly into the Tennessee River.[15]

Storm sewers are typically composed of many sections of large-diameter concrete pipe that are fitted, but not sealed, together. In many places these pipes are cracked and broken by tree roots, construction, ground movement, or the aging of the concrete itself. During dry periods, contaminants such as gasoline, paint, bleach, antifreeze, oil, and industrial effluents that are dumped into the storm sewers are not flushed through the system into the streams but lie in low spots in the pipes, perhaps leaking slowly into the soil and ground water.

Leaks in the pipes—and in some cases direct connections made by unscrupulous or ignorant plumbers—also permit the influx of sewage from sanitary sewers into storm sewers.[16] This is particularly common during heavy rains, when the soil is saturated and both sewer systems are full of rushing water, and it is one of the ways by which sewage and industrial wastes enter rivers and streams.

Not all the water that falls on asphalt evaporates or goes to the storm sewers. Much of it runs off directly into rivers and streams. A meadow, a woods, or a field absorbs rain, both in the soil and in the vegetation, but asphalt absorbs nothing. During a heavy rain, the expansive roofs and parking lots of industrial parks and commercial developments quickly shed massive torrents of water into nearby rivers and streams, increasing the frequency of damaging floods. A flood stage, for example, that used to be reached once in twenty-five years on average before development may now be reached every ten years. Recent flooding along the West Prong of the Little Pigeon River has undoubtedly been exacerbated by the increase in runoff from extensive paving associated with rapid development in Pigeon Forge and Sevierville.

Flotsam

Heavy rain falling anywhere in the bioregion may, as it collects into rivulets and streams, gathering speed and force, move objects along the ground. All across the land, from the mountain freshets to the filth of urban gutters and storm sewers, it gathers carelessly discarded trash: plastic bottles, paper and plastic wrappers, rags, cigarette butts, light bulbs, plastic shopping bags, beer bottles, steel and aluminum cans, bits and pieces of appliances, old tires, and styrofoam. Swirled and tumbled by the rushing waters, this trash moves downsteam towards the Tennessee. Because all our major rivers are pooled by dams, much of the trash eventually reaches a reservoir where the water flow is slower. There some of it sinks to the bottom, deposited in a permanent geological layer of silt, but much stays afloat, landing, when the current slackens or the water level fluctuates, on the shorelines of quiet bays.

Traveling by boat in virtually any of the bioregion's reservoirs late in a dry summer, or in the fall or winter when the water is down, one can see in these dismal bays or in the shoreline vegetation all the detritus of a throw-away culture—the plastic, paper, aluminum and broken glass; the tangled monofilament fishing line; the unidentifiable fragments of broken consumer products.

The trash that does not sink or accumulate on the shores of the reservoirs eventually backs up behind the dams. When the volume becomes large, TVA uses boats to push the trash into the main channel, then flushes it through the dam by opening the flood gates. After churning in the tailwaters, the trash stretches out into a slug of flotsam and scum as much as two miles long that travels downstream to sink or wash up along further shorelines—or accumulate behind the next dam, where the operation is repeated. TVA maintains that this flushing operation is not really polluting, since the agency did not generate the trash in the first place.[17]

To deal with this pervasive litter, communities along the river, beginning with Chattanooga in 1989, have initiated River Rescues in which hundreds of local volunteers equipped by TVA with gloves and garbage bags fan out along the shoreline to pick up trash. Knoxville's first River Rescue, organized in 1991 by the Foundation for Global Sustainability (and later supported by other organizations), netted about five hundred tires. The items collected by the river rescuers have been varied: motorcycles, refrigerators, sunken boats, shopping carts, hypodermic needles, pesticide containers, gas tanks from cars and trucks, six-foot globs of floating asphalt, dead cattle, and barrels of toxic waste—to mention a modest selection. The bulk of the trash, however, is more mundane: paper or styrofoam cups and wrappers, plastic or glass bottles and jars, and recyclable aluminum cans. In areas where River Rescues have been active, there has been a gradual reduction of litter along the shoreline, as large items (especially tires), accumulated over decades, are removed. Yet each year much of the trash is renewed as the spring rains bring a fresh influx into the reservoirs; and by the fall when TVA begins drawing water levels down, bays up and down the reservoir system have once again taken on the appearance of landfills. *(See Figure 2: Flotsam on Douglas Reservoir on page 7.)*

The Old River

From the Cumberland plateau to the Smokies, the topography of the Upper Tennessee Valley is dominated by a remarkable series of parallel ridges that run from northeast to southwest. Four major rivers—the Powell, the Clinch, the Holston, and the Tennessee—and many smaller streams traverse the rich bottomlands between these ridges. Eastward into the Smokies, though the same southwest-northeast orientation prevails, the land is more jumbled and the rivers run westward to the Tennessee through deep gaps and gorges. The waters of the Nolichucky, French Broad, Pigeon, Little Tennessee, and Hiwassee all penetrate the mountains to reach the Tennessee.

Or, at least, what is called the Tennessee. The name rests on a mistake. The Cherokees called the river the *Hogohegee*, which in their language means simply "the big river."[18] The name "Tennessee," or, more properly, "Tanasi," was first applied by white settlers to the Little Tennessee River, which joins the Hogohegee just below Knoxville. But "Tanasi" was not the Cherokee name for the Little Tennessee either; the Native Americans called that river the Settico. Tanasi was, rather, an important Cherokee town on the banks of the Settico. Ironically, the site of this town, which gave the state and the river their names, now lies with other lands sacred to the Cherokees in a watery grave beneath TVA's Tellico Reservoir.

Moral reform begins, says Confucius, with the rectification of names. But, for the Hogohegee at least, it is too late; the Old River is lost. The sparkling blue current that once rushed through deep forested gorges and over wide rocky shoals now lies buried by hundreds of thousands of acres of deep, permanent flood. Beneath the murky, sluggish water, its banks and bottomlands, with their formerly fertile and lively farms, are entombed in toxic silt. Where once the riverbanks resonated with the chirping of birds and the croaking of frogs, there reigns a watery silence, disturbed only by the occasional heavy rumble of towboat engines or the frantic whine of a speedboat far above. Those old banks were long lined with dark forests and damp vegetation—sycamore, tupelo and willows. The wider banks of the new Tennessee are often denuded and ever more frequently armored with bare, sun-bleached limestone, called riprap, which is dumped there to keep the fertile mud of the old forested hillsides or bottomland, now constantly pounded by speedboat wakes, from sloughing off and adding to the silt load.

Nowhere along the new Tennessee can the old Hogohegee be seen. From the confluence of the Holston and the French Broad just above Knoxville, where the Tennessee nominally begins, to Kentucky Dam just above its mouth on the Ohio, the water impounded and pooled by each successive downstream dam laps against the base of the one next upstream, keeping the Hogohegee totally submerged. Where the old river made a continuous, often rocky descent, these colossal dams, nine of them on the main stem, divide the modern Tennessee into a series of discontinuous steps. Behind each, the river swells out to inundate the land. Viewed from above, the new, man-made river is wider over most of its course than even the Mississippi, of which it is a mere tributary of a tributary.

Yet portions of the Hogohegee survive, for the Cherokees did not define its bounds as we do. The upper end of our Tennessee lies just east of Knoxville, where the river branches into the Holston and the French Broad. But for the Cherokees the French Broad, though carrying a larger flow, was a tributary and the Holston a continuation of the Hogohegee, which thus has its origin far up in the mountains of southwestern Virginia. It is here along parts of the Holston that the old river may still be seen.

Siltation

Before the arrival of European settlers, the Tennessee Valley was forested. But since the middle of the eighteenth century, clearing for farms and cities and later logging, mining, construction, and road building have repeatedly bared large swaths of earth. The resulting erosion has flushed much of Tennessee's rich soil into creeks and rivers, taking some of it as far as the Mississippi Delta and the Gulf of Mexico. However, with the advent of government conservation programs in the 1930's, as well as decreased farming in the Southeast, this source of sediment began to diminish. By this time, though, the valleys of smaller rivers were bulging with stored sediment, which is still making its way through the system today, and will continue to produce high sediment loads far into the future.

Then in the 1930s and 1940s TVA dammed the Tennessee. Large dams are efficient sediment traps. A reservoir whose capacity is a tenth of its annual inflow retains eighty to ninety percent of the silt that enters it.[19] This silt settles out as sediment, and as a consequence the reservoir grows shallower, until in a matter of decades, or centuries, it is reduced to a shallow lake or stream-crossed wetland behind a useless concrete cliff. (Maybe not quite useless; if the dam were removed, the released sediment would produce massive siltation downstream!)

The siltation process is most advanced in TVA's Nolichucky Reservoir and at three TVA reservoirs on the Ocoee river. Nolichucky Reservoir, also called Davy Crockett Reservoir, about eight miles south of Greeneville, Tennessee, was formed by a dam built in 1913 and acquired by TVA in 1945. Clogged by tailings from kaolin, feldspar, and mica mines located near Spruce Pine, North Carolina, the dam has been unable to generate power since 1972.[20] However, the dam has been reinforced and modified by TVA to transform the reservoir into waterfowl refuge.

Ocoee Number Three Reservoir in Polk County in the extreme southeastern corner of Tennessee silted up even more quickly. Here, over a century ago, clear-cutting combined with acid deposition from intense copper smelting operations at nearby Copper Basin reduced thirty thousand acres (about fifty square miles) of rich forestland to sterile desert and exterminated aquatic life in the Ocoee river. The barren land eroded into deep furrows and gullies as the acidified soil, laden with heavy metals, washed into the river. Decades-long reclamation efforts have recently succeeded in revegetating most of the land, and fish are returning to the Ocoee after being absent for over a century.[21] But the reservoir, created in 1943 by a nine million dollar dam 110 feet tall and 612 feet wide, is all but gone, having lost ninety-eight percent of its 8700 acre-foot storage capacity to siltation.[22] Downstream, Ocoee Number One Reservoir (also called Lake Ocoee or Parksville Lake) and Number Two Reservoir are also highly silted, as evidenced by extensive mud flats.

It is worth noting, incidentally, that maps in the most recent (1995) edition of *RiverPulse*, TVA's assessment of the bioregion's waterways, show both Ocoee Number Three and Nolichucky Reservoir as blue lakes, not as the virtual wetlands that they are, but the text fails to mention either, leaving the impression that nothing unusual has happened there.

At present rates of siltation, the larger reservoirs will take a good bit longer to silt up—several hundred to several thousand years, by TVA estimates.[23] But the current influx of paper pulp and logging industries into the Southeast following their decimation of northwestern forests (see Chapter Three) will undoubtedly add to the sediment load. So would the opening of the new mines proposed for regional national forests (see Chapter Three), new roads, new housing developments, and so on.

And though the larger reservoirs are in no immediate danger of reverting to wetlands or mud flats, siltation continually diminishes their capacity and enlarges the winter mudflat around their shores. Mudflat expansion is accelerated by the wakes of powerboats. Where shorelines are unprotected by rocks or vegetation, the wakes undercut them, leaving a rooted overhang. This overhang eventually collapses into the water, producing an outward-sloping cliff, which in turn is undercut again, perpetuating the cycle. In this way as much as two meters of shoreline may be lost in a single year. Reservoirs thus grow continually wider and shallower, the ecologically important summer riparian zone narrows, and turbidity increases as sediment clouds the water.[24]

Powerboat wakes have other, more subtle effects as well. Great blue herons fishing along the riverbanks need clear water to see their prey. When a powerboat wake disturbs the shallows in which a heron is fishing, it usually flies to clearer water, since that spot, now filled with roiling silt, will remain unusable for fifteen or twenty minutes.[25]

In the long run—yet long before the reservoirs silt up completely—progressive siltation will diminish the reservoirs' capacity for flood control. Dredging will not solve the problem. The sheer volume of the silt contained in the big reservoirs is so large that to remove any considerable portion of it would be prohibitively expensive.

Toxic Sediments

Removal of the silt would, moreover, constitute an imposing hazardous waste disposal problem. The silt has entrapped not only an enormous quantity of plain old garbage, but also deposits of toxic chemicals poured into the river through decades of industrial abuse. Most experts believe there is no practical method for removing or cleaning this silt and that the safest thing to do is to let still further layers accumulate over it until it is deeply buried.

The contaminants vary considerably from reservoir to reservoir and, within a given reservoir, from one creek embayment to the next, and the contamination migrates from time to time as currents shift the silt. Yet there are relatively stable areas in which particular contaminants are known to occur in especially high concentrations.

One, already mentioned, is the Little River Embayment of Fort Loudoun Reservoir, whose silt contains significant concentrations of PCBs (polychlorinated biphenyls). PCBs are oily liquids manufactured until 1976 (when their production was banned) for use as insulators in electrical equipment, particularly transformers, and as hydraulic fluid. PCBs are now known to cause cancer, reproductive problems, and skin eruptions. However, EPA rules concerning their disposal did not take effect until 1978 or 1979. Prior to and during this lapse, PCBs were often simply dumped onto the ground or into the water.

Once released, PCBs tend to become bound to particles of soil, which migrate into waterways, eventually sinking to the bottom as silt. There they are ingested or absorbed by microorganisms, worms, insects, or mollusks living in the sediments. Predators eat these small organisms, and they in turn are consumed by larger predators, and so on, up the food chain. Since PCBs tend to be stored in fatty tissues rather than excreted, and since each predator eats many times its own weight in prey species, the slight concentrations of PCBs in organisms low on the food chain are multiplied in their predators. This effect, called bioaccumulation, may produce dangerously high levels in the largest aquatic predators, particularly catfish and bass.

PCB contamination is serious in many of the bioregion's waterways, particularly Fort Loudoun, Watts Bar, Tellico, Melton Hill, and Boone Reservoirs and at Chattanooga Creek. Fish from all these locations contain PCBs at levels that may increase the cancer risk for people who eat them. The Tennessee Department of Environment and Conservation has issued advisories against the consumption of various species, primarily catfish and/or bass, from each of these places.

Probably the bioregion's most dangerously contaminated silt occurs in the vicinity of the U.S. Department of Energy's Oak Ridge Reservation, a legacy of the production of nuclear weapons that began during World War II. White Oak Reservoir, which collects drainage from seven nuclear and chemical waste burial grounds on the reservation, is the most radioactive lake in the country.[26] Its sediments contain extraordinary levels of both chemical and nuclear contaminants, including mercury, cesium 137, cobalt 60, strontium 89, strontium 90, plutonium 239, and PCBs.

Fed by White Oak Creek and Melton Branch, the lake empties its overflow through a small dam into the Clinch River. Here, at the White Oak Embayment, in November 1990, Department of Energy (DOE) officials discovered a "hotspot" of radioactive cesium 137 in the sediments that posed a substantial hazard to people fishing or swimming there. (This after repeated public assurances that no such contamination existed.) DOE and the Army Corps of Engineers belatedly decided to construct a coffer dam across the mouth of the embayment to contain the sediments. The dam was completed in the spring of 1992 at a cost of seven million dollars.[27]

White Oak Creek and Poplar Creek, both of which drain the reservation and empty into the Clinch River, are the chief sources of outflow of radioactive and chemical contaminants found in sediments in many areas along the lower Clinch and in Watts Bar Reservoir: primarily PCBs, mercury, and cesium 137, all of which are associated with the manufacture of nuclear weapons. Fish sampled downstream from the reservation have shown measurable amounts of mercury and PCBs, as well as Cobalt 60, Cesium 137, Strontium 89, and Strontium 90.[28] Mercury, especially, was released into Watts Bar in large quantities. Like PCBs, mercury accumulates in the tissues of fish and in the human body—where in sufficiently high concentrations it may damage the brain, nervous system, and kidneys. The Department of Energy knew all this but kept it from public attention until May of 1990, when the Foundation for Global Sustainability obtained and released to the media government documents detailing the contamination of Watts Bar. A group of resort owners later filed a twenty-four million dollar law suit against Department of Energy contractors Martin Marietta and Union Carbide for business lost as tourists and fishermen quite reasonably avoided the reservoir. Just before the trial was to begin in 1994, the plaintiffs accepted an out-of-court settlement of two million dollars.

The Foundation also learned that the Department of Energy had failed to notify the Army Corps of Engineers of the danger of disturbing the contamination by dredging, which the Corps oversees. As silt accumulates in the reservoirs, older layers are buried beneath newer ones. Since mercury, PCB, dioxin, chlordane, and radiological releases have been greatly reduced over the past few decades, cleaner layers of silt have gradually settled over the most heavily contaminated layers, insulating the water from these toxic substances. However, dredging operations or currents generated by the powerful engines of towboats may stir up the buried layers sufficiently to resuspend the contaminants. Moreover, as the silt slowly migrates downstream some of it passes through the dams where contaminants may re-enter the water as a result of the great turbulence within the turbines.[29] These disturbances may make portions of the water temporarily poisonous.

Silt along Pigeon River, and particularly in Waterville Reservoir in Haywood County, North Carolina, is contaminated with dioxin, a byproduct of a chlorine bleaching process long used by the Champion International Corporation to whiten paper. The Pigeon runs along the northern border of the Great Smoky Mountains into the French Broad which flows into the Tennessee at Knoxville. Dioxin, which is not a single chemical but a family of over seventy-five related compounds, is best known as the primary contaminant in Agent Orange, the toxic defoliant used during the Vietnam War. Its health effects are multiple and profound: cancer, birth defects, lowered sperm counts, and damage to the immune, reproductive and nervous systems.[30] The dioxin has moved from the silt into the food chain in quantities sufficient to produce deformed jaws, skeletal defects, and death in fish.[31] Both Tennessee and North Carolina have issued advisories against human consumption of fish from the Pigeon.

Recently, under relentless pressure from environmental groups spearheaded by the Dead Pigeon River Council, and regulators, including the state of Tennessee and the EPA, Champion has switched to a new incineration/evaporation process and now claims that its water emissions are dioxin-free. (They seem less willing to discuss what is coming out the incinerator stacks.) The effluent from the plant is less dark, and the odor and foam have decreased sufficiently to encourage commercial rafting operations. Yet the Pigeon still does not run clear. Even today, the black or brown liquid that pours from Champion's huge effluent pipe visibly discolors the river for dozens of miles—though the color is due primarily to lignin, a nontoxic wood component.

The dioxin, however, persists in the sediments, and it will be long before fish from the Pigeon are safe to eat. Yet lately Champion has been airing television commercials that encourage fishing on the Pigeon River.

Suffocating Waters

In free-running creeks and rivers, the water splashes and foams, absorbing oxygen from the air. Stagnant or slowly-moving water, particularly if warmed by unshaded sunlight, absorbs less oxygen, and is less able to support animal life. This is why many aquariums require aerators.

Moreover, the excessive influx of organic matter into a river or stream in the form of sewage, fertilizers, yard waste, and agricultural runoff reduces dissolved oxygen. Bacteria, protozoa, and fungi that decompose these nutrients draw oxygen from the water, sometimes generating toxic materials as wastes. High nutrient levels can also promote algae blooms, which turn the water green. As the algae grow, they create organic compounds from water and carbon dioxide by photosynthesis. Consequently, when they die and are decomposed, they return more organic material to the water than they absorbed from it, which may lower oxygen levels still further.

Dams contribute to oxygen depletion in several ways: by making the water sluggish and slow, by maintaining a pool of deep water far from surface exchange, and by piling the water up under great pressure. These problems are greatest at the tributary dams, which tend to be higher than dams on the Tennessee itself. During the warm summer months, water behind the high dams separates into two layers, a warm top layer which contains most of the dissolved oxygen, and a cooler bottom layer which contains relatively little oxygen and which therefore cannot adequately support aquatic life. TVA dams release cold and oxygen-poor water from the bottom of the reservoirs. As a result, the tailwaters below the dams suffer from unnaturally cold temperatures, low dissolved oxygen, and extreme turbulence.[32]

TVA has recently introduced technology to address the problem of dissolved oxygen and the related problem of inadequate flows below some dams when the turbines are not generating. At Douglas Reservoir, for example, liquid oxygen is injected directly into the water upstream of the dam through dozens of miles of hose laid along the reservoir bottom. At other locations, TVA has constructed downstream weirs—small dams that provide additional control of water flow and create artificial waterfalls to oxygenate the water. At several dams along the Tennessee, the agency has installed equipment to improve the turbine's natural ability to draw air into the water or to inject compressed air into the turbines or penstock, the pipe that brings water to the turbine. These innovations appear to be improving water quality.[33] Yet it is not a sign of ecological health that a river that once did an excellent job of aerating itself must now be kept on expensive forms of artificial respiration.

Moreover, such improvements generally affect only the tailwaters. Oxygen levels remain inadequate to support healthy aquatic communities in many of the deep tributary reservoirs—including Douglas, Norris, Boone, South Holston, Watauga, Cherokee, Hiwassee, Nottely, and others.[34]

Hot Water

Heating a lake, river, or stream can harm its inhabitants just as much as infusing it with silt or toxic chemicals. Ecologists have dubbed this unwanted heat "thermal pollution." TVA's power plants, both coal and nuclear, are located on rivers, which they use as sources of cooling water. After running through the plant's cooling system, the heated water is discharged back into the river. At the nuclear plants and at one coal plant the water is first passed through cooling towers (monumental structures that dominate the landscape for miles around) before being discharged into the river. Still it may be quite hot—often exceeding a hundred degrees Fahrenheit. Some TVA coal plants that do not have cooling towers must cut back generation at certain times of the year in order to meet EPA temperature limits.[35] In the winter, frozen cooling towers may be bypassed altogether. Heated water flowing directly into a much cooler river disrupts the local ecology, perhaps accelerating the growth of algae, and encouraging the growth of nonnative organisms (a problem discussed in Chapter Three). Moreover, because, other things being equal, hot water absorbs and retains less oxygen than cold, an influx of heated water also reduces dissolved oxygen.

Urban and suburban development is another source of thermal pollution. On sunny summer afternoons, streets, parking lots and roofs become sizzling hot. The sun bakes the soil of grassy lawns, too, making it much hotter than shaded soils. During a sudden thundershower, rain falling on these surfaces is heated, and the first flush of runoff into nearby streams or wetlands brings with it a sudden rise in water temperature, along with an influx of toxic chemicals, trash, silt, and bacteria. As the rain continues, the water temperature falls again just as suddenly. It is well known that sudden temperature changes can be fatal to aquarium fish. Similarly, these extreme fluctuations, which do not occur in naturally forested streams, may kill sensitive aquatic animals, and so account in part for the ecological poverty of urban waterways. Thermal pollution of creeks is increased by the widespread elimination of shade trees and other vegetation along their banks. Sunlight shining directly into a creek heats the creek bottom and raises the water temperature, decreasing dissolved oxygen, and making the stream less hospitable to many species.

Surface Water Pollution

Industrial pollution of the bioregion's waterways peaked in the 1970s. Since then, as a result of the regulation initiated by the Clean Water Act in 1972 and associated legislation, it has on the whole significantly diminished. Much of the pollution that persists in the sediments of rivers and streams is the heritage of past industrial abuse. But efforts by Republicans in the 104th Congress to weaken the Clean Water Act and cut funding for its enforcement were an unnerving reminder that this progress is not secure. Moreover, though industries generally pollute less now, many still release hundreds of tons of toxic materials into the water—with or without the blessing of regulatory agencies.

The bioregion's largest industrial source of water pollution is the Eastman Chemical Company in Kingsport, Tennessee. In 1994, the most recent year for which EPA data are available, Eastman poured 440,296 pounds of toxic chemicals into the Holston River. In that same year, the Champion International Corporation's Canton, North Carolina, paper mill dumped 283,743 pounds of toxics into the Pigeon River, and the North American Rayon Corporation in Elizabethton, Tennessee, injected 130,350 pounds of industrial toxins into the Watauga River.

These are the figures reported by the industries themselves for the EPA's Toxic Release Inventory. There is no independent check on their validity. Table 1.1 lists the specific chemicals these plants released. Some of these are carcinogens or reproductive toxins.

Table 1.1 **(1994 statistics)**

INDUSTRIES EMITTING MORE THAN 100,000 POUNDS OF TOXIC CHEMICALS INTO THE WATER[36]		
Facility and Location	**Main Toxic Water Pollutants**	**Toxic Water Emissions (lbs.)**
Champion International Corporation Canton, NC	Acetaldehyde, ammonia, catechol, cresol, formaldehyde, methanol, methyl ethyl ketone, phenol	283,743
North American Rayon, Elizabethton, TN	Ammonia, carbon disulfide	130,350
Tennessee Eastman Division Kingsport, TN	1,4-dioxane, 2,4-dinitrophenol, 2-methoxyethanol, acetaldehyde, acetonitrile, ammonia, aniline, biphenyl, bis(2-ethylhexyl) adipate, bromomethane, butyl acrylate, butyraldehyde, chlorine, chlorobenzene, chromium compounds, copper compounds, cyanide compounds, cyclohexane, di(2-ethyl-hexyl) phthalate, dibutyl phthalate, diethyl phthalate, dimethyl phthalate, dimethyl sul-fate, ethylene glycol, formaldehyde, glycol ethers, hydroquinone, m-xylene, methanol, methyl ethyl ketone, methyl isobutyl ketone, n-butyl alcohol, o-xylene, p-xylene, phenol, propionaldehyde, pyridine, quinone, styrene, sulfuric acid, toluene, xylene (mixed iso-mers), zinc compounds	440,296

TVA's coal-fired power plants also contribute substantially to water pollution by toxic metals, though comparable figures are not available, since as a federal agency TVA has been exempted from TRI reporting requirements. At many plants fly ash is sluiced to a storage pond, the water from which, though treated, still contains some toxic metals when released.[37]

The bioregion's most widespread water pollutant is fecal bacteria from sewage. Bacterial contamination is most severe in large urban areas, particularly Knoxville and Chattanooga, where the problem comes mostly from leaking sewer lines, and in overdeveloped rural areas—especially Blount and Sevier Counties in Tennessee, where failing septic tanks are the culprit. Some smaller towns, such as Red Bank, Lake City, and White Pine, Tennessee, also have inadequate sewage treatment plants. Even the relatively modern sewage facilities of the major urban areas may pour raw sewage into the rivers when they are overwhelmed by an influx of water from heavy rains. In many systems, connections between sanitary sewers and storm sewers exacerbate this problem.

In recent years the Tennessee Department of Environment and Conservation (TDEC) has begun posting some of the most dangerously polluted waterways. Table 1.2 lists the regional postings. The fact that a stream or location is not listed here does not mean that it is safe—even for body contact. TVA tests have located water failing state criteria for body contact in places not posted by state agencies, including locations along at least ten miles of the southern end of Beaver Creek in Knox County; the Blount County boat ramp on Fort Loudoun Lake; and Butternut Creek, near Blairsville, Georgia.[38]

Table 1.2

POSTED WATERWAYS IN EAST TENNESSEE[39]				
Waterway	**Portion**	**Pollutant**	**Source**	**Advisory Type**
Chattanooga Creek (Hamilton County)	TN/GA line to mouth (7.7 miles)	PCBs, Chlordane, fecal bacteria	Historic industrial waste disposal, sewage bypassing	Avoid body contact, fish should not be consumed
East Fork Poplar Creek (including embayment), Anderson and Roane Counties	Miles 0.0-15.0	Mercury, metals, organic chemicals	Dept. of Energy's Oak Ridge facilities	Avoid body contact, fish should not be consumed
Watts Bar Reservoir, Roane, Meigs, Rhea and Loudon Counties	Tennessee River Portion	PCBs	Dept. of Energy's Oak Ridge facilities and private industry	Catfish, striped bass, and hybrid striped bass/white bass should not be eaten. Precautionary advisory for white bass, sauger, carp, smallmouth buffalo, and largemouth bass.
Watts Bar Reservoir, Roane and Anderson Counties	Clinch River Arm	PCBs	Dept. of Energy's Oak Ridge facilities and private industry	Striped bass should not be consumed. Precautionary advisory for catfish and sauger.

Table 1.2 cont.

POSTED WATERWAYS IN EAST TENNESSEE[39]				
Waterway	**Portion**	**Pollutant**	**Source**	**Advisory Type**
Melton Hill Reservoir, Knox and Anderson County	Entirety (5,690 acres)	PCBs	Dept. of Energy's Oak Ridge facilities	Catfish should not be eaten.
Coal Creek Anderson County	Lake City sewage plant to Clinch River 4.7 miles	Fecal bacteria	Lake City sewage plant	Avoid body contact
Fort Loudoun Reservoir, Loudon, Knox, and Blount County	Entirety (14,600 acres)	PCBs	Historical sources include Forks of the River Industrial Park, Alcoa Aluminum, TVA Singleton Ways, Maryville sewage	Commercial fishing for catfish prohibited. Catfish, largemouth bass over 2 lbs. and largemouth bass from Little River plant embayment should not be eaten.
Tellico Reservoir Loudon County	Entirety (16,500 acres)	PCBs	Historical industrial sources	Catfish should not be consumed.
Boone Reservoir Washington Counties	Entirety Sullivan, and (4,400 acres)	PCBs, Chlordane	Historical industrial sources	Precautionary advisory for carp and catfish
North Fork Holston River Sullivan, and	Mile 0.0-6.2 TN/VA line Hawkins Counties	Mercury	Waste lagoon formerly operated by Olin Chemical Co., Saltville, VA	Fish should not be consumed
Pigeon River Cocke County	20.4 mi.-NC line to Douglas Reservoir	Dioxin	Champion International Paper Corp.	Fish should not be consumed
Nickajack Reservoir Hamilton, and Marion Counties	Entirety	PCBs	Historical industrial sources	Precautionary advisory for catfish
Oostanaula Creek McMinn County	Mile 28.4-31.2	Fecal bacteria	Athens sewage treatment plant and upstream dairies	Avoid body contact
Coops Creek Sequatchie County	Mile 0.8 to mouth	Fecal bacteria	Sewer overflows in Dunlap area	Avoid body contact
Stringers Branch Hamilton County	Mile 5.4 to mouth	Fecal bacteria	Red Bank sewage collection system	Avoid body contact

Table 1.2 cont.

POSTED WATERWAYS IN EAST TENNESSEE[39]				
Waterway	**Portion**	**Pollutant**	**Source**	**Advisory Type**
Beaver Creek Sullivan (Bristol)	TN/VA line to Boone Lake (20 miles)	Fecal bacteria	Bristol sewage plant and nonpoint sources in Virginia	Avoid body contact
Cash Hollow Creek Washington County	Mile 0.0-1.4	Fecal bacteria	Septic tank failures	Avoid body contact
Sinking Creek Washington County	Mile 0.0-2.8	Fecal bacteria	Urban runoff	Avoid body contact
Turkey Creek Hamblen County	Mile 0.0-5.3	Fecal bacteria	Morristown sewage collection system	Avoid body contact
Leadvale Creek Jefferson County	Mile 1.5 to Douglas Lake	Fecal bacteria	White Pine sewage plant	Avoid body contact
Goose Creek Knox County	4.0 miles	Fecal bacteria	Knoxville urban runoff and leaky sewers	Avoid body contact
First Creek Knox County	Mile 0.2-1.5	Fecal bacteria	Knoxville urban runoff and leaky sewers	Avoid body contact
Second Creek Knox County	Mile 0.0-4.0	Fecal bacteria	Knoxville urban runoff and leaky sewers	Avoid body contact
Third Creek Knox County	Mile 0.0-1.4, Mile 3.3	Fecal bacteria	Knoxville urban runoff and leaky sewers	Avoid body contact
East Fork of Third Creek Knox County	Mile 0.0-0.8	Fecal bacteria	Knoxville urban runoff and leaky sewers	Avoid body contact
Sinking Creek Embayment of Fort Loudoun Reservoir Knox County	1.5 miles from head of embayment to cave	Fecal bacteria	Urban runoff	Avoid body contact
West Prong Little Pigeon River Sevier County	17 miles from Gatlinburg to mouth	Fecal bacteria	Septic tank failures and leaky sewers	Avoid body contact
Beech Branch Sevier County	Entirety	Fecal bacteria	Septic tank failures	Avoid body contact

Table 1.2 cont.

POSTED WATERWAYS IN EAST TENNESSEE[39]				
Waterway	**Portion**	**Pollutant**	**Source**	**Advisory Type**
King Branch Sevier County	Entirety	Fecal bacteria	Septic tank failures	Avoid body contact
Gnatty Branch Sevier County	Entirety	Fecal bacteria	Septic tank failures	Avoid body contact
Holy Branch Sevier County	Entirety	Fecal bacteria	Septic tank failures and leaky sewers	Avoid body contact
Baskins Creek Sevier County	Entirety	Fecal bacteria	Septic tank failures and leaky sewers	Avoid body contact
Roaring Creek Sevier County	Entirety	Fecal bacteria	Septic tank failures and leaky sewers	Avoid body contact
Dudley Creek Sevier County	Entirety	Fecal bacteria	Septic tank failures and leaky sewers	Avoid body contact
Little Pigeon River Sevier County	From French Broad to Sevierville	Fecal bacteria	Septic tank failures and leaky sewers	Avoid body contact

Agriculture is another major contributor to surface water pollution—chiefly in the form of nitrate runoff from fertilizers and manure—and to a lesser extent in the form of pesticide and herbicide contamination. But the contamination is more diffuse: agriculture occupies much more land area than urban or industrial activities—about forty-seven percent in Tennessee, as compared to only two percent for urban and industrial areas.[40]

Of the bioregion's four mainstream reservoirs, Fort Loudoun is the dirtiest. It receives a massive nutrient overload from housing developments along its banks, from sewage-contaminated streams in Blount and Sevier counties, and from the filthy and malodorous waters of Knoxville's urban creeks.

The sediments of Fort Loudoun Reservoir are laced with zinc, PCBs, and other industrial wastes. Industries along the tributaries once dumped toxins openly into the waters, though regulation has generally put a stop to that. Most notorious among the recent polluters were Robertshaw Controls (which illegally discharged toxic materials as late as 1989[41]) and Rohm & Haas on Third Creek; David Witherspoon, Inc., on Goose Creek (which is now a Tennessee superfund site); and Alcoa Aluminum and TVA's Singleton Ways facility on the Little River embayment.

Siltation in Fort Loudoun from urban construction and eroded banks is intense. Knoxville's urban creeks disgorge muddy brown plumes far out into the river—a phenomenon readily observable from the bridges or the bluffs on the south bank. Trash is ubiquitous, petroleum slicks not uncommon. Extensive overdevelopment along both sides of the river and destruction of riparian corridors assures a steady influx of runoff from streets and parking lots and of fertilizers and other chemicals from suburban lawns. The toxins, the turbidity, and the silt combine to eliminate many forms of benthic (bottom-dwelling) life; nevertheless, the high nutrient levels support substantial populations of pollution-tolerant shad and enormous carp.[42]

Downstream from Fort Loudoun is Watts Bar which, though less contaminated by bacteria, still harbors within its silts the deadly legacy of decades of nuclear weapons production. In Watts Bar, the dirty waters of Fort Loudoun Reservoir are diluted by the cleaner Clinch and Little Tennessee Rivers and many smaller streams. Yet below the dam at the Lenoir City Industrial Park the Yale Lock Factory, Railroad Shed, and Public Works Garage all have contributed toxic wastes to the river, as have Staley, Viscase, and Kimberly Clark at Matlock Bend ten miles downstream. Still further downstream, at its confluence with the Clinch River, Watts Bar still receives some nuclear and chemical releases from the Oak Ridge Reservation, though these have been much reduced.[43] Moreover, toxic materials in Watts Bar's sediments continue to accumulate through the food web, producing potentially dangerous levels of contamination in some catfish, bass, sauger, buffalo, and carp. Astonishingly, TVA rated the ecological health of Watts Bar as "good" in 1994.

Watts Bar Dam empties its tail waters into Chickamauga Reservoir. Here further dilution produces somewhat lower densities of pollutants, though radioactive and chemical contaminants from Oak Ridge—including PCBs, cesium 137, and cobalt 60—have settled in the Chickamauga sediments too. The Hiwassee River empties into Chickamauga Reservoir, bringing with it the "black liquor" from the Bowater papermill upstream. Downstream, as in the Pigeon River, the sediments contain dioxin.[44]

Chickamauga in turn empties into Nickajack, where a new load of sewage and industrial contamination pours into the water from the urban and suburban sprawl around Chattanooga. At Moccasin Bend the river receives the waters of Chattanooga Creek, which drains an industrial desert of hazardous waste sites, leaking sewers, abandoned landfills and illegal dumps. High levels of PCBs, lead, arsenic, and chlordane contaminate its silt, and suspended sewage makes the water unfit for body contact. In some places a thin layer of leaves on the creek bottom conceals pits of toxic industrial tar up to six feet deep. People living in the nearby low-income African-American communities of Piney Woods and Alton Park have reported high rates of cancer, miscarriages, breathing problems, headaches, and eye and skin irritations.[45] Less than two miles downstream, the city adds the technically treated effluent from its sewage plant, a black liquid liberally dosed with chlorine. Still further down, the waters of Springer Branch discharge the inadequately treated sewage of Red Bank.

All this nutrient influx stimulates the growth of huge mats of filamentous algae and Eurasian water milfoil, which frequently clog the shallow waters of Mullins Cove and Bennett Lake. Until recently, TVA regularly combated these water plants with thousands of pounds of herbicides, adding still more toxic chemicals to the water. To its credit, however, in 1994 or 1995 the agency began to experiment with mechanical harvesters.

The silts of Nickajack Reservoir are contaminated with PCBs, which are also found in potentially dangerous amounts in catfish. TVA's Sequoyah Nuclear Plant leaked PCBs into Nickajack for many years after a transformer fire in 1982[46], but this was certainly not the only source. Elevated levels of lead and copper occur in the forebay area behind the dam. Yet TVA rates the health of Nickajack as good—indeed, as the best in the entire Tennessee River system.[47]

Of the twenty major tributary reservoirs, three on the Ocoee River are clogged with toxic and acidic silt, mostly from the Copper Hill disaster mentioned earlier. The sediment contains high to very high levels of copper, lead, zinc, cadmium, and PCBs. Nolichucky (Davy Crockett) is likewise silted up. Hiwassee Reservoir has been contaminated with chlordane—though the concentrations appear to be decreasing—and nutrient runoff.

The sediments at Nottely Lake near Blairsville, Georgia, are also contaminated, and the lake supports much algae but contains little dissolved oxygen. The sediments of Chatuge Reservoir, which straddles the Georgia/North Carolina state lines contain toxic copper and chromium.

The bioregion's healthiest tributary reservoir, according to TVA's rating system, is Blue Ridge in northern Georgia. Its sediments, too, have been toxic to test animals in the past, but were not when sampled in 1994.

The five reservoirs of the Holston watershed—Cherokee, South Holston, Boone, Watauga, and Fort Patrick Henry—are all ailing for various reasons. Cherokee receives sewage from Morristown via Turkey Creek and is also contaminated with PCBs. Boone is contaminated with sewage from Bristol, Virginia. Sediment at Fort Patrick Henry is polluted with PCBs and chlordane. Wautauga sediment contains chlordane. South Holston, on the Tennessee/Virginia line, appears not to be much contaminated, but suffers from low dissolved oxygen, which limits fish populations.

Norris lake, which has a reputation for cleanliness, has some lead-contaminated sediments and, because of its depth, low dissolved oxygen. Excessive nutrient runoff, perhaps from septic tanks, causes algae blooms in the summer. Downstream, Melton Hill Reservoir, south of Clinton, receives sewage-contaminated waters of Knox County's heavily polluted Beaver Creek. Upstream of Norris Reservoir lie the Clinch and Powell Rivers, both still in relatively good condition. The Clinch is home to the only known reproducing population of the endangered riffleshell mussel. However, some of the tributary streams of these ecologically valuable river fragments are in trouble. Big Cedar and Cooper Creeks are contaminated by agricultural runoff. The Guest River and the North Fork of the Powell are polluted by coal operations, untreated sewage, and urban runoff.[48]

Douglas Reservoir receives the dioxin-contaminated waters of the Pigeon River. A fishing advisory (consume no fish) is posted downstream from the Champion paper mill along the entire Pigeon River, but it does not extend into Douglas Reservoir.[49] Leadvale Creek used to bring sewage to Douglas Reservoir, but improvements to the White Pine sewage plant are expected to alleviate this problem.[50]

Waterville (Walters) Reservoir, on the Pigeon River in North Carolina is still contaminated with dioxin from the Champion mill upstream, and the state of North Carolina maintains a "no consumption advisory" for carp and catfish, though it has lifted advisories for other species, since improvements to the Champion plant have reduced the dioxin contamination. Waterville also has severe problems with excessive nutrients—mostly from Champion.[51]

Lake Junaluska, near Waynesville, North Carolina, a small private reservoir owned by the Methodist church, is plagued with silt and can be kept open only by dredging. It took fifty years for the lake to fill with sediment for the first time. It was first dredged in 1964. It has had to be dredged again in 1973, then in 1982, and most recently in 1992 or 1993. The sediment seems to be coming from residential and urban development in the area. Influxes of chemicals and solid waste have occasionally killed fish in the reservoir.[52]

The Sequatchie River, one of the few undammed rivers in the bioregion, drains a rich agricultural district. But it is murky with nutrients from agricultural runoff and silt from agriculture and mining operations.

River Traffic

Of people who interact with the bioregion's rivers in any significant way, most seem to value them primarily for their recreational benefits—that is, for fishing or boating.[53] Yet powerboats and jet skis degrade both the rivers themselves and the experience of those who prefer more quiet recreations: the more powerful and more numerous the boats, the worse the problems. As previously noted, the wakes of powerboats erode the banks. Powerboats also shatter the silence of the river and spread fumes—and often petroleum slicks—across the water. Poorly driven, they are a danger to swimmers and to each other. Many boaters toss their trash overboard; crews of larger boats sometimes dump sewage. Not a few vessels are ostentatiously oversized and overpowered for the Tennessee—as can be seen on any home football Saturday in Knoxville, when the "Vol Navy" docks at the municipal waterfront.

One reason for damming the Tennessee was to provide for commercial navigation. This may prove to be more of a curse than a blessing, as it provides a ready conduit for moving Southern Appalachian forests down to Mobile Bay (see Chapter Three). Yet barges are both an economically and (given that the dams and locks are already there) environmentally efficient way to transport large amounts of materials.

Unfortunately, barge terminals also bring dangerous industrial operations close to the water. At Knoxville's Volunteer Asphalt plant on the south bank of the Tennessee just below the confluence of the Holston and the French Broad, for example, a tank rupture in the early 1990s poured many tons of tar into the river. The tar now lies on the river bottom, and large globs of it, often six feet or more in length, rise to the surface now and then. Despite floating booms around the facility designed to catch these globs, they often manage to escape and may be found floating serenely downriver or permanently melted onto downstream rocks.[54]

Wetlands

In healthy, undisturbed ecosystems (of which none now are left in our bioregion) surface water is usually quite pure and safe even for drinking. In part, this is due to the operations of wetlands. Wetlands—"swamps" in less pretentious jargon—are natural water filters. The water in a wetland is shallow, diffused over a large area, and relatively slow-moving. This provides time for lush aquatic vegetation to absorb nutrients, toxic metals, and other contaminants. Water leaving a wetland is often quite pure—which is why constructed wetlands have been proposed, for example, as a means of cleaning up Knoxville's Second Creek.

In heavy rains, wetlands also serve as retention areas, absorbing a great influx of water and releasing it slowly, which helps to prevent downstream flooding. They are, moreover, crucial habitat or breeding grounds for many species of birds, fish, reptiles, insects, and amphibians.

Unfortunately, throughout most of the history of Western civilization, beginning with the draining of the malarial swamps of Rome, these functions have not been understood, and wetlands have been viewed as noxious impediments to progress. The farmers who began to till the Tennessee Valley about two centuries ago observed two things about wetlands: (1) they were a source of pesky and sometimes dangerous mosquitoes, and (2) when drained, they yielded a rich soil, ideal for crops. So industrious farmers drained them. As a result, Tennessee has already lost about sixty percent of its original wetland area.[55] Because there are few low-lying plains in Southern Appalachia, wetlands have always been few here. In this century they have become quite rare, and their unique ecosystems are disappearing. The few that remain harbor at least ninety threatened and endangered species.[56] Forested wetlands are especially important to biodiversity. Over ninety percent of the bird species living in eastern North America use forested wetlands at some time in their life cycle.[57]

Because agriculture has been diminishing in Southern Appalachia for some time, the destruction of wetlands has gradually decreased. (The wetlands that have been lost, of course, are generally not being restored.) Lately, however, more and more wetlands are being lost to development. The next to go is likely to be the Turkey Creek Wetland off Lovell Road in West Knoxville, which is home to the rare flame chub and many other aquatic species. The City of Knoxville and Turkey Creek Land Partners have applied for permits to extend a road (Parkside Boulevard) through the middle of the wetland and to fill in portions of it for commercial development. The proposal would also surround most of the twenty-two acre wetland, the largest remaining in Knox County, with industry, restaurants, and parking lots.

In an attempt to deflect opposition, the proposal also includes measures to flood some additional land to create new wetlands and turn over the remaining wetland via a conservation easement to Ijams Nature Center. There is strong evidence, how-

ever, that artificially flooded wetlands do not recreate the biological or hydrological functions of the originals.[58] Moreover the presence of large areas of asphalt contributing runoff of road slurry and trash into the wetland is likely to degrade it significantly.[59] Yet, as of this writing, the permits seem likely to be granted.

Groundwater

Much of the Tennessee Valley is characterized by karst (limestone cave) topography and faulted, fractured, and folded bedrock. This allows for rapid, voluminous,
and largely unpredictable movement of groundwater. Sinkholes abound, providing
inlets to often extensive cave systems, underground watercourses, and sometimes
even underground rivers or lakes. Water entering the sinkholes flushes whatever
has been deposited near them into the underground water system, often with sur-
prising force. During a heavy summer thunderstorm, a cave that was dry only an
hour before may rapidly fill with roiling water—a peril borne in mind by all experienced cavers. Cavers sometimes find the same sorts of trash that are so common
along riverbanks and streams, including items as large as truck tires and shopping
carts, deposited deep underground on high ledges in a cave that is, for the moment
at least, dry.

Because rainwater can plunge directly underground in a karst system, it is not fil-
tered or purified as it would be if it seeped through many layers of loam, clay, or
sand. Some people in rural areas, apparently unaware that the water that circulates
through the caves beneath their land is also the water they drink from their wells,
use sinkholes as garbage dumps or disposal pits for dead livestock. Some service
station owners in Tennessee have contaminated the groundwater by dumping waste
oil into sinkholes. But dumping any polluting substance into a sinkhole is illegal.[60]

Sinkholes and caves play an important role in Tennessee Valley drainage. In the
First Creek and Ten-Mile Creek drainage basins in Knoxville, for example, ten to fifteen percent of the runoff drains into sinkholes.[61] Development which disrupts
these natural storm sewers or causes caves to collapse may produce flooding in
areas not previously flood-prone, as has happened recently near Cedar Bluff Road
in West Knoxville.

Not all of the bioregion has a karst topography, however, and where clay soils and
more solid bedrock prevail, groundwater movement is slow. Moreover, because of
the hilly terrain there are no large, continuous aquifers; groundwater contamination
therefore tends to be localized.

In the state of Tennessee, about thirty-nine percent of the population depend on ground water as a source of drinking water.[62] Sources of groundwater contamination in our bioregion include wastewater ponds (often associated with mines, industrial sites, and coal-fired power plants); contaminated industrial or hazardous waste sites (such as the David Witherspoon sites in the Vestal community of South Knoxville); landfills (of which there are hundreds in our bioregion); leaking underground storage tanks; agricultural herbicides, pesticides and fertilizers; suburban lawn-care products; underground injection of wastes (such as occurred until 1984 at Oak Ridge National Laboratory); and failing sewers and septic tanks. The three most common groundwater contaminants in our bioregion are petrochemicals, fecal bacteria, and nitrates from fertilizers and sewage.

Petrochemical contamination occurs most frequently in the form of gasoline, diesel fuel, fuel oil, or motor oil. It is often, though not always, associated with leaking underground storage tanks. In the North Carolina portion of our bioregion, there have been 361 reported instances of leaking underground storage tanks; in the Tennessee portion, 1,200 significant releases of petroleum have been reported (releases classified as "minor" are not included in this figure, nor are releases of nonpetroleum substances).[63] Petroleum contamination of groundwater is also common beneath storage facilities, such as the tank farm just off of Middlebrook Pike in West Knoxville. Frequent spills and runoff from that facility have contaminated both Third Creek, which runs through the site, and the groundwater beneath it.

Septic wastes from failing septic tanks also contribute significantly to contamination by nitrates and fecal bacteria. In the human body, some nitrates are converted to nitrites, which reduce the blood's ability to transport oxygen, a condition especially dangerous to fetuses and young children. They may also react to form carcinogenic N-nitroso compounds.[64] Some four to five percent of wells tested in our bioregion exceed the ten part per million nitrate standard.[65]

It should be noted that the health risk from exposures to two or more pollutants may not be a simple sum of the risks of exposures to each alone. In some instances it is many times greater than this sum. Drinking water, of course, is only one of many pathways by which pollutants may enter the body.

Leaking landfills may contaminate wells with hazardous waste, a problem suffered for many years by residents of the Tennessee community of Witt in Hamblen County. Often in these cases no cleanup is possible and the only solution for residents is to move or obtain their drinking water from elsewhere.[66]

Another important problem associated with groundwater is that water from private wells is often contaminated by lead from pipes, not from the groundwater itself. In most cases (about ninety percent) these wells have pumps made before 1995 that contain lead alloy parts. Much of our groundwater is soft and acidic, which makes it corrosive enough to leach lead from the pumps. Lead in drinking water can produce irritability, anemia, blood enzyme changes, hypertension, miscarriages, and learning disabilities.[67] Fortunately, for this problem there is in most cases an easy solution: let the tap run for a few seconds to flush the system before drawing water for human consumption.

The bioregion's most contaminated groundwater underlies the Department of Energy's Oak Ridge reservation. There mercury and radioactive fission products—mainly tritium and strontium 90—are found in the groundwater down gradient from nuclear waste burial grounds at Oak Ridge National Laboratory. The Department of Energy is attempting to reduce off-site discharge of these contaminants by capping the burial grounds with clay and implementing other containment measures. Between 1951 and 1984, four seepage pits, known as the S-3 ponds, were used by the Y-12 nuclear weapons plant to dispose of over twenty-seven million gallons of various liquid wastes, including concentrated acids, caustic solutions, mop waters, and by-products from uranium recovery processes, including uranium and other heavy metals. These unlined pits were designed to allow the liquid either to evaporate or percolate into the ground. They are now capped, paved, and used as a parking lot, but the groundwater beneath them is still heavily contaminated with nitrates, cadmium, and uranium. Likewise, at the K-25 gaseous diffusion plant, numerous burial grounds consisting of unlined trenches, sludge ponds, and leaking underground storage tanks have produced complex and extensive groundwater contamination by toxic and radioactive pollutants. Most of the groundwater contamination on the Oak Ridge Reservation appears still to be confined to the watershed in which it originated; however, the contamination is migrating (at various rates for various sites), and there is no known way to eliminate it.[68] At Oak Ridge National Laboratory, for example, a plume of water about fifty feet under ground was recently discovered to be carrying radioactive strontium 90 into the Clinch River. This one plume, from an unknown source, was estimated to be responsible for at least ten percent of the strontium 90 contamination in the Clinch.[69]

Despite the enormous scope and variety of groundwater contamination, water from most of the wells in our bioregion is still safe to drink. If you drink well water, however, it is a reasonable precaution to have it tested regularly—especially if you live near potential sources of contamination.

Municipal Water Supplies

According to the Tennessee Department of Environment and Conservation, "Your water should be completely safe for you and your family to drink if the public water supply system has been approved by the Department of Environment and Conservation."[70] Modern water treatment facilities do remove most pollutants effectively, so that even if they draw from polluted waters, the resulting tap water is usually safe to drink. Pollutants can, however, enter the water after treatment. With old plumbing systems, lead may leach into the water between the treatment plant and the faucet—though, fortunately, this is becoming rarer.

It should be noted, however, that the chlorine used at the water treatment plant to kill bacteria is itself a pollutant that reacts to form carcinogenic by-products, especially chloroform. There is evidence that drinking chlorinated water slightly increases the risk of cancer of the gastrointestinal and urinary tracts.[71] Of course, water untreated with chlorine presents greater and more immediate dangers of infectious disease. Yet, to put the matter in a broader perspective, the necessity for chlorine treatment itself arises largely from human degradation of the environment. Before the arrival of Europeans, an abundance of small springs and clear streams supplied the inhabitants of the Southern Appalachians with pure, unchlorinated drinking water. Now many of the springs and all the streams are unsafe for drinking, and drinking water must be extracted by complex industrial processes from reservoirs, rivers, and groundwater that are fouled with sewage and toxic waste.

FIGURE 3: The tall stacks at TVA's coal-fired Kingston Steam Plant dwarf the original stacks. Their effluent contributes to ozone pollution, haze, and acid deposition in the Smokies.

For they have sown the wind, and they shall reap the whirlwind ...

— Hosea 8:7

The Great Smoggy Mountains

To the Cherokees they were the "land of the blue mist." European settlers named them, more prosaically, "Smoky Mountains"—which later generations glorified to "Great Smoky Mountains," presumably in order to entice tourists. All these names originally referred to the ethereal blue mist that once surrounded the mountains like a transparent veil. Today, most often in the summer months, the "smoke" of the Smokies is supplanted by a white, brown, or grey haze. The original blue mist consisted mainly of water vapor and volatile organic compounds released by trees (such as those responsible for the fragrance of pines). But the haze so evident today consists of sulfate particles from the burning of coal at power plants in the Ohio and Tennessee Valleys, smoke, and the more noxious volatile organic compounds that billow from the exhaust pipes of the millions of cars and trucks moving ceaselessly through the lands below.

To change the color of the sky may seem more appropriate to gods than to humans. Yet in Southern Appalachia we have done so. Especially in the summer, the sky itself—not just the clouds—is sometimes more grayish-white than blue. This is not its natural color. Until power plants and traffic began to fill the valleys—until the late 1960s, in fact—both the skies and the mountain mists were a healthy blue, and summer was the season of clearest air.

From the high vantage points of Thunderhead Mountain or Clingman's Dome, the smog appears as a murky grey or featureless white sea that fills the entire Tennessee Valley, hiding it from view. Usually the surface of this sea is hazy and indistinct, but during periods of pronounced temperature inversion it is flat and well-defined, marking a boundary between the thick polluted air below and the clearer air and blue skies high above.

From the valleys below, the smog is frequently visible at sunset as dirty brown or grey streaks near the horizon. At night it reflects back the light of cities, paling the sky and obscuring the stars.

Since 1948, the average visibility—the distance one can see—in the Great Smoky Mountains National Park has decreased by eighty percent in the summer and forty percent in winter. The estimated annual average visibility in the Park before we began to pollute the air was over ninety miles. The current average is twenty-two miles. In the summer the average is twelve miles. When the haze is thick, mountain peaks a mile away may be invisible.[1]

Fine sulfate particles account for most of the visibility loss (estimates range from sixty to eighty-five percent), volatile organic compounds for most of the rest. Smoke, dust, and nitrate aerosols also contribute to the problem.

The sulfate particles originate as sulfur dioxide (SO_2), an odorless, colorless gas created mostly by the burning of coal at power plants in the Ohio River Valley and the Southeast—especially the Tennessee Valley. Chemical reactions in the atmosphere, accelerated by heat, humidity, and sunlight, transform the sulfur dioxide into sulfates. The summer average sulfate concentration in the Park is now ten to forty-two times higher than the natural levels.[2] TVA's sulfur dioxide emissions peaked in 1976 at 2,376,000 tons per year and were reduced to less than a million tons by 1984 through the use of new technology mandated by the Clean Air Act. The most important innovation was scrubbers, which cleanse emissions by passing them through a spray of finely pulverized limestone mixed with water. (But while scrubbers efficiently remove sulfur dioxide from waste gases, they do not destroy the pollution but merely capture it in a toxic and acidic sludge—creating a waste disposal problem.) After 1984, however, emissions began to rise, peaking again at nearly 1,500,000 tons in 1994.[3] Sulfate particle levels in the Park increased correspondingly—twenty-one percent between 1984 and 1995.[4] Then, in the spring of 1995, TVA, responding to 1990 Clean Air Act requirements, added scrubbers to its largest remaining sulfur dioxide source, the Cumberland power plant, about fifty miles west of Nashville. The scrubbers reduced sulfur dioxide emissions from the plant by about 278,000 tons per year, which may improve sulfate levels in the Park and the bioregion slightly. Sulfate levels will remain high, however, since other TVA plants still release about a million tons of sulfur dioxide annually, and not all the sulfate that affects the Park comes from TVA. One study concludes that about thirty-seven percent of the sulfate originates from power plants in the Ohio River Valley.[5] Moreover, sulfur dioxide emissions from the two TVA coal plants closest to the Park (Bull Run and Kingston) have continued to increase—by twenty-five percent for the years 1984-1995.[6]

Sulfur dioxide and sulfate particles do more than just shroud mountains or whiten the sky. They also react with water to form sulfuric acid, a component of acid precipitation (see Chapter One), and they can cause breathing problems and lung damage.

Along with the sulfur dioxide, the tall stacks of the power plants pour out hundreds of thousands of tons annually of nitrogen oxides (NO_x—the 'x' represents a variable number of oxygen atoms, and the formula is pronounced like the word "knocks"). TVA's NO_x emissions fell between 1976 and 1982, then rose steadily from about 300,000 tons in 1982 to an all-time high of over 500,000 tons in 1994. They have since decreased slightly, to just under 500,000 tons. But since there are many other artificial sources of NO_x, TVA is responsible for only about a third of the total NO_x emissions in the TVA region. Cars, trucks, boilers, furnaces, and incinerators account for much of the rest. Agriculture also contributes, since NO_x is given off by fertilizers.[7] NO_x shares several properties with sulfur dioxide: both are colorless (or nearly so), odorless gases, both are components of acid precipitation, both can harm the lungs, and both contribute to smog. Nitrate aerosols, derived by chemical reactions from NO_x, account for about two percent of the visibility impairment in the Smokies.[8] NO_x also plays a role in the production of ground-level ozone, a pollutant considered later in this chapter.

Volatile organic compounds (VOCs) are responsible for about eleven percent of the visibility impairment.[9] VOCs constitute an extremely broad category of pollutants that includes millions of individual compounds. Some VOCs, as we noted above, are natural—part of the mountains' original "blue mist." But others are released by the burning of fossil fuels or the evaporation of solvents in paints, adhesives and similar products. The fumes that escape into the air as you pump gasoline into your car are composed of VOCs. So are the fumes of hot asphalt. Some VOCs are relatively benign; others (such as gasoline or asphalt fumes) are poisonous or carcinogenic.

The final component of the haze, accounting for about twelve percent of the visibility loss,[10] is elemental carbon, in the form of soot or smoke. Open fires, diesel exhausts, cigarettes, wood stoves, fireplaces, small engines, and poorly maintained automobiles are common sources of smoke. Smoke particles are themselves harmful to the nose, throat, and lungs. But smoke usually contains other dangerous substances—such as the tar and nicotine in cigarettes.

The smog will not soon clear. Though technical improvements to power plants could reduce sulfur dioxide and NO_x emissions still further (TVA hopes to cut sulfur dioxide emissions by about forty percent by 2003 and NO_x emissions by ten to twenty percent of current levels by 2000), there are no guarantees. Both TVA and the environmental regulations that have restrained its emissions have Congressional enemies, and both could be radically altered or eliminated.

Moreover, despite all actual and planned improvements, projected increases in demand for electrical power due to growth and development will cause emissions of both sulfur dioxide and NO_x to rise again after 2005.[11]

TVA is responsible for about thirty-three percent of the NO_x emissions in the TVA region, traffic for about thirty-one percent; the remaining emissions come mainly from homes, industries, and agriculture.[12] Attempts to reduce NO_x emissions for cars and trucks have met with troublesome design problems, and the gains that have been achieved have been largely offset by increases in the number of vehicles and in average driving times. The problem is compounded by rapid increases in the use of small machinery: leaf blowers, chain saws, lawn mowers, rototillers, weed eaters, outboard motors, and the like. The small motors of these largely unregulated devices often produce more pollution (per motor) than do the engines of cars and trucks. Working for an hour with an ordinary leaf blower, for example, generates as much pollution as driving a car a hundred miles. Using an outboard motor for an hour may produce as much pollution as driving a car eight hundred miles. The EPA has plans to regulate some small motors by the end of 1996.[13] But, given increases in population and consumption, the smog may thicken even as technology and the laws improve.

Tropospheric (Ground Level) Ozone

Dilution is the solution to pollution was industry's answer in the sixties and early seventies, when it could no longer be denied that the effluent from the stacks of factories and utility plants was sickening and sometimes killing people downwind. The way to dilute air pollution, or so it was thought, was to lift it up higher, to be carried harmlessly away by the winds aloft. So TVA replaced the modest stacks at its coal plants by spires so colossal that they seem designed for an assault upon Heaven. Such, for example, are the stacks of the Kingston Steam Plant which dominate the landscape near Interstate 40 about twenty-five miles west of Knoxville—especially at night when the pulsating flashes of their brilliant white strobe lights pierce the darkness for many miles. These huge stacks improved conditions near the plants, and the pollutants did disperse, but they did not go away. Instead they traveled east above the Tennessee Valley, directly toward the peaks of the Southern Appalachian Mountains. And so in the end they did assault Heaven—or the closest thing to it in these parts.

We have already traced the path of the acid and the smog from these stacks to the mountains. There is one more path to trace: the chemically complex trail that culminates in the production of ozone. Ozone (O_3) is a highly reactive form of oxygen whose molecules consist of three oxygen atoms instead of the usual two.

Ozone is an oxidizing agent that at high enough exposures can irritate eyes and sear lung tissue, creating scar tissue in its place. It heightens susceptibility to asthma, stuffy nose, colds, and other infections. These effects are greatest among children, asthma sufferers, and the elderly. Ozone is also toxic to certain plants.

Ozone is created in the troposphere (roughly, the lowest six miles of the atmosphere) by reactions of nitrogen oxides and volatile organic compounds in the presence of sunlight. The NO_x and the VOCs are produced not only by power plants and industry but by traffic. Ozone pollution is worst during the summer, when the sunlight is most intense. In the lowlands of the Tennessee Valley, summer ozone levels vary in a daily cycle. They are highest in mid-afternoon, as sunlight and traffic combine to maximize ozone production, and lowest at night. But ozone levels in the Smokies are not so directly tied to traffic patterns. In the summer, they remain constantly high for long periods, so that mountain plants receive exposures both day and night.[14]

Natural ozone concentrations in air are between twenty and forty parts per billion.[15] According to the EPA, concentrations in excess of 120 parts per billion for one hour are dangerous to human health, but this standard is under review and may be lowered. Evidence is mounting that healthy exercising adults show signs of lung damage at considerably lower exposures.[16] The American Lung Association advocates a standard of seventy parts per billion for an eight-hour average. Knoxville and much of the Tennessee Valley violate this lower standard frequently in the summer months—at least sixty-four times, for example, in 1990.[17]

The ozone problem is even worse in the mountains. Ozone levels at high elevations in the Great Smoky Mountains National Park frequently exceed levels known to injure sensitive vegetation. Ozone levels in the Park have reached 120 parts per billion at least three times since 1994.[18] The National Park Service has recently considered posting health risk warnings at Park entrances.

But warning signs won't help the plants. Ninety plant species in the Park show signs of ozone-like damage, ranging from leaf injury and loss to reduced growth.[19] The visible symptoms include flecking (small colored areas, metallic or brown, fading to tan, grey, or white); stippling (tiny white, black, red, or red-purple spots); pigmentation (bronzing), in which the entire leaf turns brown or reddish-brown;

chlorosis, a total death of tissue which turns leaves yellow or white; and early loss of leaves or fruit.[20] Over fifty percent of the black cherry, yellow poplar, and sassafras trees sampled near Park ozone monitors in recent years have exhibited visible ozone damage—seventy percent at the highest monitoring station. Forty-seven percent of the black cherry seedlings surveyed along trails in 1992 and eighty-eight percent of the tall milkweed plants surveyed in 1994 exhibited ozone-induced leaf damage. In general, the higher the elevation, the greater the injury. Continued exposure could extirpate some sensitive species, such as white pine or black cherry, from the mountains.[21]

Ozone also damages crops. The EPA has estimated that crop losses due to current ozone levels range on average from ten to fifteen percent. For some crops grown in the Southern Appalachian region—particularly spinach and tobacco—losses may exceed fifteen percent. The nationwide cost of these losses, according to the EPA, is between one and two billion dollars.[22]

For many years, most researchers believed that the best way to reduce ozone formation was to lessen humanly-produced emissions of volatile organic compounds. Recently, however, it has become apparent that since natural volatile organic compounds form a large portion of the ozone pollution in the Southern Appalachians, limiting human emissions may improve the ozone levels only slightly. Therefore, to significantly reduce ozone we must reduce NO_x emissions. But total NO_x emissions from internal combustion engines, industry, and TVA's power plants are now at or near all-time highs, and controlling them may require fundamental changes in the way we live.

Stratospheric Ozone

Though excess ozone in the troposphere is harmful, ozone in the stratosphere, between six and thirty miles aloft, is vital to most living things. Stratospheric ozone acts as a shield that absorbs ultraviolet radiation from the sun. Without the ozone layer, more of this radiation would reach the earth's surface, causing rapid sunburn, cataracts, skin cancer, and immune system deficiencies in humans and animals—and cell death, mutation, and growth inhibition in plants. Ultraviolet radiation can also accelerate the breakdown of plastics, such as the plastic siding now used on many houses. For every one percent decrease in the ozone layer, ultraviolet-B radiation, the harmful type, increases two percent.

Stratospheric ozone is not appreciably increased by ozone production near the earth's surface. Ozone molecules are too unstable to survive long enough to reach the stratosphere in significant quantities. Rather, ozone in the stratosphere is generated by the interaction of ultraviolet radiation with ordinary oxygen molecules. Under natural conditions, this interaction occurs at a rate which has kept the amount of stratospheric ozone stable for millions of years. But this equilibrium can be broken by ground-level release of less reactive substances—particularly chlorofluorocarbons. Chlorofluorocarbons, which are extremely stable, do last long enough to migrate to the stratosphere. There each chlorofluorocarbon molecule can catalyze the destruction of many thousands of ozone molecules. During the last few decades, tens of millions of tons of chlorofluorocarbons were manufactured, incorporated into consumer products, and ultimately released into the air. These chemicals are now eroding the ozone layer. International agreements have already phased out the manufacture of most chlorofluorocarbons, and there is hope of achieving a total worldwide ban by 2006; but because of their persistence in the atmosphere, the ozone layer is expected to continue to erode until at least 2050. By then estimates are that ten to thirty percent of the ozone layer will be lost over northern latitudes—and in particular over the Southern Appalachian region.[23]

These estimates may be too low. In March of 1993, the World Meteorological Organization reported that ozone levels over much of the Northern Hemisphere were already ten to fifteen percent below normal.[24] More recent ground-based and satellite data indicate that the stratosphere above the Southern Appalachian region has experienced up to a twenty percent loss in ozone molecules—which corresponds to a forty percent increase in ultraviolet-B radiation.[25]

Ultraviolet-B radiation can harm plants, animals, and humans. Although most terrestrial plants have some defenses against ultraviolet radiation, these are energy-consuming and usually decrease the amount of light that enters leaves for photosynthesis. Excessive ultraviolet radiation changes the pigmentation, thickness, and anatomy of leaves and may repress growth and flower formation.[26] Excessive exposure to ultraviolet rays may also make plants more vulnerable to diseases or insect infestations.

There is circumstantial evidence that ultraviolet radiation may have already damaged Southern Appalachian forests. Throughout July of 1995 the ozone layer thinned to record or near-record lows over southern West Virginia. In the last ten days of July the leaves of yellow poplars, sycamores, red maples, and redbuds turned brown and began falling along a fifty-mile stretch of the Coal River Valley, west of Charleston. In August the foliage of shagbark hickories and three species of oak—white, chestnut, and chinquapin—curled and turned brown. White pines, too, began to exhibit needle damage of a kind associated with excessive ultraviolet exposure. By August 20, damage was evident at all elevations. Though there was little rain in July and August, and drought undoubtedly contributed to the defoliation (similar drought-related damage was observed in the Tennessee Valley and on the Cumberland Plateau), the combined rainfall for May and June at the Coal River was over three inches above normal. And according to U.S. Forest Service plant pathologist Martin MacKenzie, the leaf damage was "sun-directed."[27] The evidence is inconclusive, but it is possible that the defoliation resulted from a combination of drought and intense ultraviolet radiation.

It is not just the trees, however, that are affected. The deterioration of the ozone layer is a world-historical event, marking a new stage in the power of human beings. This power has enabled us to transform the beneficent sunlight into something increasingly dangerous to nearly every living thing on Earth.

Noise

Noise, though it travels through the air, is not a substance and hence not a pollutant in the ordinary sense. But it is a common, and sometimes harmful, concomitant of many human activities. Extremely loud sounds, such as the noise of machinery, high-decibel music, or low-flying jet aircraft can cause traumatic or progressive hearing loss. At lower levels, noise increases stress, producing such symptoms as headaches, nausea, and high blood pressure.[28]

Until the European invasion, the most intrusive noises in the Southern Appalachians (apart from an occasional thunderstorm) were probably the buzzing of insects and the squawking of crows and jays. Bird song was prominent, along with the sighing of wind in the trees. Near rivers, the rushing of water was audible. On summer evenings, choirs of frogs, crickets, and katydids could be heard, punctuated now and again by the lonesome call of an owl. At night, rarely, the mountain silence might be broken by the howling of wolves—or the heart-stopping wail of a mountain lion.

Sometimes in winter—or in the dark, calm hours before the dawn—one might experience utter silence—silence so intense that within it could be heard the bombardment of air molecules against one's eardrums, playing a subtle music.

Things are different today, as the reader—if she is now anywhere within the bioregion—can verify simply by taking a moment to listen. Even on the peaks of the Smokies, one is seldom entirely out of hearing of traffic noises, gun shots, distant chainsaws, and aircraft. In most other locations, possibly excepting some isolated coves, traffic noise (the roar of engines, the blasting of horns, the squeal of brakes) is prominent—as is the noise of lawn mowers, leaf blowers, sirens, slamming doors, weed eaters, sound systems, and heavy machinery. Near interstates, the bellow and growl of diesel trucks is audible day and night.

These pervasive sounds do not harm people in any obvious way. They are ugly, of course; but most people, most of the time, have learned not to hear them. So if we were concerned only with physical health, we might dismiss most of the noise as trivial. But though common noise pollution may do little apparent physical harm, it does degrade the quality of experience, hence the health of the spirit. Seekers of silence in the Smokies, for example, are often disturbed by the invasive tree-top roar of sightseeing helicopters flying up from Pigeon Forge. This would be less troublesome if silence could be found elsewhere. It can't.

Toxic Air, Indoors

The most lethal air pollutant in the bioregion is cigarette smoke. It is not the most toxic, nor the greatest in quantity, but it kills the largest number of people because it is concentrated indoors where people spend most of their time. Lung cancer, emphysema, heart disease, and possibly breast cancer[29] are its most prominent health effects.

Second to cigarette smoke is radon, a naturally occurring radioactive gas given off by rocks and soil that can seep into buildings from the ground. In open air, radon disperses rapidly and harmlessly, but in well-sealed buildings it may accumulate to dangerous concentrations. Inhalation of radon can cause lung cancer. Radon is prevalent in the soils of Southern Appalachia—especially in upper East Tennessee and northwestern North Carolina.[30]

Because radioactive particles adhere to smoke particles in the lung, simultaneous exposure to radon and cigarette smoke results in a lung cancer risk much greater than the sum of the risks for each. This is a classic example of synergy: the multiplication of effect when two or more pollutants are present together. For many combinations of pollutants, the potential for synergistic multiplication of health effects is unknown.

Other common sources of indoor air pollution include wood stoves and fireplaces, mothballs, chlorine bleach, solvents, air "fresheners," foam insulation, plastic products, synthetic fibers, adhesives, artificial wood products, polishes, paints, pesticides, photocopiers, dust, and asbestos. Many, though not all, of the indoor pollutants are volatile organic compounds. Some are carcinogenic. Some, either singly or in combination, also cause headaches, eye irritation, nausea, allergies, memory loss, and suppression of the immune system—a suite of symptoms known collectively as "sick building syndrome."[31] Because indoor pollutants are trapped and repeatedly recirculated, indoor air pollution is usually more harmful to human health than air pollution outside. In fact it is, according to the EPA, the single most important environmental cause of cancer.[32]

The easiest and least expensive way to reduce indoor air pollution is to open the windows. But because Southern Appalachia is cold in the winter and hot in the summer, many buildings have heating and cooling systems that require windows to be closed through most, if not all, of the year. Heating, of course, is necessary in our climate. Inhabitants of Southern Appalachia have always heated their dwellings in the winter. But air conditioning, widely available only in the past few decades, is a luxury. There are alternatives: appropriate architecture, fans (preferably solar-powered), and proper placement of trees can do much to make buildings without air conditioning breezy and tolerable even when the temperature is sweltering. (And it is ironic that in our effort to escape the summer heat through air conditioning, we consume electricity generated by combustion, which releases greenhouse gases that have the undesirable side-effect of intensifying the summer heat—but more on that problem shortly.)

Living without air conditioning is initially uncomfortable, but a healthy body adapts to heat. After a few weeks, one's comfort level shifts, and temperatures that were once intolerable become comfortable, making the body hardier, more vigorous, and more resilient. Allowing the body to adjust to the temperature of the environment, rather than adjusting the environment to bodily whims by prodigal energy consumption, thus can benefit not only ecosystem health, but the health of the body as well.

Toxic Air, Outdoors

Of course, the air outside is not always healthful either. On some hot, stagnant summer days, ozone levels across the bioregion are, as we noted above, high enough to warrant serious health concerns. But most of the toxic air pollution is more localized.

In 1993 reported air emissions of EPA-listed toxic chemicals in Tennessee totaled 116,734,579 pounds, making Tennessee the second worst state in the nation for air pollution. The North Carolina total was 74,182,818 pounds.[33]   But these figures are too low, since they represent only releases that private industries report to the EPA. Emissions from government sources or individual households are not reported, and nobody is actually checking most of the industry measurements.

However enormous, these totals actually represent significant progress.   There were no reporting requirements in the 1950s and 1960s—when clothes hung out to dry in Knoxville turned black with soot, the nuclear weapons plants at Oak Ridge routinely released radioactive gases, and Chattanooga had some of the most poisonous air in the entire nation—but toxic releases in those days were certainly worse. Most of the progress can be credited to regulations mandated by the Clean Air Act.

The single most profound improvement has probably been the elimination of leaded gasoline. Lead accumulates in the body and is especially toxic to children, causing hyperactivity, learning disabilities, and decreased intelligence. In adults it may contribute to hypertension, heart attacks, and strokes. It also increases the likelihood of birth defects and stillbirths. Airborne lead has decreased dramatically over the past two decades.

Some industries, too, have made dramatic strides.   Two Polysar plants in Chattanooga, which manufacture latex and foam products, released 954,000 pounds of toxic chemicals into the air in 1987. But by utilizing thermal oxidizers, which burn volatile organic compounds, and by making other improvements, the plants reduced emissions to 44,000 pounds in 1994.[34]

Still, Southern Appalachia has more than its share of big industrial air polluters. The biggest is Lenzing Fibers in Lowland, Tennessee. Lenzing had the dubious distinction of ranking ninth in the nation in toxic air emissions in 1994, the most recent year for which EPA data are available.[35] The plant's main air pollutant was carbon disulfide, a widely-used solvent. Inhalation of carbon disulfide has produced abnormalites of the genitourinary and skeletal systems, as well as disturbances of ossification and blood formation and dystrophic changes in the liver and kidney, in test animals.[36] Lenzing reported emitting 21,400,000 pounds of carbon disulfide, plus a smattering of other air pollutants, in 1994.

The bioregion's second largest air polluter is Tennessee Eastman in Kingsport.

Eastman admitted releasing 5,982,030 pounds of toxic chemicals into Tennessee air in 1994. This may appear to be a great improvement from Eastman's 1993 total—29,027,863 pounds. But the numbers are deceptive. In 1993, the EPA required polluters to report emissions of acetone, which is suspected of enhancing the carcinogenic effect of some other chemicals, such as benzene. But objections from the chemical industry ended the reporting of acetone emissions in 1994[37] As a result, while Eastman reported emitting 22,200,000 pounds of acetone into the air in 1993, acetone amounts were absent from their 1994 report to EPA, reducing the total emissions figure dramatically. This on-paper omission may account for nearly all of Eastman's apparent reduction in air pollution from 1993 to 1994.

Champion International Corporation, better known for its clearcutting and water pollution, is the bioregion's third most largest air polluter. Champion's reported toxic air emissions for its Canton, North Carolina, mill totaled 4,672,417 pounds in 1994, more than twice its 1993 figure of 2,144,501 pounds. The increase raises serious doubts about Champion's much-touted environmental improvements.

Table 2.1 lists the bioregion's largest air polluting industries:

Table 2.1 (1994 statistics)

INDUSTRIES EMITTING MORE THAN 100,000 POUNDS OF TOXIC CHEMICALS INTO THE AIR[38]		
Facility and Location	**Toxic Air Pollutants**	**Toxic Air Emissions (lbs.)**
Ahlstrom Filtration Inc. Chattanooga, TN	Methanol, phenol	1,657,300
ALCOA Alcoa, TN	Aluminum, carbonyl sulfide, chlorine, copper, hydrochloric acid, hydrogen fluoride, manganese	942,153
American Water Heater Group Johnson City, TN	1,1-dichloro-1-fluoroethane, dichloromethane, methylenebis(phenyliso-cyanate), trichloroethylene	439,870
BASF Corp. Fiber Prods. Div. Lowland, TN	Antimony compounds, biphenyl, ethylene glycol, glycol ethers, methanol	125,165
Belding Corticelli Thread Co. Hendersonville, NC	Formaldehyde, methanol, toluene	271,000
Brooks Furniture Mfg. Inc. Tazewell, TN	Glycol ethers, methyl isobutyl ketone, toluene, xylene	162,298

Table 2.1 cont. (1994 Statistics)

INDUSTRIES EMITTING MORE THAN 100,000 POUNDS OF TOXIC CHEMICALS INTO THE AIR[38]		
Facility and Location	**Toxic Air Pollutants**	**Toxic Air Emissions (lbs.)**
Cantech Industries, Inc. Johnson City, TN	Toluene	158,000
Champion International Corp. Canton, NC	Acetaldehyde, ammonia, chlorine, chlorine dioxide, chloromethane, cresol, formaldehyde, formic acid, hydrochloric acid, hydrogen fluoride, methanol, methyl ethyl ketone, phenol, sulfuric acid	4,672,417
Chattem Chemicals Chattanooga, TN	Ammonia, ethylbenzene, hydrochloric acid, methanol, sec-butyl alcohol, xylene	363,225
CKR Ind., Inc. Winchester, TN	Isopropyl alcohol, methyl ethyl ketone, toluene	294,758
Day, International Arden, NC	Methyl ethyl ketone, toluene	498,156
Delfasco Tennessee Div. Greeneville, TN	Toluene	191,500
Du Pont Chattanooga, TN	Biphenyl, hydrochloric acid	115,279
Empire Furniture Johnson City, TN	Methanol, methyl ethyl ketone, toluene, xylene	161,316
Ethan Allen Inc. Spruce Pine, NC	Isopropyl alcohol, methanol, methyl ethyl ketone, toluene, xylene	134,471
Florida Steel Corp. Knoxville, TN	Barium compounds, chromium compounds, copper compounds, lead compounds, manganese compounds, nickel compounds, zinc compounds	139,083
Foamex L.P. Plant 1, Morristown, TN	Dichloromethane, diethanolamine, toluene diisocyanate	791,988
Fortafil Fibers Inc. Rockwood, TN	Ammonia, carbon tetrachloride, dichloromethane, hydrogen cyanide	118,787
Fruehauf Trailer Corp. Huntsville, TN	Ethylbenzene, methyl ethyl ketone, xylene	104,538
Gordons, Inc. Johnson City, TN	Methanol, methyl ethyl ketone, toluene, xylene	123,071
Henredon Furniture Ind. Inc. Spruce Pine, NC	Methanol, methyl ethyl ketone, n-butyl alcohol, styrene, toluene	217,546

Table 2.1 cont. (1994 Statistics)

INDUSTRIES EMITTING MORE THAN 100,000 POUNDS OF TOXIC CHEMICALS INTO THE AIR[38]		
Facility and Location	**Toxic Air Pollutants**	**Toxic Air Emissions (lbs.)**
Holliston Mills Kingsport, TN	Methyl ethyl ketone, methyl isobutyl ketone, toluene	2,252,566
Lea Ind. Chilhowie, VA	Glycol ethers, methanol, methyl ethyl ketone, n-butyl alcohol, toluene, xylene	163.957
Lea Ind. Plant #4, Morristown, TN	Methanol, methyl ethyl ketone, n-butyl alcohol, toluene, xylene	232,621
Lea Ind. Plant #7, Waynesville, NC	Methanol, methyl ethyl ketone, toluene, xylene	113,236
Lenzing Fibers Corp., Lowland, TN	Ammonia, carbon disulfide, chlorine, phosphoric acid, sulfuric acid	21,400,765
Marley Mouldings Inc. Marion, VA	Di(2-ethylhexyl) phthalate, methanol, methyl ethyl ketone, toluene	154,189
Mastercraft Boat Co. Vonore, TN	Dimethyl phthalate, methylenebis (phenylisocyanate), styrene	149,938
Merillat Ind. Inc. Atkins, VA	1,2,4-trimethylbenzene, ethylbenzene, glycol ethers, methyl ethyl ketone, methyl isobutyl ketone, n-butyl alcohol, toluene, xylene	340,274
Nippondenso Tennessee, Inc. Maryville, TN	1,1,1-trichloroethane, aluminum, lead, methyl ethyl ketone, toluene, xylene	131,380
North American Rayon, Elizabethton, TN	Carbon disulfide	3,066,005
North American Royalties Inc. Wheland Fndy. Div. Chattanooga, TN	1,2,4-trimethylbenzene, bis(2-ethylhexyl) adipate, chromium compounds, copper compounds, lead compounds, manganese compounds, methanol, methylenebis(phenylisocyanate), phenol, zinc compounds	161,278
Nu-Foam Prods. Chattanooga, TN	1,1,1-trichloroethane, dichloromethane, toluene diisocyanate	449,030
Olin Corp. Charleston, TN	Chlorine, dichlorotetrafluoroethane (CFC-114), hydrochloric acid, mercury	145,083
P. H. Glatfelter Co. Ecusta Div. Pisgah Forest, NC	Ammonia, chlorine, hydrochloric acid, methanol, sulfuric acid, toluene	440,109

Table 2.1 cont. (1994 Statistics)

INDUSTRIES EMITTING MORE THAN 100,000 POUNDS OF TOXIC CHEMICALS INTO THE AIR[38]		
Facility and Location	**Toxic Air Pollutants**	**Toxic Air Emissions (lbs.)**
Philips Consumer Electronics Jefferson City, TN	Methanol, methyl ethyl ketone, toluene, xylene	114,793
Polyfibron Techs. Inc., Morristown, TN	Methyl ethyl ketone, toluene, zinc compounds	246,510
Rexam Metallising Camelot, TN	Ethylene glycol, methyl ethyl ketone, toluene	185,354
Robertshaw Tennessee Knoxville, TN	Copper compounds, ethylene glycol, hydrochloric acid, nitric acid, phosphoric acid, sulfuric acid, trichloroethylene,	116,646
Sea Ray Boats (2 locations) Knoxville, TN	1,1,1-trichloroethane, styrene	235,000
Sea Ray Boats Inc. Vonore, TN	1,1,1-trichloroethane, dimethyl phthalate, methyl methacrylate, styrene	314,250
Stanley Furniture Co., Stanleytown, VA	Isopropyl alcohol, methanol, methyl ethyl ketone, n-butyl alcohol, toluene, xylene	249,397
Steelcase, Inc. Fletcher, NC	Glycol ethers, methanol, n-butyl alcohol, toluene, xylene	102,382
Tennessee Eastman Div. Kingsport, TN	1,1,2,2-tetrachloroethane, 1,4-dioxane, 2,4-dinitrophenol, 2-methoxyethanol, 2-phenylphenol, acetaldehyde, acetonitrile, ammonia, aniline, antimony compounds, benzene, biphenyl, bis(2-ethylhexyl) adipate, bromomethane, butyl acrylate, butyraldehyde, chlorine, chlorobenzene, chlorodifluoromethane, chromium compounds, cobalt compounds, copper compounds, cyclohexane, di(2-ethylhexyl) phthalate, dibutyl phthalate, dichlorodifluoromethane (CFC-12), dichloromethane, diethyl phthalate, dimethyl phthalate, dimethyl sulfate, ethylene, ethylene glycol, formaldehyde, glycol ethers, hydrochloric acid, hydrogen fluoride, hydroquinone, isobutyraldehyde, m-xylene, manganese compounds, methanol, methyl ethyl ketone, methyl iodide, methyl isobutyl ketone, n,n-dimethylaniline, n-butyl alcohol, nickel, nitric acid o-anisidine, o-toluidine, o-xylene, p-xylene, phenol, phosphoric acid, phthalic anhydride, propionaldehyde, propylene, pyridine, quinone, styrene, sulfuric acid, tert-butyl alcohol, toluene, xylene (mixed isomers), zinc compounds	5,982,030

Table 2.1 cont. **(1994 Statistics)**

INDUSTRIES EMITTING MORE THAN 100,000 POUNDS OF TOXIC CHEMICALS INTO THE AIR[38]		
Facility and Location	**Toxic Air Pollutants**	**Toxic Air Emissions (lbs.)**
Universal Bedroom Furniture Ltd., Morristown, TN	Glycol ethers, methanol, methyl ethyl ketone, methyl isobutyl ketone, n-butyl alcohol, toluene, xylene	386,250
Utility Trailer Mfg. Co. Atkins, VA	1,1-dichloro-1-fluoroethane, chlorodifluoromethane, xylene	133,315
Virginia House Furniture Co. Plant 1 Atkins, VA	Ethylbenzene, methanol, methyl ethyl ketone, toluene, xylene	170,570
Virginia House Furniture Co. Plant 2 Atkins, VA	Methanol, methyl ethyl ketone, n-butyl alcohol, toluene, xylene	108,370
Viskase Corp. Loudon, TN	Carbon disulfide	2,274,000
Whitley Prods. Inc. Franklin, NC	Methanol, trichloroethylene	159,672
Willamette Inds. Inc. Kingsport, TN	Acetaldehyde, ammonia, chlorine, chlorine dioxide, chloroform, hydrochloric acid, methanol, sulfuric acid	729,625
Wilsonart Intl. Fletcher, NC	Formaldehyde, methanol, phenol	100,288

The chemicals listed affect human health and the environment in widely varying ways; and, though all are toxic, some are much more toxic than others. It is not possible to list all their effects, some of which are in any case unknown. Some—lead, glycol ethers, styrene and toluene, for example—are reproductive toxins. Others—such as 1,4-dioxane, acetaldehyde, carbon tetrachloride, chloroform, dichloromethane, formaldehyde, styrene, and trichlorethylene—are carcinogens.[39]

Many industries not listed in Table 2.1 because their reported emissions are under a hundred thousand pounds still do considerable damage. Horsehead Resource Development, for example, (a hazardous waste processing plant in the small community of Clymersville, in Roane County), reported only 5,676 pounds of air emissions in 1994. Yet neighbors have been plagued by dust containing toxic metals, some of which have been found in elevated levels in their blood. The dust is also killing vegetation.[40]

It should also be noted that Table 2.1 does not include emissions from power plants. TVA's coal-fired power plants are a significant source of airborne mercury, a neurotoxin. TVA estimates its 1996 mercury emissions to be 4,884 pounds.[41] The coal-burning facilities also inject into the air relatively small amounts of other toxic metals, including arsenic, cadmium, chromium, beryllium, nickel, lead, manganese, selenium, vanadium, and radioactive uranium, radium and thorium. These metals may become water pollutants as they settle out of the air.[42] TVA's largest toxic emissions, of course, consist of sulfur dioxide and nitrogen oxides (NO_x), but their effects were discussed in earlier sections.

Table 2.1 also omits the DOE plants in Oak Ridge, though these have historically been significant sources of toxic and radioactive air pollutants. For a long time, little was known of the effects of their emissions, but some quantitative research is at last beginning to emerge. One study concerns the old Graphite Reactor at Oak Ridge. From 1944 through 1956 this reactor released radioactive iodine 131 into the air. The iodine, falling out on the land, was ingested by cows downwind in Bethel Valley and became concentrated in their milk. Once ingested by humans, iodine 131 is taken up by the thyroid gland, where it is especially carcinogenic to young girls. In one of the first quantitative assessments of the health effects of air pollution from the bomb plants, the Tennessee Department of Health recently concluded that the lifetime risk of thyroid cancer to girls who regularly drank milk from cows grazed two miles from the reactor was increased by about 0.6 percent. The increase in cancer risk would have been less for those who drank milk from cows farther away, for males, and for adults.[43] This is the estimated risk for only one pollutant. There are as yet no quantitative data on cumulative risks from the panoply of contaminants released at Oak Ridge.

The effect of outdoor air pollution depends to a large extent on the wind. The predominant air flow in Southern Appalachia is from the west, but local topographic features influence wind flow. The Tennessee Valley, with its northeast-southwest orientation, channels air currents so that surface winds tend to blow either up the valley from the southwest or down the valley from the northeast. (In Asheville, on the North Carolina side of the mountains, by contrast, surface winds blow most often directly from the north or from the south.) The Smokies are a formidable barrier to airflow, and Tennessee Valley weather almost never comes over the mountains from the southeast.

Unfortunately, our bioregion has nearly the highest incidence of stagnant air in the Eastern United States,[44] and because industries tend to locate in sheltered valleys, toxic emissions often linger near the site of release or slightly downwind, prolonging exposures.

Climate Change

When Hurricane Opal roared across the Smokies on October 5, 1995, flattening whole stands of trees and blocking trails, she provided a portent of things to come. The trees of the high forests, already thinned by acid deposition, ozone damage, and infestations of humanly-imported insects, could not adequately shield one another from the blast, and whole stands fell together. Red spruce in the transition zone from spruce to fir suffered heavy losses.

The Smokies are no strangers to wind and storm; the stunted and twisted trees clinging to rocks on the high peaks attest to that. But wind damage is likely to increase, not only because of the progressive thinning of the trees, but also because of the increasing ferocity of storms. For the Earth's atmosphere is heating up; and, just as water heated in a pan roils faster and faster as the heat increases, so the atmosphere will churn as it warms.

The atmosphere is warming for the same reason that a parked automobile gets hot on a sunny day: the heat is trapped by a greenhouse medium—glass in the case of the automobile, greenhouse gases in the case of the atmosphere. Other things being equal, the more dense the greenhouse gases in the atmosphere, the greater the heating. And each year humans inject trillions of pounds of greenhouse gases (especially carbon dioxide) into the atmosphere, mostly by the burning of fossil fuels. In 1850, before widespread industrialization, the atmosphere contained 250 parts per million of carbon dioxide. Today it contains about 360 parts per million— an increase of forty-four percent. The increase is accelerating.

The quantities are enormous. TVA alone releases over two hundred billion pounds of carbon dioxide annually (nearly 0.4 percent of the world's total), mostly from the burning of coal. At room temperature and sea level pressures, this amount would fill a volume of about 1.8 trillion cubic feet. A box measuring a mile square and ten miles high (as high as wispy cirrus clouds) could not contain it all.[45] And this is just from TVA; the carbon dioxide emissions of cars, trucks, furnaces, stoves, and other combustion sources are not included. Nor are other greenhouse gases, such as methane, NO_x and chlorofluorocarbons, which, while released in smaller quantities, are more effective at trapping heat.

Such gargantuan emissions, together with actual global temperature measurements, have convinced nearly all climatologists that the average global temperature is rising and will continue to rise well into the next century and beyond. Because many other factors—including cloud cover, ozone depletion, sulfur dioxide emissions, and the extent of forests—also influence global temperature, the exact amount of the increase is unknown. Models used by TVA project a rise of between 2.7 and 8.1 degrees Fahrenheit by 2050.[46]

But the temperature will not increase uniformly. Rather, the increasing fluctuation of air currents will produce more extreme and violent weather—including not only prolonged heat waves but abnormal cold snaps. Global warming may have contributed, for example, to the severe winter and damaging spring frosts in Southern Appalachia in 1996. Violent storms, hurricanes, and tornadoes are likely to increase in frequency and intensity. Hurricane Opal was the fifteenth hurricane of 1995—a record year in a record decade for hurricanes.

Average global precipitation will probably increase, but there will be wide and largely unpredictable regional variations. Nobody knows what will happen in Southern Appalachia. If precipitation does increase, so will flooding. This will have a double effect, since more precipitation means increased siltation, which makes reservoirs shallower and less able to control floods.

Rivers, lakes, and streams are also affected by increasing temperatures. Higher temperatures can produce thermal stress and promote disease in cool water fish, such as sauger and walleye. Fish populations may change significantly. Higher temperatures alter the growing season of wetland vegetation, increasing the decomposition and nutrient cycling rate. Summer heat can dry up soils and decrease runoff, lowering dissolved oxygen levels. Some aquatic plants may be eliminated and possibly replaced by species that can withstand higher temperatures, higher (or lower) pH, and increased siltation.

On land, an increase in the minimum winter air temperature would extend the range of subtropical species, bringing invasions of exotics that would compete with indigenous species, rendering the existence of certain threatened or endangered species still more precarious. Warmer temperatures might expand the range of certain infectious diseases, such as malaria, hanta virus, and dengue fever, into Southern Appalachia. Growing seasons are likely to change, so that crop varieties now suited to this bioregion may no longer be successful. The instability of climate and weather patterns may make both long- and short-term agricultural investments increasingly risky. Flooding, hail, and high winds may damage crops and orchards. New diseases or exotic insects may afflict crops and livestock.

Global warming may reduce or eliminate some tree species, altering composition of forests. If there are long droughts, forest fires will increase in frequency and intensity. Increasing temperatures may strike the final blow to the cold-adapted spruce-fir forests of the high Southern Appalachians—forests already falling to exotic insects, ozone, acid deposition, and wind.

On a larger scale, polar melting and thermal expansion of the seas will probably raise ocean levels, flooding vast areas of coastland, especially in Florida, within a century or two. While this will not affect Southern Appalachia directly, it may increase population pressure as refugees flee inland.[47]

Increasing the level of carbon dioxide in the air stimulates the growth of plants. This may be both an advantage and a disadvantage. Crop yields and forest growth may increase, but so may the growth of weeds. Increased plant growth could increase populations of insects that feed on plants.[48]

Even if we were to stop releasing all greenhouse gases immediately, the atmosphere would not return to normal for centuries. Moreover, there is a long lag time between elevated greenhouse gas levels and increased temperatures, so that the effects of the gases we introduce into the air today may not be felt for decades. At present, we are doing virtually nothing to slow carbon dioxide emissions, and two historic events—global deforestation and the industrialization of less-developed nations (China in particular)—will accelerate the increase still further. Expect rough weather.

What Will They Breathe?

Given that we are already scarring our lungs with ozone, diesel smoke, NO_x, and a panoply of toxic chemicals, it is doubtful that we ever experience a full, pure, healthy breath of air. But to these facts must be added one more—something that does not affect us significantly now, but raises a stark question for the future: for each atom of carbon added to the atmosphere by combustion, two atoms of oxygen are removed. As a result, the oxygen content of the atmosphere is decreasing by about thirteen parts per million per year.[49] This is a very small loss, since the current oxygen concentration is about 210,000 parts per million. But we should not ignore the fact that while injecting all these harmful gases into the air, we are gradually and ever more rapidly removing the one that is absolutely essential for all animal and human life.

FIGURE 4: Fraser firs near Clingman's Dome in the Great Smoky Mountains National Park. Over ninety percent of the mature Fraser firs are dead.

How long shall the land mourn, and the herbs of every field wither, for the wickedness of them that dwell therein? The beasts are consumed, and the birds; because they said, He shall not see our last end.
— Jeremiah 12:4

The first two chapters of this report surveyed degradation of the water and the air. Here we consider degradation of the system of life: the biotic community. The biotic community of the Upper Tennessee Valley and Southern Appalachian Mountains is demonstrably unhealthy, and in many respects its health continues to decline. The causes of these declines are complex, but three of the most important are habitat fragmentation, pollution (including siltation), and biological invasions resulting from human disturbance. Habitat fragmentation is most conspicuous in the bioregion's most prominent habitats: its forests.

If a Tree Falls ...

Picture the North American continent as a huge lawn. Then imagine a vast, slow lawn mower moving from east to west. The mower begins in the East about the middle of the nineteenth century. By the end of the twentieth, it has mowed virtually everything from the Atlantic coast to the Pacific Northwest.

This mower is industrial forestry. In the nineteenth and early twentieth centuries it stripped away virtually all the forests east of the Mississippi, leaving bare earth, ugliness, depleted soils, erosion, and raging floods in its wake. Eastern forests having more or less been leveled by the 1930s, it passed on to the pine forests of the Rockies and the redwood forests of California, and north to the vast rainy woods of Washington and Oregon. (Cutting began in the West, of course, with the arrival of white settlers and continued in the East as it began to devastate the West. Moreover, trees were cut, not in wide swaths across the landscape, but in a patchwork. Still, the general trend was from east to west.) The recent battles over the spotted owl in the Northwest were less about an owl than about the last fragments of the nation's old-growth forests, which the owl symbolized.

The northwestern corner of the lawn is now nearly mowed. But the eastern—and particularly the southeastern—end has been growing for many decades. Southern Appalachian hills, which less than a century ago were treeless and brown with mud, are, many of them, once again forested and green. And so the mower is turning inexorably back toward the Southeast.[1]

This historic movement of industrial forestry is one of the greatest impending threats to the diversity of life in Southern Appalachia. Its harbingers are the chip mills.

Chip Mills

A chip mill is an enormous forest-grinding machine. Fed by streams of logging trucks (hundreds per day for a large mill), it debarks the logs and grinds them into chips that are used primarily for making paper and particle board. To supply a chip mill, which may run round the clock, loggers must strip and haul away dozens of acres of forest each day from a sourcing radius of about seventy-five miles around the mill.[2] The process leaves behind scarred earth, vanished wildlife, flooded streams, and (ultimately) the broken promise of lasting jobs.

In the early nineties, three corporations—Donghae Pulp, Parker Towing, and Boise Cascade—requested permits to build barge terminals for chip mill facilities along a single twelve-mile stretch of the Tennessee River near South Pittsburgh, about twenty-five miles west of Chattanooga. Together, they said, these three mills would produce about 1,900,000 tons of chips per year.[3] Chips from the new mills would be loaded onto barges and towed down the Tennessee-Tombigbee waterway to Mobile Bay. There the chips would be transferred to ocean-going ships for export to markets as far away as Asia.[4] The result, if the barge permits were granted, would be rapid and widespread destruction of the surrounding forests.

Environmental activists, organized into a coalition called TAGER (Tennesseans, Alabamans and Georgians for Environmental Responsibility), sounded the alarm—and were pleased to find themselves seconded for once by powerful allies. In an editorial entitled "A Pending Environmental Tragedy?" the *Chattanooga Times* compared the exploitation of the Tennessee Valley forests by multinational paper corporations to the exploitation of the resources of Third World nations by colonialists.[5] Realizing that they could not compete for logs with multinational corporations, local saw mill owners and furniture manufacturers joined the opposition. The Chattanooga Area Convention and Visitors Bureau and the Chattanooga Chamber of Commerce, envisioning the impact that vistas of barren hills and mud-choked creeks would have on the lucrative tourist industry, added their political muscle.

As a result, TVA—which had originally hoped to lure chip mills to the Valley as part of its economic development strategy—agreed to do an environmental impact study on the cumulative effects of granting permits for the proposed barge terminals. This study, completed in February, 1993, issued the following judgment: "After weighing the potential benefits of the pending requests with the likelihood of substantial, cumulative localized impacts and the risk of harvesting-related impacts, TVA's preferred alternative is the denial of all proposed actions."[6] Permitting of the barge terminals, TVA concluded, would have lead to unacceptable cumulative environmental degradation.

This degradation is already apparent in Alabama and Mississippi, where existing chip mills have been cutting wood faster than it can grow since the 1980s. As Alabama has been deforested, the overcutting has moved closer and closer to the Southern Appalachians.[7]

Though the barge terminal permits were denied, at least three regional facilities are already loading whole logs to be chipped elsewhere: the Alabama State Dock near Bridgeport, just across the Tennessee state line; Nickajack Port; and the Loudon County Terminal. The first two of these are shipping hardwood, the last pine. Some of the logs from Nickajack are being chipped at the Mannington chip mill on the Tennessee-Tombigbee Waterway near Hollywood, Alabama.[8]

These facilities are competing with a number of existing chip mills in the race to gobble up Southern Appalachian forests. Among the largest are the Champion International mill in Waynesville, North Carolina; the Bowater mill near Chattanooga; the Willamette (formerly Mead) mill at Kingsport; and the Louisiana Pacific mill in western Virginia. Willamette is building another chip mill in Rutherford County, North Carolina, at Union Mills. J. M. Huber is building a chip mill in Spring City, Tennessee, which is designed to produce oriented-strand board. It will strip away enough trees to produce six hundred thousand tons of chips per year. MacMillan Truss Joist in Hazard, Kentucky, though not a chipping operation, competes with chip mills for small trees, and it "harvests" in East Tennessee.[9]

Not to be outdone, Champion International, long contemptuous of the land and people of Southern Appalachia, recently completed yet another chip mill near Caryville, Tennessee, about forty miles north of Knoxville. This large mill, whose crane is visible from Exit 141 of Interstate 75, will strip many tens of thousands of acres of trees, mostly hardwoods, from Campbell, Scott, and Anderson Counties. Champion has issued a propaganda blitz of soothing television commercials to soften the blow, but it is no more likely to respect the forest here than it did in Montana, where it clearcut eight hundred thousand acres at three times the rate of tree growth. According to Dr. Thomas Power, the chair of the Economics Department at the University of Montana, Missoula, "Champion came in here promising they would be here forever, and then just overcut all the trees and left."[10]

The Claims of Industrial Forestry

The forest products industry argues that there is room for more logging here, since tree growth currently exceeds the rate of cutting in Southern Appalachia. That depends on how and where you look. It is not true for high-quality saw timber, which is already being logged much faster than it grows.[11] (The rarity of good saw timber is evident in the scarcity of and high market price for clear boards of such hardwoods as oak, ash, hickory, cherry, and walnut.) Nor is it true for pine, which, except on pine plantations, is on average being cut faster than it grows.[12] Moreover, overall cutting exceeds growth in large portions of the sourcing areas of existing chip mills. But on average, region-wide, it may still be true—for now—that the rate of tree growth exceeds the rate of cutting.[13] With the invasion of new chip mills, however, that regional average could shift rapidly.

The industry also claims to be wiser now about forest abuses and promises to follow a code of "best management practices" (BMPs), which would reduce erosion and some of the other destructive effects of clearcutting. These promises, however, do not ensure environmental protection. Clearcutting requires extensive systems of forest roads and skid trails, where the forest soil is bulldozed and laid bare. Heavy logging equipment compacts the soil. Erosion contaminates streams with silt and nutrients.[14] These impacts may be reduced but they are not eliminated even by the strictest adherence to BMPs. In their environmental impact statement on the chip mills, TVA , the U.S. Army Corps of Engineers, and the U.S. Fish and Wildlife Service noted: *BMPs, as currently designed, do not protect all possibly impacted resources. Intensified timber harvesting and uncertain BMP compliance at least pose risks of adverse impacts on a localized or site-specific basis in the sourcing area to wildlife, karst (limestone cave) features, water quality, aquatic species, endangered and threatened species, aesthetics, and archaeological sites. Hard mast (acorn and nut) production (needed by many forms of wildlife) could be adversely affected regionally.[15]*

As to the uncertain compliance, the forest industry retorts that its compliance record is improving. Again this may be true—for the moment. Trees are still relatively abundant in the upper Tennessee Valley, so that BMPs are not too irksome to follow. But since throughout most of our bioregion they are voluntary, not legal, requirements, BMPs are still in practice often ignored. In 1995, for example, a clearcut on Champion land in Campbell County flagrantly violated BMPs by clogging a stream, diverting it to make a log-loading pad, and creating a massive sediment flow. The Tennessee Division of Water Pollution Control issued a notice of violation for the stream disruptions, but initiated no court action or fine.[16]

Violations are likely to increase as the cutting frenzy intensifies and good stands of trees become rarer and more expensive. It defies credence that in such circumstances multinational corporations under intense competitive pressures will steadfastly honor merely voluntary guidelines. TVA, the EPA, the U. S. Department of the Interior, the Alabama Department of Environmental Management, and the Tennessee Wildlife Resources Agency have all expressed doubts about the adequacy of voluntary BMP compliance.[17]

Even if BMPs were passed into law, and even if the law provided strict penalties, and even if these penalties were enforced (three big ifs), the result would still be a continual and generalized deterioration of the land: more logging roads and machinery in the forest, followed by more human intrusions, more trash, more erosion, invasions of nonnative organisms, damaged soils, and diminished wildlife habitat—not to mention the loss of the trees themselves.

Industrial forestry promotes itself as a form of agriculture, with trees as its harvestable crops. But it breaks agriculture's primary rule: give back what you take. All experienced farmers and gardeners know that if you do not return to the soil at least as much organic material (biomass) and nutrients as you take in harvest, the soil loses fertility with each succeeding crop. But industrial forestry gathers its "harvest" without giving back—except (rarely) for a little petrochemical fertilizer. The trees, which in nature would die, rot, and replenish the soil, are trucked away, and with them go the nutrients they have absorbed. Of course, the period between "harvests" is longer than for farming or gardening, so the loss is correspondingly slower. But new technologies, particularly those associated with chip mills, use younger and younger trees, promoting ever quicker cutting rotations.

Initially after a clearcut there is a rapid loss of nutrients and some loss of soil. The forest system does, however, quickly begin to heal itself and replace lost nutrients and biomass. As new trees and herbaceous plants sprout, they restore nutrients and organic matter by nitrogen fixation and photosynthesis. If the system is left undisturbed long enough, eventually the lost biomass and nutrients are restored. In northern hardwood forests, this takes sixty to eighty years.[18] In Southern Appalachian forests, the process varies widely with forest and soil type, but seems generally to be quicker.[19]

FIGURE 5: A clearcut in southeastern Tennessee.

It would be wrong, however, to conclude that in the long run there is no net loss when a forest is clearcut. An undisturbed forest not only maintains itself, but actively builds soil, enriching the foundation from which all land-based life springs. If succeeding "harvests" occur as soon as the nutrients and biomass return to pre-cut levels, this enrichment is halted and the system no longer grows richer. If they occur earlier, it is reversed and the system becomes poorer. In any case, removing the trees always makes the forest system and forest land poorer in nutrients and biomass than if it had been left alone.

We have so far considered just one measure of loss or gain—the sum of biomass and nutrients in the forest system—in relation to the enrichment or depletion of the soil. When we turn to other measures, the damage of industrial forestry becomes more evident still. For one thing, it takes well over a century for a Southern

Appalachian forest to mature and become old-growth. Some species—the endangered red-cockaded woodpecker, for example—need old-growth to survive. Without long-term forest protection, these species will be lost.

Also likely to be lost (at least locally, in the clearcut areas) are many small plants and flowers that grow on the forest floor. Examples include lilies, trilliums, bloodroot, and ferns.[20] A recent study of Southern Appalachian forests by David Cameron Duffey and Albert J. Meier of the University of Georgia compared forest plots that had never been logged to plots that had been clearcut fifty to eighty-five years before. The average understory plant density in the unlogged plots was 10.9 species per square meter versus 6.6 species per square meter in the logged plots. Average ground cover in the unlogged forest stands was fifty-three percent versus only twenty-one percent for logged forests. Neither species richness nor ground cover in the clearcut plots tended to recover over time. "If anything," they wrote, "both richness and cover appeared to be decreasing." Duffey and Meier offered several hypotheses to explain this, but were unable to confirm any of them. They did, however, reach this conclusion: "The data presented here strongly suggest that recovery requires at least several centuries, longer than the present logging cycles of 40-150 years for Appalachian cove hardwoods."[21]

Aside from the Duffey and Meier study, surprisingly little is known about the effects of clearcutting on understory plants. Most forestry research has been funded either directly or indirectly by the forest products industry, which is interested primarily in commercially valuable trees and has tended to ignore the rest of the forest ecosystem. We have heard anecdotal accounts of the declines of several important understory species, but there is little hard data.

Clearcutting does sometimes favor the growth of commercially valuable trees—oaks, for example—by reducing competition from other species. But from an ecological viewpoint such commercial gains are generally outweighed by the resulting fragmentation and destruction of habitat and degradation of soil and water.

The forest industry argues that clearcutting is better than the alternative of high-grading: cutting only the large, healthy, commercially valuable trees, leaving those that are less healthy and less marketable. It is undeniable that high-grading, which reflects the ascendancy of short-term gain over long-term care, has seriously damaged forests throughout our bioregion. Since high-grading tends to eliminate the fittest trees, leaving the weakest and most disease-prone, high-graded forests are dominated by species of little commercial worth and by damaged or unhealthy trees. The forest industry refers to such forests as "low grade." This judgment, however, reflects the commercial value of the trees, not their ecological value. Trees that are classified as low grade commercially may still serve important ecological functions, such as shading and enriching the soil, filtering and freshening the air, improving water quality, preventing erosion, and providing habitat for understory plants and for many species of animals. (Many of these specific functions are discussed below.) These "low grade" forests also have an important economic value: providing the grand, green vistas that attract tourists—and for some they satisfy the sense of beauty or deeper longings of the spirit.

Given the region's history of high-grading, the most sustainable logging practice today is probably to cull nonnative, genetically inferior, and diseased trees and leave the healthy ones—much as the traditional farmer saved the best corn for seed. In some areas, this is still best accomplished by old-fashioned horse-logging, which avoids the soil compaction associated with heavy machinery. Such painstaking practices may not have much appeal in a competitive market economy, but market economies are designed to maximize short-term productivity, not long-term health. Health is a more elusive goal, demanding, not blind obedience to the law of supply and demand, but effort, choice, self-discipline, and personal responsibility.

Southern Appalachia can support a sustainable logging industry (a massive wood-derived paper industry is more problematic), but this requires some sacrifice of immediate gain by the majority of foresters and landholders and stiffly enforced legal sanctions against the few who have no scruples.

In the long run, however, a healthy, diverse biotic community can survive only if we also protect large tracts of forest as wilderness. This requires everyone to be more thrifty in the use of wood products. But such thrift is possible. We could spare vast areas of forest, for example, simply by reducing packaging and junk mail or being less wasteful with wooden shipping pallets.

Because individual landholders control most of the region's forest land, the work of conserving the forests falls primarily upon individuals, rather than upon industry or the government. Individuals hold 73.2 percent of the region's timberland, industry six percent, the Forest Service seventeen percent, and other government agencies (including the National Park Service, which operates the Great Smoky Mountains National Park) 3.8 percent.[22] Moreover, most of the Forest Service land is or will eventually be available to private corporations for logging or mining. Of the 632,348 acres of the Cherokee National Forest, for example, only 66,469 acres

(10.6 percent) is permanently protected.[23] Further protection of public forest lands is thus an urgent priority.

But since so much of the bioregion's forest land is in private hands, the health of forests also hinges on the development of an environmental ethic among individual landholders, many of whom still allow their timber to be clearcut by less than scrupulous operators.

There are hopeful signs. The September 1995 issue of the *Journal of Forestry* heralded the appearance of a new constituency among forest landholders. An increasing number of landholders, said the journal's contributors, were managing their lands in accord with environmental values. Quoting Gandhi's remark, "There go my people. I must run and catch up with them because I am their leader," one article urged professional foresters to regain lost leadership and prestige by moving ahead with an environmental ethic of their own.[24]

Some corporate landholders, however, may be more recalcitrant. We have so far considered only damage that occurs when a clearcut forest is allowed to regrow naturally. But often on corporate holdings, the clearcut land is poisoned with herbicides and then replanted with neat, geometrical rows of pine trees to create a "pine plantation" or "tree farm." Only the pines, some weeds, and a smattering of hardy, adaptable fauna live in these sad, silent mockeries of forests. The resultant loss of biodiversity is catastrophic.[25]

The Wounds of Development

Logging is not the only threat to Southern Appalachian forests. Many other forms of industrialization and development—most importantly mining, road-building, the expansion of cities, and the damming of rivers have fragmented, scarred, smothered, depleted, and otherwise wounded the land.

Mining, particularly strip mining, has a long and grim history of destruction in Central Appalachia, but we are relatively fortunate in that coal mining in our bioregion is confined to its western edge on the Cumberland Plateau. There, however, large amounts of coal are extracted with the usual depredations. Coal mining and its effects are discussed more fully in Chapter Five.

We also have other minerals of worth, and for these, too, the land has suffered. In Chapter One we mentioned the devastation wrought on the Nolichucky River by the kaolin, feldspar, and mica mines near Spruce Pine, North Carolina and on the Ocoee by the mines of Copper Basin. Copper Basin, a thirty-thousand-acre depression in the hills of southeastern Tennessee, was extorted from the Cherokees by the U.S. government in 1836—a couple of years before the Cherokees' forced expulsion to Oklahoma along the Trail of Tears. The basin was rich in minerals, and copper mines were opened there before 1850. Copper ore, extracted from the earth, was heated over charcoal fires in large open pits to extract the copper. By 1866 these smelters had stripped virtually the entire basin bare of trees, and in 1879 the mines and smelters closed. But both reopened in 1891, using a new smelting process fueled by charcoal. From the smelters billowed thick clouds of sulfur dioxide gas, which, combining with water in the air or on the land, produced sulfuric acid. By 1907, when lawsuits forced the mining corporations to control sulfur dioxide emissions, the acid had turned thirty thousand acres (about fifty square miles) of formerly forested land to desert, poisoning all vegetation, baring and baking the red clay, and exterminating aquatic life in the Ocoee River watershed. Much of the topsoil was eroding into the streams, and heavy metals, leached out of the soil by the acid, had poisoned the water.[26]

Copper Basin is, of course, the bioregion's most extreme example of mine damage, though now, after nearly a century, its wounds have begun to heal. Today mines are better-regulated, but the regulation is only as effective as vigilance and public pressure force it to be. That vigilance must be constant, even (in fact, especially) when the land at issue is part of our national forests. Southern Appalachian national forests are under increasing pressure toward privatization and various forms of exploitation—including mining, from which, contrary to widespread belief, they are not legally protected. In 1995 a company named (appropriately enough) Broken Hill Proprietary applied to the U.S. Forest Service for a permit to conduct preliminary prospecting for copper, lead, and other metals in the Nantahala and Cherokee National Forests near the borders of the Great Smoky Mountains National Park. If ore is found, it is likely to be extracted by open-pit mining.[27]

Even more destructive, perhaps, than even the mining is the vast network of roads that provide automotive access to everything. Aside from the interior of the tourist-besieged Great Smoky Mountains National Park, few places in our bioregion are more than a mile or two from a road. Roads fragment habitat, preventing the movement and migration of wildlife. Road construction creates huge wounds of open earth, from which soil washes into streams, silting and sometimes acidifying them. As roads grow and widen, they bring more traffic and fouler air, and development flows out along them, radiating across the countryside. (Pigeon Forge and in West Knoxville are extreme examples.) Where roads go, development inevitably follows; subdivisions, gas stations, convenient marts, shopping malls, golf courses and industrial areas multiply, devouring rural land and rural life. To the asphalt of the roads is added the asphalt of parking lots, creating vast areas of biological desert, devoid of life.

In the summer, these deserts are unbearably hot. Bare asphalt absorbs and radiates the sun's heat, baking the immediate environment. With the asphalt come unshaded lawns of closely-cropped grass, which also quickly dry out in the sun and require frequent artificial watering—in contrast to natural forests, which remain much cooler and can store water efficiently in shaded loam and leaf litter. The heat and drought of these degraded environments make them unsuitable for many forms of life—including human life. Thus, during the warm months, the people of Southern Appalachia spend most of their time in air-conditioned buildings or automobiles. These insulated, encapsulated spaces produce hot exhausts which further heat the environment, and their voracious consumption of fossil-fuel generated energy adds to global warming, which compounds the heat in the long run.

Like road construction and the development it brings, road maintenance also degrades natural vegetation. To maintain roads—and also railways and utility rights of way—nearby plants are often sprayed with herbicides. The herbicides may run off into streams, killing aquatic life, or harm rare and sensitive plants. Bunched arrowhead, a small flowering plant that grows only in Henderson County, North Carolina, and Greenville County, South Carolina, has been nearly lost to road, railroad, and utility maintenance and to the clearing and development of the wooded swamps in which it grows.[28] Salt used to melt snow and ice may also damage streams or roadside vegetation.

Dams, too, have radically altered the land. The reservoirs they have created are huge permanent floods that have drowned many thousands of acres of prime forest and farmland. This land is already lost. But the constant fluctuation of the water level continues to damage vegetation along the shores. To balance the demands of recreation and flood control, TVA raises reservoir levels in the late spring and lowers them in the fall, a pattern not synchronous with the natural cycles of Southern Appalachian rivers, which run high in the winter and low in the summer. As a result, the reservoirs are bordered by mud flats of a kind which did not originally occur in this bioregion. Few native plants and animals are specifically adapted to living there, and they are ecologically unproductive.[29]

Fires

Even our well-intentioned efforts to prevent forest fires can reduce biodiversity. The table mountain pine, *Pinus pungens*, is a part of a family of yellow pines including shortleaf pine, Virginia pine, and pitch pine, all which are found in the Smoky Mountains. But it is different from other pines in that it needs fire to reproduce. Its cones do not open automatically in the fall, but remain closed, protecting the seed inside, until opened by the intense heat of a fire. Before the establishment of the Park and the surrounding national forests, fire was a common and natural occurrence in the tree's native habitat. Thirty to fifty percent of Swain County, North Carolina, for example, burned every year, and every acre burned within five years, enabling the table mountain pine to reproduce regularly. But for most of this century fires have regularly been extinguished, and as a result the table mountain pine has been dying out.[30]

Oak trees, which are less fire-sensitive than competing beeches and maples, tend to grow best where there are occasional fires. Where burning has been suppressed, oaks are crowded out by the beeches and maples, which can tolerate more shade. Thus fire suppression gradually shifts the dominant forest composition from oak to beech and maple.[31] This has ramifying effects, since acorns are a staple in the diet of many forms of wildlife. Before we consider existing wildlife, however, it would be well to recall what we have already done to the wildlife that once was here.

Mammals

The history of human destruction of wildlife in the upper Tennessee Valley is long. The earliest known human inhabitants, the Paleo-Indians, were well-established here by the end of most recent ice age, about 10,000 B.C.[32] Nomadic hunters of large animals, they seem to have overexploited their food sources. The mastodon, the horse, the camel, and a prehistoric bison, all of which inhabited large portions of North America until 10,000 B.C. were extinct by 7,000 B.C.—the victims, so many now think, of overhunting.[33]

Later inhabitants seem to have understood the immorality and ultimate futility of such behavior. The Cherokees had legends of a long-gone time when overhunting threatened animals with extinction. (The great time lapse, however, makes it unlikely that these legends spring from Paleo-Indian sources.) The hard-pressed animals, said the legends, retaliated by inventing diseases, which they inflicted upon humans by magic. To avoid disease, the Cherokees believed, the hunter must

apologize to the animals he killed and take certain ritual precautions that in practice limited the extent of the kill. Implicit in this mythos was a concept of human
forbearance in preserving the natural balance.[34]

Yet during the eighteenth century even the Cherokees, in concert with the incoming settlers, hunted the white-tailed deer almost to extinction in a frenzy comparable to the slaughter of the Great Plains bison a century later. This, it has been
argued, shows that the Cherokees were just as exploitative as the settlers, though
ineffective until they acquired guns. That conclusion, however, is hasty. By the
time the deer were being slaughtered, war, disease, and whiskey were already dis-
solving the bonds of Cherokee culture. To survive, the remnants of the tribe
needed guns to defend themselves against the Europeans and iron tools to work the
marginal land to which they had been forced to retreat. These could be obtained
only through trade, and the only marketable commodity the Cherokees could provide was deerskin. (A "buck," our slang word for a dollar, originally meant a deerskin used in trade.) Whether the Cherokees would have overhunted the deer if
their own survival had not been at stake is uncertain.[35]

The slaughter of the deer may also have a more intriguing explanation. Diseases
brought by European explorers had been decimating native American tribes at least
since the early sixteenth century. In 1738 a smallpox epidemic killed nearly half the
Cherokee people.[36] Given their account of the origin of disease, it would have been
natural for the Cherokees to conclude that the animals had invented new diseases
and were engaged in magical aggression against them. Such reasoning could easily
have eroded the original reluctance to overhunt and perhaps even sparked retalia-
tion against the deer. Thus the very ideology that supported sustainable hunting
before the European invasion may have served to rationalize overhunting as the
plight of the Cherokees became desperate.[37]

The white-tailed deer ultimately survived, but the bison did not. Bison are associated in the American consciousness with the vast spaces and open skies of the
Great Plains: Nebraska, the Dakotas, and the Sioux. Yet when the Europeans first
arrived, a variety of woodland bison (not to be confused with the *bison antiquus*
mentioned above, which had disappeared about nine thousand years earlier)
were still plentiful in what is now middle Tennessee, perhaps ranging into the
forests of the upper Tennessee Valley, black shadows in the mottled green.
Though large and powerful, they were no match for firearms. Hunters waited in
ambush at natural salt licks, where the bison had congregated for long ages. At
Bledsoe's Lick, thirty miles northeast of Nashville, a French-Canadian fur trader

reported in 1790 that "One could walk for several hundred yards at and in the lick on buffalo skulls and bones, and the whole flat around the lick was covered with their bleached bones." By 1800 woodland bison had become rare. Within a decade or two they were extinct.[38]

Eastern elk, too, once inhabited the forests of Southern Appalachia. Like the woodland bison, the elk sought the salt licks, and, like the bison, there they were relentlessly slaughtered. They were extinct by the start of the Civil War.[39]

The elk often traveled with the white-tailed deer, which, as we noted above, were also targets of the hunters. By the middle of the twentieth century, few deer remained, hiding warily in mountain fastnesses. In the 1950s, state wildlife officials began to reintroduce white-tailed deer, using individuals from as far away as Wisconsin. The reintroduction effort, in concert with the creation of large no-hunting preserves, such as the Great Smoky Mountains National Park, has restored deer populations, and since the 1950s herds have been increasing throughout the bioregion.

In fact these efforts may have succeeded too well. Statewide, the deer now number over eight hundred thousand,[40] well in excess of the population prior to European settlement.[41] As the deer increase and range more widely over the humanly redesigned landscape in their search for food, new problems arise. Deer are now common in many suburbs, raiding gardens and eating pesticide-poisoned vegetation. Many collide with automobiles. The populous deer transport the deer tick, the bearer of lyme disease, an increasing threat to humans. Near Oak Ridge, some deer are radioactive, a consequence of eating vegetation growing in soil contaminated by the spoils of the nuclear weapons industry, and hunters must be wary of eating their meat.

Because the deer's predators (wolves and mountain lions) have been eliminated, there is no natural check on deer populations. So human predation in the form of hunting has become necessary to prevent the deer from ravaging crops, wildflowers, and forest plants and reducing the understory cover needed by songbirds.[42] Deer are already damaging many endangered and threatened plants.[43] Unfortunately, while nonhuman predators tended to cull the sick and weak and so promote the herd's long-term health, hunters prefer to shoot the biggest and strongest—with what long-term evolutionary effect remains to be seen.

Deer, as Aldo Leopold so eloquently notes, are enemies of mountains, and the defense that mountains have evolved against them is the wolf: *I have lived to see state after state extirpate its wolves. I have watched the face of many a newly wolfless mountain, and seen the south-facing slopes wrinkle with a maze of new deer trails. I have seen every edible bush and seedling browsed, first to anemic desuetude, and then to death. ... I now suspect that just as a deer herd lives in mortal fear of its wolves, so does a mountain live in mortal fear of its deer. And perhaps for better cause, for while a buck pulled down by wolves can be replaced in two or three years, a range pulled down by too many deer can fail of replacement in as many decades.*[44] Leopold was writing of the mountains of the Southwest, but (though vegetation recovers more quickly here) the principle is the same in the Southern Appalachians. Our mountains, too, once defended themselves with wolves. But now, though the deer are recovering and nonnative wild hogs ravage the land, the mountains' long-evolved defense is gone.

The Southern Appalachians were originally home to two kinds of wolves: the red and the gray. (There is, however, controversy as to whether the red wolf is a distinct species; genetic studies suggest that it is a mix of wolf and coyote.[45]) Both wolves were hunters of deer, bison, and elk. As the settlers eliminated their prey, they turned increasingly to farm animals instead. The result was an escalating war of extermination that lasted until about 1920 when, somewhere deep in the Smokies, the last wolf cry was silenced.[46]

Though driven from the East and in constant retreat, gray wolves maintained substantial refuges away west in the Rockies, in Alaska, and in Canada. But the smaller red wolf, whose range never extended beyond the Southeast, was hunted almost to extinction. By the mid 1970s, there were maybe a hundred red wolves left in the entire world, mostly in Louisiana and Texas. Many of these could not find mates and had begun breeding with common coyotes, so that the strain was rapidly disappearing. A captive breeding program was established using seventeen captured red wolves in 1976. In January of 1991, wolves from this program were released in Cades Cove in the Great Smoky Mountains National Park. Five pups were born that spring. At least seven of the wolves released in the first few years were killed by disease (canid parvo virus), by fights with other wolves and coyotes, or by drinking spilled antifreeze.[47] But efforts continued, and by the summer of 1996 there were twenty-three red wolves in the Smokies.[48] One day, if we are both careful and lucky, the mountains may once again defend themselves with wolves.

Nobody knows when (or even if) the eastern cougar, mountain lion, or "painter" disappeared from the Southern Appalachians. Wary hunters, they were themselves hunted mercilessly for over two centuries. Sightings are still sometimes reported, but many wildlife officials believe that if there are any big cats here they are released or escaped western cougars, not the native eastern variety.[49]

The black bear was nearly eliminated early in this century by hunting and the massive logging which destroyed much of its habitat. After the creation of the Great Smoky Mountains National Park in 1934, the bear population began to increase, but it dropped suddenly again as a result of the chestnut blight (discussed below), which eliminated one of the bears' main food sources. Eventually the bears switched to acorns and began to rebound, but drought and the decline of the oak trees brought the bears to the brink of starvation in 1992, and many came out of the mountains to forage on the edges of suburbs. There are now about five hundred bears in the Smokies. But these are still threatened by the relentless development that is hemming the Park in from all sides and by poachers, who kill forty-five to eighty bears per year.[50]

River otters were gone from Southern Appalachia by the middle of the twentieth century, primarily as a result of hunting, trapping, and habitat loss. A reintroduction effort was begun in 1984. Between then and 1994, 487 otters were released in Middle and East Tennessee. Several otter pups have been spotted in the wild.[51]

The large, sociable Carolina northern flying squirrel and its cousin the Virginia flying squirrel may still be found in the high spruce-fir forests of the Southern Appalachians, the southernmost extent of their ranges. But not for long. As the spruce-fir forests die and the greenhouse effect warms the peaks, their ranges will contract northward. Being endangered species, these squirrels are likely never to return.[52]

Fourteen kinds of bats occur in Tennessee. Nine of these live in caves and mine shafts; the others live in trees. Two of the cave dwellers, the gray bat and the Indiana bat, are endangered. Both have been hard hit by pesticides, which make the insects they eat poisonous. Many of the caves in which these bats are found have been fitted with gates to prevent human intrusion and disturbance while enabling the bats to come and go freely. But this has recently been found to kill some bats by altering cave temperature. The gray bat occurs in two caves in our bioregion: Pearson Cave in Hawkins County, Tennessee, and Nickajack Cave, just north of Chattanooga. Their populations seem to have stabilized, or even increased somewhat, but the Indiana bat, which lives in New Mammoth Cave in Campbell County, continues to decline. (Both bats also inhabit other places outside our bioregion.) Some researchers think the decline of the Indiana bat is due in part to logging, which eliminates the big trees in which they forage and sometimes roost.[53]

Birds

We hear much these days of the evils of government regulations, but government regulations—specifically hunting restrictions and the banning of the pesticide DDT—have saved many native birds from extinction. DDT, first widely used in the 1940s, was manufactured in such enormous quantities that it quickly became distributed throughout the environment. In the early 1960s, researchers began to suspect that DDT was responsible for an abrupt decline in the populations of many predatory birds, including eagles, ospreys, pelicans, herons, and falcons. The prey animals of these birds had consumed contaminated food, and the DDT was stored in their fatty tissues. When female birds consumed these fatty tissues, the DDT migrated to their reproductive systems, altering the composition of egg shells. The eggs became so thin and fragile that they broke in the nest. In 1962, Rachel Carson alerted the American public to the dangers of DDT and other pesticides with the publication of her classic book *Silent Spring*. DDT use subsequently declined, and was banned by the federal government a decade later.

One bird that was saved by the ban was the bald eagle, the symbol of the American republic. A big bird, with a wingspan that can exceed seven feet, it was gone from Southern Appalachia by 1961 and in danger all across North America. But in 1980, with environmental DDT levels falling, the state of Tennessee began a reintroduction program. By 1995 there were fifteen successful nests.[54]

Another bird that was rescued by the DDT ban was the osprey. Sometimes confused with bald eagles, ospreys are large fish eaters with a wing span that can reach six feet. They were never completely eliminated from the bioregion, but by 1980 there were only about five remaining nests, all on Watts Bar Lake. In the succeeding years, they enlarged their territory and by 1995 the number of active nests had risen to over sixty.[55]

Peregrine falcons were gone from Southern Appalchia by about mid-century. They are still endangered, but restoration efforts have begun to bring them back. Peregrines like to nest on skyscrapers and eat urban pigeons, and one has recently taken up residence in downtown Knoxville.[56]

Great blue herons have recovered dramatically. Originally rare in the upper Tennessee Valley, they have become more common, in part because of the building of the dams, which created suitable habitat. Their numbers, however, declined precipitously nationwide in the 1950s as their prey became contaminated with DDT. By

1973 there were only 135 active nests could be found in the entire Tennessee valley. Today there are thousands. All along the valley the great blues can be seen standing stiffly like silent sentinels along the banks, stalking fish and frogs in the shallow waters, or winging their way gracefully along the river, issuing from on high an occasional throaty squawk. The reduction of toxic industrial discharges has aided their recovery, as has the protection of wetlands, but the single most important factor was probably the banning of DDT.[57] Black-crowned night herons seem to be making a similar recovery.

Other birds have been saved from near extinction by restrictions on hunting. Wild Turkeys were common throughout Southern Appalachia until the 1930s, when over-hunting, poultry diseases, and the chestnut blight (which eliminated one of their main food sources) caused a sudden population decline. By 1952 there were only about a thousand wild turkeys in Tennessee, mostly in inaccessible mountain areas. Restocking and conservation programs directed by the Tennessee Wildlife Resources Agency have brought the turkeys back, and their statewide population had reached seventy-five thousand by 1993.[58]

Giant Canada geese, a subspecies of Canada geese, were hunted relentlessly throughout the nineteenth century. By 1920, they were thought to be extinct, but a small population was found in the midwest in 1960. Carefully managed, it has recovered, and flocks of these large, beautiful waterfowl are once again plentiful on the Tennessee River.[59]

Wood ducks, which nest in the cavities of old trees, were almost lost to hunting and to the logging of the trees in which they nested. But hunting restrictions and the installation of millions of nesting boxes have begun to restore this colorful and distinctive bird.[60]

In all these cases, the foresight, persistence, and hard work of a few dedicated individuals have redeemed the apathy of many. But what remains to tell is more grim.

Two remarkable Southern Appalachian birds, the passenger pigeon and the Carolina parakeet are gone forever, both having been hunted to extinction early in the 1900s. The Carolina parakeet, the only member of the parrot family native to the United States, was a large and flamboyantly colored bird, about thirteen inches long, mostly bright green, but with a yellow head and neck and orange cheeks and forehead. These birds flew and roosted in large flocks, but people shot them because they raided orchards, because ladies prized their feathers for hats, and because their bright colors made them useful for target practice.

Their unwariness undoubtedly hastened their extinction. When one was wounded, its distress call caused the rest of the flock to circle around until all were shot.[61] Ornithologist Alexander Wilson described this behavior: *Having shot down a number, some of which were only wounded, the whole flock swept repeatedly around their prostrate companions, and again settled on a low tree, within twenty yards of the spot where I stood. At each successive discharge, tho showers of them fell, yet the affection of the survivors seemed rather to increase; for after a few circuits around the place, they again alighted near me, looking down on their slaughtered companions with such manifest symptoms of sympathy and concern, as entirely disarmed me.*[62] The last known member of the species died in the Cincinnati Zoo in 1914.[63]

Nearly everyone knows the story of the passenger pigeon, a bird once so numerous that its flocks used to darken the sky for hours as they passed overhead. Ornithologists estimate their precolonial population at two to three billion, making them probably the most abundant bird species on earth.[64] Their extensive winter roosting grounds along river bottoms in the Southern Appalachians are still recalled in the names of two rivers, the Pigeon and the Little Pigeon, and in the name of the city of Pigeon Forge.

They ranged widely. Simeon Pokagon, a Michigan Pottawottomi chief, wrote in 1850 of their mating ritual: *I was startled by hearing a gurgling, rumbling sound, as though an army of horses laden with sleigh bells was advancing through the deep forest toward me. ... While I gazed in wonder and astonishment, I beheld moving toward me in an unbroken front millions of pigeons ... I now began to realize they were mating ... I tried to understand their strange language and why they all chattered in concert. In the course of the day, the great on-moving mass passed me, but the trees were still filled with them sitting in pairs in convenient crotches of the limbs, now and then gently fluttering their half-spread wings and uttering to their mates those strange bell-like wooing notes which I had mistaken for the ringing of sleigh bells in the distance.*[65] Though the pigeons tended to mate further north, they wintered in Southern Appalachia in great numbers.

Despite their profusion, the passenger pigeons were quickly exterminated. The initial blow was habitat destruction. As settlers cleared the forests, the beech nuts and acorns the pigeons ate became too scarce to support the huge flocks, and populations declined. Then, in the last half of the nineteenth century, market hunters across the eastern United States blasted hundreds of millions from their roosts or from the sky. The meat was shipped by rail to New York and Chicago, where it had become fashionable to dine on squab (young pigeon). The business was lucrative, and the big city cash did much, no doubt, to silence consciences. Then, as now, the excuse that soothed was money.

Not everyone accepted that excuse. Well before the passenger pigeons vanished, there were warning signs and scattered calls for conservation, but most people seemed to think that so numerous and familiar a bird could never be eliminated.

Their last precipitous decline surprised even the conservationists. As their numbers fell, the pigeons ceased to mate.[66] Apparently their mating instinct was triggered in a way that we will now never understand by something in the presence of the great flock. Perhaps it was the sound of sleigh bells in the distance.

By a strange coincidence, the last known passenger pigeon, a female named Martha, died in the Cincinnati zoo in 1914, the very place and year when the last known Carolina parakeet died.[67]

Bachman's warbler once inhabited the dense undergrowth of river swamps across the Southeast. It may have occurred sporadically in our bioregion; but, if so, it was long ago driven away by lumbering and the draining and filling of wetlands. For awhile, it clung to life along the Carolina coast, but it has not been spotted since the 1960s. It had wintered in Cuban forests, and the conversion of these forests to sugarcane fields may have been the fatal blow. The last of these birds that anyone saw were adult males. They sang for weeks, apparently in a futile effort to attract mates.[68]

Today, more birds are jeopardized than ever before, not by hunters, but by roads, suburban development, and clearcutting. Some of the worst losses are among the songbirds—a fact that anyone with a long memory and an eye or ear for birds knows well. Worldwide, two-thirds of all songbird species are declining, and Southern Appalachia is no exception.[69] Many Southern Appalachian songbirds migrate in the winter to the tropics, where the destruction of the rainforests has created intense competition for habitat. In the tropics they also encounter DDT, which is still sold by American chemical companies to Central and South American nations, despite the ban on domestic use. Radar studies over Louisiana indicate that the number of migrating songbirds fell fifty percent between the mid sixties and the late eighties.[70]

If, despite the perils in the south, the songbirds manage to return, they will find their northern habitat, too, under attack, as roads, suburbs, industrial parks, and clearcuts fragment the forest. Many songbirds must nest in large uninterrupted forest stands, for only there are their eggs and young safe from predators. Nest predators, such as blue jays, crows, grackles, chipmunks, weasels, possums, cats, and raccoons, live mostly at the forest edges. So do brown-headed cowbirds, which lay their eggs parasitically in the nests of other birds. Deep in the forest these enemies are rare. As forests are fragmented, deep forest habitats disappear and fewer birds survive.[71] This effect is measurable and profound. One researcher simulated songbird nests by setting out artificial nests containing quail eggs in small, medium and large forest tracks. In some of the smaller tracts nearly all the nests were raided by predators. But in the largest only one in fifty were. This largest tract was the Great Smoky Mountains National Park.[72]

Populations of many Southern Appalachian songbirds have dropped in recent years; the cerulean warbler, Swainson's warbler, Bachman's sparrow, grasshopper sparrow, Bewick's wren, yellow-billed cuckoo, least flycatcher, baltimore oriole, worm-eating warbler, and blackburnian warbler are all in decline. (Bachman's sparrow and Bewick's wren may already be gone from the bioregion.)[73] Spring is not yet silent, but the music is fading and becoming more monotonous.

For some birds, the crucial factor in survival is not only the size of the forest habitat, but its age and composition. The red-cockaded woodpecker is a small bird with black-and-white-striped sides, a black back and a red patch just behind the eye. It nests only in cavities in living pine trees that are infected with a fungal disease, and these are found primarily in old-growth forests, most of which have been eliminated by logging. As a result, only a few thousand red-cockaded woodpeckers still exist. About fourteen make their home in the Daniel Boone National Forest of southeastern Kentucky. For these, some hope was kindled in the summer of 1994 when Kentucky Heartwood, the Heartwood Coalition, the Sierra Club Legal Defense Fund, and the Foundation for Global Sustainability's Southern Appalachian Biodiversity Project successfully sued the U.S. Forest Service to halt logging of old-growth pines in the Daniel Boone.

Other birds that nest in tree cavities—bluebirds, red-headed woodpeckers, and barn owls, for example—have also diminished because clearcutting has eliminated many of the old, dead, or dying trees that provide the habitat they need.[74]

Ruffled grouse populations have fallen in recent decades, but this may be a return to a more natural pattern, as the forests mature. Grouse require young succes-sional forests (saplings), so their habitat tends to increase after logging.[75]

Many birds are declining because of the destruction of wetlands. The American bit-tern, least bittern, woodcock, king rail, and common gallinule (common no longer) are fading into memory as the swamps in which they live, nest, or breed are hemmed in or bulldozed for agriculture or development.[76] Ducks and other water-fowl have declined nationwide as a result of the draining of the prairie wetlands in which they breed.[77]

The death of the spruce-fir forest is likely also to take its toll on certain birds. The small, yellow-eyed saw-whet owl ranges from Canada south to Guatemala, but almost all the recorded sightings in our bioregion have occurred in the dense high-elevation spruce-fir forests of the Smokies. As these forests decline still further, the owl is likely to disappear from the Southern Appalachians. The rare olive-sided fly-catcher also uses spruce-fir forest for breeding and nesting ground, and is equally likely to vanish with the forest.[78]

The merger of small farms into bigger farms has eliminated much of the habitat of quail, as fence rows and wild borders that used to provide food and cover have been torn out and plowed over. This problem is compounded by the fact that newer, more efficient farm machinery leaves less plant material in the fields for for-age and nest-building, and agricultural herbicides kill native plants on whose seeds quail and other birds depend for food.[79]

Not all bird species, of course, are in decline. Urbanization and the fragmentation and destruction of forests seem to have benefited mockingbirds, pigeons, mourning doves, robins, cardinals, blue jays, English (house) sparrows, grackles, and star-lings. Many birds have learned to feast on garbage or the leavings of a littering fast-food culture. Crows enjoy cornfields and the bountiful road kill.

Amphibians

Amphibians—frogs, toads, salamanders and newts—inhabit worlds smaller than ours and move in a different sort of time. Often furtive and silent, they easily escape notice. Yet many are extraordinary. In the early spring, most amphibians lay their eggs—each a soft transparent sphere with a jet-black core—in gelatinous masses, in shallow pools or ponds. In a week or so the tiny tadpoles hatch. Fishlike at first, most soon sprout legs, many lose their tails, and, in a microcosmic re-enactment of evolution, the newts and salamanders gradually come to resemble proto-reptiles.

Unlike most other amphibians, frogs and toads have voices, and use them to sonorous effect. There are few sounds so enchanting as the rhythmic chorus of hundreds of frogs in a swamp or canebrake at midsummer twilight—and few so comic as the deep-throated wonk of a bullfrog on a summer afternoon. During the winter, frogs and toads hibernate a foot or more underground in tomb-like burrows, to emerge resurrected as the spring sun warms the earth. Though cold-blooded, some amphibians have a kind of antifreeze in their circulatory system which makes them hardy enough to survive temperatures well below freezing.

Cave-dwelling salamanders, sculpted by the dark, have over millennia evolved huge eyes or grown pale, but the small, shy ones that inhabit the leaf mold of the forest floor or the moist hollows under rocks are often slick and brightly colored. Still others are aquatic, like the big (up to thirty inches), ugly, voracious hellbender that still lurks in the shadows of stony streams in upper East Tennessee and western North Carolina and Virginia.

Yet out of sight, out of mind, amphibians suffer many depredations. Development, clearcutting, siltation, acid rain, toxic water pollution, and the destruction of wetlands all take their toll. But something else is at work which the scientists do not yet fully understand. Amphibians everywhere—in Australia, in Central and South America, in Europe, and in the western United States, even in remote and relatively undisturbed habitats—are declining in unprecedented numbers. Many species have abruptly disappeared.

The causes are still in debate. Initial speculation centered on pesticides, but lately attention has turned to ozone depletion (see Chapter Two). The eggs of many amphibians float close to the surface of the water, where they are exposed to sunlight. Ultraviolet-B radiation in sunlight, intensified because of the thinning of the Earth's ozone layer, reaches the larvae through the transparent egg casings. Recent experiments have shown that excessive ultraviolet-B radiation reduces hatching rates, especially when combined with acid precipitation, and that it also increases developmental abnormalities and death rates in immature frogs.[80]

Because research is scanty and underfunded, nobody is sure what is happening to the amphibians of Southern Appalachia. The Great Smoky Mountains National Park is one of the world's most important centers of salamander diversity, boasting twenty-seven species.[81]   Somewhat surprisingly, these are concentrated at the higher elevations.   But whether their populations, or the populations of other regional amphibian species, are declining is not known.[82]

One thing, however, is certain: clearcutting devastates salamanders. Salamanders need shade, moisture, and cool soils. Clearcutting crushes burrows, eliminates shade, dries out the soil, and exposes the bare earth to the baking heat of the sun. One recent study concludes that clearcutting kills over three quarters of the salamanders in a mature forest stand.[83]   There is no research on how the herbicides often used by loggers affect the amphibians of our bioregion. Not only the existence of the forest, but also its quality, affects amphibian life. When a natural deciduous forest is replaced by a pine plantation, for example, the number and diversity of amphibians never returns to anything like its natural levels.[84]

Amphibian populations have always been subject to wide fluctuations. A drought or a cold snap may eliminate a species from a particular habitat in a given year; yet a year or two later, it may return in number. This is possible, however, only if populations are not too isolated, so that they can be replenished by migration. If the habitat is broken and fragmented by roads, urban development, or clearcutting, these natural population swings may be halted and the species extirpated.

Road building and mining can also kill amphibians by exposing rocks with toxic leachates. When U. S. Highway 441 was rebuilt through the Great Smoky Mountains National Park in 1963, for example, leachate from the construction exterminated nearly all the salamanders in the streams below.[85]

Finally, global warming is likely to reduce or eliminate some Southern Appalachian salamanders, especially those endemic to the cool higher elevations. As the peaks heat up and the spruce-fir forests fall, these salamanders will have nowhere to go.[86]

Fish

It is the sport fish that come first to mind when we think of fish in the Tennessee Valley: bass, sauger, crappie, pike, sunfish, walleye, catfish, carp—and, in the mountains, brown, brook and rainbow trout. Many of the most prominent game fish—including the brown trout, rainbow trout, carp, striped bass, yellow perch and some varieties of walleye and muskellunge—are not native, having been introduced mainly for the benefit of fishermen. But the greatest species diversity is in the small, largely unnoticed fish of the creeks and streams: darters, madtom catfish, daces, chubs, and other minnows. In fact, because of the profusion of these little fish, Tennessee is home to about three hundred species—the greatest diversity of freshwater fish in the nation.

The reservoirs provide ample habitat for most of the sport fish, which generally remain plentiful. However, three large species became extremely scarce or disappeared from the upper Tennessee soon after the closing of the dams: the huge lake sturgeon, the bizarre shovelnose sturgeon, and the fierce muskellunge. (Muskellunge occasionally caught at Norris Reservoir and elsewhere are not native fish, but stocked individuals of a northern variety that are apparently incapable of reproducing in Tennessee waters.)[87] None of these three species are yet extinct, but all are extirpated from much of their original range and in decline elsewhere. Recently there have been efforts to reintroduce the lake sturgeon into the Clinch River, but it is too soon to know whether these will succeed.[88] Old-timers say that big paddlefish (spoonbills) used to be caught regularly up on the Holston and French Broad before the building of the dams. They are scarce or nonexistent there now, though they still inhabit the bigger reservoirs of the Tennessee.

It is the smaller, less-noticed fishes, however, that have been most threatened by human intrusions. Many of these can feed or reproduce only on clean gravely or rocky stream bottoms and thus are very sensitive to silt. The harelip (or rabbit-mouth) sucker, which once ranged widely in the upper Tennessee Valley, was probably the first fish in our bioregion to fall victim to human negligence. This silvery fish, which needed extremely clear water, vanished quickly in the late 1800s as the streams became turbid with silt from clearcutting and agriculture. Last seen in 1893, it is now almost certainly extinct.[89]

The slender chub, an inhabitant of gravel shoals, has nearly disappeared as a result of habitat degradation. One important cause appears to be coal-washing operations along the Powell River in Virginia. Despite repeated searches, it has been seen only once in the last ten years: a single specimen was found in the Clinch River in the fall of 1996.[90] The western sand darter has not been found in the Clinch since 1980 and the Powell since 1987 and may now be gone from our bioregion, though it persists elsewhere. A gravel quarry on US 25E is thought to have destroyed its Powell River habitat. The yellowfin madtom, a three-inch catfish with venomous stinging spines, originally ranged through much of the Tennessee Valley. Dams and pollution degraded most of the streams and rivers it once inhabited, confining it to three widely separated locations: Copper Creek (a tributary of the Clinch river in southwestern Virginia), a small section of the

Powell River, and Citico Creek in Monroe County, Tennessee. These populations are all small and precarious.[91]

The blotchside logperch, one of the largest darters, with a length approaching eight inches, is missing from seven of its fifteen known locations. Its isolated populations are separated by reservoirs, and more may disappear soon, threatening the species with extinction.   The channel darter disappeared from the Tennessee below Knoxville shortly after the closing of the dams. For a while it remained fairly abundant in the Clinch and the Powell, but recent investigations have failed to detect it, though it is still relatively abundant in Big South Fork. Two of six known populations of the duskytail darter have vanished, and at least one more (in the Little River) is unstable.[92] The longhead darter is gone from half of its known locations, and other populations are declining. Seven of sixteen known populations of the ashy darter have probably been extirpated, though it remains common at Big South Fork and has apparently expanded its range into the New River.[93]   The palezone shiner was found in only one place in our bioregion: Cove Creek in Campbell County, Tennessee. Norris Dam and mining-related pollution extirpated it from that habitat half a century ago, but it still exists in some locations in Kentucky and in the Paint Rock River system in northern Alabama. The spotfin chub is also gone from most of its former range, but persists in North Carolina above Fontana dam and at several other locations.[94]

Much is unknown about these and other small, unobtrusive fishes, some of which have not even been classified biologically. Because there is little funding to study them, it may well be that some long-unobserved species still exist and that some that are not yet classified as extinct are in fact already gone.   Yet it is clear that many of these small fish are declining, and that the main causes are siltation, the damming of rivers, and toxic pollution.

Until the late 1950s, some of the rarest of these fish inhabited the relatively pristine Abrams Creek, which meanders though Cades Cove and out of the National Park into the Little Tennessee River. But in June of 1957 the creek was intentionally poisoned with rotenone for fourteen miles below Abrams Falls in an effort to exterminate "rough" fish and enhance fishing for nonnative rainbow trout. The poisoning was a joint effort by the National Park Service, the U.S. Fish and Wildlife Service, TVA, and the Tennessee Wildlife Resources Agency (then called the Tennessee Game and Fish Commission). A number of specimens collected as their bodies floated to the surface after the poisoning were sent to the Smithsonian museum, and it was among these specimens that the Smoky madtom was first discovered many years afterward. At first presumed already extinct, it was later found to be clinging to life in nearby Citico Creek.[95] Reintroduction efforts are now underway at Abrams Creek, but these have been hampered by siltation created as the cattle that are grazed in Cades Cove trample the stream banks and tourists disturb the banks and stream bed. Recent efforts by the National Park Service and other agencies to fence the cattle away from the stream and restore streamside vegetation appear to be improving the situation.[96]

One small denizen of Tennessee waters has made international news. The snail darter was catapulted into prominence after a population was discovered in the Little Tennessee River during construction of the Tellico Dam. In one of the first and most controversial applications of the newly passed Endangered Species Act, a court decision halted construction of the dam. But in the waning hours of the 1978 session, Congress hastily passed a rider exempting the dam from the Endangered Species Act and mandating its completion—to the delight of powerful real estate interests, who would soon reap a financial bonanza selling the "lakeside" housing units. In November of 1979 the gates closed and the dam flooded the valley, creating Tellico Reservoir and obliterating the snail darter's entire breeding habitat on the Little Tennessee. In the meantime, however, the snail darter has been found elsewhere, and some have been captured and introduced into the lower Hiwassee and the Holston, where they appear to have established healthy breeding populations that have expanded into the French Broad.[97]

One of the most abundant species in the Tennessee River, particularly in turbid, sewage-laden Fort Loudoun Reservoir, is the common carp. Carp are not native to Southern Appalachia. They were imported from Eurasia in the nineteenth century. But they are tolerant of silt and of low dissolved oxygen levels and so have competitive advantage in degraded waters. Canoeists, who can move quietly enough to observe them in the shallows, are familiar with the long, thick clouds of mud they stir up as they dart along the bottom. These mud clouds decrease light penetration, impairing aquatic plants and feeding waterfowl. The mud may also settle on the eggs of more desirable fish, depriving them of the oxygen needed for normal development.[98] Large carp occur in extraordinary numbers in Fort Loudoun Reservoir, and they are prominent along the Knoxville waterfront, where visitors enjoy exciting them into a slurping, frothing feeding frenzy by dropping food scraps into the murky water.

Southern Appalachia's only native species of trout, the brook trout, has been declining since about 1900. Brook trout are smaller than the nonnative rainbow and brown trout, which have been introduced into many clear mountain streams. They are, however, exceedingly beautiful; the dark-green to slate-grey breeding male has a strikingly spotted dorsal fin and an orange or scarlet belly with spots of orange or scarlet along the side. Much of their initial decline was probably due to heating and siltation of streams resulting from clearcutting early in this century. Overfishing and competition from the nonnative rainbows and browns accelerated the losses. Slight acidity in streams gives the brook trout an advantage over its competitors, so that they have increasingly retreated to the more acidic higher-elevation streams.[99] However, increases in acid runoff are making some of these streams so acidic that they may soon no longer support brook trout either.[100] Then brook trout may be caught in a squeeze between competitors moving up from below and acidity moving down from above.

Mussels and Snails

The Tennessee River Valley still holds the richest diversity of freshwater mussel species in the world. But probably not for long. Our native mussels are nearly all declining, smothered by silt, poisoned by toxics, and deprived of fresh, rapidly flowing water by the dams. Silt interferes with the filter-feeding of mussels and may prevent reproduction. Some of the remaining mussel populations consist entirely of fifty- to sixty-year-old individuals, which have been incapable of reproducing since the dams were built. Mussels have also been injured or killed by low dissolved oxygen, acid mine drainage (which erodes, and sometimes eats holes in, their shells), fertilizers, pesticides, and other toxic pollutants. They are more vulnerable than many other species to local disturbance, since they are stationary and cannot move to cleaner water.

Before the European invasion, Tennessee was home to 130 mussel species. It now has seventy-nine.[101] Of those that remain, thirty-five are on the federal endangered species list.[102] Many species that were once widespread are now clinging to life only in isolated and endangered communities. Some of these communities consist entirely of aged individuals that have not been able to reproduce for decades. A freshwater mussel sanctuary at Chattanooga that harbored nearly a hundred species in 1939 had forty-four in 1969, and eleven in 1978.[103] Because of the dams, losses have been greatest on the main stem of the Tennessee, but they are severe even in the tributaries. The headwaters of the Clinch River contained eighteen mussel species in 1918; a 1978 survey found only five. The headwaters of the Powell harbored twenty-one species in 1918; this has dropped to seven. The species count for the lower section of the North Fork of the Holston dropped from thirty-two to nine between 1918 to 1978. Similar losses have occurred in other tributaries.[104]

The names of these endangered or threatened creatures are poetic, quaint, and sometimes downright queer: Appalachian elktoe, rough pigtoe, fine-rayed pigtoe, rough rabbitsfoot, birdwing pearlymussel, Dromedary pearlymussel, yellow blossom pearlymussel, green blossom pearlymussel, tuberculed blossom pearlymussel, cracking pearlymussel, little wing pearlymussel, shiny pigtoe pearlymussel, white wartyback, orange-foot pimpleback, clubshell, fanshell, Cumberland combshell, tan riffleshell, Cumberland monkeyface, Appalachian monkeyface, oyster mussel, pink mucket, ring pink, purple bean, Cumberland bean, winged mapleleaf, pale lilliput ... and on and on. Some produce freshwater pearls. Some are strikingly beautiful. All are passing.

Several native species of snail are also in trouble. The beautiful painted snake coiled forest snail is found only in Franklin County, Tennessee. Its conical shell is a light cream color with chocolate-brown blotches. It lives in limestone crevices in dense forest cover, much of which has been destroyed by lumbering. The brownish-yellow noonday snail, or noonday globe, small and dome-shaped, has been found only at Blowing Springs, Cliff Ridges, and Nantahala Gorge in Swain County, North Carolina. U.S. Highway 19 through Nantahala Gorge has disrupted its forest habitat.[105] Both are considered threatened species. Five others are endangered (see Table 3.1).[106]

The loss or decline of the mussels and snails may seem of little consequence to humans. Yet mussels and snails produce mercenene, a substance which reportedly prevents or delays two types of cancer in mice and has produced no side effects when tested on humans.[107] Inconspicuousness is no guarantee of unimportance.

The dams, siltation, and pollution would probably by themselves have extirpated most of the mussel species eventually. But recently boats and barges have been bringing upriver a lowly assassin that will probably eliminate not only many more native mussel species, but other species of aquatic life as well. This new peril is the zebra mussel.

A fingernail-sized mollusk native to the Caspian sea in Russia, the zebra mussel is so-named because its shell is striped by alternating bands of dark and light. During the last century and a half, it extended its range through much of Europe by hitching rides on the hulls of boats and taking advantage of canals and other connections between formerly isolated waterways. In 1985 or 1986, a few zebra mussels were inadvertently dumped into Lake St. Clair near Detroit when a European freighter flushed its freshwater ballast. From there, their descendants hitchhiked down the Illinois River to the Mississippi, then up the Ohio and the Tennessee. Within the last few years, Zebra mussels have been observed as far upriver as Knoxville.

Ironically, the same dams that have smothered so many of the native mussels have opened the river to the advance of the zebra mussel. Before the building of the dams, the Tennessee posed formidable barriers to navigation—especially the shallows at Muscle Shoals, Alabama, and the perilous narrows near Chattanooga. But the dams created a deep, calm navigation channel all the way to Knoxville, enabling boats to travel the length of the river, spreading the hardy and adaptable zebras.

Zebra mussels reproduce at an astonishing rate, blanketing the muddy bottoms of rivers or lakes and coating any hard object they can find. In Lake Erie, less than a decade after their introduction, researchers were finding as many as a hundred thousand per square meter of lake bottom. Zebra mussels clog water intake pipes and the cooling systems of powerplants, forcing expensive cleaning and prevention measures. They also build colonies on top of other mussels, competing for their food and smothering them. Thus they may virtually eliminate other mussels from the Tennessee River.

Perhaps their most dramatic effect will be to clarify the water. Zebra mussels consume microscopic algae that color the water green. They also filter out brown particles of silt. When present in large numbers, zebra mussels can make the water visibly clearer, as they have in Lake Erie. This has several important consequences. Because sunlight penetrates deeper in clear water, aquatic plants will be able to grow deeper than before and will likely colonize new areas. Portions of the river now suffering from nutrient overload might be cleaned up as zebra mussels remove algae and nutrients from the water.

But because algae are eaten by insects and microscopic animals, which in turn are eaten by fish and aquatic birds, effects will ripple up the food chain as the zebra mussels deplete the algae. Many fish and bird species are likely to decline; others—particularly bottom-feeders such as catfish and drum that could learn to eat zebra mussels—may increase. Fish that spawn in gravel, such as smallmouth bass, may decrease as zebra mussels crowd the gravel beds.[108]

The zebra mussel, incidentally, is not our first bivalve invader, though it will certainly be the most destructive. Corbicula, an Asiatic clam, has already become ubiquitous in the Tennessee River and its tributaries.

The zebra mussel explosion is not a natural phenomenon, but a disquieting side effect of rapid global transportation systems. It is, moreover, an instance of a larger pattern: unique native plants and animals are increasingly being pushed aside and replaced by tougher imports from around the world. This is happening not only in the water but on the land and not only in Southern Appalachia but everywhere.

The Homogenization of Nature

Many of the most prominent plants and animals in the Southern Appalachian landscape are nonnative—and they are the same plants and animals that now occur in climatologically similar regions around the world.

Two of the bioregion's most common bird species, English sparrows and starlings, are European imports. In the nineteenth century, the sparrows expanded with the British empire around the world. Starlings were first introduced to North America at a Shakespearean play in New York in the early 1900s. From there they swept across the continent in a matter of decades, becoming one of the most numerous of birds.[109] Vast flocks now darken Tennessee Valley skies in the fall.

The homogenization of nature extends also into the wild—or what passes for the wild in these days of human dominance over everything. The wild hogs of the Smokies, which root up and destroy so much of the native forest vegetation, are European in origin.

Many Tennessee Valley fish, including the rough and undesirable carp, are nonnative, as was noted above. Eurasian water milfoil, an imported ornamental aquatic plant, grows so thickly in some eutrophic reservoirs that it fills swimming holes and tangles outboard motors.

Red clover, timothy, and bluegrass were brought to Southern Appalachia from Great Britain by settlers whose livestock (also imported species) did not thrive on the native American grasses.[110]

Pink-blossoming mimosa, foul-smelling ailanthus (tree of heaven), and rough, lilac-flowered paulownia (princess) trees, all three of which are prominent in disturbed landscapes across our bioregion, are imports from Asia. Some unattended urban lots are dominated by these species and appear more Asian than American. Princess trees are especially troublesome on rocky outcrops in the mountains, where they can outcompete rare native flora.

Common privet, a bushy semi-evergreen European hedge plant, has become naturalized throughout Southern Appalachia and now dominates the understory of many regenerating forests. English ivy, escaped from suburban plantings, also grows aggressively on the forest floor, smothering native plants. Japanese grass and the invasive periwinkle do likewise.[111] Multiflora rose, a native of East Asia with numerous small, white, sweet-smelling blossoms, chokes pastures with its briars and weed-like growth. Shrub honeysuckle and especially the fragrant Japanese honeysuckle, with its tough and tenacious vines, can easily strangle or overgrow many native species. Both were imported from the orient.

The champion strangler and overgrower, of course, is another Japanese import, kudzu. Kudzu was introduced into the U.S. at the 1876 World's Fair in Philadelphia. A legume and nitrogen-fixer, it was used effectively during much of this century to fertilize and loosen soil that had been worn out and compacted by overfarming, and also to control erosion, though for the latter purpose it has proved ineffective. Now thoroughly naturalized, it grows rapidly on disturbed land, smothering all other plants, from the tiniest mosses to the tallest trees.

Such invasive aliens leave their natural biological controls (such as insects and fungi) behind, and so acquire a competitive advantage over native species. Some hybridize with the natives, threatening their genetic distinctiveness.

More damaging still are the imported insects, fungi, and microorganisms that attack native plants. The Japanese beetle, now a prominent lawn and garden pest, is a familiar example.

Southern Appalachian forests—already fragmented by roads, logging, and development and degraded by acid rain and ozone pollution—are also facing a mounting accumulation of biological assaults. Logging, road-building, and other forms of human disturbance facilitate the spread of disease and invasive organisms by opening routes of infection into the heart of the forest.

The first massive disease outbreak was the chestnut blight, which was caused by a fungus imported early in this century with chestnut trees from China. By the late 1930s this blight had killed virtually all the mature chestnut trees of Southern

Appalachia, depriving many forest creatures, including black bears, of the nuts that were until then a staple of their diet. The rotting stumps of the huge old chestnuts are still visible here and there in the Smokies. Chestnut sprouts still emerge from old root systems, but generally die of the blight within a decade. The Allegheny chinquapin has also been decimated by the chestnut blight.[112]

Many dogwood trees have been killed by dogwood anthracnose, a fungus thought to have been introduced with imported Chinese dogwood trees in the late seventies. The infection begins as leaf spots that may enlarge to kill the entire leaf. Later it spreads to the main stem, where cankers develop. Mature trees often die within two or three years as a result of repeated defoliation. This is a foreboding loss, since dogwoods are prime soil builders and important sources of high-protein fruit for migratory birds.[113]

Beech trees are ailing from two invaders, an insect and a fungus, which work together. The beech scale (the insect) feeds on bark, leaving tiny holes which provide entry for the Nectria coccinea fungus. Both were introduced into Nova Scotia around 1890 and progressed southward, reaching the Smokies in 1993.[114] Stands of dead beech are now common in the Park.

The European mountain ash sawfly, probably introduced from Europe into Canada early in this century, defoliates American mountain ash, which grows at high elevations along the crest of the Smokies. These trees have been dying at unusually high rates, and the sawfly is a likely explanation.

Many native elms have fallen to the Dutch elm disease, which was introduced into the United States in 1930. The disease has hit urban trees the hardest, but it is slowly felling forest elms as well. A new outbreak of the disease in the 1980s killed hundreds of American elms in the Little River area.[115]

Butternut trees have been decimated by the butternut canker, a disease that first appeared here in 1967. In the years since, it has killed ninety percent of the butternut trees in the Southern Appalachians. In 1990, the U.S. Fish and Wildlife Service recommended that butternut trees be listed as an endangered species, though they have not yet received that listing. Many private landowners have cut their butternut trees to cash in on them before the disease strikes, but this destruction of uninfected trees, which may be genetically resistant to the disease, has further imperiled the species.[116]

After the chestnuts died, oaks took their place. Now the oaks are declining, too. Part of the problem is that fire suppression has prevented development of the forest openings where oak trees get their best start. As a result, oak seedlings are being crowded out and killed by the faster-growing maples, beeches, and black gum. But the oaks are also suffering from invasive pests. The Asiatic oak weevil has infected many, and all are likely soon to face the devastating attack of the gypsy moths.[117]

Introduced from Europe into Massachusetts sometime between 1867 and 1869, gypsy moths have advanced gradually down the Appalachian Mountains, defoliating forests as they come. They are especially fond of oak leaves. Infected forests literally crawl with caterpillars, which at times drop from the trees like rain. By the time the caterpillars spin their cocoons, few leaves remain. A few gypsy moths have already reached the Smokies, but there have been no serious infestations yet. When the main "front" moves in, perhaps in the first decade of the next century, yet another major stress will be added to our already beleaguered forests.[118]

This presents the forest stewards with painful dilemmas. There are, for example over eight hundred species of arthropods—including many delicate moths and butterflies—in the oak forests of the Great Smoky Mountains National Park. If chemical or biological controls are used to fight the gypsy moth, many relatively benign creatures may be killed as well. If not, the gypsy moths may kill them anyway by destroying their habitat.[119]

In 1993, a related invader, the Asiatic gypsy moth, was inadvertently introduced into North Carolina by a munitions ship docked near Wilmington. More voracious and faster-spreading than its European counterpart, this moth could do even greater damage.[120]

Sometimes an invasion has ramifying effects across whole ecosystems. We noted in Chapter One that the balsam woolly adelgid, an insect carried here on plants from Europe earlier in the century, has almost eliminated Fraser fir trees from the high Southern Appalachian mountains, which are their sole habitat.[121] Ninety-one percent by volume of the mature Fraser firs are dead. Only a few small stands are left, and these are infested.[122] The Fraser firs are therefore in fact an endangered species, though, like the butternuts, they have not yet officially been listed as such.

Because of the complex interdependence of other species with the Fraser firs, their elimination has initiated a cascade of further declines. The most prominent side effect is the blowdown of red spruce trees, some over two centuries old, which used to be shielded from the wind by the Fraser firs. We have already observed that the Carolina northern flying squirrel, the saw-whet owl and the olive-sided flycatcher depend on the spruce-fir forest and will likely disappear. But there are also more subtle effects. At least eight specialized species of moss and liverworts grow mainly or only on the bark of Fraser firs. As the firs die, these tiny plants die with them. Moreover, the dead trees have allowed sunlight to penetrate the forest canopy, drying out the moss mats that once dappled the moist forest floor. And the loss of the moss in turn threatens other species, including the spruce-fir moss spider.[123] Where this cascade of effects will end remains to be seen. *(See Figure 5 on page 61.)*

The balsam wooly adelgid has recently been joined by the hemlock woolly adelgid, an import from Asia so destructive that it may kill every eastern and Carolina hemlock tree that is not actively protected by pesticides. The loss of the hemlocks is expected to initiate further cascades, since the eastern hemlock is crucial habitat for already-stressed neotropical migrant birds and an important component of streamside ecosystems, providing cooling shade and vital nutrients to the flowing waters.[124]

Yet another cascade has already begun to affect humans. Within the past few years, honey bees (which, incidentally, are themselves nonnative, having been brought here by settlers from Europe) have become rare, victims of tiny Varroa mites and tracheal mites from Europe, Asia, and South America. In the 1980s there were about two hundred thousand honeybee colonies in Tennessee, about half of them wild. By 1996 that number had been reduced by eighty percent to forty thousand— nearly all of them domesticated. Beekeepers have managed to keep some hives going by the careful use of pesticides, but regional fruit and garden crops, which depend on bee pollination, have already suffered substantial losses. And since bees pollinate many wild plants as well, these plants and the animals that depend on them will also experience losses, of a degree as yet unknown.[125]

These are merely examples. The problem is global in scope. It is as if we had thrown all the world's species into a blender and turned on the juice, mixing competitors, diseases, parasites, and predators from each unique ecosystem with competitors, diseases, parasites, and predators from all the others. Delicate, unique, and rare species are too fragile to survive this treatment and are being lost. And, across the planet, tough, aggressive, and weedy species are moving in to replace them. We are blurring the outlines of Creation, leaving a homogenized, standardized, scrambled, and depleted world in its place.

Table 3.1

This table includes only those species listed as endangered or threatened or proposed for one of these statuses by the federal government. (A species is listed as endangered if it is likely to become extinct throughout all or a major portion of its range, and as threatened if it is likely to become endangered in the near future.) State governments and conservation agencies list many additional species, and many more are in fact in decline, threatened, endangered, or already extinct.   Many groups of organisms (lichens, mosses, or arthropods, for example) are underrepresented in this list, simply because few people know or care about them. This table is compiled from several sources; though nearly all the species listed here inhabit (or used to inhabit) our bioregion, a few may occur only in the Tennessee River Basin to the west.

THREATENED AND ENDANGERED SPECIES OF THE TENNESSEE RIVER BASIN AND THE SOUTHERN APPALACHIAN MOUNTAINS[126]			
Common Name	**Scientific Name**	**Status**	**Habitat**
MAMMALS			
Red wolf	*Canis rufus*	Endangered	Forests, Fields
Eastern cougar	*Felis concolor cougar*	Endangered	Mountains, wide-ranging
Carolina Northern flying squirrel	*Glaucomys sabrinus coloratus*	Endangered	Spruce-fir/hardwood ecotone
Virginia Northern flying squirrel	*Glaucomys sabrinus fuscus*	Endangered	Wide-ranging
Virginia big-eared bat	*Corynorhinus townsendii virginianus*	Endangered	Caves
Gray bat	*Myotis grisescens*	Endangered	Caves, rivers, lakes
Indiana bat	*Myotis sodalis*	Endangered	Caves, riparian areas
BIRDS			
American peregrine falcon	*Falco peregrinis anatum*	Endangered	Cliffs, large rivers, reservoirs
Bald Eagle	*Haliaeetus leucocephalus*	Threatened	Lakes, large rivers, wooded shores
Red-cockaded woodpecker	*Picoides borealis*	Endangered	Mature old-growth pine forests
AMPHIBIANS			
Cheat Mountain Salamander	*Plethodon nettingi*	Threatened	High-elevation spruce-fir forest
Shenandoah Salamander	*Plethodon shenandoah*	Endangered	Rock outcrops and cliffs
FISHES			
Pygmy sculpin	*Cottus pygmaeus*	Threatened	Cool streams
Blue shiner	*Cyprinella caerulea*	Threatened	Clear, cool pools
Spotfin chub	*Cyprinella monacha*	Threatened	Small rivers, large creeks
Slender chub	*Erimystax cahni*	Threatened	Small rivers
Slackwater darter	*Etheostoma boschungi*	Threatened	Small creeks, springs
Duskytail darter	*Etheostoma (Catonotus) sp.*	Endangered	Small rivers, large creeks
Cherokee darter	*Etheostoma scotti*	Threatened	
Boulder darter	*Etheostoma wapiti*	Endangered	Small rivers, large creeks
Palezone shiner	*Notropis albizonatus*	Endangered	Small rivers, large creeks
Smoky madtom	*Noturus baileyi*	Endangered	Large creeks
Yellowfin madtom	*Noturus flavipinnis*	Threatened	Small rivers, large creeks
Pygmy madtom	*Noturus stanauli*	Endangered	Small rivers
Amber darter	*Percina antesella*	Endangered	Rivers
Goldline darter	*Percina aurolineata*	Threatened	
Conasauga logperch	*Percina jenkinsi*	Endangered	Deep gravel runs, pools
Snail darter	*Percina tanasi*	Threatened	Large rivers, small rivers
Blackside dace	*Phoxinus cumberlandensis*	Threatened	Small upland streams
Alabama cavefish	*Speoplatyrhinus poulsoni*	Endangered	Cave streams

Table 3.1 cont.

THREATENED AND ENDANGERED SPECIES OF THE TENNESSEE RIVER BASIN AND THE SOUTHERN APPALACHIAN MOUNTAINS[126]			
Common Name	**Scientific Name**	**Status**	**Habitat**
MUSSELS AND CLAMS			
Appalachian elktoe	*Alasmidonta raveneliana*	Endangered	Small rivers, creeks
Birdwing pearlymussel	*Conradilla caelata*	Endangered	Small rivers
Fanshell	*Cyprogenia stegaria*	Endangered	Rivers
Dromedary pearly mussel	*Dromus dromas*	Endangered	Rivers
Cumberland combshell	*Epioblasma brevidens*	Proposed endangered	Small rivers
Oyster mussel	*Epioblasma capsaeformis*	Proposed endangered	Small rivers
Yellow blossom pearlymussel	*Epioblasma florentina florentina*	Endangered	Large rivers
Green blossom pearlymussel	*Epioblasma torulosa*	Endangered	Small rivers
Tuberculed blossom pearlymussel	*Epioblasma torulosa torulosa*	Extirpated	Large rivers
Turgid blossom pearlymussel	*Epioblasma turgidula*	Endangered	Creeks
Tan riffleshell	*Epioblasma walkeri*	Endangered	Small rivers, creeks
Shiny pigtoe pearlymussel	*Fusconaia cor*	Endangered	Small rivers, creeks
Fine-rayed pigtoe	*Fusconaia cuneolus*	Endangered	Small rivers, creeks
Cracking pearlymussel	*Hemistena lata*	Endangered	Rivers, large creeks
Pink mucket	*Lampsillis abrupta*	Endangered	Rivers
Alabama lampmussel	*Lampsillis virescens*	Endangered	Creeks
Ring pink	*Obovaria retusa*	Endangered	Rivers
Little-wing pearlymussel	*Pegias fabula*	Endangered	Creeks
White wartyback	*Plethoblasus cicatricosus*	Endangered	Large rivers
Orange-foot pimpleback	*Plethoblasus cooperianus*	Endangered	Large rivers
Clubshell	*Pleurobema clava*	Endangered	Rivers, large creeks
James spineymussel	*Pleurobema collina*	Endangered	
Rough Pigtoe	*Pleurobema plenum*	Endangered	Rivers
Rough rabbitsfoot	*Quadrula cylindrica strigillata*	Proposed endangered	Small rivers
Winged mapleleaf	*Quadrula fragosa*	Extirpated	Small rivers
Cumberland monkeyface	*Quadrula intermedia*	Endangered	Small rivers
Appalachian monkeyface	*Quadrula sparsa*	Endangered	Small rivers
Pale lilliput	*Toxoplasma cylindrellus*	Endangered	Creeks
Purple bean	*Villosa perpurpurea*	Endangered	Small rivers, creeks
Cumberland bean	*Villosa trabalis*	Endangered	Small rivers, creeks
SNAILS			
Painted snake coiled forest	*Anguispira picta*	Threatened	Forested bluffs
Anthony's river snail	*Athearnia anthonyi*		
Endangered Royal marstonia	*Marstonia ogmorhaphe*	Endangered	Spring runs
Noonday globe	*Mesodon clarki nantahala*	Threatened	Cliffs
Virginia fringed mountain snail	*Polygyriscus virginicus*	Endangered	Alkaline or mafic habitats
Royal snail	*Pyrgulopsis ogmoraphe*	Endangered	
Turtuloma livebearing snail	*Turtuloma magnifica*	Endangered	
ARTHROPODS			
Madison cave isopod	*Antrolana lira*	Threatened	Caves
Spruce-fir moss spider	*Microhexura montivaga*	Proposed endangered	Spruce-fir forests
Alabama cave shrimp	*Palaemonius alabamae*	Endangered	Caves
Lee county cave isopod	*Lirceus usdagalun*	Endangered	Caves

Table 3.1 cont.

THREATENED AND ENDANGERED SPECIES OF THE TENNESSEE RIVER BASIN AND THE SOUTHERN APPALACHIAN MOUNTAINS[126]			
Common Name	**Scientific Name**	**Status**	**Habitat**
FLOWERING PLANTS			
Appalachian elktoe	*Alasmidonta raveneliana*	Endangered	Small rivers, creeks
Pool sprite	*Amphianthus pussilus*	Threatened	Rock outcrops, cliffs
Price potato-bean	*Apios priceana*	Threatened	Hardwood forests, forest edges
Shale barren rock cress	*Arabis serotina*	Endangered	Rock outcrops, cliffs
Cumberland sandwort	*Arenaria cumberlandensis*	Endangered	Rock outcrops, cliffs
Virginia roundleaf birch	*Betula uber*	Threatened	Creek terraces
Small anthered bittercress	*Cardamine micranthera*	Endangered	Seeps, springs, streamsides
Morefield's leather flower	*Clematis morfieldii*	Endangered	Hardwood forests
Alabama leather flower	*Clematis socialis*	Endangered	Seeps, springs, streamsides
Cumberland rosemary	*Conradina verticillata*	Threatened	Riverine gravel bars
Smooth coneflower	*Echinacea laevigata*	Endangered	Alkaline or mafic habitats
Glade spurge	*Euphorbia purpurea*	Threatened	Rich or swampy woods
Spreading avens	*Geum radiatum*	Endangered	High-elevation acidic rock outcrops
Roan mountain bluet	*Hedyotis purpurea var. montana*	Endangered	High-elevation acidic rock outcrops
Eggert sunflower	*Helianthus eggertii*	Proposed threatened	Hardwood forests
Swamp pink	*Helonias bullata*	Threatened	Bogs, meadows, edges of meandering streams
Dwarf-flowered heartleaf	*Hexastylis naniflora*	Threatened	Mixed mesic habitats
Mountain golden heather	*Hudsonia montana*	Threatened	Rock outcrops, cliffs
Peter's mountain mallow	*Iliamna corei*	Endangered	Rock outcrops, cliffs
Small whirled pogonia	*Isotria medeoloides*	Threatened	Hardwood forests
Heller's blazing star	*Liatris Helleri*	Threatened	High-elevation balds
Morh's Barbara buttons	*Marshallia mohrii*	Threatened	Marshes, wet meadows
Ruth golden aster	*Pityopsis ruthii*	Endangered	Boulders in rivers
Eastern prarie fringed orchid	*Plantanthera leucophaea*	Threatened	Fen or pond wetlands
Harperella	*Ptilimnium nodosum*	Endangered	Gravel bars, rocks in rivers
Bunched Arrowhead	*Saggitaria fasciculata*	Endangered	Non-forested seepage areas
Kral's water-plantain	*Saggitaria secundifolia*	Threatened	Gravel bars, rocks in rivers
Green pitcher plant	*Sarracenia oerophila*	Endangered	Bogs, wet meadows, moist woodlands
Mountain sweet pitcher plant	*Sarracenia rubra ssp. jonesii*	Endangered	Mountain bogs and streamsides
Northeastern (barbed) bullrush	*Scripus ancistrochaetus*	Endangered	Fen or pond wetlands
Mountain (large-flowered) skullcap	*Scutellaria montana*	Endangered	Hardwood, mixed forests
White irisette	*Sisyrinchium dichotomum*	Endangered	Alkaline or mafic habitats
Blue ridge goldenrod	*Solidago Spithamaea*	Threatened	Acidic, sandy balds
Virginia spiraea	*Spiraea virginiana*	Threatened	Habitat generalist
Persistent trillium	*Trillium persistens*	Endangered	Mixed mesic habitats
Tennessee yellow-eyed grass	*Xyris tennesseensis*	Endangered	Forested seeps
FERNS			
American harts-tongue	*Phyllitis scolopendrium var. americanum*	Threatened	Cave, sinkhole mouths
LICHENS			
Rock gnome lichen	*Gymnoderma lineare*	Proposed endangered	High-elevation cliffs

FIGURE 6: The climate in our bioregion is mild enough that row covers and cold frames allow year-round harvests, as in this herb garden.

Neither say they in their heart, Let us now fear the Lord our God, that giveth rain, both the former and the latter, in his season: he reserveth unto us the appointed weeks of the harvest.

— Jeremiah 5:24

How Are We Fed?

Day and night, seven days a week, in any weather and in all seasons, constantly and without interruption, streams of smoke-spewing eighteen-wheelers rush noisily along the interstates to feed us. They roll in from California, from Mexico, from the Pacific Northwest, from Florida, and via Gulf ports from Brazil, Guatemala, Costa Rica, and points south, carrying food to a land once peopled by some of the most rugged, independent, and self-sufficient farmers on earth. But the new inhabitants of this land are beholden to the trucks, for they can, for the most part, no longer be bothered to feed themselves.

As Southern Appalachia's population has grown, its agriculture has declined. Recent data on imports and exports are hard to come by, but according to a 1984 estimate, about fifty-three percent of Tennessee's food and eighty-four percent of its fresh fruits and vegetables are imported from outside the state.[1] Since Tennessee's richest agricultural regions are in the middle and western portions of the state, it is likely that these figures were higher for East Tennessee. And since the trend of growing population and declining agriculture has continued since the 1980s, it is likely that they are still higher today.

Local figures for urbanized counties are even more extreme. In Knox County in 1992, for example, vegetables were grown on only thirty-seven farms totaling 185 acres, and fruit was produced on only eighty-five acres. The only grains grown were corn (1,334 acres, mostly for livestock) and wheat (275 acres). The largest acreage was devoted to growing hay. Most of the farms that still exist specialize in cattle.[2] According to a University of Tennessee study done in 1977, "It can be stated with assurance that less than five percent of the produce passing through the Knoxville market is locally grown."[3] Since then, much, if not most, of Knox County's remaining farmland has been lost.

The trucks, of course, keep the warehouses, grocery stores, and restaurants well stocked. But fresh food is not always easy to come by. Supermarkets and even small neighborhood markets have abandoned many inner city communities. The only food available in these neighborhoods is at the convenience stores, often attached to gas stations. This food is mostly junk: highly processed, fattening, low in quality, of little nutritional value, and expensive. Thus it reinforces the familiar cycles of poverty, disease, and dependence.

Even in the suburbs, most of the available produce has been transported long distances and much of it is treated with chemical sprays, waxes, and colorings to preserve "freshness"—or at least the illusion thereof. And even where high-quality produce is available, many people—ignorant, befuddled by advertising, or demoralized beyond caring—still choose junk, as can be confirmed by a few minutes' observation of any supermarket check-out line.

The results are all too apparent. About fifty-nine percent of Tennesseeans consider themselves overweight. Sixty-nine percent say they would like to weigh less.[4] Most of our diet-related illnesses (obesity, cancer, diabetes, heart disease) are problems of excess, not problems of want.

It is not easy to motivate people so little cognizant of their own health to care about the health of the world around them. Yet many people do strive for health, and so have begun a venture whose logical conclusion will take them beyond themselves; for personal health requires healthful food, and healthful food requires a healthy land.

Food and the Land

Our current food system damages the land, not only here, but wherever the food is grown, and everywhere in between. Because our food comes from around the world, our eating habits in Southern Appalachia promote environmental damage almost everywhere. Rainforests in Costa Rica may be felled to provide grazing land for the cattle that become the fast-food hamburger we eat in Chattanooga. A hillside in the Philippines may be deforested and soaked with herbicides and pesticides to grow the pineapple in the sundae we have for dessert. The lettuce on the hamburger may be grown in Southern California on an irrigated desert whose shrinking water supply will dry up within a decade or two. The bread for the bun may be baked in Cincinnati from flour ground in Minneapolis that is made from grains grown on Iowa farms that douse their crops with pesticides and chemical fertilizers. The onion may be raised in Texas on eroding land that is thin and compacted by heavy farm machinery. In one way or another, all these forms of agriculture degrade the land that produces the crops that feed us.

To that damage we must add the further degradation involved in getting the food here. The exhausts of the ships and trucks that transport our food pollute the air with carbon monoxide, particulates, nitrous oxides (NO_x), volatile organic compounds, and ozone, the effects of which are discussed in Chapters One and Two. As local agriculture declines, population grows, and tastes become more cosmopolitan, the transportation system also grows, crowding the interstates with trucks and the landscape with the truck stops, fast food joints, and service stations that support the transportation system.

All this moving from place to place requires enormous amounts of fuel—as, in most cases, does the growing and processing of the food itself. This fuel is made from crude oil. Since our domestic supply of crude oil is nearly used up, the crude must be shipped from Saudi Arabia and other oil-producing nations on supertankers (which themselves use still more fuel). When it reaches the United States, typically on the Gulf coast of Texas or Louisiana, the oil is refined and processed in one of the innumerable polluting chemical plants of that industrial nightmare known as "cancer alley," then pumped or trucked (again at great expense of energy and fuel and with considerable pollution of the air) to truck stops and gas stations all across the country, where the diesel trucks that bring the food receive it.

Those same Gulf-coast chemical plants may supply the plastics, styrofoam, coloring, and inks in which the food is packaged—unless it is packaged in paper or cardboard, in which case forests are cut and chipped to supply the paper mills. The packaging is generally used once, after which it becomes a waste disposal problem (see Chapter Six). Much of our food is refrigerated over long times and distances. The refrigeration requires more fuel—or electricity generated chiefly by the burning of strip-mined coal.

Most of the food bought in Southern Appalachia is processed. Precise recent percentages are unavailable, but a good estimate may be obtained by considering the stock of any regional supermarket. The unprocessed foods are the fresh fruits and vegetables, fresh meats, eggs, and some dairy products. Compare the floor area in the grocery store devoted to these items with the area devoted to such products as soft drinks, processed meat, beer, canned and frozen foods, specialty foods, mixes, snacks, sugary breakfast cereals, and candy. Since most people buy most of their food from grocery stores, this proportion is a good estimate of the preponderance of processed food in our diet. All these processed items pass through at least one and often several industrial operations, each of which requires additional truck transportation and energy. The resulting food is almost invariably less nutritious than produce fresh from the garden or farm.

To these energy and transportation costs we must add the fuel burned by our auto-mobiles as we drive to the grocery store or restaurant to buy the food and the fuel required to bring the fuel for our automobiles to the gas station where we buy it, and the energy and pollution required to refine that fuel—and so on. All these things are now integral components of our food supply system, and all degrade the land.

Not only do most people in Southern Appalachia no longer grow their own food; many seldom even prepare it. Thus we endure the seemingly endless proliferation of strip malls teeming with restaurant upon fast-food restaurant. Many of these go out of business almost as soon as they open, yet they continue relentlessly to expand across the land, leaving boarded-up buildings and desolate parking lots behind. This is said to be a side effect of the "efficiency" of our economic system.

Agriculture: A Long, Steep Decline

As the strip malls, roads, and housing developments expand, farms die, and more and more of our food comes from somewhere far away. This is a disturbing trans-formation for a land that was once self-sufficient and agriculturally independent. Given the exponential growth of world population, worldwide loss of croplands, competition for fresh water, and global climate change, it is prudent to have a reli-able bioregional food supply.

The statistics are not encouraging. Southern Appalachian agriculture has suffered a long, steep decline over the last century. Table 4.1 gives some idea of its magni-tude, though the figures are for the entire state of Tennessee. Since most of the state's remaining agricultural land lies in Middle and West Tennessee, the decline in East Tennessee and Southern Appalachia has almost certainly been steeper.

Table 4.1

(Source: U.S. Census Bureau. Farm data are not collected every year. Except for the year 1995—the most recent data—we have selected data from available years closest to the turn of the decade.)

TRENDS IN FARM POPULATION AND ACREAGE IN TENNESSEE				
Year	Number of Farms	Total Farm Acreage	Average Acreage per Farm	Total Farm Population
1900	225,000	20,342,000	90	1,246,000
1910	246,000	20,042,000	81	1,278,000
1920	253,000	19,511,000	77	1,290,000

Table 4.1 cont.

	TRENDS IN FARM POPULATION AND ACREAGE IN TENNESSEE			
Year	Number of Farms	Total Farm Acreage	Average Acreage per Farm	Total Farm Population
1930	246,000	18,003,000	73	1,219,000
1940	248,000	18,493,000	74	1,276,000
1950	232,000	18,534,000	79	1,016,000
1959	158,000	16,081,000	101	715,000
1969	121,000	15,057,000	124	412,000
1980	96,000	14,000,000	146	176,000
1992	88,000	13,000,000	148	(unavailable)
1995	80,000	11,800,000	148	(unavailable)

Just since 1950, the state of Tennessee has lost 6,734,000 acres of farmland, much of it to sprawling development.[5] That, in more familiar terms, is over ten thousand square miles: more than enough land to fill a square a hundred miles on a side, an area roughly equal to all of East Tennessee. Though much of this land has reverted to forest, and so is healing and growing richer, and some was so steep that it should never have been farmed in the first place, much of the best agricultural land is being damaged or made barren by development.

The advocates of development sometimes herald this loss as a good thing, signaling the transformation of an agricultural economy into a modern, diversified economy. King Midas may celebrate his power to turn everything into gold, but if he turns his farms and fields into gold, he may eventually come to regret it.

It is astonishing how little care we have taken, for example, to insure a fresh supply of locally grown vegetables. The soils and climate of the Tennessee Valley are quite good for the cultivation of many vegetables, including asparagus, broccoli, cauliflower, carrots, lettuce, onions, green peas, and many others. Some of these can be grown in multiple crops per season. Certain highly nutritious greens—cabbage, kale, collards, and brussels sprouts, for example—can be cultivated well into the winter months. But we do not commonly grow any of these vegetables commercially.[6] Some of the vegetables that are raised here—tomatoes and eggplants, for example—are often sold outside the bioregion, while we import tomatoes (mostly tasteless) and eggplants from elsewhere.[7] A large portion of our fruits and vegetables come from the irrigated deserts of California.

Despite the losses in farm acreage and farm population, Tennessee still produces (or did produce in the early 1980s) surpluses of dairy products, strawberries, snap beans, spinach, soybeans, and wheat.[8] With the exception of the dairy products, however, these are grown mainly in Middle and West Tennessee.[9] Therefore, it seems probable that the only farm products from our bioregion (if any) for which exports exceed imports are dairy products. If that is so, then the unavoidable conclusion is that Southern Appalachia no longer comes even close to feeding itself.

Regional farm losses have been partially offset, of course, by increases in productivity. Production per acre of virtually all crops has increased with the development of new crop varieties and new agricultural chemicals, and Tennessee's total production of corn, soybeans, and tobacco (though fluctuating widely from year to year with shifts in rainfall and weather) has generally held steady or increased. Yet the production of many vegetable crops has steadily declined, either in absolute quantities or per capita.[10] This indicates a state-wide movement away from agricultural diversity and towards monoculture—the reliance on a single kind of crop, or at most a small group of crops. Monoculture is economically efficient in the same way that factory mass production is economically efficient, but it is also risky. A single crop can be destroyed by a single kind of insect, a single disease, a single shift in climate or precipitation. In agriculture, as in nature, diversity makes it probable that much will survive. Monoculture makes it probable that, in a widespread agricultural plague, very little will survive.

Such plagues remain possible, despite the advances of modern chemistry. Many weeds, fungi, and insects have evolved rapidly in response to the pervasive use of herbicides, fungicides, and pesticides, and are now immune to much of the contemporary chemical armory.[11] Crops are also under stress from changing climate and weather patterns, increasing ultraviolet radiation due to ozone depletion, and ground-level ozone (see Chapter Two)—factors which make them more vulnerable to plagues. Putting all our agricultural eggs into one basket, then, is imprudent. Yet the farms of Southern Appalachia are mostly monocultural, their chief products— apart from hay—being cattle, sorghum, soybeans, corn, and tobacco.

An especially unsettling aspect of the agricultural decline has been the disappearance of the small farm. Table 4.1 shows that average farm acreage has more than doubled since 1930, as small farmers have been driven out of business by low crop prices and stringent competition. Small farms are important—strategically, eco-logically, and culturally—for they have, at least historically, served as the main-stays of local food supply systems, as havens of crop diversity, and as molders of the sturdy, independent character of Southern Appalachia. Thomas Jefferson—that great visionary of the American union—was emphatic in insisting that the small farmer is indispensable to preservation of democracy and the spiritual life of the nation.

But many today regard Jefferson's view as outdated. When the most recent farm statistics were announced in the summer of 1996, showing yet further declines in Tennessee agriculture and in the small farm, a University of Tennessee agricultural economist, was quoted in the *Knoxville News-Sentinel* as saying, "The smaller farms are not inherently less profitable, but they may have to change if the market condi-tions require that they get bigger, and I think they have done that."[12] It seems that the structure of late twentieth century agriculture is to be determined not by Jeffersonian wisdom, but by the dictates of the inexorable god Market Conditions, a being whose demands we must obey, though they undermine much that we once thought good.

The demise of the small farm is a nationwide phenomenon, more prominent in many other places than it is here. In portions of the Midwest and Southern California, much of the agricultural land has been acquired by huge corporations—Tenneco, Goodyear, Exxon, Prudential Insurance, Bank of America, and others—which have rooted out and exterminated the culture of the family farm. Not so in Southern Appalachia. In this respect, as in many others, we have been protected by the rugged hills, which naturally divide the land into small holdings and have so far made large-scale corporate farming impractical. As a result, Southern Appalachian farms (those that remain) are still on average much smaller than farms nationwide. Most are still in private hands, and remnants of the traditions of the family farm survive here.

But these remnants are fast disappearing as farm population declines. While overall population has grown exponentially, farm population is now much less than a tenth of what it was in 1920. The skills and experience of food production are vanishing, along with the frugal character and solid spirit that once grew from the land. Correspondingly, there is a rise of dispiritedness, improvidence, and dependence among those who live in detachment from the soil that gives them life.

The Squeeze on Farmers

Why have we lost so much of our agriculture? The answers, of course, are primarily economic, but the direction of the economy is determined by the choices of individuals. The ultimate answer lies with each of us.

One cause has been increasing urbanization and the rising land costs and property taxes that it brings. As suburbs swallow up the countryside, available land becomes scarce and land values increase. Rising values attract speculators who buy up large tracts, wait for the value to increase still further, and then sell them to real estate developers. This further reduces the available land, driving costs still higher. Nearby farmland also increases in value, raising property taxes and often erasing the farmer's thin profit margin. The farmer then has no choice but to sell. Those who would like to start new farms are deterred both by the taxes and the cost of the land itself. This is due in large part to population growth, which in turn stems at least in part from the most intimate of personal choices—but more of that in Chapter Eight.

A second cause of the agricultural decline is the "corporatization" of food production. The activities involved in producing food may be divided into three categories: farming, the production and sale of inputs to farming (chemicals, seeds, and equipment purchased by the farmer), and marketing. The nature of this "corporatization" can be understood by considering the amount of money generated by activities in each of these three categories since 1910. Table 4.2 gives the essentials:

Table 4.2

WEALTH GENERATED BY THE SECTORS OF U.S. AGRIBUSINESS SINCE 1910[13]		
Sector	Percentage of American Agribusiness in 1910	Percentage of American Agribusiness in 1990
Farming	40%	8%
Input	14%	25%
Marketing	46%	67%

In constant 1984 dollars farming was a thirty billion dollar enterprise in 1910 and accounted for about forty percent of the money generated by food production. In absolute dollars, this figure has remained stagnant, but the money generated by marketing and inputs has increased dramatically. The result is that, farming currently accounts only for about eight percent of the wealth produced by agribusiness. The wealth generated by America's farmland is, in other words, no greater than it was in 1910—despite the fact that farmers feed a much larger population and are much more productive.[14] The money has instead flowed primarily to the corporations that control inputs and marketing.

Corporate dominance of marketing is largely the result of choices of individual consumers. It is we who have acquiesced to the advertising that teaches us to prefer convenient, heavily packaged, far-transported, highly processed food to nutritious produce direct from local farms. Thus many of the local farms have withered and died from lack of consumer support.

The corporations, of course, have planned and promoted this process. With the rise of television advertising in the 1950s, many people were conditioned to esteem corporate food products as symbols of modern affluence. Tasteless, textureless, highly processed Wonder Bread replaced the fresher and heartier breads that had been baked locally from locally milled flour. As corporate marketers of farm products inserted themselves between farmers and consumers, many of them—Del Monte, General Mills, Ralston Purina, Kraft, and Tyson, for example—obtained monopolies or virtual monopolies in various areas of distribution, undercutting and destroying local distribution systems, forcing farmers to sell through them, and siphoning away the profit.[15]

The squeeze came from the input side as well. As mechanization and competition intensified, farmers were forced to rely less on their own labor and ingenuity and more on mechanical and chemical inputs. And among the suppliers of these inputs, as well as among the marketers of farm outputs, there was all too often a conspicuous lack of competition. Tires, petroleum products, chemicals, and rail transportation were controlled by a few large corporations. There were many farming communities where feed had to be bought from Ralston Purina or not at all.[16] Twenty years ago, Texas agricultural advocate Jim Hightower noted: *Before the first sprout breaks ground, American farm families are over their heads in debt to such corporate powers as Bank of America (production loans), Upjohn Company (seeds), The Williams Companies (fertilizer), International Minerals & Chemical (pesticides), Ford Motor Company (machinery), Firestone (tires), Ralston Purina (feeder pigs), Merck & Company (poultry stock), Cargill (feed), Dow Chemical (cartons and wrappings), Eli Lilly (animal drugs), Exxon (farm fuels), and Burlington Northern (rail transportation).[17]* The situation is little different today, except that those farmers whose debts were most precarious are no longer farming.

So the squeeze on farmers continues. The corporations that control inputs and marketing have huge reserves of capital and can withstand wide fluctuations in markets and weather, leaving the financial risks to fall almost entirely on the farmers. Money, not land, must therefore be the farmers' central concern. Eighty-three percent of farmers interviewed in a national survey in 1994 said that their biggest challenge was simply making a profit.[18]

Wendell Berry, who farms and writes in Kentucky, describes the demoralizing effects of the forced priority given to money by those whose discipline should be directed first toward the land: *The concentration of the farmland into larger and larger holdings and fewer and fewer hands—with the consequent increase of overhead, debt, and dependence on machines ... forces a profound revolution on the farmer's mind: once his investment in land and machines is large enough, he must forsake the values of husbandry and assume those of finance and technology. Thenceforth his thinking is not determined by agricultural responsibility, but by financial accountability and the capabilities of his machines.*[19]

The farmer, squeezed between the profit-taking corporations that supply inputs, on the one hand, and those that market the produce, on the other, is forced to adopt the corporate values of specialization, efficiency, mechanization, and growth simply to survive. Many don't, and have given up in disgust.

The squeeze exists because the rise of mechanized and chemical agriculture and industrially processed foods has diminished the productive role of the farmer relative to the food industry as a whole, transferring more and more of the responsibility (and hence more and more of the profits) to the suppliers of inputs and the marketers. The farmer is thus crunched between the jaws of a vice—the corporations that control inputs on one side, and the corporations that control marketing on the other. One obvious way to loosen the vice is to return to the farm or farming community some of the productive functions (and hence the profits) that have been usurped by these corporations.

There are many strategies for doing this: using cover crops, compost, or manure produced on the farm rather than chemical fertilizers; bartering among farm households; using draft animals or human labor instead of petroleum wherever possible; making greater use of wind power and solar energy; avoiding routine spraying of pesticides and herbicides (using them only as needed); marketing more directly to local consumers rather than to corporate food processors; organizing marketing co-ops or schemes of community-supported agriculture (discussed below); experimenting with small-scale processing on the farm of such items as cheese, preserves, or cured meats; and minimizing debt.[20] The recent development of a Farmer's Market in Knox County is a useful step in the right direction, though much of the food sold there is trucked in from out of state.

We will probably never return to a healthy agriculture, however, if we expect the initiative to come from hard-pressed farmers (the few who are left). The crucial element is an educated public who appreciate the advantages of a sound, healthful local food supply and are prepared to pay somewhat higher prices (at least initially) or take some financial risk to secure it.

One way to accomplish this is community-supported agriculture—an arrangement whereby a number of consumers pay to the farmer in advance a fixed price for a year's supply of certain specified foods. If the harvest is good, they get a bounty and a bargain; if it is poor, they accept the loss along with the farmer (who also has less to eat). This guarantees the farmer a livable income and spreads the risk normally borne by the farmer among the consumers, each of whom carries only a small portion of it. Such an arrangement enables small farmers to avoid debt and to hold their own against competition cushioned by greater capital. It also knits communities together and increases their independence, cuts out middlemen, provides consumers with nutritious produce direct from the farm, lowers the cost and environmental impact of food transportation, and increases everyone's care for the land. Several farms in our bioregion have promising community-supported agricultural projects already underway, and with greater consumer demand there could be more; for many are the people—both old and young, both experienced and inexperienced—who would love to farm, if only they could make a living at it.

Organic vs. Chemical Agriculture

What is nowadays known as "conventional" agriculture did not become conventional until after World War II. It began with the wide availability of cheap petrochemical fertilizers (made possible by the conversion of munitions plants to fertilizer plants) and of pesticides, such as DDT. For the greatest part of human history, all farming was organic. Farmers adopted the new technologies, not because the old methods did not work, but because the short-term efficiency of chemical agriculture generated fierce competitive pressures that forced compliance. That situation is now changing. Advances in organic agriculture (achieved mostly outside the dominant agricultural institutions) have steadily increased its efficiency, so that some farmers are now able to compete on the open market using organic methods. Other organic growers have sought niches not dominated by the competitive pressures of the marketplace, niches in which they can work slowly and responsibly to heal the land. Community-supported agricultural projects are one sort of example.

There is some controversy over the definition of the word "organic," but certain general points may be stressed: Organic farms avoid the use of artificial pesticides and fertilizers. For fertility they rely on manure, compost (genuine compost, not ground-up municipal waste), and cover crops that are plowed into the soil (often referred to as "green manure"). For pest control, organic farms employ various combinations of crop rotation, physical pest removal, and biological controls. Large organic farms may use standard farm machinery, though often with modifications to avoid soil compaction, but the smaller ones tend to rely solely on muscle power (human or animal) for tillage.

By nearly all measures of ecological health, organic agriculture is far superior to conventional techniques. A recent Washington State University study, for example, compared two adjacent farms in Washington, one of which had been operated organically for over eighty years, the other of which had used fertilizers and pesticides since 1948. (We would prefer to report regional research, but we have been unable to find studies of organic agriculture in Southern Appalachia. Funding for agricultural research is dominated by chemical companies and other corporate interests that do not support scientific investigation of organic techniques.)

In the Washington study, soil samples were taken from adjacent areas with identical slopes on each farm. Soil from the organic farm contained much more moisture and was richer in nutrients (especially nitrogen and potassium) than the soil of the nonorganic farm. This was due in part to greater microbial activity. (Microbes, which generate nutrients that enrich the soil, are often killed—along with beneficial insects and worms—by conventional agricultural chemicals.) The organic farm had sixty percent more organic matter (which improves soil structure and increases the soil's ability to store moisture) at the soil's surface. It also had a lower "modulus of rupture"—a measure of how easily seedlings can break through the surface of the soil—and was superior in overall tilth. The topsoil on the organic farm was over six inches thicker than on the nonorganic farm. This was due in part to differences in the erosion rates; erosion was nearly four times greater on the nonorganic farm. But it was also due to the practice on the organic farm of plowing in cover crops to build topsoil. The researchers concluded that the nonorganic farm was gradually becoming less productive as a result of the erosion, though the impoverishment of the soil was masked by the use of higher-yielding plant varieties and more effective chemical fertilizers, but that the organic farm could maintain its productivity in the long term.[21]

Most organic farms strive for diversity, growing many varieties of fruits and vegetables, and rotating crops to keep pests from becoming established or from infecting the whole crop. Many use biointensive methods, which concentrate the plants into highly enriched beds of soil. Unlike traditional row cropping, this method of concentrating plants simulates natural growing conditions by creating a cool, shady microclimate near the surface of the soil that maintains constant moisture and discourages weeds. Though the biointensive method requires more labor than "conventional" methods, its yields are in many cases much higher.[22] Moreover, through the use of terracing, biointensive growing is adaptable to Southern Appalachian hillsides, where conventional row cropping creates unacceptable erosion, thus permitting the production of fruit and vegetable crops on lands that might otherwise be suitable only for pasture. Connie Whitehead, using biointensive methods at Planted Earth Farm in Strawberry Plains, Tennessee, has been easily able to grow on two acres nearly all the vegetables needed over a period of five months by twenty families, who participated with her in a community-supported agricultural project.[23] Her methods were strictly organic.

There is no question that organic farms are superior in almost every environmental measure to "conventional" farms. The only serious objection to them is economic. Primarily because they require more labor than conventional farms, their produce usually costs more. If not biointensive, they may also have lower yields. In one sense, the additional labor is an advantage, since organic farms create more jobs than nonorganic farms. But cost is still the great deterrent.

The True Cost of Food

Market price, however, is not the true cost of food. Conventional agriculture imposes high environmental costs, which eventually become financial costs, though the bill may not come due for many years. One important hidden cost is siltation. Since "conventional" agriculture increases erosion, it can substantially add to the sedimentation of streams and rivers. A 1981 study found that conversion of previously unfarmed land to conventional cropland in a Southern Appalachian ridge-and-valley landscape increases the influx of sediment into streams by over twelve tons per acre annually (about an inch of topsoil every fourteen years)—an unacceptably high figure by any standards.[24]

Silt makes rivers and streams less suitable for fishing and recreation, which can hurt the businesses that support these activities. Furthermore, as it settles into reservoirs, it hastens the day when the reservoirs become so clogged that they are no longer effective for flood control.

But silt is not the only problem caused by erosion. The loss of the soil is itself a cost. Early farming and logging in the Southern Appalachians were so reckless that in effect they mined the soil. As the steep hillsides were clearcut and then plowed and plowed again, more and more topsoil washed away, until sometimes only the subsoil remained. The losses were monumental. In 1977, long after most farmers had become aware of the need for soil conservation, a national resource inventory indicated that the soil of Tennessee's croplands was still eroding at an average rate of one inch every eleven years.[25] Earlier in the century, the losses were no doubt much greater. By now, much of the soil of Southern Appalachia lies beneath the waters of the Gulf of Mexico.

Erosion continues, though agricultural reforms and soil conservation programs have substantially slowed the rates.[26] (Recent advances in "no-till" agriculture can reduce soil losses still further, but no-till systems may also require larger applications of herbicides or pesticides.[27])

Soil loss is partially counteracted by the creation of new soil due to the erosion of underlying rock and the deposit and decay of organic material, such as wood and leaves. Yet most forms of human land use (organic agriculture being a notable exception) erode soil more rapidly than it forms, creating net losses. Because humans use virtually all the land, except for the forests (when they are not being logged), this means that net gains of topsoil occur primarily in the forests. Topsoil accumulates at a rate somewhere between an inch a century and an inch every three or four centuries.[28] Since much of Southern Appalachia has already lost many inches of soil, merely to restore the losses we have already inflicted would take many centuries of forest growth. And since topsoil is a prime necessity for all land-based life, this is another reason (if more were needed) for defending Southern Appalachian forests.

Loss of topsoil is in effect loss of capital; the land grows poorer each year, so that over time it becomes less suitable for growing crops and requires more chemical inputs. Food production thus becomes increasingly expensive, though we may not notice the loss or pay the price for many years.

And conventional agriculture imposes other hidden costs as well. It adds substantially to the nutrients (especially nitrogen and phosphorus from chemical fertilizers) and pesticides that contaminate streams and groundwater (see Chapter One), increasing the risk of cancer for those who drink the groundwater and harming fish and wildlife that use the streams. The results are higher health-care costs (which must ultimately be borne by everyone) and a further generalized degradation of water quality, which is likely to reduce income from tourism, hunting, and fishing.

With chemical agriculture, there are also more direct health care costs to consumers of food which contains pesticide residues and to the farmers themselves, for some percentage (albeit small) of these people will get cancer or suffer other health problems from pesticide exposures. The purchase of these pesticides draws down the inventories of pesticide suppliers, stimulating new orders to manufacture more. In this manufacturing process, too, people are exposed to dangerous chemicals and still more pollution is released. Further pollution is generated by the trucks that transport the chemicals to the supplier and on to the farm. These activities, too, contribute to the cost of health care.

It is probably impossible accurately to assess all these hidden costs. But, though fraught with uncertainties, they are real and eventually will have to be paid. Once we take them into account, it is by no means certain that nonorganic food is cheaper in purely monetary terms, on the whole and in the long run, than organic food.

Consequently, even though organic produce generally costs more in dollar amounts than nonorganic, many people are willing to pay the higher price, the true cost, as an investment in their own health, in the health of the land, and in the future. A good selection of high-quality organic produce, some of it locally grown, is available at the Knoxville Community Food Co-op and at several other outlets in our bioregion.

Food that is healthy (in all the senses of the word "health") is not only local and organic—that is, healthy for its consumers and the land; it is also healthy for its producers. When we demand (by our buying habits) that food be as cheap as possible, we often inadvertently harm farmers. Fruits and vegetables from California, for example, are cheap in part because they are grown by underpaid migrant workers. Decently paid local growers can't compete, even factoring in the transporation costs. In fact, in order to produce their crop as cheaply as possible, some of the few remaining fruit and vegetable growers of Southern Appalachia have begun to employ migrants, who are forced by social circumstance to work for low wages. The situation is much worse elsewhere—in Central America, for example—where low wages are enforced by repressive governments, which violently suppress labor organizations. This makes food from Central America *very* cheap in monetary terms, though its true cost (in lives and land) is extraordinarily high.

We are conditioned by the rewards and punishments inherent in our market economy to buy food according to monetary cost, rather than according to its true cost, preferring cheap food to food that is, in the widest sense, healthy. As a result, local farmers can't make a living, and our food is produced in ways that degrade both people and the land.

Meat

As farm after farm wore out in the first half of this century, more and more farm families packed up and moved west—to the dust bowl (but that is another story). Those who stayed adapted their methods to the impoverished soil. When the hills would no longer bear a healthy crop of corn, wheat, or tobacco, they would still grow grass. So the grain and tobacco farms gave way to beef and dairy operations, which are the mainstays of Southern Appalachian agriculture to this day.

But the cow, though less destructive than the plow, is still hard on the land—especially when confined to small, steep acreage. Many a Southern Appalachian hillside is grazed almost bare and criss-crossed with muddy or dusty paths, its thin compacted clay, once overlain by rich forested topsoil, now receding to reveal the underlying skeleton of rock. Where pasture land is crossed by a spring or stream, the cattle are often allowed to trample its banks, contaminating the water with sediment and manure and sending the soil riverwards.

Still, cattle operations are more compatible with the land of Southern Appalachia than they are with the denuded rainforest of Central or South America or the water-starved, overgrazed land of the American West, from which we now get much of our beef. And cattle can be, and often are, raised sustainably here—provided that the herds are not too large and the pastures are rotated and not overgrazed. Local cattle growers, most of whom are small, private operators, generally take better care of their animals than the large corporate operations, and many refuse such pharmaceutical novelties as growth hormones. Moreover, local grass-fed beef is leaner than grain-fed beef.[29] Anyone who eats beef, then, would do well to insist that it be locally raised, not only because the local product is generally higher in quality, but also because buying locally helps to minimize wear on the land, reduce transportation impacts, and preserve Southern Appalachian agriculture. The same is true for dairy products.

An increasing minority, however, have chosen to eat no beef at all, and some have gone still farther, becoming vegetarian (eating no meat) or vegan (using no animal products). The East Tennessee Vegetarian Society has a growing and active membership. Often these choices are motivated by concern for personal health. (Red meat has been implicated in heart disease, various forms of cancer, and a number of other maladies.[30]) But often, too, the welfare of the animals themselves is decisive—especially in view of the appalling suffering routinely inflicted on animals at factory farms.[31] There are also such ecological considerations as the impact of cattle on the land. These considerations will increase in salience as population grows and the world food supply becomes more precarious, for it generally takes much less land, energy, and environmental disruption to support a vegetarian diet than to support the food habits of a carnivore.[32]

Eating with the Seasons

Throughout all of human history up until the last few decades, diet had a seasonal rhythm. In Southern Appalachia, greens came in the early spring, then peas and other spring vegetables. Strawberries appeared in May, blackberries in June. July, August, and September were the months of the corn and bean harvest and of fresh tomatoes and watermelons, and later in the fall there were nuts, squashes, and persimmons. Meat, dried beans, and stored grains made up the bulk of the winter diet, though the careful gardener knew how to extend a fall crop of greens long into the winter.

But these rhythms, which once gave texture and tempo to life and provided cause for anticipation and celebration, have long been broken. Processed food, which makes up the bulk of our diet, has no seasonal rhythm and is available on demand, constantly. Even "fresh" produce of virtually any variety, is now available year round, trucked in from Mexico or California, or shipped up from Chile, New Zealand, or Brazil—the only seasonal variation being a fluctuation in price.

What is true of the food supply generally is also true in particular for the bioregion's restaurants. The fast-food restaurants, of course, get their stock from regional or national suppliers which standardize it so rigidly that it varies not at all from franchise to franchise or season to season. But even the more up-scale and unique local restaurants which offer changing menus usually buy from a few corporate suppliers, such as Robert Orr/Sysco or IJ, which may truck in just about any food from just about anywhere in just about any season.

Perhaps this constant availability of everything has contributed in some measure to human happiness, but nearly all now take it for granted and many find it blasé. Correlatively, celebrations of the seasonal rhythms and harvests have for many lost their meanings.

However we assess its effect on the quality of our lives, this much, at least, is clear: this vast supply of exotic and luxurious foods is procured at great environmental cost. The energy required to transport and refrigerate all this food is tremendous, and most of it is generated by the burning of fossil fuels, with all the attendant effects described in Chapters One, Two, Five and Seven.

Progress toward a sustainable food supply would require in part a return to eating with the seasons. Much more of our produce would be locally grown, farm-ripened, transported only short distances, and consumed while still fresh. This would certainly enhance the health of the body and of the land. It is not unreasonable to hope that it might also improve the health of the spirit.

Growing Your Own

The ultimate local food source is the home garden. Its ecological advantages are manifold. Fruits and vegetables grown at home are eaten at home, with no consumption of fossil fuels for transportation. In fact, the home garden is usually small enough to be worked entirely by hand—especially by biointensive methods—so that fossil fuels need not be used at all; and most other inputs can be reduced or eliminated by organic techniques.

Yard waste, kitchen waste, and leaves, which might otherwise be landfilled or incinerated at considerable ecological cost, can, with very little effort, be made into compost that continually enriches the soil and eliminates the need for industrial fertilizers. A family can grow most or even all of its fruits and vegetables on an acre or two, saving hundreds or even thousands of dollars annually in food bills. And almost anyone can gain some advantage and make some contribution by gardening. Even apartment dwellers usually have access to a nearby patch of ground or, lacking that, a set of planters and pots, in which tomatoes, peppers, fresh herbs, or greens may be grown. Rainfall in Southern Appalachia is abundant in most years, and the climate is so mild that it is possible, using such simple methods as row covers or cold frames, to harvest something every month of the year.[33]

The home gardener enjoys exercise in the open air and the freshest and most healthful of foods. She eats with the seasons, rejoices in harvests, develops a weather eye, becomes acquainted with a whole world of small creatures (both helpful and frustrating) that once lived beneath her notice, learns discipline of keeping and improving the soil, and—in taking personal responsibility for the source of her nourishment—taps a wellspring of meaning that is inaccessible to those who consume only the cargo of eighteen-wheelers.

FIGURE 7: On-demand hot water heaters use much less energy than heaters that maintain a constant reservoir of hot water.

It shall not be quenched night and day; the smoke thereof shall go up for ever; from generation to generation it shall lie waste ...

                                                    — Isaiah 34:10

Energy Consumption

We consume energy for heat, light, the manipulation of information, and motive force in a myriad residential, commercial, and industrial applications. This chapter considers the consequences of that consumption. We also use energy to move people and things across the land, but transportation raises special issues, which are reserved for Chapter Seven. Here the topic is the non-transportation uses of energy, and, especially, of electricity.

It is, of necessity, a topic already broached, for consumption of electricity affects the water, the air, and the whole system of life. Chapters One and Two, for example, traced the paths of acid, smog and ozone pollution from the tall stacks of the coal-fired power plants to the imperiled spruce-fir forests of the Great Smoky Mountains National Park. This chapter traces other paths: those that run backwards from the ends of electric power lines of homes and businesses to the power stations—hydroelectric, coal-fired, and nuclear—and beyond, to the depths of the oxygen-deprived reservoirs, to the ravaged coal country, to the uranium mines, the contaminated enrichment plants, and the places where nuclear waste is to be buried deep in the Earth.

We pride ourselves on having learned to control energy, yet our control is only local and brief. We can generate enormous power, send it across wires, and make it do almost anything. But in the process we set loose social, ecological, and even geological forces that we only dimly understand and have neither the knowledge nor the will to control.

The most immediate effect of our energy consumption, the one we notice, is the work that the power does for us. But even this effect sometimes has unwanted consequences. Take, for example, the cumulative effects of electric lighting. A few electric lights here or there may have little effect on the world, but a landscape aglow with millions of streetlights, house lights, and advertising signs on poles fifty feet in the air is utterly transformed. In such a landscape there is no darkness, for the light streaming upwards is reflected back from the clouds or the particulate pollutants in the air to illuminate everything—often in unearthly tones of yellow or orange. Moths that instinctively navigate by moonlight become disoriented, spiraling madly and fatally around sources of brilliance for which nothing in their evolutionary past has prepared them. People lose touch with the stars, which can be seen, if at all, only faintly, as a few lonely points of light amid the brighter, flashier moving lights of airplanes—never as the silent, scintillating celestial vault that inspired the ancients with thoughts of a pure, transcendent Heaven. Minor matters, one might suppose, in comparison with the lofty purposes served by the lights themselves—but perhaps worthy of mention.

Electric lighting is, as Table 5.1 indicates, by far the single largest commercial use of electricity. Much of it is devoted to the all-night illumination of the gigantic billboards and advertising signs that fill the skies above the strip malls. Much is also consumed by interior lighting during the day—which on most days could be accomplished at no expense and with negligible environmental impact by the sun. Many businesses also keep their interior lights burning through the night, though the building is empty. This may provide a measure of advertising or security—but at what human and environmental cost? Equal security, moreover, can be provided by occupancy sensors that turn the lights on automatically when someone enters the building.

The most wasteful of all regional commercial lighting displays is the one that runs for twenty-three miles through the towns Gatlinburg, Pigeon Forge, and Sevierville, from the Smokies to Interstate 40 during the holiday season. This ostentatious extravagance, designed to milk money from off-season tourists, violates the night well up into the mountains.

Table 5.1

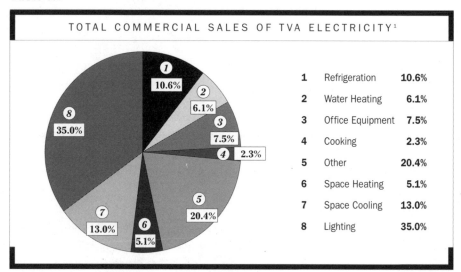

TOTAL COMMERCIAL SALES OF TVA ELECTRICITY[1]

1	Refrigeration	10.6%
2	Water Heating	6.1%
3	Office Equipment	7.5%
4	Cooking	2.3%
5	Other	20.4%
6	Space Heating	5.1%
7	Space Cooling	13.0%
8	Lighting	35.0%

Besides commercial uses, electricity also has multiple manufacturing and residential uses. Manufacturing uses are highly varied, from chip mills to food production, but the greatest amount of electricity is consumed by the chemical industry.[2]

TVA sells some power directly to regional industries and some through various distributors. Some of the largest direct sales are listed in Table 5.2, though it should be noted that many large industries, such as Tennessee Eastman, are not included here, since they are not direct customers:

Table 5.2

DIRECT POWER SALES TO INDUSTRY IN THE UPPER TENNESSEE VALLEY, YEAR ENDING SEPTEMBER 1992[3]		
Direct Sales to Industries	**Kilowatt-hours**	**Cost in dollars**
Aluminum Company of America Alcoa, TN	2,383,081,000	54,913,664
BIT Manufacturing, Inc. Copperhill, TN	24,061,000	1,016,394
Bowater Incorporated Calhoun, TN	1,802,864,000	54,454,128
H-R International, Inc. Jasper, TN	2,593,000	139,255
Kimberly-Clark Corporation Loudon, TN	51,262,000	1,403,553
Olin Corporation Charleston, TN	1,016,765,000	24,190,927
Skyline Coal Company Dunlap, TN	14,287,000	430,719
A.E. Staley Manufacturing Company Loudon, TN	286,712,000	8,862,693
Total	5,581,625,000	145,411,333

Electricity is also used to power a vast array of residential appliances, many of which are inefficient and outdated. The worst of these is the electric water heater (see Table 5.3). Electric water heaters, still used in over three-quarters of the homes in the TVA region, are remarkably inefficient. To maintain a constant supply, they heat a large volume of water even during long periods when no water is being used. The heat, moreover, is usually provided by electrical resistance, which is itself inefficient and expensive.

Better alternatives are readily available. Merely switching to natural gas increases energy efficiency, though water is still being heated when it is not being used. Moreover, the combustion of natural gas releases considerably less sulfur dioxide and carbon dioxide into the air than the combustion of the coal that is usually used to generate electricity. Thus gas appliances are not only more efficient; they also contribute less to pollution, acid rain, and global warming. More efficient still are "on-demand" gas heaters, which have no storage tank at all, and heat the water only when the tap is turned on *(see Figure 7 on page 121)*. Widely used in Europe, they provide piping hot water efficiently and almost instantly. Any water heater can in addition be made more efficient still by fitting it with a passive solar preheater. This simple device does no harm to anything and, once installed, heats the water for free, so long as the sun is shining.[4] In the early 1980s, TVA actively promoted the residential use of solar energy, especially solar water heaters. But as the political winds shifted and the agency fell deeply into debt (matters soon to be discussed in more detail), these progressive initiatives were eliminated.

Table 5.3

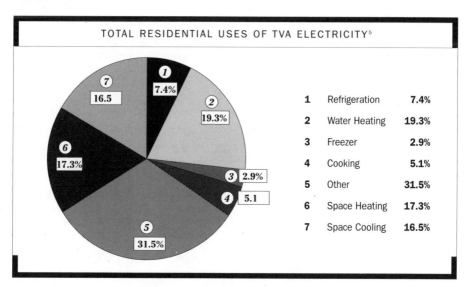

TOTAL RESIDENTIAL USES OF TVA ELECTRICITY[5]

1	Refrigeration	7.4%
2	Water Heating	19.3%
3	Freezer	2.9%
4	Cooking	5.1%
5	Other	31.5%
6	Space Heating	17.3%
7	Space Cooling	16.5%

Heating and cooling comprise the next largest categories of home electrical use. About twenty-nine percent of the homes in the TVA distribution area still use electrical resistance for space heating, and many additional homes whose primary heat comes from wood also use electrical resistance as a backup.[6] Electrical resistance is even less efficient for space heating than for water heating, and should be regarded as obsolete. Electric heat pumps are more efficient, but gas is more efficient still. Good insulation and passive solar architecture can reduce both the financial and environmental costs of heating to a minimum. Wood heat has the advantage of using a more-or-less renewable energy source that a person can procure independently, but without pollution control equipment it heavily pollutes the air. About eighteen percent of the homes served by TVA still heat with wood.[7]

Air conditioning, discussed briefly in Chapter Two in connection with increasing exposures to indoor air pollutants, has become so common that many people now regard it as a necessity—an opinion that would have been unintelligible to earlier inhabitants of this land, who were hardier and knew a trick or two about keeping cool on a hot summer day. About eighty-four percent of homes in the TVA distribution area are air conditioned, and the percentage is steadily rising.[8] Whatever common opinion may decree, the fact is that we keep ourselves cool primarily by burning coal and nuclear fuel—which entails certain risks and harms. The comfort we receive should therefore be weighed against these risks and harms.

The "other" category in the residential chart represents such uses as lighting, microwave ovens, dishwashers, clothes washers and dryers, and other electronic equipment. The relative amounts of electricity used by some of these common appliances are shown in Table 5.4. Appliances that use resistance heating (electric water heaters, electric ranges, fully electric clothes dryers, blow dryers, most dishwashers, irons, toasters, hot plates, electric frying pans, and so on) are especially high consumers. However, the actual energy used also depends on the amount of time an appliance is drawing power. A thousand-watt air conditioner running twenty-four hours a day, for example, consumes forty-eight times as much electricity as a thousand-watt iron used only half an hour each day.

Table 5.4

APPROXIMATE ELECTRICITY CONSUMPTION OF COMMON APPLIANCES[9]			
Appliance	**Watts**	**Appliance**	**Watts**
Air conditioner, room	1000	Garage door opener	350
Air conditioner, central	2000-5000	Hot plate	1200
Blow dryer	1000	Iron	1000
CD player	35	Light bulb, 100w incandescent	100
Clock radio	1	Light bulb, 100w equivalent compact fluorescent	30

Table 5.4 cont.

APPROXIMATE ELECTRICITY CONSUMPTION OF COMMON APPLIANCES[9]

Appliance	Watts	Appliance	Watts
Clothes dryer, electric heat	4000	Microwave	600-1500
Clothes dryer, gas heat	300-400	Printer for PC	100
Coffee maker	800	Refrigerator/freezer, 16 cu. ft.	475
Coffee pot	200	Refrigerator/freezer, 20 cu. ft.	540
Computer, laptop	20-50	Sander (3" belt)	1000
Computer, pc	80-150	Satellite dish	30
Dishwasher	1200-1500	Saw, 7 1/4" circular	900
Drill 1/4"	250	Saw, 8 1/4" circular	1400
Drill 1/2"	750	Shaver 15 Electric blanket	200
Television, 19" color	70	Electric heater, portable	1500
Television, 25" color	150	Electric range (per burner)	1500
Toaster	800-1500	Fan, ceiling 10-50 VCR	40
Fan, table	10-25	Washing machine	500
Frying pan	1200	Water heater, electric	4500-5500
Furnace blower	300-1000	Weed eater	500

Especially significant in Table 5.4 are the entries for "Light bulb." Standard incandescent bulbs, which shine by electrical resistance, also produce waste heat and so are highly inefficient. Equivalent compact fluorescent bulbs (available at most large hardware or department stores) shine coolly, but just as brightly, and so use less than a third as much electricity. Their purchase price is higher, but the investment is returned in electric bill savings—not to mention environmental savings.

All this power usage adds up to astronomical numbers. Table 5.5 gives the total electrical consumption for the TVA portion of the Upper Tennessee Valley region, excluding federal facilities. A kilowatt-hour is the amount of electricity used by a thousand-watt appliance (such as a typical room air conditioner) in an hour.

Table 5.5

POWER DEMAND IN THE UPPER TENNESSEE RIVER WATERSHED, YEAR ENDING SEPTEMBER 1992[10]		
Power Purchaser	**Kilowatt-hours**	**Cost in dollars**
Municipal and County Systems	21,597,242,000	936,943,000
Cooperative Systems	5,125,026,000	220,787,000
Industrial Direct Purchasers	5,581,625,000	145,411,000
Total	32,303,893,000	1,303,141,000

Municipal and county systems include such distributors as the Knoxville Utilities Board. Cooperative systems, such as the Powell Valley Electrical Cooperative, operate mostly in rural areas. Direct purchases by industries were listed in Table 5.2.

Table 5.5 does not account for all the energy consumed in our bioregion, since it leaves out not only usage by federal facilities, such as the Department of Energy's Oak Ridge Reservation, but also usage in a part of western North Carolina, including Asheville, that lies in the upper Tennessee watershed but is serviced by Nantahala Power and Light, Carolina Power and Light, or Duke Power, rather than TVA. Even so, the amounts are enormous. And we are clearly using more than our share. Crude estimates indicate that the average person in the United States consumes about forty times as much energy as the average person in the less-developed world.[11]

Power Transmission

Some of the uses we make of electricity, such as commercial lighting, affect the environment directly, but all affect it indirectly. To trace the indirect effects, we must follow the incoming current backwards through the plug, into the junction box, back along the power line to the transformer, the substation, the generating station, and beyond.

Transformers, the dark cylinders high up on telephone poles or the larger devices protected by the chain-link and barbed-wire fences of the substations, have contaminated much of the soil and water of Southern Appalachia. Until the late 1970s, nearly all transformers contained an insulating oil consisting largely of polychlorinated biphenyls (PCBs). When they leaked or exploded (as transformers sometimes do), this liquid leaked out onto the ground. Heavy industrial users of electricity, such as Alcoa Aluminum or the nuclear weapons plants at Oak Ridge, employed many large transformers and were especially troublesome sources of PCB leaks. When transformers wore out, they were taken to scrap yards, such as David Witherspoon, Inc., in the Vestal community of South Knoxville, where they were broken open, allowing the oil to spill out on the ground, in order to salvage the copper wire inside. PBCs, as was noted in Chapter One, are now widespread in the silt of regional waterways, and in some places they still contaminate the soil. In the 1970s, it was discovered that ingestion of PCBs or PCB-contaminated food can cause cancer, reproductive problems, and a host of other maladies. Their manufacture was banned in 1976, and since then many older transformers have been replaced or provided with a substitute insulating oil. Still, PCB contamination remains one of the most important residual problems of an incautious industrial era.

Beyond the transformers are the power lines. These lines form a grid that distributes electricity everywhere the roads go—and some places where they don't. Power lines may appear to be inert and nonpolluting, but they are in fact sites of high electrical activity, which surrounds them with invisible and impalpable, but nonetheless real, electromagnetic fields. Several studies have suggested a link between long-term exposure to the electromagnetic fields of power lines and childhood leukemia or other forms of cancer; but other studies have found no such link, and the issue is still open.[12]

Power lines do, however, have obvious and visible effects on the environment. Where long-distance transmission lines cut across the land, vegetation must be cut or suppressed with herbicides in corridors a hundred or more feet wide and many miles long. These swaths are prominent from the air, running often in perfectly straight lines, even over rugged mountainous or forested terrain.

Power line cuts fragment forests, facilitating entry for disease organisms, exotic invasive species, and the predators of songbirds. Many songbirds, as was noted in Chapter Three, require deep forest habitat, well away from open edges, in order to have a fair chance at reproduction. Power line cuts deny them that throughout much of our bioregion.

Vegetation in the power line cuts must be kept constantly short to prevent interference with the wires. This used to be done almost entirely by tractor or by hand, but nowadays it is often accomplished by the spraying of herbicides—Arsenal, Accord, Escort, and Big Sur, for example—from helicopters. This is a dangerous practice. In the fall of 1994, one of these herbicide-spraying helicopters crashed in the driveway of an upper East Tennessee residence.[13] Moreover, some of the herbicides used can have acute toxic effects on human beings and may harm fish or other wildlife. American Cyanamid, the manufacturer of Arsenal, warns against spraying the chemical on water, food, crops, wetlands, gardens, and in winds greater than five miles per hour. A helicopter rotor generates a wind much stiffer than five miles an hour, and springs, crops, wetlands, and gardens are often located in or very near to powerline cuts. People in upper East Tennessee and in western Virginia have reported the spraying of streams and springs, sometimes despite repeated pleas to stop it.[14]

TVA

Tracing the power lines back far enough leads ultimately back to the power's source: a generating station. Most of the generating stations that supply power for Southern Appalachia are owned and operated by TVA, and there can be no adequate understanding of power generation in the Tennessee Valley without a sense of the history, politics, and economics of that unique agency.

One of the largest power producers in the country, TVA generates between four and five percent of all the electricity used in the United States. Serving more than eight million people in seven states, it can produce over twenty-eight billion watts of power.[15]

TVA was established in 1933 to help the Tennessee Valley recover from two scourges: the Great Depression and decades of egregious environmental abuse. At that time, the Tennessee River watershed had been almost entirely clear-cut, which, together with destructive mining and farming practices, was causing massive erosion and contributing to catastrophic flooding. TVA aimed to solve these problems by building dams on the Tennessee River and its major tributaries. The dams were to help control flooding, promote river traffic, and generate electricity. By the beginning of World War II, the agency had completed twelve hydroelectric dams. The dams, together with exemplary programs to reforest the hillsides and promote responsible agriculture, brought the flooding under control—though at the expense of permanently drowning some of the best farmland in the Valley.

During World War II, regional demand for electricity soared as a result of wartime aircraft production by Alcoa Aluminum and the enrichment of uranium for the first atomic bombs at Oak Ridge. In 1945, TVA completed its first coal-fired power plant at Watts Bar. Over the next twenty years, the agency built eleven coal-fired plants, which provided power at rates among the lowest in the nation.[16] Electrification proceeded rapidly. By 1970, about thirty percent of the homes in the valley were heated with electricity, and TVA customers used nearly twice as much electricity as the national average.[17] Low electric rates and a cost-effective river transportation stimulated industrial growth.

In the 1960s, it became apparent that the electricity demand in the Tennessee Valley could not be met by coal and hydroelectric power alone. TVA had already used most of the feasible hydroelectric sights and was under increasing pressure to reduce the emissions from the coal facilities. The agency saw nuclear power as the clean, cost-effective answer. By the late 1960s, TVA had announced plans to build seventeen nuclear units at seven sites. In 1967, it broke ground for Browns Ferry, the nation's largest nuclear power facility.

The energy crisis of the 1970s brought a new wave of conservationism to TVA, revitalizing the agency's vision. TVA's fifty-year retrospective, published in 1983, proudly proclaims that "Energy consumers throughout the Valley are now encouraged to use electricity efficiently and to substitute solar and renewable resources where possible."[18] TVA sponsored a million residential energy audits and provided many low-interest or no-interest loans to finance energy-saving improvements—including thousands of residential solar water heaters. Over six hundred thousand residences were weatherized, saving over 1,400 megawatts of power, the equivalent of two medium-sized nuclear reactors. These initiatives were internationally recognized, catapulting TVA to the forefront of the push for sustainable energy. Yet, despite their well-documented success, most were abruptly canceled in 1988 in cutbacks initiated by Chairman Marvin Runyon, a Reagan appointee. They have never been restored.

In the meantime, instead of introducing a new age of abundance and energy "too cheap to meter," TVA's nuclear program, tainted by mismanagement, became increasingly mired in debt and shaken by rumblings of financial disaster. In 1975, an electrical insulation fire at the Browns Ferry plant, caused by a worker using a candle to check for air leaks, destroyed several core-cooling systems. A catastrophic meltdown was narrowly averted. This harrowing accident caused the Nuclear Regulatory Commission to issue a host of new regulations, which significantly increased TVA's costs. The still more serious partial meltdown at Three Mile Island in 1979, though not involving TVA directly, produced still more regulations and increased costs further. In 1985, whistleblower complaints prompted the Nuclear Regulatory Commission to shut down TVA's entire nuclear system, to correct repeated errors in

operations and maintenance and flagrant safetly violations. The reactors were eventually restarted, but delays and cost overruns plagued the entire program—especially
the ill-starred Watts Bar plant. Construction on the two Watts Bar reactors began in
1973, but Unit 1 did not come on line until 1996. Unit 2 was canceled in 1995. TVA
originally projected the cost for both reactors at about 370 million dollars.[19] The
actual cost for completing just Unit 1 was about seven billion dollars.[20]

Although by 1995 TVA's nuclear program comprised roughly sixty-nine percent of
the agency's net investment in property, plants, and equipment, nuclear power generation made up only fourteen percent of its generating capacity.[21] Since then, two
additional nuclear plants have come on line, but these are projected to boost the
nuclear share of generating capacity only to twenty percent.[22] Largely as a result of
the nuclear debacle, TVA was, by the end of 1996, about twenty-eight billion dollars
in debt[23] and was paying about thirty-five percent of its revenue (approximately two
billion dollars per year) in interest charges. In contrast, the utilities in surrounding
power districts pay an average of about sixteen percent of their revenue in interest.
This will, in the foreseeable future, make it difficult for TVA to charge competitive
rates for its power.[24]

To compound the difficulty, there is within the entire utility industry a strong tendency toward deregulation and stiffer competition. Power producers outside TVA's
operating area may soon be able to bid on contracts to provide power to utilities
and industries within TVA's electricity market. Producers will then have to cut their
rates to retain their customers.

So far, TVA has been protected from competition by two factors. First, a 1959
ammendment to the TVA Act, reinforced by the Energy Policy Act of 1992, makes it
very difficult for outside producers to sell power to TVA customers, because it does
not compel TVA to bring outside power into its service area. To get their electricity to customers in the TVA area, low-cost power suppliers must acquire rights of
way to install new power lines. There is, however, increasing pressure in Congress
to allow them to do so. Secondly, TVA distributors (such as the Knoxville Utilities
Board) are under contractual commitment to give a ten-year notice when they
decide to switch to another supplier.[25] This prohibits them from seeking out the
most competitive power producer. Some distributors have recently made efforts to
cancel TVA contracts and obtain cheaper power elsewhere,[26] but TVA has prevented
them from doing so. Nevertheless, this may signal the beginning of a trend.

In 1995, the United States General Accounting Office (GAO) concluded that TVA's high debt made the agency uncompetitive in the long run and that keeping the agency solvent might eventually require a federal bailout. In the words of the GAO: *...TVA has far more financing costs and deferred assets than its likely competitors have, which gives TVA little flexibility to meet competitive challenges. To the extent that TVA cannot compete effectively and improve its financial condition, the federal government is at risk for some portion of TVA's debt. ...Although protected from competition by legislation and its customer contracts in the short run, TVA will have to compete with other utilities in the long run. Because of its heavy debt burden and high financing costs, TVA lacks the ability to successfully compete in this environment.*[27] The GAO also pointed out that one of Congress's options for solving TVA's debt crisis was to privatize the agency—that is, in effect, to eliminate it and sell the remains to the highest bidder.[28]

Ironically, these developments have shifted the momentum of TVA, which was created to help conserve the Tennessee Valley, directly against urgently needed conservation initiatives. Struggling to survive, TVA is concentrating on reducing its debt; but to do so, rather than encouraging conservation, it must generate and sell as much electricity as possible. As a result, in 1995, TVA, in flagrant contradiction to its original mission, began promoting the wasteful use of energy among its customers, who already use more electricity per capita than the national average. In a crass series of television advertisements, costing at least 4.6 million dollars, TVA showed an unattended television running pointlessly while a lone dog watches or a person sleeps, as the voice-over proclaimed the value of cheap TVA electricity. This ad campaign was selected by a Washington-based coalition of consumer, health, and environmental groups to receive the tongue-in-cheek Hubbard Award as one of the "most misleading, unfair, and irresponsible ad campaigns" of 1995.[29]

The message, however, seems to have been lost on TVA. The euphemism for the agency's current policy is "beneficial electrification," which TVA defines as "promoting the use of electricity and electrical technologies in processes that will improve a customer's productivity, quality of life, or economy over existing energy sources or technologies"—that is, to put it plainly, getting people to buy more electrical technology, while avoiding natural gas, so that TVA can sell more electricity.[30]

So, within a mere decade, TVA has plummeted from national leadership in energy conservation to the status of a bureaucracy adrift and visionless, in contradiction to its original mission, and preoccupied with self-preservation.

In line with the recent "downsizing" of government, many are now calling for the privatization of TVA. But this would only deepen the tragedy. In the process, much of TVA's public land would be sold to private developers, who would destroy it as they have already destroyed so much of the Tennessee Valley, and the valuable scientific work that TVA still supports (and which is the basis for much of this *State of the Bioregion* report) would be further curtailed or lost. What is needed is not a dissolution of the agency, but a return to its original vision.

Power Generation

To generate electricity, TVA uses twenty-nine hydroelectric dams, a pumped-storage hydro facility at Raccoon Mountain, eleven coal-fired power plants, forty-eight natural-gas or oil-powered combustion turbines, and five nuclear reactors. Each has specific advantages and disadvantages. TVA uses some as much as possible and others (such as combustion turbines and pumped storage) mainly during peak hours. Table 5.6 shows the contribution of these sources to total electricity generation.

Table 5.6

TVA'S POWER PRODUCTION SYSTEM, FISCAL YEAR 1994[31]				
Generator Type	Capacity (watts)	% of total capacity	Energy produced (kilowatt hours)	% of actual generation
Hydroelectric dams and pumped storage	5,576,000,000	22	20,200,000,000	15.4
Coal	14,743,000,000	57	92,100,000,000	70.4
Combustion Turbines	1,952,000,000	8	200,000,000	0.2
Nuclear	3,282,000,000	13	18,400,000,000	14.0
Total	25,553,000,000	100	130,900,000,000	100.0

By 1996, the capacity for nuclear generation was expected to increase to 5,157,000,000 watts, with the reopening of one reactor at Browns Ferry and the completion of another at Watts Bar. TVA also occasionally buys power from other utilities.

Energy from Running Water

In 1995, TVA was operating a total of 109 conventional hydroelectric generators at twenty-nine different dams with a total capacity of 3,408,000,000 watts, and four pumped-storage generators at Raccoon Mountain with a capacity of 1,532,000,000 watts. Not all the hydroelectric generators are located within our bioregion. Those that are are listed in table 5.7.

Table 5.7

TVA HYDRO FACILITIES WITHIN OUR BIOREGION[32]			
Facility	River	Number of generators	Summer capacity (watts)
Appalachia	Hiwassee	2	76,000,000
Blue Ridge	Ocoee	1	10,000,000
Boone	Holston	3	99,000,000
Chatuge	Hiwassee	1	10,000,000
Cherokee	Holston	4	135,000,000
Chickamauga	Tennessee	4	130,000,000
Douglas	French Broad	4	136,000,000
Fontana	Little Tennessee	3	235,000,000
Fort Loudoun	Tennessee	4	140,000,000
Fort Patrick Henry	Holston	2	36,000,000
Hiwassee	Hiwassee	2	135,000,000
Melton Hill	Clinch	2	75,000,000
Nickajack	Tennessee	4	96,000,000
Nolichucky	Nolichucky	0	0
Norris	Clinch	2	100,000,000
Nottely	Nottely	1	17,000,000
Ocoee	#1 Ocoee	5	22,000,000
Ocoee	#2 Ocoee	2	18,000,000
Ocoee	#3 Ocoee	1	27,000,000
South Holston	Holston	1	40,000,000
Watauga	Watauga	2	60,000,000
Watts Bar	Tennessee	5	179,000,000
Wilbur	Watauga	4	11,000,000
Subtotal		59	1,787,000,000
Raccoon Mountain Pumped-Storage	Tennessee	4	1,532,000,000
Total		63	3,319,000,000

Some of the generators, particularly those on the Ocoee River, are threatened by siltation (see Chapter One). The damage occurs when sediment from upstream settles into the lake and takes the place of the water, reducing the holding capacity of the reservoir, eroding generating equipment, and ultimately clogging water intakes. Siltation forced the closing of the Nolichucky power station in 1972.[33]

Hydroelectric generation is TVA's cleanest and cheapest source of electricity. As a result, it might be expected that the hydroelectric units would be used as much as possible. However, hydroelectric generators are more easily adjusted to variable demand than are nuclear or coal-fired generators. And TVA must also regulate the flow of the rivers to control flooding and maintain high water levels for recreation in the summer, and these activities sometimes prevent the release of water for generating electricity. Furthermore, some of the generators on the smaller tributaries do not have enough water flow to provide constant electricity. For these reasons, hydropower is often used only intermittently.

While the impacts of hydroelectric generation have been small compared to the impacts of other TVA sources, they are not negligible. The most dramatic social effect was the forcible removal of thousands of families from their valleyside homes and farms as the dams were constructed. The largest ecological impacts have been the permanent submersion of large areas of rich agricultural bottomland and sensitive riparian habitat, and the transformation of swift-flowing rivers and streams into large, relatively stagnant reservoirs.

The damming of rivers, as was explained in Chapter One, deprives the deep waters behind the dams and the tailwaters that flow from the bottoms of the dams of oxygen, especially at the deep tributary reservoirs. As a result, most of the dammed tributaries of the Tennessee River are less productive fisheries than they once were, and many species of native fish have declined as more adaptable exotic species have moved in. Damming and siltation have, as was noted in Chapter Three, also decimated the once flourishing mussel beds of the Tennessee Valley.

Another biological effect of the reservoirs is the fragmentation of habitats and populations. The rivers of the Tennessee Valley were nearly all, during dry periods, shallow enough at some places for animals to swim or wade across. But the big, deep reservoirs are for many terrestrial species impassable barriers, preventing dispersal, migration, and genetic exchange. This may hasten the extirpation or extinction of some species.

In addition to the dams, TVA operates a pumped-storage generating facility at Raccoon Mountain on the Tennessee River west of Chattanooga. This installation uses low-cost power generated during periods of low electrical usage to pump water uphill to a reservoir. The water in the reservoir stores potential energy, functioning in effect as a huge battery. During periods of peak demand when additional power is needed, the water in the reservoir is released back down the mountain to a bank of four generators, which convert its momentum back into electricity. The result is a net loss of power but an increase in TVA's peak generating capacity.

To create a pumped-storage facility, trees must be cut down and a mountain top reshaped into areservoir. The reservoir cannot be used for recreation or wildlife habitat because it is constantly being emptied and refilled. Since pumped storage uses more energy than it produces, its environmental impact also includes the effects of whatever generating source (coal, hydro, or nuclear) is used to pump the water up the mountain.

Recently, a private corporation, Armstrong Energy Resources, has proposed building two new pumped-storage facilities above the Sequatchie River in Bledsoe and Sequatchie Counties. If approved, these facilities would inundate over two thousand acres. The project would create two huge transmission-line corridors on the ridges above the river and would expose the acidic Sewanee coal seam on Walden Ridge, which could easily contaminate downslope streams.[34] Such continuing miseries are among the largely unnoticed effects of our voracious appetite for energy.

Energy from Fossil Fuels

Most of TVA's electricity is generated by burning coal. Unfortunately, of all the common methods of power generation under normal operating conditions (that is, barring a catastrophic nuclear accident), burning coal is the most destructive. In the upper Tennessee Valley there are fourteen active coal-fired units at three sites and four idle units at the Watts Bar Reservation. These plants were completed between 1952 and 1967. Table 5.8 lists the coal-fired plants in our bioregion.

Table 5.8

COAL-FIRED GENERATING PLANTS IN THE UPPER TENNESSEE VALLEY[35]				
Plant	Location	Number of Generators	Capacity (watts)	1994 Coal Burn (tons)
Bull Run	Oak Ridge, TN	1	879,000,000	2,119,542
John Sevier	Rogersville, TN	4	704,000,000	2,047,223
Kingston	Kingston, TN	9	1,434,000,000	3,925,284
Total		14	3,017,000,000	8,092,049

Some of their effects on the air and the water were discussed in Chapters One and Two. We merely recount them here: acid rain; haze; carbon monoxide pollution; low-level ozone; thermal pollution of rivers; depletion of atmospheric oxygen; air-borne emissions of radionuclides, mercury, and other toxic metals; global warming.

There are other effects as well. One is the production of ash and slag, which pile up in huge mounds at the coal-fired plants. There are two kinds of ash: fly ash and bottom ash. Fly ash is material precipitated out of the coal smoke before it is released into the atmosphere. Bottom ash is the ash left in the furnaces, along with the slag. The primary components of ash and slag—silica (SiO_2), alumina (Al_2O_3), and iron oxide (Fe_2O_3)—are relatively harmless minerals, though smaller quantities of toxic metals and radioactive materials are also present. The use of scrubbers to absorb the sulfur from exhaust gases also creates many thousands of tons of flue gas desulfurization sludge. Coal-washing residue creates yet another form of waste. Some of these wastes are used to create cement products, asphalt products, roofing granules, road-bed and road-resurfacing materials, grit for snow control, or blasting grit. Some are also used for fill. But much of the waste must be landfilled or stored on the plant site in ash ponds. This landfilled or stored waste may contaminate groundwater.[36]

Since coal contains relatively small, though hardly negligible, amounts of radioactive materials, the burning of huge amounts of coal can also release significant quantities of radionuclides. An Oak Ridge National Laboratory report reckons that a typical coal-fired power plant releases 5.2 tons of radioactive uranium and 12.8 tons of radioactive thorium per year. Nearly all of this is concentrated in the ash. The report concludes that "although trace quantities of radioactive metals are not nearly as likely to produce adverse health effects as the vast array of chemical by-products from coal combustion, the accumulated quantities of these isotopes over 150 or 250 years could pose a significant future ecological burden and potentially produce adverse health effects, especially if they are locally accumulated."[37]

These releases do not exhaust the environmental impacts of coal-generated electricity, for the coal plants themselves are merely the endpoints of yet another series of vast, destructive processes. The coal that fuels them is carried from the mines to the plants by truck or rail. As new mines are opened, new roads or railroad links must be built. These transportation corridors fragment forests, destroy wildlife habitat, and add to the general degradation of the land. The railroad engines and trucks burn diesel fuel, which is supplied by the usual array of energy-consuming and polluting processes (see Chapter Seven).

Tracing backwards along paths by which the coal arrives, we find an expanding lattice of highways and railroads leading back into the coal country of Tennessee, Illinois, or Kentucky or westward to the vast open mines of the Rocky Mountains (see Table 5.9). At the coal tipples, these give way to dusty or muddy mining roads traversed by huge dump trucks with wheels taller than a man.

Table 5.9

TVA COAL PROCUREMENT BY STATE, FISCAL YEAR 1994[38]		
State	**Tons**	**Percent of total**
Colorado	1,196,000	3.2
Illinois	3,907,000	10.3
Kentucky	27,091,000	71.7
Ohio	213,000	0.6
Pennsylvania	567,000	1.5
Tennessee	1,008,000	2.7
Utah	365,000	1.0
Virginia	1,282,000	3.4
West Virginia	2,118,000	5.6
Wyoming	29,000	0.1
Total	37,776,000	100.0

The mining roads open out at last onto scenes of utter desolation. Especially when the coal is taken by strip mining (though also in the various forms of underground mining), the living hills, farms, and forests are reduced to bare earth, caked mud, protruding rock, subsiding land, and flowing silt on a geological scale.

It is not as bad as it once was. The federal Surface Mining Control and Reclamation Act of 1977 outlawed some of the worst mining abuses and required coal companies to restore the land to its original contour before closing a mine. (Here, again, federal regulation has ameliorated catastrophic damage with some success—contrary to the fashionable myth that governmental restraint of industry is counterproductive.) But the new law did nothing to restore the older mining areas, particularly in West Virginia, eastern Kentucky, and parts of East Tennessee, where operators simply pushed the overburden downslope from mountain mines, causing landslides, acid drainage, massive erosion, sedimentation, and flooding. There, the mining companies pillaged, profited, and proceeded on, leaving behind thousands of square miles of tortured moonscape—land that will never be reclaimed and may take centuries to heal.[39] But the law at least ensured that future strip-mining would be monitored more carefully and that destroyers of the land could be penalized.

Yet strip-mining is inherently destructive, even if the law is followed to the letter, and even the best reclamation does not wholly heal the wound. A strip mine begins with a clearcut, with all the attendant environmental effects described in Chapter Three— more than a clearcut, in fact, since all the vegetation is bulldozed down to the bare earth. Then the topsoil is scraped away and (if the mine is well-operated) stored or used separately. This exposes the overburden (subsoil and rocks overlying the coal seam), which is drilled and blasted. The pulverized overburden is removed to expose the coal, which then is fractured by blasting and hauled away. After the coal is gone, dump trucks and bulldozers replace the overburden, then the topsoil. (The original overburden and topsoil are usually used elsewhere, so that the replacing overburden and topsoil come from a newly mined area.) Since the blasting decompacts the overburden, its volume increases, so that the excess must usually be deposited in a fill somewhere else. Finally the topsoil is sowed and replanted.[40]

This process greatly increases erosion and siltation, even under the best of conditions. Watercourses and aquifers are disturbed or destroyed, and water both on the surface and beneath the ground may be contaminated with acid drainage from sulfur-bearing rocks, or with toxic metals or minerals. Aquatic life may disappear as springs and streams turn red with iron oxide or yellow with iron hydroxide ("yellow boy"). Nearby wells may become cloudy, dry up, or be poisoned. Residents are sometimes forced to choose between leaving their homes and living with water they can't use—water that looks like apple cider, kills house plants, and burns eyes, nose, and mouth when they take a shower.[41] Coal-hauling trucks create potholes and other road hazards. The blasting and moving of earth may buckle or crack the foundations of buildings. The noise produces stress for both miners and residents and can lead to loss of hearing. Sometimes the blasting is deadly—and not only to miners. In 1994, a sixteen-year-old boy was killed when rocks and debris from a blast at the Flatwoods Mine in Campbell County hit the car in which he was riding with his family on Interstate 75.

The mines are also haunted by disease. The classic miners' disease is black lung, but miners also have higher-than-average incidences of lung and stomach cancer. This is predictable, since coal dust contains at least thirteen carcinogens. Disease may affect nonminers as well. People living near the mines sometimes show symptoms of black lung, apparently from the fugitive dust of mines and tipples.[42]

When a mine opens, the land and the people suffer stress, damage, and disease for many years; but, in the end, the mine falls silent, and the land, at least, begins to heal. A few years after replanting, a reclaimed strip mine may look healthy and green, but the land is never the same. The new topsoil may be mixed with less fertile subsoil, decreasing fertility. The activity of beneficial insects and microorganisms, which were killed during the mining, may not be entirely restored.[43] Acid drainage is likely to continue. A 1992 survey of twelve reclaimed sites in the Sewanee coal seam of southeastern Tennessee found indications of continued acid mine drainage at ten of them.[44]

Revegetation of reclaimed strip mines usually involves some tree planting, but to obtain a quick, complete cover, many operators use a seeding mixture dominated by Kentucky-31 fescue, a tall grass. The fescue shades the tree seedlings and competes with them for moisture. After a few years, it forms a thick sod cover that discourages both forest growth and the return of wildlife such as quail and wild turkeys. Moreover, the soil compaction that occurs as the topsoil is hauled in and bulldozed into place can stunt tree growth by more than thirty years.[45] As with clearcuts, if the land is allowed to revert to forest, the understory vegetation probably takes well over a century to recover—if it ever does.[46]

These damages occur at the best of mines, under conditions of compliance with the law. Unfortunately, some coal companies have enough money and political influence to stave off law enforcement, while others move in quickly, violate the law, and then vanish into a cloud of legal shenanigans. From the time of its passage in 1977 until 1984, the Surface Mining Control and Reclamation Act was supposed to have been enforced in Tennessee by the state Division of Surface Mining. The enforcement, however, was so lax that in 1984 the federal Office of Surface Mining Reclamation and Enforcement stepped in and took over the administration of the state's permitting program.

Enforcement, however, has remained inadequate. A study by SOCM (Save Our Cumberland Mountains) of fifty-two sites that were in violation of the law during the years 1988-1991 found that as of 1992 only seventeen had been reclaimed. The reclaimed sites had remained unreclaimed for an average of four years with outstanding violations. The unreclaimed sites had so far remained unreclaimed for an average of three and a half years. During this time, it is likely that substantial and preventable environmental degradation was occurring at most or all of these mines.[47]

Underground mining is less damaging than strip-mining, since it disturbs less surface area, though the harm from mining roads and initial cuts may still be considerable. Moreover, like surface mining, underground mining can disrupt aquifers.
Old underground mines may fill with water, which builds up pressure and may eventually create a "blow-out," sending toxic or acidified water into aquifers or streams.
Underground mines may collapse unpredictably decades after their abandonment,
disturbing water flow, opening sinkholes, or damaging buildings on the surface.

More sinister problems sometimes occur in the transfer of the coal to TVA power
plants. Much of the coal of Southern Appalachia is so high in sulfur that it creates
unacceptably high levels of sulfur dioxide (which contributes to acid rain and
smog) when burned. To meet federal regulations, TVA must burn relatively low-sul-
fur coal. In 1996, investigators from the Tennessee Valley Energy Reform Coalition
and the Foundation for Global Sustainability video-taped a large and politically well-
connected coal operator loading trucks bound for TVA power plants with high sulfur coal and then placing a layer of low sulfur coal on top to conceal the substan-
dard shipment. The effects of this criminal practice, known as "layer-loading," on
regional air quality are at present unknown.

Coal is not the only fossil fuel used to produce electricity in the Tennessee Valley.
TVA also operates forty-eight combustion turbine generators. Twenty-eight of
these can burn either natural gas or fuel oil. The other twenty burn oil only. Due
to their relatively high fuel costs, these generators are used only during peak
demand. They are located at four of TVA's coal fired plants, none in our bioregion.

Fossil fuels are also used to generate energy in a variety of other ways. The
University of Tennessee, for example, consumes trainloads of coal at its Physical
Plant on Neyland Drive. (This plant, incidentally, has been seen on occasion to emit
heavy clouds of thick, black smoke.) Many businesses, industries use boilers or furnaces that burn coal, oil, or natural gas. Some use high-sulfur coal. Natural gas,
propane, and coal are also used to heat homes. Diesel, gasoline, and propane-pow-
ered generators are legion. These all, to various degrees, add to air pollution,
ground-level ozone, haze, oxygen depletion, and global warming.

There is, moreover, some question about whether we really gain anything in burning fossil fuels—coal, in particular—for energy. Extracting and transporting the
coal, reclaiming the strip-mined land, and maintaining the infrastructure by which
all this is accomplished are themselves energy-consuming processes. Could it be
that more energy is used to obtain the fuel than is generated by its burning? This

question becomes more vexing the more deeply we trace the less obvious, but real, energy expenditures entailed by coal production: the energy required to provide medical care for disabled coal miners, for example. An energy analysis of the coal fuel cycle in Anderson County, Tennessee, performed at Oak Ridge National Laboratory in the early 1980s attempted to account for all these expenditures. It concludes: "Unless new data to the contrary are made available, it appears that the coal fuel cycle in Anderson County presently consumes more energy than it produces." The study also predicts that this problem will worsen in the future, since the remaining coal is less accessible, so that still more energy will be required to mine and transport it.[48]

Studies coming out of Oak Ridge have often displayed an ideological tendency to criticize any form of energy production that competes with nuclear power and so must be read with caution. Energy analysis is a tricky business, and much depends on how you cut the pie. Yet it is clear that to generate energy from coal we must also consume vast quantities of energy. And, whether the final energy balance is positive or negative, when we consider the totality of effects on the health of people, the air, the water, and the land, and the frivolous and wasteful purposes for which much of the energy is used, the morality of generating electricity by burning coal is profoundly questionable.

Energy from Nuclear Fission

The final source of TVA electricity—and the agency's financial bane—is atomic energy. TVA currently operates five nuclear reactors at three sites on the Tennessee River. Two of the sites are in our bioregion: Sequoyah, on Chickamauga Reservoir above Chattanooga, and Watts Bar, near the Watts Bar Dam. Sequoyah has two working reactors with a net capacity of 2,217,000,000 watts. Watts Bar has one with capacity of 1,170,000,000 watts.[49] The remaining two reactors are at Browns Ferry near Decatur in northern Alabama. Though TVA began work on seventeen reactors, all the others have been mothballed or abandoned.

Since the normal daily operations of a nuclear power plant are relatively inexpensive and since nuclear reactors cannot readily be switched off and on, TVA runs the nuclear power plants, like the big coal plants, as much as possible.

All nuclear power plants routinely release small amounts of radioactive material into the air and water. The evidence is inconclusive as to whether these routine releases can harm people living nearby; some studies show no effect, while others find elevated rates of cancer or leukemia. (It is worth noting, however, that until very recently nearly all significant research on the health effects of radiation was funded by institutions ideologically committed to the proliferation of nuclear energy.)

The greatest concern with nuclear plants, however, is the possibility of a major release of radionuclides. The worst example of this sort was the explosion and meltdown that occurred at Chernobyl in 1986. Hundreds, perhaps thousands, of people have already died from this accident, and it is likely that many thousands more will die from radiation-induced cancers. Over three hundred thousand people had to be relocated. About 3,900 square miles of land were heavily contaminated, and much of Europe received dangerous levels of fallout.[50] Though American reactors are better designed than the Chernobyl reactor, they are not foolproof. TVA has had one near-meltdown (at Browns Ferry in 1975), and an American-built reactor at Three-Mile Island in Pennsylvania underwent a partial core melt in 1979, exposing thousands of people to dangerous radiation. These incidents indicate that the risk of a serious accident in the Tennessee Valley is not negligible. The possibility of terrorist attack compounds the peril. Efforts have been made to quantify these risks, but these depend heavily on guesswork. Single accidents and terrorist attacks are by nature unpredictable, and, with a nuclear reactor, one such event is all it takes.

The damage to Southern Appalachia from a large radiation release at Watts Bar or Sequoyah could be enormous. Signs along the roads near both plants mark the evacuation routes, grim reminders of the scramble that must ensue if the sirens sound. If an air release occurred at Sequoyah when the wind was blowing down the valley from the northeast, the cloud of radiation would move directly into Chattanooga twenty miles away. A southwest wind blowing up the valley could drop radiation from a release from Watts Bar onto Knoxville and Oak Ridge sixty miles downwind. If the wind were blowing from the west, a major release from either plant could fall out largely in the Great Smoky Mountains National Park and the surrounding national forests. The extent of the damage would depend on many factors besides the wind—most crucially on the amount of radiation released. In the worst case, thousands of lives, billions of dollars, and the health of much of the land of Southern Appalachia could be lost.

FIGURE 8: The twin cooling towers of TVA's Sequoyah nuclear plant dominate the landscape north of Chattanooga. Here they are seen from a distance of about nine miles.

TVA's nuclear power plants use partially enriched uranium for fuel. Together all five reactors consume about 1,250 tons of uranium per year.[51] The mining of uranium, like the mining of coal, harms both people and land. In the 1970s, the nuclear industry's greed for uranium, like the forty-niner's greed for gold in the gold rush of the previous century, prompted thefts of Native American land. Efforts by TVA, former Oak Ridge DOE Contractor Union Carbide, and other large corporations to secure uranium rights on or near tribal lands in South Dakota were strands in a complex pattern of intrigue, oppression, and violence that led to the bloody siege at Wounded Knee in 1973 and the shoot-out at the Pine Ridge Reservation in 1975. The details of this sad, tangled, and little-known story are recounted in the book *In the Spirit of Crazy Horse* by Peter Matthiessen. One of the FBI agents in charge of the suppression of Native American resistance to these land grabs was Norman Zagrossi, who is now Chief Administrative Officer at TVA.[52]

Today, the uranium that fuels TVA's reactors comes from Canada, Australia, South Africa, Niger, Russia, Namibia, Uzbekistan, Tajikistan, and Kazakhstan, as well as the United States. The uranium is mined in open pit, deep pit, or leaching operations. The mining and milling processes produce heaps of radioactive tailings and release carcinogenic radon, which is a danger primarily to the miners. The commercial-grade uranium that is used in the United States is transported to one of two conversion plants in Illinois and Ontario for processing, then transported again for enrichment to one of two federal facilities at Paducah, Kentucky or Portsmouth, Ohio. Commercial uranium may in the future also be derived from nuclear warheads decommissioned as a result of post cold-war treaties.[53]

TVA claims that the reuse of weapons material in civilian reactors is "in the true sense of swords to plowshares."[54] Given the state of Southern Appalachian agriculture (see Chapter Four), the reference to plowshares is disingenuous; microwave ovens, air conditioners, and advertising signs would be nearer the truth. Moreover, the agency is just as eager to turn "plowshares" back into swords. TVA's Watts Bar reactor was recently selected by the Department of Energy for an eighteen-month test project to produce tritium, a radioactive form of hydrogen that will be used to boost the megatonnage of thermonuclear weapons. If successful, this test may lead to a more permanent tritium production program at Watts Bar.[55] This would be the first use of civilian reactors for nuclear weapons production, a move that is likely to weaken the American argument for nuclear nonproliferation. The operation would also entail the transportation of more nuclear weapons materials on the region's railroads and highways.

In another shift that likewise blurs the line between civilian and military uses of nuclear power, TVA is also negotiating with the Department of Energy for disposal of weapons-grade plutonium at its mothballed Bellefonte nuclear power plant in northeastern Alabama.

Nuclear energy is touted by its proponents as "clean," yet it inevitably creates large volumes of radioactive waste. Radioactive waste is classified as either low-level or high-level. Low-level waste consists of such objects as filters, cloth wipes, paper wipes, plastic shoe covers, tools, water purification devices, and various residues—all contaminated with varying quantities of radioactivity. Much of the radiation decays away within a decade after disposal, though some persists for much longer. TVA's low level waste is sent to a land burial facility in Barnwell, South Carolina. That facility was supposed to have been closed at the end of 1995, but plans now call for it to remain open for several years, while a new burial ground in Wake County, North Carolina, is readied to replace it.[56]

High-level waste, which currently consists mostly of spent fuel rods, is another matter. TVA's five reactors produce about 115 metric tons of used fuel per year. A large additional volume of high-level waste (as well as low-level waste) is likely to be created within several decades when the plants wear out and are dismantled. High-level waste, when first removed from the reactor, is extraordinarily "hot" and must be handled with utmost caution. Most of the radioactivity subsides within several months, but the waste remains deadly to humans for tens of thousands of years—longer than civilization has existed on Earth.

There is no practical way to make the waste non-radioactive. Other means of eliminating the waste, such as shooting it into space or injecting it deep into the earth, are too expensive or too dangerous. Storage is, for the present at least, the only acceptable option. Storage facilities must be safe from earthquake, climate change, rising water tables, and so on, and must also be constantly guarded against terrorists, since the waste could be used to make nuclear weapons. Whether this can be done successfully over a period of tens of thousands of years is doubtful.

There is no permanent disposal facility for high-level nuclear waste anywhere in the world. The only place in the United States currently being considered for such a facility is Yucca Mountain, which is located on Shoshone tribal lands in Nevada. But Yucca Mountain is surrounded by geological faults and volcanoes, one of which erupted as recently as five thousand years ago. Since 1857, there have been eight major earthquakes within 250 miles of the site. It remains unclear when, if ever, the Yucca Mountain depository will open.[57]

In the meantime, TVA is storing all its high-level waste on site. As of 1995, 760 metric tons of spent fuel were being stored at the Brown's Ferry nuclear plant and 417 metric tons at Sequoyah. If Yucca Mountain ever opens, this waste will be sent by truck or rail to Nevada for burial.

Eventually, nuclear plants wear out. Over time, the high temperature and extreme radiation inside a reactor cause metal parts to weaken and become brittle. If operation continues beyond this point, the reactor becomes increasingly dangerous. Many researchers think that the appropriate life span for a nuclear reactor is thirty to forty years. The two Browns Ferry reactors (TVA's oldest) came on line in 1975 and 1977. Their operating licenses expire in 2014 and 2016, though TVA expects these licenses to be extended.[58] In any event, these reactors will have to be closed and decommissioned within a few decades. Nobody knows exactly how expensive it will be to dismantle them and dispose of the resulting waste. TVA says it will cost between two and six hundred million dollars per reactor,[59] but TVA cost estimates in matters nuclear have a history of optimism. Independent estimates run as high as 5.86 billion dollars for the Watts Bar reactor alone.[60] The money TVA has set aside for decommissioning all five reactors was projected to amount to 373 million dollars by the end of fiscal year 1996.[61] Given TVA's deep debt, there is likely to be pressure to scrimp on this fund. Who, then, will pay for decommissioning?

Sustainable Energy Sources

All the ways in which TVA generates electricity are harmful on a grand scale. None offers much hope for the future. Though hydropower generation could be increased by modernizing existing hydropower projects[62], there is little room for new dams, except perhaps for some small generators on tributary streams, even given a (foolish) willingness to flood more land. Over the long term, the reservoirs will silt up and become less useful for power generation.

Fossil fuels offer still less hope. For one thing, fossil fuel reserves are nonrenewable and finite. We have already used up much, if not most, of this nation's once vast oil supply. Considering all the world's known reserves and estimating the unknown reserves, at current rates of consumption, all the world's oil will be gone by the middle of the next century. Natural gas may last another 120 years at current rates, much less if we begin to rely heavily on it. Coal is more abundant; it may last 1,500 years—if consumption rates are steady (a big "if").[63]

But the consequence of burning all the world's remaining fossil fuels would be massive pollution, immense mining operations, and (perhaps most dangerously) unavoidable carbon emissions leading to climate change so rapid and extreme that it would threaten the stability, not only of planetary ecosystems, but of human civilization. This is simply not an option.

Nuclear energy has so far proved unexpectedly expensive and less than reassuringly safe. Yet on the whole, even considering Chernobyl, nuclear power plants have probably done less harm than coal plants. Still, any technology that passes radioactive trash on to generations ten thousand years into the future is morally bankrupt. If we do not know how to clean up our mess, but only how to shovel it under the rug (or under Yucca Mountain, as the case may be), we have no business making it in the first place.

One of our most urgent needs, therefore, is to develop new sources of energy that are safe, reliable, and sustainable. Biological fuels, wind power, and solar energy are all practical means of generating electricity, and each can be used sustainably.

Among biological fuels, the most practical for large-scale power production consist of various forms of biomass. Three general types are readily available: (1) waste or residue consisting of wood or the byproducts of agriculture and food processing, (2) energy crops, and (3) whole logs.

Wood residue from pulp operations is already being used by the regional paper industry to generate thermal energy. In addition, TVA has successfully experimented with burning a mix of wood waste and coal at its coal plants. This practice, called "co-firing," decreases coal consumption, reduces emissions of sulfur and toxic metals, and may divert some wood waste from landfills. But the source of the "waste" is important. If it includes material that would otherwise be left on forest sites to reduce erosion or provide wildlife habitat or organic matter for the soil, energy is generated at the expense of the forests. Materials which are now landfilled, such as used wooden pallets, might be good biomass fuels.[64] There is the additional advantage that the ash from the burning of such materials is an excellent organic fertilizer, which can be returned to the land to enrich the soil.

A second source of biomass energy is energy crops: typically, fast-growing trees and grasses, particularly switch grass. Since these energy crops actively remove carbon from the air while growing, the net carbon emission from such a fuel process is practically nil; nearly as much carbon is absorbed by the growing plants as is released in combustion. Thus energy crops add very little to global warming. (There is, however, an increase in carbon emissions relative to other possible uses of the land; for example, if the land were left as undisturbed forest, the trees would continuously remove carbon from the atmosphere, rather than removing and re-releasing it, as energy crops do. Some carbon is also released in harvesting the crops and transporting them to the power plant—especially if these operations are powered by fossil fuels.)

Other environmental effects of energy crops depend on where and how the crops are grown. Transportation impacts (and costs) are high if the crops are not grown close to the power plant. If industrial fertilizers, pesticides, and herbicides are used, air, water, and soil suffer pollution. Heavy machinery may compact soils and enhance erosion. Moreover, though the burning of biomass fuels releases very little sulfur or toxic metals, it does, like coal combustion, produce NO_x and volatile organic compounds and therefore contributes to smog. Finally, given the precipitous loss of regional farmland (see Chapter Four), there is a painful trade-off between using the remaining farmland for energy crops and using it to enhance the local food supply.

The worst biomass fuel is whole logs. Southern Appalachian forests are already under intense pressure from pulp and paper and lumbering operations and from a host of other insults (Chapter Three). Any increase in the cutting of existing Southern Appalachian forests is therefore unacceptable. This is especially true for cutting for biomass; because biomass operations can use whole trees—wood, limbs, roots, leaves, and all—they are potentially even more destructive to forests than chip mills, which use only logs.

On a smaller scale, biomass energy can be obtained by the collection of the methane gas that is released from landfills, sewage plants, and composting manures. Methane is an excellent substitute for natural gas. It burns cleanly, releasing only water and carbon dioxide. And, since methane is a very powerful greenhouse gas (up to thirty times more effective at trapping heat than carbon dioxide[65]), collecting and burning it, rather than releasing it into the atmosphere, is a big help in mitigating global warming. What is otherwise an obnoxious waste is thus converted into a relatively clean and beneficial source of energy.[66] This is entirely feasible; methane collected from rotting garbage at the Chestnut Ridge Landfill in Anderson County is already being used to run four electrical generators, whose output is sold to the Knoxville Utilities Board.

Wind energy is another reliable and cost-effective energy source. Though windmills are noisy and may be hazardous to birds, their overall environmental impact is much smaller than that of biomass, hydroelectric, coal, or nuclear power generation. They have, however, the additional disadvantage of operating only when the wind is blowing. Therefore, their primary use is to supplement existing power systems (though for home or farm use, a small windmill plus batteries may be adequate). On a larger scale, a recent study by Kenetech Wind Power, Inc., has identified a wind power generating capacity of between seven hundred million and two billion watts in or near TVA's service territory. (For comparison, TVA's entire generating capacity in 1995 was slightly under twenty-six billion watts.) This capacity may increase somewhat over the years if global warming increases the average wind velocity. TVA, however, currently has no plans to utilize this capacity.

The ultimate source of biomass, fossil fuel, hydropower, and wind energy is the sun. Fossil and biomass fuels store in a chemical form energy that originated as sunlight captured by plants. The sun's heat drives the rain cycle that fills the rivers that generate hydropower. And it is the sun's heat, again, that stirs the atmosphere and moves the wind. Why not, then, use the sun to generate power directly?

Photovoltaic cells do just that. Recent advances in photovoltaics have made them economically competitive with conventional power sources for remote rural applications. Increasing use will bring the price down still further. Current commercial photovoltaic panels can generate 120 watts per square meter in the noonday sun. They are less effective, but still operable on cloudy days and when the sun is low, and they provide almost no power at night. Photovoltaic panels must therefore be combined either with power storage devices, such as batteries, or some other form of power generation to provide a continuous supply of electricity.

Unlike most other power sources, photovoltaic panels are poorly suited for large, centralized power plants. A plant equalling the hundred-million-watt output of Norris Dam, for example, would require a square mile of panels.[67] But one of the beauties of solar panels is that they need not be centralized into immense power plants to operate efficiently. Indeed, they work best if not thus centralized. The roofs of buildings already provide a vast, though scattered, area, much of which is well-suited for solar collection. Utilizing this roof area, each household can generate much or (if energy is carefully conserved) all of its own electricity.

Regional demand for electricity is highest on hot, sunny summer days—precisely the times at which photovoltaic panels reach maximum output. Solar panels used to supplement centrally generated electricity would therefore alleviate pressure to build destructive peak generating facilities, such as the two new pumped-storage plants proposed for the Sequatchie Valley. Moreover, in hybrid systems that integrate photovoltaic panels with conventional powerlines from a central utility, there is no need for storage batteries, since when the solar panels are not generating, the system automatically reverts to the conventional power source. During periods when the solar panels are generating more power than is being consumed, the excess can be fed back into the commercial grid. Federal regulations require utilities to buy back power generated in this way, effectively running the electric meter in reverse and subtracting dollars from electric bills.

Photovoltaic systems work even when there is a general power failure. In the blizzard of 1993, power was out for nearly a week in Hogskin Valley in Grainger County. The only electric lights in the valley in all that time were at Narrow Ridge Earth Literacy Center, which generates its electricity from solar energy.

Solar power has become increasingly cost-effective, and will continue to do so as rates for conventionally generated power rise. TVA has been holding its power rates artificially low for the last decade, but its accumulated debt is likely soon to force a steep rise, while advances in solar technology continue to lower the price of solar electricity. This will make solar generation increasingly feasible.

The main obstacle to increased use of solar energy is the initial cost of installing a home system, which can run into the thousands or tens of thousands of dollars. If low-interest loans were available for buying such systems, increasing usage would bring down the price still further and make them yet more widely affordable. In the 1980s, TVA actively encouraged conversion to solar energy. Advances in technology make that conversion even more feasible now. But little help is to be expected from an agency whose primary aim is to sell, not conserve, electricity.

Changes, however, are in the wind. The likely deregulation of the utility industry may soon allow customers to select the utility from which they buy electricity. If that happens, it is likely that the utilities will, like the phone companies, try to increase their market share by offering customers special options. One widely discussed option is "green pricing," a plan which allows customers to pay a premium in order to receive energy generated from environmentally benign sources, such as the wind and sun. This may give conscientious users of electricity another tool for change, and utilities which do not offer "green pricing" may eventually find themselves loosing "green" customers.

Energy Conservation

In the first section of this chapter, we surveyed some of the purposes for which energy is used and found many of them wasteful, frivolous, or unnecessary. In the succeeding sections, we traced that energy back to its sources and surveyed the damage that is done and the risks undertaken to produce and deliver it. We saw that the damage is immense and the risks considerable. It follows that we can and should reduce energy consumption.

That is a moral imperative. But there are economic imperatives as well. Demand for electricity is increasing. But new generating facilities are expensive and financially risky, as TVA's nuclear power program clearly illustrates. Many utilities have therefore found it less risky and yet still profitable to increase the overall efficiency of the entire power system by simultaneously raising rates and offering conservation programs aimed at decreasing demand. These conservation programs provide ways for customers to become more efficient energy users, which would, of course, decrease the utility's profits if the rates were not raised. The purpose of raising the rates, then, is to ensure that the utility can still make money. But because customers use less electricity, their bills remain about the same, despite the rate increase. Thus the utility retains its profits and customers on average pay no more, but the whole power system becomes more efficient, less electricity is generated and used, and less damage is done to the environment. This win-win strategy is called "demand-side management."

Demand-side management programs may provide discounts on or even giveaways of compact fluorescent light bulbs, offer low-interest loans for weatherization, install solar energy systems or solar water heaters, promote passive solar architecture, provide incentives for industries to replace old electric motors with newer, more efficient ones, and so on. TVA pioneered some of these strategies in the eighties, but abandoned most of them in the nineties, though many utilities are still using them with considerable success.

The reason TVA has scaled back demand-side management is apparently the agency's concern that if it raises rates, as the electricity market is deregulated, it will lose customers to more competitive (and less debt-burdened) utilities. This concern is valid, and little can be done on a regional level to address it. TVA can return to its mission of conservation only if the federal government develops a strong, far-sighted energy policy. That may take years.

In the meantime, the Tennessee Valley must endure a vacuum of conservation leadership. The responsibility for using energy sanely and wisely thus falls by default to individuals. There are three things we can do: (1) support and vote for public officials who understand the energy dilemma and are willing to take strong steps to move TVA back toward conservation, (2) complain to businesses that misuse electricity, especially for ostentatious lighting displays, and refuse to patronize those that continue to do so, and (3) reduce home energy use.

One of the simplest and most effective ways to reduce energy use at home is to obtain a solar clothes dryer—otherwise known as a clothes line. A conventional clothes dryer, particularly one that uses electrical resistance heating, is one of the most wasteful home appliances, and its solar replacement costs a few dollars at most. The solar clothes dryer pays for itself within a month or two in reduced electricity bills, and thereafter saves both money and energy.

Slightly more expensive initially, but equally cost-saving in the long run, is the replacement of incandescent lights with compact fluorescents. Compact fluorescents last longer than incandescents, and they provide the same amount of light for less than a third of the electricity. Of course, forming the habit of turning off all lights (and televisions) that are not being used is an easy way to conserve that requires no investment and begins to save both energy and money immediately.

The largest home savings can be realized in water heating, but these may require a larger investment. The simplest step is to wrap the water heater and hot water pipes with additional insulation. Replacing electrical resistance heaters with electrical heat pumps or gas heaters saves more energy, installing a timer that turns the heater off when hot water is not needed saves still more, and an on-demand heater more yet. Supplementing any of these with a passive solar pre-heater reduces energy consumption dramatically.

Using fans instead of air conditioning for cooling not only saves energy but reduces indoor air pollution. Other effective cooling measures include installing a white roof, planting shade trees near the house, and using awnings or other forms of window shading.

These are some of the easiest and most effective ways to reduce home energy use. There are hundreds of others. Most homes could probably cut their electric bills in half with no serious loss in quality of life and palpable improvements to the health of the air and land.

FIGURE 9: Warning sign at the fence surrounding White Oak Embayment on the Department of Energy's Oak Ridge Reservation. The sediments are contaminated with radioactive waste.

*And I brought you into a plentiful country, to eat the fruit thereof and the
goodness thereof; but when ye entered, ye defiled my land, and made
mine heritage an abomination.*

— Jeremiah 2:7

Litter

Along the berm of any highway, in the dust of any urban alley, in gutters and parking lots, in fields, along stream banks and river banks and the shores of reservoirs,
on the most remote trails of the Great Smoky Mountains—anywhere, in fact, where
people do not regularly clean up the land—lies the debris of a throw-away culture.
Bottles, cans, soft drink cups, wrappers of endless composition and variety, bags
(both paper and plastic), small plastic articles, bits of metal, broken glass, chewing
gum, food remnants, old tires, cigarette butts innumerable—these are now as
prominent or more prominent in the landscape than flowers, mushrooms, or rocks.
If future archaeologists excavate our soil, they will be easily able to identify the layers that begin about the middle of the twentieth century by their large component
of nondegradable trash.

A mile of an average highway contains about sixteen thousand pieces of litter—
mostly cigarette butts. These are surprisingly durable. It takes about fifteen years
for a cigarette butt to decompose. Styrofoam cups last ten to twenty years, plastic
milk jugs fifty to sixty years, aluminum cans several centuries. Glass, though it may
be broken into smaller pieces, leaves sharp shards that last practically forever.[1]

Besides the individual pieces of litter, the entire bioregion is plagued by illegal
dumps. Much of this surreptitious dumping is the work of individuals or small businesses seeking a way to discard construction debris, landscape waste, tires, and
gasoline tanks—and leave the cleanup bill for the rest of us.

If natural environments lift the spirit, trashed environments depress it. The effect
may not be measurable, but it can hardly be doubted. Litter, however, is only the
surface of the problem.

Landfills

In sheer volume, modern solid-waste landfills are among the largest structures ever
created by human beings. The Chestnut Ridge Landfill, for example, located in
Anderson County near the intersection of Interstate 75 and Raccoon Valley Road,

has grown to the size of many of the surrounding mountains. Its eastern flanks—treeless, despite its name (chestnut trees having long ago died off anyway)—now loom over the interstate, seeded with close-mown grass, studded with groundwater-monitoring wells, and frequently crowned by a circlet of wheeling buzzards.

But the height to which garbage can be piled is limited. As of the end of 1996, the Chestnut Ridge Landfill had about a nine-year life expectancy, although its operator, Waste Management, Inc., hoped to receive permission from the state to expand the landfill and hence extend its period of operation. In 1994, there were seventeen per-mitted landfills within a seventeen-county region centered on Knox County. At that time their average life expectancy was twelve years. This figure, however, includes a thirty-five year expectancy for the Shoat Lick Hollow landfill near Oliver Springs in Anderson County, which, though permitted, has not yet opened and is bitterly opposed by nearby residents.[2]

EPA Subtitle D regulations, which require municipal solid waste landfills (those that accept "ordinary" trash) to install plastic liners, leachate-collection systems, groundwater-monitoring wells, and other precautionary measures, while crucial in protecting groundwater, have made small landfills increasingly unprofitable, forcing many to close. As a result, many of the landfills that remain are "mega-fills" designed to accept enormous amounts of garbage.

Because landfills are so big, because unused land has become increasingly scarce, because many places are geologically unsuitable for landfills, and (not least) because people will fight to keep landfills out of their neighborhoods, it is more and more difficult to find new landfill space. Yet, so far at least, it has been found. We are not in danger of running out of places to put our garbage any time soon. New landfills, however, are often less conveniently located than the older ones, forcing garbage trucks to travel longer distances to the dumping-ground. The increased transportation distance entails an array of negative environmental consequences (see Chapter Seven).

Increased transportation also increases costs, both for the transportation itself and in the form of "host fees" which some communities that have landfills charge other communities to dump there. Anderson County, for example, charges host fees to Knox County for depositing its trash at Chestnut Ridge.

Recently, to Knox County's relief, a new landfill has been opened in Union County by the TransAmerica corporation. This landfill, which has been accepting some of

Knox County's wastes, is not yet operating under federal Subtitle D regulations, having received a variance that expires in May, 1998. Like most landfills, it has been opposed by neighbors worried about groundwater contamination. Its life expectancy is not yet known. Ironically, this landfill offers a spectacular view of the Southern Appalachian Mountains, though it seems unlikely that many will take advantage of the scenic opportunity.

Attempts to site new landfills or expand existing ones often have significant social effects. Neighbors usually oppose them, and sometimes violence ensues. When Chambers Development Corporation announced plans to build the Shoat Lick Hollow landfill in the early nineties, residents quickly organized and took their concerns to the Anderson County Commission. After one commission meeting, an elderly man who had opposed the landfill was beaten by thugs, some wearing Chambers tee-shirts.[3]

Opposition to landfills may exemplify the NIMBY ("not in my back yard") syndrome, but it is not irrational. Besides the obvious noise, odor, and aesthetic problems, landfills bring with them a high volume of dangerous truck traffic (and garbage trucks are not the most pleasant of trucks). Moreover, though Subtitle D regulations may help reduce the hazards, many landfills still leak, contaminating groundwater with whatever toxic stuff oozes out of the garbage. Such contamination threatens the health of nearby residents who get their water from wells, and who may not want to move.

At Roane County's landfill, for example, which is located in the Midtown area, rain has carried trash from the landfill into the Tennessee River, and leachate has contaminated residential water wells. Monitoring wells have revealed mercury contamination of the groundwater. A proposed sixty-nine acre expansion to handle waste from, among other places, Knox County (which has no municipal waste landfill of its own) met with staunch local opposition, which has apparently halted the project.[4]

Municipal Solid Waste

Though nobody wants a landfill next-door, we continue to generate more garbage, so that more people will have to live near landfills. To understand the problem, it is important to know something about the composition of the waste stream.

Table 6.1 lists the EPA's estimate of the typical composition of municipal solid waste:

Table 6.1

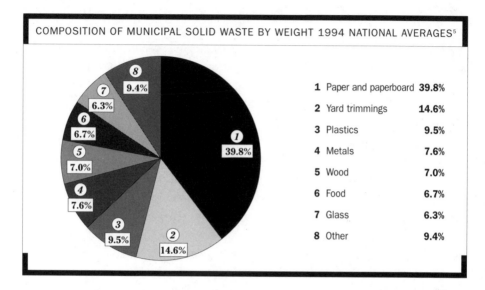

COMPOSITION OF MUNICIPAL SOLID WASTE BY WEIGHT 1994 NATIONAL AVERAGES[5]

1 Paper and paperboard	**39.8%**
2 Yard trimmings	**14.6%**
3 Plastics	**9.5%**
4 Metals	**7.6%**
5 Wood	**7.0%**
6 Food	**6.7%**
7 Glass	**6.3%**
8 Other	**9.4%**

Between thirty and thirty-seven percent of this waste is from homes. The rest is from commercial, institutional, and industrial sources.[6] In Knox County, which has a fairly progressive recycling program compared to much of the rest of the region, only about fifteen percent of this material is being recycled or composted,[7] as compared to about twenty-four percent nationwide.[8]

In the late 1980s municipal solid waste became a hot political issue. Concerns about air pollution and disappearing landfill space led the Tennessee legislature to enact the Solid Waste Management Act of 1991, which mandated a twenty-five percent per capita reduction by 1995 in the amount of waste that is burned or buried.[9] But this goal was not met, and in some areas the amount of waste burned or landfilled increased instead. In Knox County, for example, per capita waste generation was 1.160 tons in 1991. By 1995 it had risen to 1.233 tons—an increase of over six percent. Since population also grew in the interim, this amounted to an even larger increase in the amount of waste sent to landfills, which rose thirteen percent, from 394,445 tons in 1991 to 445,481 tons in 1995.[10]

The increase exceeded most expectations. In 1989, for example, the Knox Metro Solid Waste Authority projected that, though waste production would rise continuously, even by 2000 the county would be landfilling only 419,135 tons annually.[11] Much of the additional garbage was from businesses, which have little incentive to recycle or reduce waste, primarily because disposal is so cheap.

Statewide, Tennesseeans produced about 6.5 million tons of waste in 1991, 7.3 million tons in 1995.[12] Despite this increase, the state claims to have reduced the amount of solid waste going into landfills by an average of about twenty percent per capita.[13] But progress has been uneven. Some regions reportedly have reduced solid waste disposal by as much as seventy-four percent. In other places it has increased by as much as 110 percent.[14]

Moreover, the official numbers conceal some funny business. The state-mandated reduction was supposed to apply to waste diverted from sanitary landfills *or incinerators.* Yet some waste that is being burned (as, for example, in Blount County's incinerator, discussed below) is actually counted in this saving. So is some waste that is actually landfilled. Sevier County, for example, "composts" its garbage—glass, plastic, furniture, television sets, household chemicals, and all. Since the resulting product is understandably of low quality, there are few buyers, and most of the "compost" is spread on Sevier County's landfill as "landfill cover." This, according to the state, counts as not landfilling the garbage. Moreover, putting construction and demolition waste in a construction and demolition landfill instead of a municipal solid waste landfill also counts in the state definition as diverting waste from landfills.

Yard "Waste"

The greatest progress in diverting waste from landfills has been achieved with yard waste (grass clippings, leaves, tree trimmings, etc.), the second largest component of municipal solid waste (see Table 6.1). In Knoxville, for example, yard waste, which used to be sent to Chestnut Ridge, is hauled to the Knox Ag facility just off Central Avenue, where it is converted to compost and sold inexpensively for lawn and garden use. This facility diverts about a hundred dump truck loads of yard waste from the landfill each day.

This is a commendable improvement, convenient for urban and suburban residents, but not an optimal solution. Its main disadvantages are air pollution and the consumption of nonrenewable fossil fuels. The hundred diesel truck trips a day needed to haul the material burn a lot of petroleum and add to regional smog—though, of course, the same number of trucks would have had to travel at least as far to take the yard waste to the landfill. Large, polluting diesel motors are also used to operate the chippers that grind the yard waste into mulch. The composting operation itself releases methane, a greenhouse gas (though this effect is balanced in part by the fact that the compost is used to grow plants that remove greenhouse gases from the air). And, finally, the front-end loaders used to load the finished compost and the pickup trucks that customers use to haul it away both consume petroleum and emit noxious effluents.

Arguing that the total air pollution from this method is excessive, neighboring Blount county has adopted a different procedure: incineration. Yard waste from Blount county is hauled to Alcoa and dumped into a high-tech Pactherm air-curtain incinerator. The incinerator burns the organic matter thoroughly and emits (according to the incinerator's manufacturer) mainly carbon dioxide and water.[15] But this process, too, requires diesel trucks to bring the waste to the incinerator, and the carbon dioxide it generates is also a greenhouse gas. With respect to carbon, at least, incineration is directly counterproductive. There is too much carbon in the air already (see Chapter Two). We should be removing it from the air and feeding it into the biotic system, not removing it from the biotic system and injecting it into the air. In the long run, moreover, burning yard waste worsens the problem of soil nutrient depletion (discussed in Chapter Four).

Yard "waste" is in fact not waste at all but nutritious organic matter—an essential commodity in the economy of life. Without such "waste" returning to the soil year after year, the land would eventually grow barren. When people remove leaves, twigs, and grass cuttings from their land, they interrupt the natural cycle of growth and decay. Growth continues for awhile, but the decay that replenishes the soil ceases and fertility is gradually lost. Eventually, to maintain healthy greenery, landholders must import nutrients—which all too often take the form of petrochemical fertilizers, the products of another long chain of polluting industrial processes.

This is folly upon folly. The only ecologically sound way to deal with yard "waste" is to compost it on site—that is, simply to pile it up and let it rot, then return it to the soil. Everything necessary for home composting (bacteria, rainwater, and a little heat) is available everywhere free of charge, and the process is neither time-consuming nor difficult. Even apartment dwellers can compost indoors, using worm bins. The worms eat the food scraps and produce clean, sweet-smelling, nutrient-rich soil, which can be added to beds for shrubbery, vegetables, or flowers. To cycle organic matter through polluting transportation and industrial processes is, by comparison, enormously wasteful and inefficient. To landfill or burn it is just stupid.

Recycling

Recycling (as distinguished from composting) has proved most successful with aluminum, steel, and other metals. Nationwide, more than fifty-five percent of steel cans and sixty-two percent of aluminum beverage cans were recycled in 1995.[16] Bauxite ore, from which aluminum is made, must be imported. Extraction of the metal from the bauxite consumes enormous amounts of electricity and so is quite expensive. Using recycled aluminum instead saves between ninety and ninety-seven percent of this energy.[17] This economic advantage makes aluminum recycling consistently profitable.

The production of steel requires iron ore, coal, and limestone, the mining of which creates vast amounts of waste and likewise consumes much energy and capital. But steel is easy and economical to recycle, and has the advantage that it can be separated from other waste with magnets.

For glass and plastic, the economic incentive to recycle is not so great, and markets fluctuate in ways that sometimes make recycling risky or unprofitable. Glass is made from cheap, abundant sand, but it is heavy and hence expensive to transport for recycling. Plastic is made from oil and natural gas, which are likewise (for the present) relatively cheap. Consequently, it is difficult for recyclers to compete with suppliers of the inexpensive virgin (primary) materials from which plastic and glass are made. Some small recycling enterprises have opened, only to close a year or two later, as prices for recycled glass or plastic plummeted.

It is thus an unfortunate fact that, even though there is a steady supply of recyclable materials, artificially low landfilling and incineration costs and the undervaluing of virgin materials often make recycling the most economically expensive disposal option—though it is far from the most expensive ecologically. The economic cost is particularly high for recycling household waste, which is diverse in composition and difficult to collect and separate. The waste streams of businesses, by contrast, are often more uniform and more easily sorted and collected; as a result, hundreds of regional businesses have long found recycling profitable.

Yet profit is not the only sort of value, and there are some exceptional businesses and many conscientious individuals who practice recycling and waste reduction simply in order to do the right thing—whether it saves them money or not.

The success of recycling efforts depends in part on the convenience and availability of recycling opportunities. The 1991 Solid Waste Management Act took an important step in the right direction by requiring each county in Tennessee to have at least one drop-off center. These centers are much used, but too often they require an out-of-the-way stop in the car or truck.

Some are also poorly managed. During the spring of 1996, for example, Hancock County's recycling center was often unattended and badly littered, the bins and barrels filled to overflowing. The new baler sat idle, never having been operated, and aluminum collected by school children for their schools was allegedly stolen from the center.[18] (Because of the value of aluminum, theft has been a problem at other recycling centers as well). Such difficulties discourage recycling—which is already a good bit less convenient than simply throwing out the garbage—and squander the good will of those who want to do their part.

The crucial step in making recycling work is to "close the loop" by finding markets for the recyclables, manufacturers to use the recyclables, and customers for the recycled products. Since consumer demand drives the markets, anyone can help, simply by buying recycled products in preference to nonrecycled products.

With no single commodity is this more important than paper. Paper and paperboard comprise about forty percent of the waste stream (see Table 6.1), and less than half the recyclable paper is actually recycled at present.[19] Paper is made from trees, and since the pulp and paper industries have targeted Southeastern forests for an increasing portion of their supply, each time we use virgin paper, we promote the deforestation of our own land. It is important to demand not just paper that is labeled as "recycled," which may be made from scraps that are part of the virgin paper-producing process, but paper labeled "post-consumer," which indicates that it has actually been used at least once already. Non-tree fibers, such as kenaf or hemp, may be ecologically sound alternatives where high-quality virgin paper is needed. (Both kenaf and hemp are cash crops that can be grown locally.)

It is also important to recycle plastics, since most of them degrade very slowly, and so contribute disproportionately to the trash which we are depositing on a geological scale everywhere on Earth. Plastics can be burned, but in the process they may release dioxin, which is highly carcinogenic, and so incineration is generally unwise. More than five hundred types of plastics are in common use. Unfortunately, while it is technically possible to recycle many of these, most regional recycling centers accept only two. These are polyethylene terephthalate (more commonly known as PETE or PET), which is used to make plastic bottles or jars marked with the number one inside the recycling logo, and high-density polyethylene (HDPE), which is used to make milk jugs and other containers that are marked with a two inside the recycling logo. In addition, a few of the larger grocers offer plastic bag collection. Some businesses recycle shrink wrap and a few other forms of plastic, but these services are not available to the public.[20]

Because plastic bottles can absorb chemicals that are stored in them, recycled bottles are generally not made into new food containers, but are refabricated instead into such products as carpet, fabric, "plastic lumber," and detergent bottles. Unfortunately, many of these once-recycled items cannot be recycled a second time and will ultimately end up in a landfill. Still, using the plastic twice is better than using it only once.

Used motor oil, a toxic and hazardous waste, is now collected at most service stations and many recycling centers. For years, an untold number of backyard mechanics (and some professional mechanics) have unwittingly polluted soil, surface water, and groundwater by dumping oil on the ground, often to kill weeds. Oil poisons the soil and may run off into surface water or seep into ground water, contaminating wells. The used motor oil collected in our bioregion, however, is not recycled to make new oil or petroleum products, but is burned as industrial fuel. "Recycling" used oil thus creates air pollution—which, however, is preferable to dumping the stuff directly on the ground. In some places outside our region, oil is actually recycled for use as a lubricant, and this re-refined oil is available at some auto stores. Buying it can help to stimulate markets that could eventually lead to true recycling of oil here.

Old tires are a big disposal problem. They are prominent in illegal dumps and in most rivers and streams. Volunteers for Knoxville's first River Rescue in 1991 pulled over five hundred muddy tires from the Tennessee River and nearby creeks. Hundreds more have been collected each succeeding year. Whole tires are now banned from landfills, since they degrade very slowly and tend over the years to "float" to the top, where they destabilize the landfill cover and may catch fire. Landfills may accept shredded tires, but shredding is wasteful and expensive, both economically and environmentally. Some regional recycling stations ship tires to the Signal Mountain Cement Company in Chattanooga, where they are burned to fuel a cement kiln.[21] Here, too, "recycling" contributes to air pollution and global warming, though using tires for fuel is better than firing the kiln with nonrenewable fossil fuels.

One good way to both save money and extend the life of tires is to buy retreads. Retreads have a bad reputation because of the poor quality of retreads made many years ago, but newer versions are quite reliable.

Incineration

Incineration has the beneficial effect of reducing waste and thus saving landfill space. But not all the waste is burned, and there is generally a residual ash, the volume and toxicity of which vary depending on the type of incinerator, the fuel, and the competence of the operators. Moreover, though incinerators have been vastly improved in recent years, they still pollute the air. All are sources of carbon dioxide, a greenhouse gas (see Chapter One) Many also release smog components—especially nitrogen oxides (NO_x).

Incinerators used to burn municipal garbage emit many other toxic materials as well. An early 1990s state-of-the-art municipal waste incinerator meeting all EPA requirements and burning 2250 tons of garbage a day would emit the following quantities of harmful or toxic contaminants annually:

NO_x . . . . 2248 tons
Sulfur dioxide. . . . . 853 tons
Hydrogen chloride. . . . . 777 tons
Dust particles . . . . 98 tons
Sulfuric acid . . . . 87 tons
Fluorides. . . . . 18 tons
Mercury . . . . 17 tons
Lead. . . . . 5 tons
Cadmium . . . . 580 pounds
Nickel. . . . . 580 pounds[22]

Moreover, municipal-waste incinerators also release significant quantities of dioxin, a potent carcinogen, largely from the burning of plastic.

Incineration is also expensive, and efficient operation requires a steady influx of garbage. This discourages recycling and source reduction, since incinerator operators lose money unless the hungry monster is fed. The pressure to burn rather than reduce or recycle is especially great when the incinerator is also used to generate energy, typically in the form of electricity.

In the early nineties, Knoxville and Knox County were planning a five-hundred-ton-per-day mass-burn municipal solid waste incinerator to relieve pressure on the rapidly-filling Chestnut Ridge landfill. There was immediate, strong, and vocal public opposition, and Knoxville mayor Victor Ashe wisely withdrew the city's support from the project, effectively killing it. The Knoxville Recycling Coalition has since provided valuable leadership in moving Knoxville and Knox County toward more sustainable alternatives.

But, while there is no longer much enthusiasm anywhere in the bioregion for incineration of municipal solid waste, incineration of other kinds of waste has proceeded apace. We have already mentioned Blount County's yard waste incinerator. Many hospitals incinerate medical waste. The Champion International paper mill now incinerates some of the "black liquor" that it used to dump into the Pigeon River, thus replacing water pollution with air pollution.[23] Dixie Cement in east Knox County burns hazardous chemical waste in its cement kiln—16,320,000 pounds in 1994. The waste incinerated by this facility that year included such toxic and/or carcinogenic compounds as 1,2,4-trimethylbenzene, butyl acrylate, di(2-ethylhexyl) phthalate, ethylbenzene, methyl ethyl ketone, methyl isobutyl ketone, styrene, toluene, and xylene.[24]

Roane County is the unhappy home of four incinerators that burn waste which is not only hazardous but radioactive. Three of these incinerators are corporate ventures: two by Scientific Ecology Group (SEG)—which, despite its name, is not a nature study club but a subsidiary of Westinghouse and the largest handler of radioactive waste in the country—and one by Diversified Scientific Systems, Inc., a subsidiary of the gigantic transnational WMX conglomerate.[25] The fourth, located not far away, at the old K-25 site on the Oak Ridge Reservation, is operated by the Department of Energy.[26] This is the Toxic Substances Control Act (TSCA) incinerator, which burns mixed waste containing both radioisotopes and other hazardous materials, including PCBs.[27] The TSCA incinerator was slated to burn about 2,900,000 pounds of toxic and radioactive waste in 1996, some of it shipped in from DOE facilities outside the state of Tennessee.[28]

All these, and many other incinerators, both large and small, add to the pollution of Tennessee Valley air. When state air-pollution permits are issued for an incinerator, only the emissions of that particular incinerator are taken into account, not the cumulative emissions of regional incinerators. Thus it is possible to site many incinerators in close proximity, which, though none individually violates air pollution standards, together regularly produce emissions well in excess of current standards.

Mine Waste

Mines may be overlooked as sources of waste, but in fact the host rock, tailings, slurry, and waste water from mining and mineral washing produce high volumes of what is, in effect, garbage. Waste may be generated from the mining process itself as the overburden (the soil and rock covering the ore) is removed. Concentrating the ore creates additional waste, called tailings. Finally, smelting and refining may produce large amounts of slag. When toxic, these wastes can poison the soil and water. Even when not, they can be so voluminous as to clog rivers and streams. Nolichucky Reservoir south of Greeneville, Tennessee, has been almost completely filled by mine tailings.

Aside from coal, which is mined in large quantities on the western slopes of the upper Tennessee Valley, there are mines in our bioregion for mica, olivine, crushed granite or limestone, marble, shale, clay (for bricks), gemstones, and feldspar. Sand is mined by instream dipping. Barite mining occurs in the Sweetwater area, zinc in the Cherokee Dam area, silica sand mining to the northeast of this. Shale is mined at the far eastern tip of Tennessee.

Mine tailings are normally stored near the mine behind dams (called tailing or slurry impoundments), which are usually constructed in hollows, depressions, or valleys, and left as an after-mining "new contour" of the land. Where mining is well-regulated, the surfaces of these dams are covered with top soil and vegetated when the mine site is closed. Still waste-water, tailings, and slimes sometimes find their way into surface water or groundwater if the impoundments are inadequately lined or if cracks develop in the embankments or underlying rock.[29]

Industrial Waste

Then there is industrial waste. The world generates about twenty billion tons of industrial waste per year, of which six hundred million tons are hazardous. Industrial wastes in the U.S. are estimated at thirteen billion tons per year, about fifty tons per person annually. Two hundred million tons of this are hazardous.[30]

Before the enactment of strong environmental legislation, industries dumped their waste just about anywhere they wanted to—in the water, in the air, and on or under the ground. Much of it was poisonous or carcinogenic. While enormous discharges (both legal and illegal, both accidental and intentional) still occur, regulations have done much to curtail them. Some of the worst polluters have fled—to places like Mexico or Southeast Asia, where they can exploit the cheap labor and poison the land and the people with little interference from authorities. Others have closed up shop.

As a result, our bioregion is dotted with old industrial sites, many trashed and abandoned, some still in use, where the earth or water is contaminated with hazardous materials. Zoning and city planning having never been much practiced in Southern Appalachia, many of these sites are near people's homes. Almost without exception, the people whose homes they are near are poor. Many are people of color.

So it is that those who benefit least from the profits and products of industrial society are the ones harmed most by its poisons—the classic pattern of environmental injustice. Nowhere in our bioregion is this more apparent than in the low-income, predominantly African-American Alton Park and Piney Woods neighborhoods around Chattanooga Creek. About ten thousand people live near the creek, which is contaminated by at least forty-two hazardous waste sites, twelve of which are Tennessee Superfund sites, and one of which is a federal Superfund site. The contaminants include PCBs, heavy metals such as lead and arsenic, coal tar, and pesticides. Health studies by the federal Agency for Toxic Substances and Disease Registry (ATSDR) have indicated that exposure to creek water, soil, fish, and the surrounding air, can increase the risk of skin rashes, throat and stomach irritations, nervous system effects, leukemia, and liver or kidney cancer. Residents have reported increased instances of cancer, miscarriages, breathing problems, headaches, and eye and skin irritations. Since clean-up will take many years, recent educational efforts near the creek have focused on teaching children that it is dumb or uncool to be a "Creek geek,"—that is, to play in or near the creek.[31]

Chattanooga Creek is the worst example of private industrial contamination in the bioregion, but it is far from the only one. As of August 1, 1995, the state of Tennessee recognized 154 sites as superfund sites. Nineteen of these are in Hamilton County, which includes Chattanooga Creek. Sullivan County has fourteen. Knox County has eleven.[32]

Of the Knox County sites, the most notorious are the three dismal junkyards operated by David Witherspoon, Inc., in the impoverished Vestal community of South Knoxville. For many years beginning in 1948, Witherspoon used these three parcels of land along Maryville Pike to process scrap-metal parts, many of which were contaminated with radioisotopes, asbestos, and various toxic chemicals. Much of the metal was sold to Witherspoon by the Atomic Energy Commission (AEC)—later, Department of Energy (DOE)—nuclear weapons facilities at Oak Ridge.[33]

Internal DOE memos obtained by the Foundation for Global Sustainability through the Freedom of Information Act also reveal that Witherspoon may have handled scrap contaminated with plutonium—one of the most deadly of radioactive metals. A memo dated April 21, 1969, states that "the purchaser [Witherspoon] should emphatically be made aware that the material he is contracting to handle does contain a plutonium potential and we cannot guarantee a specific level below which all the material will read."[34] A second memo, dated June 4, 1969, said that although most of the potentially plutonium-contaminated material sold to Witherspoon remained in Oak Ridge, "four or five pickup truckloads have been taken to Knoxville."[35]

Radioactively or chemically contaminated metal in the form of large pieces of equipment, pipes, parts, chips, or tailings was hauled to the Witherspoon scrap yards from Oak Ridge and elsewhere by truck and by rail. Using Geiger counters, neighborhood women working for slightly more than minimum wage—often with no protection other than gloves—sorted the radioactive metal by hand, placed it into barrels and carried it into a warehouse. This operation was performed in an area called the "hot field." Metals were identified by using a grinder to remove the outer layer of rust and dirt and then applying acid to see what color the metal would turn. The grinding operation undoubtedly released radioactive particles into the air. Dorothy Hunley, who worked at this job for twelve years, died in 1985 of osteogenic sarcoma, a form of bone cancer associated with ingestion or inhalation of radioisotopes. Her doctor thought it likely that exposure to radiation was the cause.[36]

Former workers also report that transformers shipped from various locations were smashed open with a wrecking ball in order to salvage the copper wire inside, and the liquid they contained (presumably consisting largely of PCBs) was spread on the ground to control dust. Neighbors and former workers tell stories of large pieces of heavy equipment being off-loaded from trains and buried. Tires—and just about anything else combustible—were piled up and burned in the open air. Tire fires continued sporadically, at least until the fall of 1992, when Witherspoon finally received some heavy fines for air pollution. Witherspoon operations also included the smelting of radioactively contaminated metals, for which permission was granted by the state, beginning in December, 1968.

Tennessee Department of Environment and Conservation and Tennessee Occupational Safety and Health Administration files on Witherspoon are voluminous with complaints and reports of violations. A 1971 state inspection found incoming scrap metal with radioactivity measuring fifty millirems per hour, a level sufficient to be of concern for worker safety. A 1973 inspection found a pipe leaching uranium near Goose Creek, which runs through the property. Inspectors also found unmarked piles of highly radioactive scrap iron and barrels of uranium turnings—which Witherspoon was not licensed to handle.

In 1976, the Tennessee Division of Occupational and Radiological Health tried to collect from Witherspoon a fine of $120, for inadequate restrooms. The Attorney General's office recommended that the state not pursue the fine, because Witherspoon was declaring insolvency. Witherspoon, however, continued to do business.

Through the years, Witherspoon resold a great deal of the contaminated scrap to the Knoxville Iron Company. A 1981 investigation by the Nuclear Regulatory Commission (NRC) found that Witherspoon had bought over two hundred thousand pounds of steel contaminated with uranium 235, never reported the shipment, and then resold the steel to the Knoxville Iron Company, all in violation of NRC regulations. NRC was unable to determine what happened to the steel after that. No fine was levied, though Witherspoon's NRC license to handle enriched uranium was eventually revoked. Witherspoon's response to an NRC query as to why he did not know where the metal had gone was: "Iron is iron."[37]

In the early eighties, there was a partial cleanup of the hot field. Soil contaminated with PCBs and uranium was removed, placed in barrels, and moved to a second site at Candora Avenue. In May of 1985, the Tennessee Department of Health and Environment ordered Witherspoon to dispose of these barrels within six months or pay a fifty-thousand-dollar fine. Witherspoon failed to meet the deadline, which was then extended. The extended deadline also passed, and the fine still was not paid. Witherspoon's reason for not disposing of the barrels was that no facility in the country was willing or able to accept this sort of mixed waste. Thus it remained onsite in leaking barrels—immediately adjacent to a residential neighborhood. It was not until 1993 that the Department of Energy was finally persuaded under intense legal pressure from the state to remove all the remaining barrels. Cleanup of the sites is still under way, and the Candora property has been secured with razor wire. Witherspoon's fines and penalties are tied up in the courts.

Sampling conducted by the state and by the Department of Energy has revealed widespread contamination, including radioactive contamination as high as 129,700 picocuries per gram.[38] The applicable state cleanup guideline is thirty-five picocuries per gram. In places where PCB-contaminated items were burned, the state has found dioxin, which suggests that residents were exposed to airborne dioxin (a severe carcinogen) while the burning was occurring. There are also excessive mercury and PCB levels both in the soil and in the sediments of Goose Creek, which flows through the site. The groundwater at the Candora site is contaminated with lead, mercury, chromium, beryllium, antimony and several organic compounds in excess of state standards. Small amounts of plutonium have also been detected in the soil at the Candora site.[39] Concerning radiological and chemical risks to human health at that site, a 1996 Department of Energy study concludes, "In almost every current and future scenario, the EPA's target risk range is exceeded, indicating unacceptable current and future risk."[40]

Nuclear Waste

The most egregious dumping in our bioregion, and the most expensive to correct, occurred on the Oak Ridge Reservation during World War II and the cold war years that followed. There nuclear weapons—and, later, commercial nuclear fuels—were produced by novel and sophisticated industrial processes that brought some of the brightest minds in the country to Oak Ridge. This genius was mustered, however, in the service of urgent and immediate goals; less thought was given to the more mundane matter of waste disposal. Because Oak Ridge was cloaked in the secrecy of "national security," there were few to raise questions when orders were issued to take the stuff out back and bury it. So take it out and bury it they did—often in unlined trenches dug with a backhoe, sometimes penetrating the water table.

On the grounds of the Oak Ridge National Laboratory (ORNL), for example, there are six solid waste disposal areas (with a seventh under construction), all located in the drainage basin of White Oak Creek. An almost unbelievable variety of toxic and radioactive trash has been dumped there, contaminating the soil, the groundwater, the creek, White Oak Reservoir, the Clinch River, and Watts Bar Reservoir. The contaminants include biological wastes, mercury, toluene, naphthalene, and both high-level and low-level radioactive wastes contaminated with such radioisotopes as tritium, strontium 90, cobalt 60, cesium 137, and plutonium. *(Please see Figure 9).*

In the late 1950s ORNL mixed radioactive waste with concrete and injected it into fractured rock deep underground. This practice, called hydrofracture, continued until 1984 when it was discovered that groundwater near the hydrofracture sites had become contaminated. The current disposal practice at ORNL is to store waste above ground in concrete casks within concrete tombs.

A variety of initiatives have been undertaken to reduce the contamination flowing from the old waste-burial grounds. Many of these involve rerouting the flow of water. The most innovative is *in situ* vitrification, a process whereby electrodes are inserted into the ground and charged with enormous amounts of electricity in order to melt the earth into a kind of glass. Radioactive and chemical contaminants are encased within the glass where, presumably, they are stabilized and cannot contaminate groundwater. But moisture in the soil sometimes interferes with this process, unpredictably producing large quantities of contaminated vapor. In one incident, on April 21, 1996, vapors from the operation exploded from beneath a fifteen-thousand-pound hood built to collect them, lifting it a foot off the ground, and expelling approximately twenty tons of radioactively-contaminated molten earth.[41]

Bear Creek Valley, just west of the Y-12 plant, was also used for nuclear and chemical waste disposal, beginning in 1951. From then until 1984, four unlined seepage pits, known as the S-3 ponds, were used for the disposal of over 2,700,000 gallons of liquid wastes. These wastes contained concentrated acids, caustic solutions, mop waters, and byproducts of uranium recovery processes. The pits were designed to allow the liquid either to evaporate or percolate into the ground. From there it flowed into the headwaters of Bear Creek and East Fork Poplar Creek. The S-3 ponds were closed in 1984 and paved over to create a parking lot.

Also located in Bear Creek Valley was the Oil Landfarm Site. A "farm" only in the twisted nomenclature of the bureaucrats' imagination, this thirteen-acre site was, in fact, a dumping ground for PCB-contaminated oily wastes, which were spread out and plowed into the ground. The oil also contained toxic beryllium compounds and radioactive uranium. This "farm" has been closed and covered with a waterproof cap.

Like ORNL, Bear Creek Valley also has burial grounds. These are located along the southern flank of Pine Ridge. They received PCB-contaminated oils, radioactive mop waters, radioactive asbestos wastes, and items contaminated with beryllium, thorium, and uranium. In 1961, an open-topped tank was placed in one of the burial grounds and filled with 180,000 gallons of various toxic liquids, which were then set on fire. After the burning, the residues were dumped into nearby trenches. In 1990, monitoring wells south of Burial Ground A revealed PCB contamination 274 feet below the surface at a concentration of 29,000 parts per million—almost three thousand times the acceptable limit. All the Bear Creek burial grounds are now closed and covered.

In 1951, the Atomic Energy Commission began to use the abandoned Kerr Hollow Quarry, off Bethel Road, as a dumping ground for explosive materials. Containers of these materials were dropped into the quarry from the ridge above and then shot to release or explode their contents. Disposal continued at Kerr Hollow until 1988.

The K-25 complex southwest of Oak Ridge is dotted with more unlined open-trench burial grounds. For many years, radioactive scrap metal was stored there in a twenty-two acre site along the banks of the Clinch River. The river flooded in 1984, inundating this scrap yard and carrying radioactive materials downstream. The scrap has since been moved to higher ground.[42]

The most abusive practices on the Oak Ridge Reservation have ceased, and some remediation has begun, but much of the Reservation is likely to remain contaminated for the foreseeable future, a testimony to our monumental lack of foresight.

The Three R's

In 1989, the EPA announced a strategy to improve the way America handles municipal solid waste. The heart of this strategy has come to be known as the "three R's": reduce, reuse, recycle. The order of the terms is significant. "Reduce" is listed first to indicate that the highest priority is source reduction: generating less waste to begin with. Second in the hierarchy is reuse—an idea aimed at reversing the momentum of the throw-away culture. Recycling is third. These three primary strategies are followed by composting, incineration and landfilling—in that order. Landfilling, be it noted, is dead last.

Unfortunately, the two top priorities—source reduction and reuse—have largely been ignored by most communities in our bioregion, which continue generate large quantities of waste and send most of it to landfills. There have been notable improvements in recycling and composting, but these do not address waste and inefficiency resulting from overproduction and overconsumption. Recycling and composting are beneficial, but we have yet to deploy the most effective strategies: reduction and reuse.

Source reduction has been difficult to achieve because our current waste disposal system provides few incentives. Many localities still pay for residential (and in some places even commercial) disposal through general tax revenues. The cost of disposal is the same no matter how much garbage you throw away. Most private residential services also charge a flat rate, regardless of the amount of garbage customers generate. In both cases, there is no monetary incentive to reduce. Incentives can be introduced by various "pay-as-you-throw" schemes, which charge for waste disposal either by weight or by volume. One simple way to charge by volume is to require that the garbage be placed in special bags, the purchase price for which is the disposal fee for the volume they can hold. Paying by weight is more complicated, since it requires garbage trucks to be fitted with scales.

Pay-as-you-throw policies may cause a temporary increase in illegal dumping, especially in rural communities, as freeloaders seek to evade the fee. But ultimately, as the fees gain acceptance, they promote a community ethic of thrift.[43]

Pay-as-you-throw plans have beneficial ripple effects through the whole economy. Aiming to reduce their garbage bills, people demand products that are reusable, recyclable, or less wastefully packaged. This in turn impels producers to increase product quality, reduce packaging, and eliminate throw-aways. Consumers also have greater incentives to reject planned obsolescence, motivating manufacturers to build sturdier, longer-lasting products. These adjustments increase efficiency in the use of materials, promote conservation, and help protect the land from which raw materials are extracted.

Pay-as-you-throw pricing also promotes reuse, since money is saved by repairing, selling, or donating items rather than throwing them away. Reuse was, until fairly recently, a tradition imposed by hard necessity on Southern Appalachia, but that tradition has faded with burgeoning wealth. Yet age-old patterns of reuse still survive in garage sales, flea markets, and donations to Goodwill, the Salvation Army, and other charities. A new twist to these patterns is the notion of a waste exchange where businesses or individuals can deposit items they no longer want so that others can use them. Tennessee operates a statewide waste exchange, which has proven useful as an inexpensive source of raw materials for businesses; and smaller waste exchanges (such as the one operated by the Knoxville Recycling Coalition) have promoted the same ideal on a more local level.

Pay-as-you-throw pricing also encourages the third process in the EPA hierarchy: recycling. People will be motivated to recycle when they can reduce their garbage bills by doing so.

The benefits of recycling are many. Communities can sell recycled materials to offset waste collection and program costs, reduce their budgets for collection and disposal of non-recyclable waste, postpone investment in siting and construction of new landfills, and create jobs, as businesses collect and process recyclables and remanufacture them into new products. Manufacturing products from recycled materials can also reduce environmental and energy costs associated with logging, mining, and other extractive industries.

By using recycled materials in manufacturing, industries can reduce materials and energy costs, as well as the cost of complying with environmental regulations—and reinvest the savings in regional economies. The recycling of aluminum, for example, has dramatically lowered the consumption of energy (and associated costs) at the Alcoa Aluminum Plant.

Unfortunately, recycling is often hampered by unfair competition from suppliers of virgin materials. Federal subsidies or tax incentives for lumbering, mining, and oil and gas exploration, for example, keep the prices for virgin materials artificially low, discouraging the recycling of paper, metals, and plastics. These subsidies include depletion allowances for the extraction of oil, natural gas, and various minerals; below-cost timber sales, road-building, and other federal subsidies for timber operations, especially in the national forests;[44] tax provisions for energy development, including the funding of exploration and development, and tax-exempt bonds; and various other tax provisions.[45] Inheritance taxes, for example, often treat timber as an investment, which encourages logging as a way of avoiding the tax.[46]

Changing the tax structure could, therefore, reduce the extraction of virgin materials and increase recycling. Much higher rates of recycling with much greater economic efficiency have been achieved in the more advanced waste management systems of Western Europe and Japan. We could do as well or better if the disincentives were replaced with positive incentives.

We have already discussed the benefits of the fourth process in the EPA hierarchy: composting. Composting is the only reasonable method for dealing with yard trimmings, food scraps, and other organic materials. Inorganic materials, however, cannot be composted, and companies which claim to compost them are running a scam.

Incineration and landfilling should be regarded, as the EPA pointedly indicates, as last-ditch measures, to be used only when all else has failed. Unfortunately, we have so far had our priorities backwards, sending most of our trash to landfills.

This is a monumental waste. The used metals, glass, wood products, plastics, and chemicals that we dump into landfills once had to be mined or logged or pumped from the earth, and then refined, separated from ores, or processed—all at great expense of money and energy, and considerable cost to the air, water, and land. By keeping these used materials separate and relatively intact for recycling or reuse, we could preserve much of the value originally created by their extraction and processing, to the benefit both of the ecology and the economy. To jumble them together into an entropic mess from which they are once again difficult and expensive to extract and then bury them in the ground, degrading still more air, water, and land, is, therefore, highly irrational.

In sum, while there have been some notable improvements, waste-disposal policy in our bioregion has so far amounted to little more than crisis management and political expediency. Because landfill space continues to be found, albeit at increasing cost, the perception of crisis is fading and business is returning to usual. The underlying problems, however, remain unsolved. We constantly generate more and more waste, and landfill most of it. Without a restructuring of taxation and the widespread acceptance of an ethic of thrift, the waste will continue to grow.

Table 6.2

APPROACHES TO WASTE REDUCTION

Waste prevention, or source reduction, is the design, manufacture, purchase, and/or use of materials and products that serve to reduce the amount and/or toxicity of discarded waste. Sometimes the most effective waste prevention is simply doing without.

Reuse pertains not only to those items that can be donated to charity, such as used furniture, but also reusing discarded one-sided copies as scratch paper, and reusing envelopes, boxes and manila folders. Using reusable goods such as cloth napkins, real glasses, refillable pens, rechargeable batteries, and refillable printer and toner cartridges also helps to cut down on waste.

Exchanges can be set up so that what one person or company regards as waste can be used by another. Pallets, plastics, and construction debris are some of the materials that can be usefully exchanged. Recycling is the separation and collection of materials that would otherwise have been discarded as waste, which are then used as raw materials in the manufacture of new products.

Composting is a natural process by which food scraps, landscape debris and other organic materials are collected and allowed to decompose under controlled conditions into a rich, soil-like substance called compost.

Purchasing is the procurement of products made from recycled materials and/or designed to result in less waste after their useful life.

FIGURE 10: Traffic jams up and halts in Gatlinburg, Tennessee—a common occurrence, especially during the tourist season. Mount LeConte, shrouded in mist and haze, looms in the background. This juxtaposition of prominent ugliness and obscured beauty aptly symbolizes what we have done to the land.

The chariots shall rage in the streets, they shall jostle one against another in the broad ways: they shall seem like torches, they shall run like the lightnings.

— Nahum 2:3-4

Masters or Slaves?

It takes no science, no computers, no satellite-borne instrumentation, to detect the trouble wrought by our transportation system. Anyone can see it. The roads are widened and widened again. Still they fill with speeding cars and trucks. New roads are built to relieve the burgeoning traffic. They only bring more development and more traffic. Asphalt reaches out across the land. The farms are swallowed up, the mountains hemmed in. Noise and fumes are everywhere. The highway culture blurs local distinctions, making every place like every other. The pace of life constantly quickens. Cities, neighborhoods, homes, and individual lives shape themselves around the automobile.[1]

It is not unreasonable to suppose that the average American spends about an hour a day driving or being driven somewhere. Over a lifetime of seventy-two years, that amounts to three years sitting in the confinement of a motor vehicle. Since the interior of a motor vehicle is scarcely more commodious or healthful than a prison cell, it is questionable whether these three years are well spent—even if the cell is equipped with a cellular phone.

To the years spent in cars and trucks, we might also add the time served working to pay for them—and for their financing, their upkeep, their fuel, their parking, their licensing, and their insurance. The rewards of this service are, moreover, not always what we hope: hurling across the land in capsules of steel and glass, we routinely risk impacts that no human body is built to sustain, and many of us bear scars of the body, or scars of sorrow as a result.

Though in some ways the private automobile has enlarged our freedom, in others it has diminished it. Cities have been reorganized around the automobile so that most people are no longer free to walk or bicycle where they choose, but are compelled by the structure of the roads and consequent elimination of neighborhood businesses to drive in order to obtain the simple essentials of life. Children, especially, must constantly be shuttled here and there, since (primarily because of changes wrought by the automobile) few places can safely be reached on foot. Thus, between the automobile and its owner, it is sometimes doubtful who serves whom.

The True Cost of Oil

The statistics confirm what we know already: we drive too much and burn too much petroleum, and the quantities are constantly increasing. In 1992, Tennessee had 85,144 miles of roads, 3.7 million registered automobiles, and 3.5 million licensed drivers—sixty-nine percent of the population. These numbers represent a 466-percent increase in the number of licensed drivers since 1940, and a 924-percent increase in the number of registered automobiles since 1940. By 2010, the number of registered automobiles in Tennessee is expected to increase to 4.75 million, and the number of licensed drivers to 4.3 million, or seventy-nine percent of the population. Tennesseeans drove over 49 billion miles in 1992[2]—a distance equivalent to more than a hundred thousand trips to the moon and back.

About a quarter of our total energy usage is for transportation,[3] but not all of this is used directly to power cars and trucks. For every barrel of oil burned by motor vehicles, about a quarter of a barrel is used to produce, refine, and distribute the oil. Additional energy is expended in manufacturing and repairing vehicles and in building and maintaining roads.[4]

Tennessee drivers consume more than three billion gallons of gas and diesel fuel annually.[5] This fuel is not always used efficiently. In 1992, the average fuel consumption for registered vehicles in Tennessee was only 16.11 miles per gallon. Still, this was a great improvement over previous years; in 1970, for example, the average per registered vehicle was 11.81 miles per gallon. Because of this increase in efficiency, total fuel consumption increased only about three percent per year between 1970 and 1992, though travel increased at a rate of 5.5 percent per year— for a total increase of about 325 percent. In 1993 the Tennessee Department of Transportation estimated that highway travel would continue to increase at an average annual rate of about 2.4 percent over the next twenty years, causing fuel consumption to increase about 1.5 percent per year.[6] These projections assume continued improvements in fuel efficiency. But after two decades of cheap and readily available gas, RVs, vans, jeeps, big pickup trucks, and other low-mileage vehicles are becoming increasingly popular. As a result, average mileage could decrease, causing much larger increases in total fuel consumption.

Increases in fuel consumption are costly to the environment in ways already discussed in previous chapters. But they are also costly to the economy and to national security. Domestic oil production peaked in 1970 and has been steadily declining ever since, as oil well after oil well runs dry.[7] We have so little oil left that over the past few years there have been intense congressional debates over whether to open up our last big remaining sanctuary, the Arctic National Wildlife Refuge on Alaska's northern coast, to oil exploitation.

Since we are running out of oil at home, much of our oil is imported from the Middle East. We fought a war there in 1991 to protect our oil supply, and we still maintain an expensive military presence. A full accounting of the cost of oil ought therefore to include the cost of the military forces that protect the oil supplies—and the cost in lives when it comes to a fight. Fighting itself adds enormous new environmental costs: oil well fires and oil spills, as was the case in the Gulf War—and, perhaps, the costs to health and the environment of the use of chemical weaponry.

Since money spent importing oil is largely responsible for the trade deficit, there are also substantial economic and political costs to dependence on foreign oil.

Then there are the direct environmental costs. The most obvious of these are output effects—the ones that begin with the hot medley of pollutants and poisons pulsing from the tailpipe. One prominent output effect is the stifling brown or gray smog that hangs over the cities on still, hot summer days. This smog is a mixture of various noxious substances, many of which are generated by the exhausts of traffic. These include nitrogen oxides (NO_x) and volatile organic compounds, which contribute to ground-level ozone (discussed in Chapter Two). Nitrous oxides also react with moisture to form nitric acid, creating acid rain (see Chapter One). In addition, automotive exhaust contains smoke particles, which can increase the probability of respiratory disease[8], and carbon monoxide, which can damage the nervous system. At high concentrations, as in a closed garage, carbon monoxide is quickly lethal. Most of the carbon in the exhaust of a well-tuned motor vehicle, however, takes the form of carbon dioxide, a greenhouse gas (see Chapter Two).

Not all cars pollute equally. According to a study conducted by researchers at the University of Denver, a mere ten percent of the cars were responsible for fifty percent of the automotive pollution. Interestingly, the study also found that a car's polluting level is not dependent on its age alone. Poorly maintained newer cars pollute more than well-maintained older cars. Surprisingly, this holds true even for early 1970s models, which lack pollution-control equipment. According to the study, "a well-maintained 1972 car emitted 10 grams of hydrocarbon pollution per mile, while a poorly kept 1992 car emitted nearly 100 grams." However, new technology has significantly improved the emissions of automobiles which are maintained properly. In fact, "a well-maintained 1992 car emitted just one gram per mile" of hydrocarbon pollution.[9]

Some of the less obvious effects of oil consumption come to light when we turn from the output side to the input side, starting at the gas station and tracing the input process backwards. As gas is pumped into the fuel tank, vapor escapes into the air. One significant component of this vapor is benzene, inhalation of which can cause cancer and leukemia.[10]

The fuel is pumped from underground storage tanks beneath the asphalt of the filling station. Many of these tanks leak, contaminating soil and groundwater. Dribbles from the gasoline hose or overflows from the fuel tank splash onto the asphalt and are eventually washed down the gutter and into the nearest river or stream.

The fuel comes to the filling station in tank trucks, which compound the environmental costs of oil as they roar down the highways belching black diesel exhaust. The trucks themselves are loaded at petroleum storage depots, such as the one just off Middlebrook Pike in Knoxville. Fuel leaks are common at these depots, and the soil beneath them is contaminated with petrochemicals. At the Middlebrook Pike depot, there is visible (and olfactory) evidence of petroleum runoff into Third Creek.

The depots themselves are supplied by pipelines, trucks, trains, or barges from refineries where the fuel is distilled from crude oil. Much of the gas used in Southern Appalachia comes from refineries along the Gulf Coast of Texas and Louisiana, an area known as "cancer alley." The crude is shipped largely from the Middle East aboard supertankers. These tankers occasionally leak or break up— with familiar consequences.

The true cost of oil includes all these costs. And oil is not the end of the story.

Other Effects of Cars and Trucks

Cars and trucks are virtual storehouses of hazardous materials. The fluids in the radiator, transmission, windshield washer reservoir, braking system and oil sump are all, to varying degrees, toxic. As motor vehicles age, these substances tend to leak into the environment. Brake linings contain asbestos, which sloughs off as brakes abrade and may accumulate in street dust. Asbestos exposure increases the probability of several forms of lung disease, including lung cancer.[11]

People who drive or ride too often tend to grow fat, and their muscles atrophy and weaken, unless they make special efforts to exercise. But to reach a place suitable for exercising, many people drive, further compounding the problem.

Cars and trucks also add significantly to the problem of waste disposal. Tires, used oil, and lead-acid batteries are difficult and costly to dispose of properly, and so are often improperly handled, at considerable environmental cost (see Chapter Six).

Motor vehicles fill the air with noise that commonly reaches volumes of nearly ninety decibels in city traffic—loud enough to cause progressive loss of hearing with prolonged exposure.[12] More subtly, traffic noise overpowers the more beautiful and ancient voices of birds and the wind.

Automotive accidents kill or maim hundreds of people and millions of animals each year. Many of these accidents are the result of speeding. But even when it causes no accidents, speeding takes its toll in frayed nerves. Rare is the driver who consistently stays within designated speed limits. Truck drivers, especially, are pressed to speed to deliver their cargo quickly. The newer rigs are lighter and longer than the older ones, so that they can carry more cargo at higher speeds. The monster truck suddenly filling the rearview mirror, then blasting by at seventy-five miles an hour is an increasingly familiar experience.[13]

Speed is also an important factor in pollution. According to models constructed by the EPA, NO_x emissions increase gradually with speed above forty-four kilometers per hour (twenty-seven miles per hour), and increase more dramatically after seventy-six kilometers per hour (forty-seven miles per hour). Emissions of volatile organic compounds, by contrast, decrease with speed until about eighty-eight kilometers per hour (fifty-five miles per hour), but dramatically increase thereafter. Emissions of both pollutants increase with distance traveled, all other factors being held constant.[14]

Fuel consumption also increases with speed. As speed is increased from fifty-five to seventy-five miles per hour, fuel consumption increases thrity percent.[15]

Driving with underinflated tires has a surprisingly large effect on fuel consumption. If the rolling resistance of tires is decreased by only ten percent, fuel economy can increase by three to four percent. The Department of Energy estimates that underinflated tires waste a hundred thousand barrels of oil nationally each day.[16]

The Proliferation of Roads

Perhaps the most profound environmental effect of our transportation system is the proliferation of roads. We use more land for roads and for the parking, fueling, and repairing of automobiles than for housing. Nationwide, nearly sixty thousand square miles are paved, about two percent of the total surface area of the country.[17]

Southern Appalachia has done its best to keep up with this trend. The only large roadless areas in the bioregion occur within the Great Smoky Mountains National Park. An area counts technically as "roadless" if it is relatively untouched and contains no more than half a mile of improved road for each thousand acres.[18] Hence an area that is technically roadless may contain dirt roads that allow motor vehicle access—and even some stretches of paved roadway. Yet even by this relatively lax criterion, there are no roadless areas at all in the upper Tennessee Valley (see Figure 12). The few places that remain unscathed by roads are confined to the roughest terrain, high in the mountains. These comprise about three percent of the land of Southern Appalachia—by far the greatest part of which lies within the bounds of the Great Smoky Mountains National Park. No other roadless area is even a twentieth the size of the Park.[19]

FIGURE 12: Roadless areas in the Southern Appalachian region. The big roadless area on the Tennessee/North Carolina border is the Great Smoky Mounatins National Park. (SAMAB 1996d, p. 179; dark outline designates the Southern Appalachian Assessment area, which is larger than the bioregion covered in this report.)

Though roads are virtually everywhere already, the drawing boards of the planners are busy with many more. New areas of pavement accompany each new housing development or industrial park. Where traffic is most dense, as on highway 441 through Sevier County, new road projects are planned to relieve the congestion. But, historically, such projects have been only a temporary fix. New roads bring in new development, which in the long run worsens the problem, and the cycle of road-building and development rapidly gobbles up the land.

The most important ecological effect of roads is habitat fragmentation. Large roads with heavy traffic flows are almost impossible for animals to cross. Thus today migration and movement across the landscape are restricted to a degree unprecedented, so far as we know, in all of ecological history. And, just as the penetration of the skin opens the body to infection by microorganisms, so the penetration of the landscape by roads opens ecosystems to invasion by nonnative organisms, furthering the homogenization of nature (see Chapter Three).

Each new road runs over unique fragments of humanity or nature and imposes a standardized regime of strip development in their place. Some of the oldest and most established neighborhoods of South Knoxville, for example, will likely be destroyed by the huge four-lane extension of the South Knoxville Boulevard, which is meant to shoot traffic from I-40 and I-75 more rapidly toward Sevier County and the Smokies. When this road was first planned over twenty years ago, the question apparently was never asked whether the Smokies need more traffic more quickly. (We have always assumed that bigger and faster is better.) Nor did anyone consult residents in the new road's path, some of whom have lived in their quiet neighborhoods for half a century and had planned to die there. Some of these residents will be forced to move. Others must choose either to stay and endure the sights, sounds, and smells of traffic where once they enjoyed the sounds of birds in the green woods—or leave and find a new home in a landscape in which woodside homes are increasingly rare and expensive.

On the other side of Knoxville, at Turkey Creek, between Lovell and Campbell Station roads, it is a unique natural area, not a neighborhood, that is threatened by road construction. The Turkey Creek wetland, the largest remaining wetland in Knox County, and one of the highest quality wetlands left in the bioregion, is to be bisected by a long mound of earth bulldozed across the swampy ground and capped with a seven-lane expanse of asphalt. This road, too, is advertised as a congestion reliever. But its primary motivation is to promote new development,[20] which will tightly ring this unique natural habitat with asphalt, while adding still more traffic to an already sadly overdeveloped area.

Roads are also degrading the mountains. Section 8D of the Foothills Parkway just north of the Great Smoky Mountains National Park threatens the quiet and ecological integrity of the Smokies' northern foothills. The proposed section extends from Wear Valley Road (US 321) to the Gatlinburg/Pigeon Forge spur (US 321/441). Construction and operation would directly destroy about a hundred plants of pink lady's slipper, a species listed by Tennessee as endangered, and three plants of the lesser ladies' tresses, listed by the state as a species of special concern.[21] But its indirect effects would be far greater. By further fragmenting the already severely fragmented buffer zone around the Park, the road would constrict wildlife habitat and open new routes for invasive species, further impairing the Park's function as a last haven for native biodiversity. It will also degrade the quiet and historic quality of Wear Valley.

Yet another example of destructive road-building is US highway 19-74 which runs southwest into the Nantahala National Forest from Asheville, North Carolina. Construction on the last link in the highway began in May 1995. Originally, the highway was supposed to follow the most direct route through breathtaking Nantahala Gorge. When that proposal was squelched a decade ago and a new route was found, opposition faded. Still, this expensive highway through very rugged terrain makes little sense either environmentally or economically. The cost of the twenty-seven mile highway is estimated conservatively at 280 million dollars, making it perhaps the most expensive highway per mile ever built in North Carolina. The construction and subsequent use of the highway will degrade the wilderness character of an area crossed by the Appalachian Trail. It will also expose bands of rocks which, when exposed to air and water, create acid runoff that may contaminate pristine streams.[22]

These are merely examples. The asphalt network is expanding everywhere in the bioregion, and contracting nowhere, and with each new expansion something of value is lost.

Asphalt

Whether it is homes, woods, mountains, wetlands, farms, or fields that are bulldozed away to make a road, what is laid down in their place is usually asphalt. Asphalt surfaces, while well-suited for cars and trucks, are poorly suited for just about everything else. Biologically, they are death zones, fatal to almost all organisms that venture onto them.

From a hydrological perspective, their most important property is imperviousness to water. Nearly all soils are porous and capable of quickly absorbing great amounts of water from rain or melting snow. Vegetated soils can absorb even more, discharging the water slowly into creeks or underground water systems. But asphalt absorbs no water. Rain or melting snow rushes off in sheets, quickly swelling streams and increasing the potential for floods.

Runoff from asphalt is contaminated with whatever drips, falls, drifts, runs, or is sprayed onto the pavement: dirt and dust, rubber and metal deposits from tire wear, asbestos from brakes, antifreeze, grease, gasoline, engine oil, road salt, heavy metals, pesticides, and litter.[23] Toxic oils may also seep from the asphalt itself, which is composed largely of sticky residues from the oil refining process.

When first laid down, hot asphalt releases a noxious vapor known as "blue smoke." This vapor contains two important precursors of tropospheric ozone formation, nitrogen dioxide (NO_2) and volatile organic compounds (see Chapter Two). Prominent among the volatile organic compounds in blue smoke is benzene, inhalation of which may cause cancer, leukemia and suppression of the immune system. Other carcinogens—including benzo(a)pyrene, benzo(k)fluoranthene, ideno(1,2,3-cd)pyrene, and naphthalene—are present in smaller amounts. There is evidence that some components of blue smoke—e.g. fluoranthene and benzo(a)pyrene—interact synergistically, becoming more carcinogenic in combination than in separate exposures.[24] Given these facts, it is troubling that road construction workers and others who are regularly exposed to asphalt fumes almost never wear respirators.

Barges

Roads are not the only means of transportation in our bioregion. There are also about 265 miles of commercially navigable waterways in the upper Tennessee Valley above Chattanooga. These include the Tennessee River (up to Knoxville), the Hiwassee River (up to Charleston, Tennessee), and the Clinch River (up to Clinton, Tennessee).[25] The barges that use these waterways are the most efficient means we have of moving large quantities of raw materials such as logs, wood chips, asphalt, coal, and coke, at low cost.

Commercial river traffic tends to fluctuate with the markets for such commodities. Net tonnage of river freight traffic grew from 26,006,000 tons in 1981 to 47,289,000 tons in 1988, then fell in 1989 to 43,452,600 tons. By 1992, the traffic had grown again to 46,167,000 tons.[26]

River traffic provides access to international markets via the Tennessee-Tombigbee Waterway, a 470-mile-long canal extending from Pickwick Reservoir on the Tennessee-Mississippi border to Mobile, Alabama, a port on the Gulf Coast.[27] Before the opening of this waterway in 1985, barges could reach the Gulf only by traveling the length of the Tennessee River to its juncture with the Ohio and then down the Ohio and the Mississippi to New Orleans. The "Tenn-Tom" reduced the distance to the Gulf by 882 miles.[28]

Barges use fuel efficiently and are a relatively minor source of pollution. Thus, given that a system of locks and canals is already in place, they have important advantages over other less efficient and more polluting forms of transportation— especially truck transportation. Barge traffic has, however, one grave drawback from an ecological point of view: it facilitates the exploitation of Southern Appalachian forests (see Chapter Three). The advantages of any attempt to increase river traffic must therefore be weighed against the disadvantage of increased deforestation.

Several such attempts are under consideration. The locks at the three big dams above Chattanooga (Chickamauga, Watts Bar, and Fort Loudoun) are all small, old, and deteriorating. While locks lower down the river are six hundred feet long and 110 feet wide, these three are only 360 feet long and sixty feet wide. They can only accom- modate one barge at a time, whereas the newer locks below Chattanooga can accom- modate eight.[29] Consequently, the Army Corps of Engineers and TVA are studying the possibility of enlarging the old locks—especially the decrepit ones at Chickamauga Dam. If the locks are enlarged, pressure to cut the forests may increase.

Trains

Civilization is shaped in part by the possibilities of transportation, and transporta- tion in turn is sculpted by regional geography. The early economic development of West Tennessee, for example, was based largely on Mississippi river traffic. But the swifter and shallower rivers of Southern Appalachia, though serving as conduits for settlement, were not easily navigable and did not play as large a role in economic development. The mountainous terrain of Southern Appalachia became economi- cally accessible only after the introduction of the railroad.

By the beginning of the twentieth century, the United States had the most extensive railroad system in the world. But now, a hundred years later, the railroads have declined and extensive sections of track have been abandoned or dismantled. No longer, for example, can tourists ride the Smoky Mountain Railway from Knoxville to the Smokies, as they could earlier in this century. The track has been dismantled, many of the rights of way no longer exist, and even the old rail bed is becoming difficult to discern as it winds its way through a bulldozed and rebulldozed countryside.

Yet, from an environmental standpoint, trains are superior in almost every respect to cars and trucks. Railroad tracks generally do not fragment habitats as severely as do big roads, or the canals and reservoirs that support barge traffic. Animals can cross railroad tracks more easily than they can cross big highways or reservoirs. And trains are more efficient and less polluting than either cars or trucks: *If railroads are used as a baseline of 1, studies have shown trucks coming in at 13.6 on diesel particulates, 12.5 on hydrocarbons, 3.7 on nitrogen oxides, and 3.6 on carbon monoxide. It is much the same when fuel efficiency is considered, with railroads producing about 2.5 times the ton-miles of trucks per gallon of fuel.*[30] Yet trucks predominate in the transportation of goods, and there is, so far as we are aware, no passenger-train service anywhere in our bioregion. There was some talk back in 1992 of opening an AMTRAK stop at Knoxville (and perhaps also at Sweetwater and Morristown) with connections to Washington, DC; Birmingham; and New Orleans. But AMTRAK has since suffered budget cuts which make this desirable improvement highly improbable.[31]

On a smaller scale, light rail lines could help relieve traffic congestion in crowded urban areas. The average daily traffic count at Interstate 40 near Knoxville's West Town mall, for example, has skyrocketed, rising from 24,170 in 1967 to 112,490 in 1994.[32] The inevitable consequence is frequent, anxiety-provoking slowdowns and traffic jams. Much of this traffic is due to commuting by lone drivers. If a light rail line or some other form of public mass transportation were built in this area—say, between Knoxville and Oak Ridge—traffic, transportation times, and fuel consumption would all decrease, the air would become cleaner, and West Knoxville's way of life would become palpably more sane.

In the meanwhile, a useful stopgap measure would be to dedicate certain lanes of Interstate 40 as carpool lanes (lanes which can be used during rush hours only by vehicles carrying more than one person). These encourage carpooling and hence reduce the number of vehicles on the road. Carpool lanes have been instituted with apparent success on some of the interstates near Nashville.

Toward a Healthy Transportation System

Any transportation system encumbered with all the side-effects discussed in this chapter is destructive to both human and ecological health. The challenge, then, is to construct one that is healthier.

The single most important variable in the whole thorny transportation problem is how much people drive. Even the most progressive technologies imaginable (solar-powered electric cars, cars powered by natural gas, fuel cells, or hydrogen) can only reduce pollution and oil dependence; they cannot remedy the broader social and ecological damage caused by the proliferation of traffic and asphalt. We will not, therefore, achieve a healthy transportation system until we can reduce the number of motor vehicles on the road and the number of miles they travel. Such a reduction, however, runs contrary to the inertia of historic forces. It will not be easy.

The most important of these forces is suburbanization. For much of this century, people have been moving in from the countryside and out from the cities to the sub-urbs, where they have come to rely more and more on the automobile. Unlike the farms of an earlier era, suburban homes lack any semblance of self-sufficiency. Their existence depends on a constant inflow of products, services, and cash, and a constant movement of people to and from other places: stores, schools, recreational facilities, and places of employment. And, unlike traditional urban homes, suburban homes are generally located far from these other places. People who cannot provide for their own needs at home and who live far away from outside sources have no other option: they are forced to drive—far and often.

This compulsion is seldom recognized. On the contrary, the automobile is usually touted as essential to our freedom. Consider this excerpt from the 1994 Tennessee Transportation Plan: *Our society is based upon the principle that people must be free to choose among its opportunities ... Adequate personal transportation or mobility is one of the basic requirements for personal freedom. The provision of such mobility can be a significant means for enhancing the quality of life.*[33] There is no question that mobility enhances freedom. But our current transportation system has diminished the possibilities for all forms of mobility (on land at least) except one: the automobile. It is now more difficult than in former times to get where you want to go by walking, taking a train, riding a street car, riding a horse, or bicycling—all healthier forms of transportation (in an ecological—and, often, in a human—sense) than driving or riding in a car. The diminishment of these healthier possibilities of mobility is a real restriction on our freedom. If we add to this the host of negative side-effects catalogued in this chapter, it is at least debatable whether our transportation system does on the whole enhance the quality of life.

This diminishment of nonautomotive forms of transportation is due in part, of course, to the distances created by suburbanization. If you live twenty miles from where you work, you can't walk there and back every day. But such distances are no hindrance to trains or buses. What prevents *their* use is a general disorganization and lack of planning. These issues will be considered in Chapter Eight.

But while twenty miles is near the outside limit for bicycle commuting, five or ten miles is a practical distance for biking, and up to about two miles is practical for walking. Yet even people who commute only these shorter distances tend to drive. According to 1990 census data, in Knox County, for example, 129,699 workers usually drove to work alone and 19,966 carpooled, but only 4,324 usually walked and only 153 usually road a bike.[34]

One of the main impediments to bicycling or walking is the road system itself, which is for the most part ugly, dangerous, and obstructive to pedestrians and cyclists. That problem, however, has a remedy: comprehensive networks of sidewalks, bike lanes, and greenways in all urban areas. Greenways, especially, can enhance not only possibilities for healthy transportation, but also the beauty, air quality, peace, and habitat potential of cities. A greenway is a linear park, often containing a path for walking, jogging, biking, or horseback-riding, that serves to link together more traditional parks, schools, residential areas, businesses, or other important destinations.

Greenways already exist in Chattanooga (along the riverfront and Chickamauga Creek), Knoxville (along the waterfront and up Third Creek), Knox County (between Knoxville and Oak Ridge along the Pellissippi Parkway), Maryville, Sevierville, Townsend, and elsewhere. The region's most visionary greenway scheme is the Great Smoky Mountains Regional Greenway System, a plan to link Knoxville to the Smokies and various other regional locations, including Gatlinburg and Newport, via an interconnecting greenway network. If the plan—which is supported by all the relevant local and federal agencies—can be funded and implemented, it will become possible to bicycle between these locations safely, enjoying the green countryside, and avoiding the nerve-wracking traffic snarls that plague Sevierville, Pigeon Forge, and Gatlinburg.

Still, it is unlikely that large numbers of people will soon forego the comfort and convenience of the private automobile, either for healthy muscle-powered transportation or for somewhat less convenient public transportation. The transition to a healthy transportation system will take time, for it will require changes in the way we think and, more importantly, in the way we live.

Suburbanization, as was noted earlier, has two consequences that practically necessitate the automobile: the decline of self-sufficiency and the increasing distances that must be traveled to obtain life's needs. Long-range solutions to the transportation problem must address one or both of these causes of automobile-dependence.

To address the first is to make home a more self-sufficient place—a place which we need not always leave to obtain food, clothing, education, recreation, or work. The farmers who first settled this land—and the Native Americans who preceded them—didn't need cars, because they could grow, find, or make virtually everything they needed close to home. Thus one approach to many of the problems created by our transportation system is simply to find ways to stay put.

Staying put, of course, cannot now take the forms it took in earlier days. But the principle is still applicable. Some people, to take a high-tech example, can now "commute" electronically, performing their work tasks through the internet from their homes. A simpler instance of the same principle, applicable to virtually everyone, is to plan automobile use carefully, reducing the number of shopping trips by bulk buying, for example, or eliminating trips to purchase one or two small items.

A more potent way of staying put is to move toward independent living. People who grow some of their own food or make some of their own necessities are likely to spend more time at home and need less from outside. They are also, if part of a family, less likely to need two paychecks, and so to have still less need of automotive transportation. Such efforts toward home-making and simple, independent living, though they may seem unrelated to the transportation problem, are in fact at the heart of its most hopeful and healthful solutions. They will be further discussed in Chapter Ten.

A second approach to the transportation problem is to reduce the distances created by the chaos and sprawl of suburbanization. Ideally, homes should be within safe walking or biking distance of places of work, shopping, education, and recreation. Where this cannot be achieved, they should be reachable by inexpensive, swift, and reliable mass transportation. Since individuals have little control over the organization of cities, solutions on this scale can be achieved only by collective political effort. But there is no reason in principle why such an effort could not, by ecologically and socially sound planning, reshape the senseless and unsightly crazy-quilt of the urban and suburban landscape, restoring a measure of efficiency, beauty, and reason. These ideas will be taken up again near the end of Chapter Eight.

FIGURE 12: Riprap at Melton Hill Reservoir. Though it may look tidy, this shoreline is biologically dead. A healthy and biologically rich riparian zone would be lush with vegetation, which would extend into and overhang the water. The stormwater pipe carries into the reservoir anything deposited on the nearby pavement. Riprap and runoff are typical forms of degradation associated with shoreline development.

*Woe unto them that join house to house, that lay field to field, till there be
no place, that they may be placed alone in the midst of the earth!*
                                                                    — *Isaiah 5:8*

Population Growth

In 1930, National Park Service Director Horace M. Albright rode from Knoxville to
Gatlinburg to inspect what was to become the Great Smoky Mountains National
Park: *Mr. Albright was treated to a wonderful show of native white dogwoods. The
countryside—both in the park and en route from Knoxville to Gatlinburg—was an
almost endless array of brilliant bloom flanking the road and making fascinating borders between fields or meadows and adjoining woodlands. For contrast there were
also the beautiful flowers of occasional redbuds and service (pronounced "sarvis")
trees, and millions of small spring flowers. After several miles of such scenes, still
some distance from the park boundaries, he exclaimed [to Colonel David C. Chapman,
the man for whom Chapman Highway was named], "Dave, this whole section has the
beauty of a national park."*[1]   What would he say today? That same landscape is a
tangle of traffic, foul air, screaming billboards, and tacky tourist traps, stretching
from Sevierville through Pigeon Forge to the Park boundary and then picking up
again in Gatlinburg. And not only there.

Throughout our bioregion, crowded urban scenes are becoming more common and
open rural scenes less common, as population increases. The growth is uneven—
slow in places, very rapid in others—but on the whole it is relentless.

Population growth exacerbates all environmental impacts discussed in previous
chapters. This chapter will analyze the intensity of the population growth and identify the places where it has occurred most rapidly and least rapidly. It will look at
some of the environmental impacts which growth must inevitably have on a region
such as ours, as well as some which we know it has had already.

While the title of the chapter is "Population and Urbanization," it could as well be
called "Increased Human Presence." Just as rapidly as our census population has
grown, so too our tourist population and our transportation throughflow have
grown. Tourists put the same stresses on our environment and our infrastructure
as do the people who live here permanently: they too need housing, utilities, recreation, and places to eat and shop; they too create garbage and pollution. They, too,
are part of the population problem, no less real because their numbers can't always
be tracked.

Population Figures

Our bioregion has historically not been densely populated. In 1910, there were only two cities with populations over twenty-five thousand: Knoxville and Chattanooga. Of the other towns, only Asheville had a population of over ten thousand. As late as 1970, only six urban places had populations over twenty thousand.[2] Knoxville and Chattanooga were over one hundred thousand (neither has reached two hundred thousand today), Asheville had slightly less than fifty and, and Bristol, Kingsport, and Johnson City ranged from around twenty thousand to thirty-five thousand. The population of the bioregion has, however, grown dramatically since the late 1960s. By 1990, when the average U.S. population density was 70.6 persons per square mile, our bioregion had eleven counties with population densities greater than 150 persons per square mile (the highest was Knox, with over five hundred).[3]

Significantly, those eleven grouped into four clusters: Knox, Anderson, and Blount in Tennessee (in another decade, Sevier is expected to join that group); Hamilton and Bradley in Tennessee, along with Georgia's Catoosa, largely a Chattanooga suburb; the Tennessee Tri-Cities region of Sullivan, Washington, and Carter; and the rapidly growing Buncombe and Henderson counties in North Carolina. Between 1970 and 1990, the four metropolitan areas just mentioned—Knoxville, Chattanooga, Asheville, and Tennessee Tri-Cities—all continued to gain population at a troubling rate.

Knox County has grown from 276,293 in 1970 to an estimated 357,447 in 1994. The Knoxville metropolitan area (Knox, Anderson, Blount, Sevier, Grainger, and Jefferson counties) was home to 424,586 people in 1970. By 1992, that figure had risen to 631,097, an increase of 44.3 percent. Just two years later, the same counties were estimated to have added another twenty-two thousand people. Since 1970, Sevier County, home to Dollywood, Pigeon Forge, and Gatlinburg, has more than doubled in population: 28,241 residents have become 58,184. Neighboring Blount County has grown from 63,744 to 94,565.

The Chattanooga area has also grown significantly, although Hamilton County has not grown at the same rate as Knox. Knox County's increase represents approximately a thirty- percent population growth from 1970 to 1992. Hamilton County's population grew from 255,077 in 1970 to 287,643 in 1980; but since then estimates are that it may have grown by as little as five thousand. The city of Chattanooga actually lost population during the 1980s, a period during which it had just begun to recover from severe pollution and urban decay. The counties around Hamilton seem to have witnessed major population booms, while the center briefly stabilized. Bradley County has grown by more than ten thousand since 1980. It is also worth noting that from 1960 through 1994 Bradley grew from 38,324 to 77,570. Rhea County and Meigs County in Tennessee, both on Hamilton County's northern border, experienced booms of greater than thirty-nine percent in the 1970s. The rate has since slowed, but they are still growing; in fact, Meigs County's population more than doubled between 1970 and 1990, in part because of development along TVA's reservoir system. Catoosa County in Northwest Georgia, immediately south of Chattanooga, grew 19.7 percent from 1980 through 1992.

The Tri-cities area in upper East Tennessee also showed significant population increase during the period 1970-1994. Sullivan County gained an estimated twenty thousand residents, Washington twenty-three thousand, and Carter eleven thousand. In the Asheville area, Buncombe County increased in population from approximately 140,000 to 180,206 from 1970 through 1992, and Henderson County more than doubled in population to 71,774 by 1992. Another Asheville neighbor, Haywood County (home to the infamous Champion paper mill), had a population in 1992 of 48,019, although it had grown by "only" a few thousand since 1970.

It has not only been the metropolitan areas which have gained. The 1980 national census revealed that over the previous decade every county in our region, from the most rural to the most urban, was more populous than it had been ten years before. Some of the increases were marginal, some striking. From 1980 through 1990, the growth continued in most counties, although usually at a slower rate than during the previous decade. And even though some counties lost population during the 1980s, the net change from 1970 through 1992 was still positive in every county in the bioregion.

In addition to counties which have already been mentioned as having doubled their populations from 1970 through 1990, there was one other which almost did: Cumberland County on the extreme western edge of the bioregion. Other counties have grown at varying rates, and some have hardly grown at all. Trying to identify subregions within our region, and to attempt to find demographic trends within each, is well beyond the scope of this study. Nevertheless, a few generalizations can be made.

Except for Buncombe and Henderson, the mountainous counties of western North Carolina have generally grown between five and fifteen percent over the last two decades. Some of those whose populations were small to begin with grew by only a few hundred people. On the other hand, Macon grew by over twenty-five percent, Watauga by approximately forty percent. The latter, not coincidentally, is home to Appalachian State University, and is one of the hubs of the Southern Appalachian ski boom. Even though these counties are still not densely populated—Watauga is the most populous with approximately 38,500 citizens—their growth raises concerns, because they are almost all within or adjacent to national forests or the Great Smoky Mountains National Park. Most of these counties have poverty rates of greater than twelve percent (Graham County has a rate in the twenty-two to thirty-two range), so the temptation to spur economic development by logging (see Chapter Three) or other destructive forms of commercial or industrial development is likely to be intense.

Every county in southwest Virginia experienced modest growth during the 1970s, and then every one lost population during the 1980s. Russell County declined from 31,761 to 28,667, while Wise dropped from 43,863 people in 1980 to 39,573 in 1990. Residents say that a poor coal market was to blame and that the region will rebound. Yet, whatever the reason, what has happened in southwest Virginia, the only large area in our bioregion where population has not noticeably increased, has not been depopulation; there are more people living there today than in the early 1970s, and projections indicate that stabilization is already giving way to another period of steady growth.

Other counties scattered throughout the region generally showed gains since 1970 in the ten- to twenty-five-percent range. A few remained at virtually the same levels: Hancock, perhaps the most rural county in east Tennessee, had a population of 6719 in 1970, 6753 in 1992. Unicoi County, a geographically small county on the North Carolina border, increased from 15,254 to 16,743 by 1992. But even that is a 10.4 percent gain. At the same rate of increase, Unicoi County will have a population of approximately 18,500 in another twenty years—eighteen hundred more people, perhaps 750 more dwellings.

Future Population Trends

There is every reason to believe that these trends will continue. In 1992, Knoxville was the nation's primary destination for immigration of any city. An incredible one hundred forty-one households moved in for every one hundred which left. On the same scale, Chattanooga was fifth nationally. Mild climate, a relaxed atmosphere, and a healthy environment for families were cited as some of the reasons.[4]

Once there was massive poverty in our bioregion, yet the percentage of families living in poverty in Southern Appalachia as a whole declined from twenty percent in 1970 to eleven percent in 1990.[5] All but seven of the counties in our bioregion moved from a higher to a lower category in the Southern Appalachian Assessment's poverty index, meaning that poverty was reduced.[6] None moved into a higher category.

The four metropolitan areas defined in the previous section are projected to continue to grow through 2010.[7] Not that there is evidence that growth will stop in 2010: that is simply a conveniently near and relatively safe target for predictions. Knox, Blount, and Anderson counties are all expected to increase by as many as twenty persons per square mile. (Knox is projected to show the largest leap—108 persons per square mile.)[8] At the lower end of the bioregion, Hamilton, Bradley, and Catoosa counties are also expected to add more than twenty persons per square mile. The same is true of Buncombe, Henderson, Sullivan, and Washington counties. In several of these counties, an increase of twenty-five persons per square mile is a net population increase of fifteen percent in two decades.

A few, such as Hancock in Tennessee and Graham in North Carolina, will probably lose slightly or increase hardly at all; but most are expected to gain in the five- to twelve-persons-per-square-mile range—not staggering, but steady growth.[9]

There is an emerging populous zone which includes Hamblen County in Tennessee and parts of three contiguous Tennessee counties: Jefferson, Greene, and Hawkins. From 1970 through 1992, those four counties grew from a total population of 134,013 to 188,019—approximately a forty-percent increase. Hamblen, a county small in size, is projected to have grown in population by more than twenty persons per square mile by the year 2010. Morristown, the economic center of Hamblen County, is located directly between Knoxville and Kingsport. If the predicted area of new growth occurs, there may be, in the near future, some seven to eight hundred thousand people living in a Tri-Cities area expanded to include the Morristown hub. Assuming that the Knoxville and Chattanooga areas continue to grow, an almost continuous line of development would then stretch from northwest Georgia to extreme upper East Tennessee, and beyond into Washington and Scott counties in southwest Virginia, which are expected to return to a pattern of growth after their losses during the 1980s. The two most important natural features of our bioregion, the Appalachian Mountains and the Tennessee River and its drainage system, both lie in or near the path of the development.

Effects on Flora, Fauna and Agriculture

As people spread throughout the bioregion, using more land, there is less available for other life forms. As was noted in Chapter Three, one of the primary threats to our bioregion's wildlife is loss of habitat. The Southern Appalachian Assessment notes that there has been a slight loss of privately held forest land in the region and that this is "mainly the result of the growing population in the Southern Appalachians."[10] As we noted in Chapter Four, large amounts of farm and pasture land, some of which are valuable to small mammals and birds, have also been lost to urban development.

Residential and commercial development are the most direct devourers of land. But to support more people, more infrastructure is also needed: highways, sewers, power stations, transmission lines, landfills, recreational facilities, government buildings, schools, and so on. (And, since local governments typically bill the cost of new services on an average basis rather than an incremental basis, those who enjoy these new developments and services are effectively subsidized by all taxpayers.)

In some areas, we are running out of undeveloped land. Even green space which is not completely used up is fragmented, and, as we have seen, many species cannot survive without large expanses of true, unbroken wilderness.

There is perhaps no better example of the perils animals face in our midst than the case of the beaver "invasion" of the Knox County metropolitan area in recent years. By the turn of this century, the beaver population of East Tennessee had almost been eliminated by the rifle, the trap, and habitat destruction. The beavers' defeat was most complete, of course, in the most developed spots. They survived in rural stream systems such as the Clinch and Powell Rivers.[11]

Yet recently they have reappeared in urban areas, and again find themselves in intense competition with humans. Often species extermination by people is unintentional; the case of the beaver is different. Beavers kill trees, and property owners do not like that. But their primary affront is dam-building, an activity which can, if unchecked, seriously alter the water-flow patterns in a community, flooding property and creating permanent ponds out of previously dry land (some of which will be stagnant and mosquito-infested).

In the fall of 1993, beavers began to build a dam in downtown Oak Ridge. The resulting pond soon grew to three acres, and stood twelve feet deep in spots.[12] For a time,

Oak Ridge tried to accommodate its growing beaver population. But ultimately attempts were made to relocate the animals. Oak Ridge, a city of twenty-five thousand where deer are allowed to run wild (usually in late-night safety, to be sure), is probably a more ecologically sensitive community than most. But even there, coexistence with some of the original inhabitants of this land has proved problematic. The problems will grow with the population.

Other than reducing their sheer quantity, population growth and urbanization have essentially the same effects on flora as they have on fauna. We do not "hunt" plants in the same way we have hunted certain creatures out of our region, but our development brings more species into immediate contact with the paver, the developer, the bulldozer. Anyone who thinks plants are not much affected by population development is invited to watch fifty acres of forest being cleared for new homes. And we bring with us pollution of water, soil, and air, as well as new competitors and diseases (see Chapter Three).

Urbanization and population growth also consume agricultural land. From 1986 through 1995, over six hundred thousand acres of cropland and pasture land were converted to suburban use in Southern Appalachia.[13] How much of that happened in our bioregion is not documented, but if the rate throughout the larger area has not been highly disproportionate, we accounted for as much as two hundred thousand acres of that loss.

Comparing land in farm use in 1969 and 1987, regrettably the last year for which figures are available, nineteen counties in our bioregion have shown significant declines in farmland; none have shown increases.[14] The counties showing declines are not randomly situated. One group lies in a broad belt extending from Chattanooga's North Georgia suburbs through the Knoxville metropolitan area. Another falls neatly around the growing urban area of which Buncombe County, North Carolina, is the center. These regions of agricultural decline include three of the four significant metropolitan areas in our bioregion—an indication of the role of urbanization in farm loss.

Effects on Air and Water

More people mean more cars; and unless we centralize business and housing areas and institute public transportation, those people will drive their cars longer distances. When fossil fuels begin to run out, of course, this will become a matter of extreme concern to everyone. (It ought, in fact, to be a matter of extreme concern *now*, for all the reasons catalogued in Chapter Seven)

As we saw in Chapter Two, *industrial* air pollution is generally decreasing. We can be pleased that our skies are cleaner, but hardly satisfied. Seven counties in our bioregion remain on the list of the 210 worst counties in the United States in toxic releases.[15] Four—Hamblen, Carter, Hawkins, and Sullivan counties in upper East Tennessee—are closely bunched in that rapidly growing area combining the Tri-Cities and a Hamblen County hub. In crowded urban areas, toxic pollution threatens large numbers of people with pollution-related diseases.

Urbanization and population growth also affect the water. Urbanization, or any population increase, tends to crowd waterways, denuding the banks and inviting erosion (and increased pollution and siltation). If they are inconveniently located in the way of new buildings, streets, or housing, streams may be routed underground through tunnels, or diverted to artificial channels, destroying many of their ecological functions.[16]

It is ominous, therefore, that three counties which are among the five most densely populated in our bioregion, and which are predicted to increase significantly in population in the next decade, are among those with the most miles of creeks: Knox and Washington in Tennessee and Buncombe in North Carolina.[17]

Urban streams, like any bodies of water, are crucial for floodwater management. They are not located by accident; they are almost always where they are because water (sometimes in large quantities) has flowed in that direction for a long time. If that flow is interrupted or carelessly rerouted, flooding may result. But if the streams are left to continue through their natural floodplains—or rerouted carefully—and kept clean without the banks being harmed, they can do their tasks very well.

Flood control is not the only benefit of informed urban stream management. Some others are more aesthetic, and are related to the need to re-create our urban places as centers for sustainable living. If streams are not stripped of vegetation, they can serve as wildlife corridors, sorely needed when urbanization destroys or fragments habitat, and they make excellent greenway connectors for enjoyment and transportation.

In the city of Knoxville, there is a walking and biking trail along Third Creek. Here one can see the possibilities for such a stream/greenway system. In places, there is enough wild space contiguous to the waterway for small to medium-sized mammals and reptiles to move with ease. But those densely vegetated areas, some wider than fifty feet, alternate with areas where the bushy corridors are no more than a few feet wide or are absent. And the creek is infamously dirty: foul to the nose, the eye, and the touch. In at least one neighborhood through which it passes, it has on more than one occasion become cluttered from bank to bank with thousands of refuse items ranging from soft drink cans to sinks and commodes to metal cables that create miniature dams by snagging branches and junk. Apparently the city is not able to enforce dumping regulations, nor regularly to clear the garbage out of one of the principle elements of its natural drainage system. Local citizen-inspired river rescues have, however, done much to ameliorate this problem. Third Creek is today a reminder that urban waterways can serve multiple useful purposes, provided that there is a strong commitment by public agencies and private citizens to keep them healthy and clean.

Groundwater is also vulnerable to pollution. In Washington County, near Johnson City, for example, the dumping of landscaping, construction, and demolition wastes into a large sinkhole has contaminated the groundwater. The Tennessee Department of Environment and Conservation recently issued notices of violation to the alleged perpetrators.[18]

Shoreline Development

Not only the water itself, but also the ecologically valuable shorelines which it creates, are threatened by expanding populations. The reservoir system created by the Tennessee Valley Authority's many dams is in danger of becoming a huge residential neighborhood rather than the largely green and blue recreational resource it has been until now. Rather belatedly, TVA is attempting to respond to the forces of change, for some of which the agency itself must be held accountable.

About thirty-eight percent of the reservoir shoreline is today open to development, either because it is privately owned or because access rights were purchased years ago. Of this, seventeen percent had been developed by 1995.[19] The percentage may seem small, but in certain places the visual evidence is already striking. Watts Bar, for instance, despite being lined with toxic sediments, is in many places becoming crowded residential development, a considerable portion of which is due to retirees seeking their dream home on the water. Much of the Fort Loudoun shoreline, near Knoxville, has already become so crowded, and the banks so denuded, that it is nearly useless as riparian habitat. At Chickamauga Reservoir, near Chattanooga, houses line the shore in many places two-deep.[20]

Unfortunately, as was explained in Chapter Five, TVA is deeply in debt, and is not popular with the current Congress. To raise revenue, it is considering selling or leasing shoreline property for further development. As a result, plant and wildlife diversity, which are already declining, will decline still further.[21] Aquatic habitats, especially those nearer shore, will be adversely impacted,[22] which is worrying in that TVA shoreline ecosystems support several plant and animal species that are endangered.[23]

Residential development along shorelines sometimes endangers wetlands and can adversely affect floodplains.[24] Typically, vegetation is cleared, and often the land, including embankments, is scraped. Banks are degraded structurally, their vegetation is stripped, entire stands of trees are uprooted, and erosion accelerates. It would be bad enough were it soil erosion alone; however, construction wastes also find their way into the water.[25] And after construction is completed, thousands of shoreline homes, sewage systems, and all the various by-products of human presence continue to pollute the river system.[26]

All this is to say nothing of aesthetics or recreation. Ann Murray, executive director of the Tennessee Conservation League, said of the proposal to encourage shoreline development: "We're going to end up with lakes being pier to pier and very little public access. It's going to affect wildlife, crowding, and pollution."[27]

TVA has recently proposed standards for shoreline development and dock maintenance at its reservoirs.[28] For example, residents could be required to leave a one-hundred-foot vegetation zone along shorelines—no mowing or tree removal—to slow erosion, preserve natural habitat for wildlife, and act as a filter for pollutants. There are several alternative plans, ranging from one which allows for little future land sale and controlled development, to one which is openly pro-development. TVA estimates that, under even the most restrictive plan, total shoreline impacted by development, new and previously existing, would be up from the current seventeen percent to thirty-eight percent by 2022. Were the least restrictive plan to be adopted, perhaps sixty-three percent of TVA's reservoir shoreline land will be welcoming houses, condos, boat docks, speed boats leaking oil, bulldozers, chain saws, and apartment buildings, and there would be virtually no restrictions on their placement or use.[29]

TVA asserts that if the most restrictive of the plans were adopted, virtually no new land would be sold, development would be carefully scrutinized and regulated, and some of the past ecological degradation would be repaired. However, that is not likely to be the plan we get. When TVA first aired its proposals, the Rhea County

Commission passed a resolution opposing the "wild" zone because they feared it would devalue property already developed and would discourage future development along the waterfronts, thereby reducing county tax revenues.[30] At a handful of public meetings, opponents loudly lambasted the proposal of a deposit to be paid by dock owners to TVA as a guarantee of proper dock maintenance, and TVA quickly took the proposal off the table.

The issue of the preservation of the Tennessee River and its reservoir system is central to more than one question about the future of our bioregion. If TVA proceeds with sales and adopts a weak oversight plan, it will have abandoned its responsibility to protect the river that it opened to these insults.

Effects on Natural Areas

Our bioregion contains a treasure that some would call intangible, yet which, if carefully preserved, can provide employment without destruction, while helping to preserve the region's traditional character. This treasure is natural beauty, the most precious examples of which are our national forests, the Big South Fork National Recreation Area, and the Great Smoky Mountains National Park. These are all endangered. Though we are beginning to remedy some of the pollution that has damaged our landscape for many years, we are now endangering it simply by being here, by being so many.

One need only drive through the old Wautaga area of Washington, Carter, and Greene counties to see what is happening. Where once there were broad, green expanses marked by only the occasional farm or gas station, there are now tracts for homes, small factories, truck distribution centers, and, of course, mega-convenience stores. (The latter are at least preferable to the gas station, fast-food joint, and package store being in three separate buildings.) And, notes the Southern Appalachian Assessment, "As the population centers grow, high density use patterns will creep toward the center of the mountain ranges."[31]

The problem of permanent population growth is compounded by aggressive marketing of the outdoors as a recreational resource. Until a few decades ago, Sevier County, Tennessee, was a rural county whose southern boundary was the high crest of the Smoky Mountains on the North Carolina border. The environment there has changed drastically, as is well known, by the Gatlinburg-Pigeon Forge complex. In Pigeon Forge alone there are 7,395 hotel rooms and over eight hundred log cabins and chalets.[32] And the growth is continuing. The gaudy sprawl which is coming to define Sevier County was until recently a single vein running along Highway 441 from the Knox County line, through Sevierville and Pigeon Forge, into Gatlinburg; now it is threatening such little-known places as Pittman Center, Wear Valley, and Kodak.

Pittman Center is an unincorporated community a few miles east of Gatlinburg on Highway 321. Its location, immediately outside the Great Smoky Mountains National Park, provides a fine setting for the residents, but it is also providing them with a challenge the older families probably only recently considered: development of golf courses, clubs, and housing.

Just to the north of Pittman Center, another off-shoot of development stretches from Sevierville to I-40 in the form of Highway 66. New hotels, recreational parks, and restaurants have occupied that corridor rapidly, and with a major theme park being constructed, it is likely to rival Pigeon Forge soon enough.

More recently, there are signs that development will turn west from Pigeon Forge through Wear Valley, a scenic, sparsely populated section of Sevier and Blount Counties lying hard against the Great Smoky Mountains National Park. It also lies hard between Pigeon Forge and Townsend, Tennessee, another park-access point which is beginning to develop commercially. The Tennessee Department of Transportation has announced that one of the principle roads through the valley will be widened at a cost of nine million dollars.[33] The city of Pigeon Forge will fund the engineering and right-of-way acquisition. Even if development of the valley is not itself imminent, Pigeon Forge clearly intends to foster its own growth by making it easier for tourists and others to find their way there.

Residents of the area and friends from the region have taken, and continue to take, steps to save some of the threatened land from development. The Foothills Land Conservancy, with the participation of thousands of citizens, had by the summer of 1996 purchased 6,114 acres near the Great Smoky Mountains National Park for wilderness protection. This small but extremely effective organization continues doggedly to raise funds, with the goal of establishing a wild buffer zone around the Park. It is too late to establish a complete buffer, but the Conservancy hopes to purchase as many reserves as possible.[34]

The Importance of Planning

It is obvious that if our region is to adjust to its changing density patterns, planning is necessary: planning at the urban level, as well as at the rural or semi-urban level.

The first step a polity can take to counter the undesirable effects of increasing population density is to attempt to stabilize the population. One way to do this is to provide skills training for residents, to make it more likely that employment will go to people already in the community rather than to immigrants. We must also utilize humane population control strategies such as education, counseling, and family planning to encourage "zero population growth" within the resident population. It is also important to encourage sustainable enterprises that are already in the community and, if it is necessary to attract outside employers (preferably employers in "green" businesses), strive for those which can use the skills already found in the local work force. Above all, we must not assume that community well-being requires growth.

As we have seen, one of the principle unwanted effects of urbanization is increased pollution. A city can use tax-and-fine structures to reduce pollution and promote clean industry; at the same time, it can use incentives to recruit environmentally friendly employers—not merely those which do not pollute, but those which are involved in "green" enterprises. (Examples of such enterprises will be discussed in Chapter Nine). Cities must carefully plan so that waterways are protected from pollution and erosion. In this context, we offer this note from a prominent business monthly: in 1995, Knoxville, Tennessee, had the lowest state and local taxes of any of the one hundred largest metropolitan areas in the United States.[35]

Urban sprawl can be defined as the unplanned and erratic spread of population, commerce, and infrastructure away from an original center. In geographical areas where there is ample room to spread, the typical signal that urban sprawl is approaching irreversibility is the dying of that original center. If a metropolis continues to sprawl, with or without a vital center, it can eventually lose the ability to provide basic necessities such as water, clean air, transportation, health services, and waste disposal for its population.

Thus far, no municipality in our region has failed severely, though, in terms of air quality, Chattanooga experienced a partial failure thirty years ago. Still, urban sprawl is detrimental to those living in metropolitan areas. As we noted in Chapter Seven, it requires the use of the automobile and the truck. More transportation using conventional carbon fuels and conventional engines means more draining of oil and other toxic fluids and, of course, more exhaust. More vehicles also mean more paving: more roads; more parking lots; less green space; more intrusion on streams, wetlands, and other ecosystems; and the destruction of green land that could be used for agriculture, recreation, or wild space. Urban sprawl also tends to diminish the quality of life because, by abandoning what is old in the city, it abandons what is traditional and leaves in its place only the sameness of whatever generation is doing the sprawling.

Most of the negative effects of urbanization can be reduced by limiting the geographic area over which the urbanization spreads. And it is not necessary for people to live unnaturally close together to resist the phenomenon (although it may be useful to discourage the desire to live in a four bedroom on four acres in the suburbs). Control of sprawl and its effects can be facilitated by providing incentives to reuse buildings rather than demolishing them and building new ones miles away, by encouraging a new transportation philosophy, and by reshaping the uses and locations of public recreational land.

One obvious way to combat urban sprawl is by revitalizing the older areas, both commercial and residential, of our towns and cities. It has already been noted that in the largest cities in our region—Knoxville, Chattanooga, and Asheville—city planners and the business community have cooperated on such projects. Chattanooga will be discussed in Chapter Nine. Asheville's downtown revitalization project has created a high-quality entertainment district, well-known throughout the South, and, among jazz musicians, throughout the nation. In Knoxville, the Old City has brought shops of all varieties, eateries, night clubs, and offices back into an inner-city district which had been declining since the 1920s. Life, art, and excitement have returned to downtown Knoxville, although the heart of the city's downtown business district still displays a depressing number of empty storefronts and underused office buildings.

Work is now in progress on Knoxville's waterfront development, a project to bring condominiums, shops, restaurants, greenways, and recreation space to the north side of the Tennessee River as it passes through the downtown area. This type of development, which centralizes rather than disperses consumer destinations, is in itself a positive step, an antidote to unplanned energy-wasting urban sprawl, as are major shopping malls and downtown redevelopment projects. But this particular project is not perfect. For one thing, it relies almost exclusively on new buildings rather than old. But then, heretofore, there were no old buildings contiguous to the river. The worst aspect is that the development not only stretches beside the river, it impinges on the banks, disrupting the ecologically vital riparian zone, and even extends fifty feet into the stream of the waterway in at least one spot.[36] This is, then, a mixed case.

Knoxville's historic Fort Sanders district is also resurgent. At the turn of the last century, and well into this one, Fort Sanders, named after a Civil War embattlement, was a solid middle-class neighborhood adjacent to the University of Tennessee at Knoxville. It became somewhat worn as the century progressed, and when the campus population exploded in the late 1950s, family homes rapidly were converted to student apartments by realtors who bought up everything they could. Naturally, little thought was given to maintenance of the buildings. Now many of them are grossly deteriorated, and many more could be soon. But Fort Sanders is not in danger of being abandoned. Rather, the opposite. Some property has been cleared for large, modern apartments—not particularly aesthetic, but a practical way of re-using inner-city space. Other houses have been purchased by commercial realtors, restored, and occupied by dentists, architects, attorneys, and art galleries.

Thus at least a few businesses and people who could have been forced out of central Asheville, Chattanooga, and Knoxville, have remained or have in fact returned downtown. These are small steps. They need to be multiplied by long-term planning for transportation, for zoning, for tax incentives, for power and water dispersion, and for recreational sites. If they are not, areas such as Fort Sanders will continue to be the exception and the nearby Mechanicsville area will be the more typical example of what happens to an older neighborhood.

Throughout the latter twentieth century, Mechanicsville gradually declined, until now many of its homes and buildings stand empty. Empty houses and shops mean that people and businesses have gone elsewhere. Some of the people have moved into public housing. Other people and businesses are occupying land which was once green, having become part of the ex-urban culture symbolized by the advertising sign and the automobile. The remaining residents now face the problems typical of decaying inner city neighborhoods: poverty, crime, lack of new investment, unemployment, and inadequate access to healthful food and necessary services.

A similar phenomenon has occurred among businesses along Knoxville's Kingston Pike: as the center of economic gravity has moved further and further west with the sprawl, businesses closer to the center of town have been abandoned and left empty. In part this is due to the development further west of shopping centers and shopping malls, beginning with West Town Mall.

Malls and shopping centers have in most cases been built as alternatives to downtown shopping districts. They provide many shops and services within reasonably easy walking distance. Most people (quite rightly) prefer not to drive all over town (or several counties) for shopping, eating, and entertainment. The mall is downtown moved to a different location—except for one factor: it is no longer at the center of things and thus cannot easily be reached by walking, biking, or public transportation. Instead, malls are designed almost exclusively to serve customers who drive private automobiles; they have enormous parking lots and tend to be located near major traffic arteries. This extreme reliance on automotive transportation compounds all the problems discussed in Chapter Seven.

Any ecologically sound urban design must provide for public and nonmotorized forms of transportation. Public transportation should, if at all possible, run on electricity, using the cleanest possible system of power generation. Chattanooga has an electric public-transportation system, and Knoxville is considering one.

The most energy-efficient (and one of the most healthful) of all means of transportation is the bicycle. Bicycle lanes for new streets should be mandated where feasible. With buses replacing many automobiles, older streets as well should have room for bicycle lanes. Greenway paths for foot and bicycle travel are also part of the solution.

Automobile traffic must be discouraged, but so should delivery-truck traffic. There are at least two excellent means of reducing truck traffic which environmentalists, carriers, and consumers should all be eager to explore. One is to build 'transportation parks' where truck terminals, freight distribution centers, and warehouses belonging to many trucking companies would be clustered.[37] Transportation middlemen and local distributors also operate out of the parks. Commercial enterprises providing services to the firms and their employees are assembled in the area: equipment repair shops, refrigeration services, tire dealers, restaurants, and so on. The trucks, the distributors, and the service people all have less driving to do. They consume less fossil fuel, they produce less waste, and they make less noise. And because they operate more efficiently, their goods can be sold more cheaply.

As an extension, there is no reason why several distributors cannot combine to load their goods onto a common carrier, thus reducing driving distances. This is essentially what happens now when one distributor contracts to deliver the products of multiple manufacturers.

Finally, land with recreational potential in an urban area should be used wisely. Greenways and small parks, for example, provide pleasure for a diversity of citizens

of all ages, but golf courses use land prodigally, require chemical-intensive maintenance, and serve a limited clientele. For many years, the Cherokee Country Club
and the Deane Hill Country Club and their golf courses occupied many valuable
acres just west and south of what were, even by the 1930s, established urban and
suburban Knoxville neighborhoods, forcing the city to grow around them. Such
space-eaters should be built away from the city's center, if they are built at all.

The impending development at Turkey Creek in West Knoxville is another example
of poor urban planning. When Interstate 40 came to Knoxville, commercial centers,
small at first, began to grow up around the interchanges. Two of those interchanges, then distant from the city limits, were Campbell Station Road and Lovell
Road. But over the next twenty years, Knoxville developed steadily in their direction, incorporating land along the way, until the city limits reached just beyond
Lovell Road, the nearer of the two.

With the expansions came new roads. Parkside Drive was built as an east-west corridor, extending out to Lovell Road, beyond which lies a twenty-two-acre functioning wetland, the largest left in Knox County, situated within a larger complex of several wetlands. In 1996, to accommodate still further development, the Knoxville
City Council adopted a plan to extend Parkside Drive over or through (the cheaper
and thus preferred method) the wetland. But Tennessee Department of
Environment and Conservation staffer Paul Stodola, writing of the importance of
the Turkey Creek Wetlands for flood control and filtering urban runoff, questioned
why, in plans for the development, the wetlands were not taken into consideration:
"A route for this *additional* thoroughfare should have been planned around the wetlands! We find the City of Knoxville extremely deficient in environmental planning
in respect to this project."[38]

The city administration and a majority of the Council are favorably disposed to the
development project, which will enhance the city's tax base. The administration
has argued that the connector road is necessary to make the Campbell Station area
as accessible as possible; that a road in that part of the city is needed anyway to
reduce traffic on existing routes; and that due to current land-use patterns in the
area, there is no other feasible location for such a road.

Given conventional thinking (that commercial development is something to be
judged on the basis of quantity, that urban sprawl is acceptable although regret-
table, and that commercial development always rates a higher priority than ecology) construction of the road may seem warranted—even though, in fact, it will not

relieve the area's traffic problems.[39]   But from the viewpoint of ecological health, the road and the associated new development are beyond justification. Unfortunately, until city governments learn to incorporate ecological values into planning and decision-making, the land will continue to suffer such insults.

We have discussed planning issues at the urban level and the regional level. What about the rural areas which population growth is threatening to engulf? Let us look back to Pittman Center, near Gatlinburg and Pigeon Forge. Most of the citizens of Pittman Center do not want their town to be overrun by the same commercialization, at least not without a say in the process and the product. Thus, the community has been working with the East Tennessee Community Design Center to review zoning ordinances, slope and soil conditions, water-quality and wastewater-treatment strategies. At the heart of the project is a desire to "balance the demands of development with a desire to maintain the character of the community and the beauty of the natural and built environment."[40] This is a prime example of thoughtful planning.

The Upshot

The total estimated population of our sixty-one-county bioregion in 1992 was approximately 2,750,000 people, an increase of at least 230,000 (over eight percent) since 1980. In the four major urban areas, the increase has been much greater. We have chronicled the special problems of urban areas and the need to reinvent the ways we think about urban growth and urban sprawl; however, the severest threat is to the very character of the region. Our land has historically been praised for the beauty of its remote mountains and valleys, and for the breadth of its biodiversity. Now people, both residents and tourists, are crowding the land from the highlands to the lake shores. Outside of the Great Smoky Mountains National Park, the bioregion is almost devoid of roadless areas. The Park itself appears doomed to being fronted on its Tennessee side by a wall of development. And the banks of the reservoirs of the Holston, French Broad, and Tennessee Rivers are well on their way to being crowded with more of the same.

These are signs of excess, not of health. We must learn to accommodate the new without obliterating the old. That will require moderation—in our desire to reproduce, in our desire to attract tourists and jobs, and in our desire for ever-increasing wealth. The last of these is the topic of the next chapter.

FIGURE 13: Ethanol production facility at Marc Cardoso's EcoGenics operation in Sevierville — one of the bioregion's best examples of industrial ecology.

Take heed, and beware of covetousness; for a man's life consisteth not in the abundance of the things which he possesseth.

— Luke 12:15

Shop 'til You Drop

"Buy more stuff" is a theme that resounds across our bioregion from West Knoxville to the most remote rural mountains—and just about everywhere else. But, beyond our usually momentary delight with our new "stuff" (which all too often ends up collecting dust in the closet or basement), lies the waste, pollution, and degradation documented in previous chapters.

Our consumerism is a product of the growth-oriented economics prevalent in much of the world. The view that ever-increasing consumption is essential to a sound economy is now a dogma of industrialized and developing countries alike. Growth has become a new religion, and consumption so pervades our values that the term "consumer" is has become synonymous with "person." Consumption is our most conspicuous way to gain group-status and respect. We compete with the family down the street as we struggle for more than we had in previous years. Our happiness comes not simply from high consumption, but from ever-rising consumption. Last year's luxury becomes a necessity, while we pursue new luxuries.

Buying things has displaced many of the functions of neighborhoods, churches, and families. Today, family time often means shopping to buy children new video games and toys. Consumerism dominates our religious holidays. While our vehicles, tools, entertainment centers, and computers have provided some degree of independence, we have lost many of the benefits of working together and socializing with our families, neighbors, and churches.

The pursuit of consumer goods requires us to work longer hours. So we increasingly turn to convenience in our foods and home life, and our households make the change from "producer to consumer."[1] Even in the rural parts of our bioregion, once known for home-cooked country meals, many families have all but abandoned cooking from scratch, turning instead to packaged goods, microwave meals, and "take-out." Today's home no longer has a pantry, but merely a compact kitchen complete with a built-in shelf for the microwave. Once the producers of homespun crafts and handmade clothes, increasingly we consume the offerings of the chain discount store.

Local retail shops in neighborhoods and downtown areas are steadily replaced by shopping malls, "strips," and superhighways. The mall has replaced the town square as the American gathering place, and Americans spend an average of six hours each week shopping.[2] The places we shop are increasingly impersonal: Wal-Mart, K-mart, Big Lots, and the rest. As a result, we lose community. Moreover, while discount stores facilitate consumption by those who previously could not afford common luxuries, they promote products that may be cheap, but often do not last. The VCR we buy one year may break the next, and, when it breaks, buying a new one will be cheaper than repairing it. This only worsens the waste problem (see Chapter Six).

We live, it would seem, in order to consume. In the consumer economy typical of most industrialized (or developed) nations, two-thirds of the gross national product is comprised from consumer expenditures.[3] "Consumer confidence" lies at the heart of national economic policies, the stock market, politics, and the very consciousness of the American people.

The prime motivator of consumption is advertising. Advertising proclaims that there is a product to solve any problem—bad breath, pores, pimples, skin color, wrinkles, curly hair, straight hair, no hair—thus creating an endless procession of artificial needs. And advertising is ubiquitous; it saturates the air waves, assaults us from flashy billboards, insinuates itself into our minds from every direction. Packaging, for example, has far surpassed its original role of safeguarding our goods and has become a bait for attracting consumers. Four cents of every dollar Americans spend on products goes to packaging.[4] Our children are walking billboards of corporate advertisement, our schools a fountain of corporate thought. Schools use curricula developed by corporations, while corporate logos and advertisements deck school grounds. Ronald McDonald is prominently displayed in many of the region's schools.

Let It Grow, Let It Grow, Let it Grow . . .

Yet there are many who believe that this is as it should be. Mainstream economists hold that a free market economy cannot simply stand still. High levels of employment and wealth can be maintained, they argue, only by continual growth. Thus they maintain that businesses must grow and expand, accumulate profit, invest in surplus capital, and create new markets in order to survive changes in consumer demand and spending, the instability of existing markets, the threat of recession and depression, and, of course, competition from other businesses.

But continual growth requires an ever-increasing consumption of resources. The industrialized nations of the world, with just one-fourth of the planet's population, consume between forty and eighty-six percent of the earth's natural resources, including eighty-six percent of the world's aluminum, eight-six percent of its chemicals, eighty-one percent of the paper made, eighty percent of the iron and steel, seventy-six percent of the world's timber, seventy-five percent of the world's energy, fifty-two percent of the cement, and forty-eight percent of the grain.[5]

Moreover, the transformation from raw material to consumer product inevitably generates wastes—some of which can be economically reclaimed and recycled, some of which cannot.[6] When nature's capacity to assimilate wastes has been exceeded, they accumulate. Even if population and current economic activity are kept stable, pollutants and wastes will continue to accumulate wherever our production of them exceeds nature's assimilative capacity.[7]

Most of the world's hazardous wastes are generated by industrial nations. Industrialized countries are responsible for ninety-six percent of the world's radioactive wastes, as much as seventy-five percent of the sulfur and nitrogen oxides causing acid rain, and ninety percent of the chlorofluorocarbons.[8] Fuels, chemicals, metals, and paper—the materials upon which our consumer society is based—are those that are also the most damaging to the planet. Extracting coal, oil, and natural gas from the planet persistently damages ecosystems. Burning these fossil fuels produces a large portion of the world's air pollution. Yet we burn them with few scruples. Half of all American households can brag that they have two cars to fill their two-car garages.[9] Passenger cars consume about one-fourth of the world's oil each year, while their manufacture requires additional energy.[10] In the U.S., oil refining is the most energy-intensive industry and the fourth largest generator of toxic emissions.[11]

Our endless construction in the name of growth also has significant effects. Buildings consume one sixth to one half of the physical resources we use.[12] About forty percent of the materials that enter the global economy go into the construction of buildings; each year, some three billion tons of raw materials are converted into the foundations, walls, pipes, and panels that we call our homes and offices.[13]

Current tenets of business economics do not consider the necessity of biodiversity, the limits of the planet's carrying capacity, or ecosystem health. Our economy—regional, national, and international—operates blindly from the dogma that money and growth can overcome all ecological constraints—and social constraints as well.

The Haves and Have Nots

The growth economy is also creating a dichotomy of "haves and have-nots." The gross national products of two-thirds of the world's nations are lower than the value of worldwide sales of luxury goods. The world's average annual income, amounting to about five thousand dollars, is below the U.S. poverty line.[14]

Though in this country the Gross National Product (GNP) has grown tremendously since World War II, the gap between the wealthy and the poor has grown with it. There has been a dramatic and undeniable shift of wealth from the bottom to the top classes of the U.S. economy. According to the U.S. Census Bureau, in 1970, the bottom twenty percent of U.S. families received only 5.4 percent of the income, while the top five percent received 15.6 percent. By 1994, the bottom fifth's share of income decreased to 4.2 percent, while the top five percent had increased its share to 20.1 percent. The disparity between blue-collar workers and white-collar management continues to grow. Twenty years ago corporate executives were making approximately thirty-five times as much as the average manufacturing employee. Now they make 150 times as much.[15]

Despite the growing income gap, and despite this nation's heritage of strong workers'-rights movements, labor activity has declined. In 1970, some 2.5 million workers nationwide participated in some form of work stoppage. In 1993, this number dropped to less than two hundred thousand.[16] In much of the South, labor has historically been still weaker, enabling the region to attract large manufacturing companies in search of "contented" workers.

The economy of the Southern Appalachian mountains has been historically distinguished by absentee land ownership of coal mines, timber stands, and industry. Chemical refineries and other industries, including a wide range of manufacturing facilities, have been attracted to the region's low-wage workers and low land prices. Once a rich agricultural region yielding a variety of produce and grain, today Southern Appalachia has only a small and declining agriculture, relying rely mainly on cattle and tobacco (see Chapter Four).[17]

Yet most of our bioregion has seen steady economic growth in recent years, especially in the service sector. Poverty (with its attendant lack of social services, economic opportunities, and capital accessibility) still lingers in the Appalachian Mountains, but is increasingly limited to isolated pockets.[18] One historical reason for this poverty was the "colonial" nature of the region, whose vast timber and mining resources have been held mainly by large absentee landowners and mineral and timber corporations. One of the most important documents for understanding this history is the Appalachia Land Ownership Study (ALOS).[19] This study analyzed property-tax records and similar accountings from eighty counties, gathering data on over twenty million acres, including thirteen million acres of surface rights and seven million acres of mineral rights.[20]

A key finding was that only one percent of the local population, along with absentee landholders, corporations, and government agencies, controlled at least fifty-three percent of the total land surface in the eighty counties. Therefore, the remaining ninety-nine percent of the population owed, at most, forty-seven percent of the land. Of the twenty million acres of land and minerals owned by over thirty thousand owners in the survey, forty-one percent (over eight million acres) were held by only fifty private owners and ten government agencies.

Of the thirteen million acres of surface sampled, seventy-two percent were owned by absentee owners, forty-seven percent by out-of-state owners, and twenty-five percent by owners residing out of the county of their holdings, but within the state. The top one percent of the owners in the sample owned forty-four percent of the land. This figure is more than 1,400 times what was owned by the bottom one percent of the owners in to sample. The top five percent owned sixty-two percent of the land, in contrast to the bottom five percent who owned 0.25 percent. The study further determined that the top half of the landholders owned ninety-four percent of the land, while the bottom half controlled under six percent.

The study concluded that absentee ownership and concentrated land ownership have shifted natural resource capital away from those who live in the Appalachian area: "...through control of the region's land and natural resources, these forces prevent the formation of the indigenous financial control and other requisites for economic development. For development to occur, in this view, strategies must be developed that deal with the problems of ownership and control of land and mineral resources."[21]

Employment in Forestry and Farming

Close to 9,300 jobs in the East Tennessee region are tied to the forest-products industry, including sawmills and planing mills, as well as the production of wood furniture, cabinets, hardwood flooring, paperboard containers, and stationery.[22] But farming and forestry workers, like workers in the manufacturing sector, are losing their jobs to technology. While agriculture, forestry, and fishing in the state are projected to grow by 14.7 percent between 1990 and 2005 (an addition of 4,765 jobs), the percent of total employment will fall from 1.4 to 1.3 percent because of the growth of other occupational groups. Moreover, higher productivity in farming and forestry methods will require less land per unit output and therefore less labor. The trend toward fewer and larger farms will continue to result in fewer farm operator positions, while growth in the sector will be largely in such jobs as gardener and groundskeeper.[23]

The national shift toward large-scale farming or agribusiness is reflected in the decline of small farms in our bioregion. Chapter Four documents the steep decline of agriculture (see especially Table 4.1.) Currently, the majority of farmers in Tennessee, as with other states in the South, rely primarily on a few limited crops for production—tobacco, soybeans, and corn (in addition to cattle). Increasingly, the small farmer is finding it difficult to compete with larger farms in the growing of these conventional crops. In the case of tobacco, there is also increasing competition from overseas markets.

Tennessee ranks third in the nation in the tobacco production,[24] and the tobacco crop consistently ranks at or near the top in cash receipts for Tennessee farmers. Yet foreign producers are putting increasing pressure on U.S. tobacco farmers because of differences between foreign and domestic burley tobacco prices, increases in domestic burley production costs (specifically labor, quota, and marketing costs), and erratic and low domestic yields. These effects combined are reducing the U.S. and regional share of the tobacco market.[25] Yet the annual worldwide demand for tobacco continues to grow at one percent, maintaining the market for American-blend cigarettes, which use burley tobacco grown in our region.[26]

Nevertheless, uncertainty regarding the future of tobacco is growing. So, since many small farmers depend on the supplemental income they receive from growing tobacco, it is becoming increasingly important to find viable replacement crops. Tobacco-production employment in the state is expected to decline forty-two percent by 2005.[27] As David Altman, an associate professor in the Department of Public Health Sciences at Wake Forest University, said: "No one is saying get out of tobacco entirely. On the other hand, the handwriting is on the wall. The farmers' dream may be going up in smoke."[28]

A recent survey sponsored by a Kentucky research center and the Bowman Gray School of Medicine at Wake Forest University indicates that young tobacco farmers are more interested in growing crops other than tobacco than older farmers. Moreover, young tobacco farmers would support increased taxes on tobacco if the money went to help finance changes in planting. Of the farmers surveyed, two-thirds of those under forty-five said they were "interested" or "very interested" in trying other ventures to supplement tobacco. When asked to identify barriers to diversification, seventy-two percent of the farmers surveyed mentioned a shortage of processing facilities for other crops, sixty percent referred to a lack of money to finance alternatives, and sixty percent cited a shortage of places to sell other crops.[29]

Tobacco farmers still benefit from price supports. According to one report, through the supports, the annual gross income per acre of tobacco is twelve to fifteen times that of an acre of corn or soybeans. The total value of these subsidies for tobacco growers is more than a billion dollars per year.[30] As the public grows increasingly concerned with the health effects of tobacco products, these price supports are likely to diminish.

Is There a Fast-Food Job in Your Future?

Different economic concerns trouble the urban areas. Corporate downsizing, movement of manufacturing facilities overseas, and a general shift toward service-oriented work are the economic themes of the 1990s. Employment trends in our bioregion generally reflect what is happening in much of the industrialized world: we are moving from an industrial economy to a service-oriented economy. Here, as elsewhere, technology is replacing workers: labor-based manufacturing sector has been beset by upheavals brought on by computerization and automation. This has induced a "skill bias"; fewer highly skilled workers have replaced larger numbers of less skilled (and lower-paid) workers.

Manufacturing industries, though still growing in absolute terms, are declining relative to other sectors. The reasons for this decline include diminishing and more costly resources and rising overseas competition. Plant closings have led to high unemployment rates in rural and some industrialized urban regions of the country. Many of the displaced workers do not have the necessary skills to find employment in the service or technology sectors.

In Tennessee, the *operators, fabricators, and laborers* group has the slowest projected growth rate of any group in the state: 9.7 percent, for the period between 1990 and 2005.[31] This group's total employment percentage for the state is expected to drop from 20.9 percent in 1990 to 18.7 percent in 2005.[32] According to the

Tennessee Department of Employment Security, workers in the *operators, fabricators, and laborers* group are "susceptible to job losses resulting from more efficient uses of technology and production processes such as computer-integrated production processes."[33]

The volatility of the manufacturing sector produces swings of euphoria and insecurity. In early December 1996, for example, it was announced that Alpine Industries would locate a manufacturing plant and corporate headquarters in Greene County, Tennessee. This facility, which is to manufacture air-purification systems, will employ a reported 2,700.[34] Just the day before, however, Philips Electronics had sold its Green County facility to GC Capital. The sale left uncertain the fate of Phillips' employees, who numbered some 2,300 during peak production periods.[35]

Yet, despite its volatility, the region's manufacturing sector is strong relative to the nation as a whole. Tennessee's total employment is expected to grow 23.2 percent between 1990 and 2005, nearly three percentage points higher than the expected national average growth rate of 20.5 percent.[36] This higher growth rate is at least in part attributable to Tennessee's strong goods-producing sector.[37] Tennessee's manufacturing sector is expected to grow by 9.0 percent from 1990 to 2005, while, nationally, this sector is forecast to grow by only 0.2 percent during the same period.

Agriculture is expected to grow by 7.5 percent between 1990 and 2005, and construction by 11.6 percent, while mining should show a significant drop in employment, down 25.5 percent by 2005 (coal mining alone is expected to decline by 56.6 percent).[38] The state's once active textile industry will continue to decline, with employment in apparel and textile products decreasing by 11.3 percent between 1990 and 2005, leather and leather products declining 52.9 percent during the same period and textile mill products declining by eleven percent.[39]

As with the rest of the nation, the most noteworthy employment trend in our bioregion is the rise in the service industry. Between 1990 and 2005, it is expected that employment in the service sector in Tennessee will rise by 28.5 percent, surpassing even the national growth in this sector, which is anticipated to be about 26.6 percent by 2005.[40] The service sector is made up of such industries as transportation, communications, and utilities; wholesale trade; retail trade; finance; insurance and real estate; government; and food services. It currently includes nine of the top ten industries in employment in Tennessee. It represented seventy-three percent of Tennessee's employment in 1990 and is expected to grow to seventy-six percent of total employment by the year 2005— and to include all ten of the top ten industries in the state by that year.[41]

Health services, educational services, and self-employed workers hold the top three rankings in terms of numbers of employees in the service arena for 1990 and in the projections for 2005. These three industries have a substantial number of highly paid employees, from managers and doctors to teachers and other educators. However, the fourth-ranked employer in the sector is eating and drinking places, while food stores and general merchandise stores rank eighth and ninth respectively (general merchandise stores ranked eleventh in 1990, but are expected to move to ninth by 2005).[42] Thus, three of Tennessee's ten largest industries in 2005 will be those which traditionally hire the lowest-paid workers—from burger flippers to bag clerks. Moreover, in terms of employment numbers, eating and drinking places are expected to rank third in the top ten industries in the state by increases in actual employment from 1990 to 2005.[43]

An encouraging employment outlook for the state, at least in terms of employee skill requirements (and, we may hope, corresponding pay levels), is that of the top twenty rapidly expanding occupations, fourteen require training levels beyond a high school education, while eleven of the top twenty are in the professional, paraprofessional, and technical group. The occupational groups usually regarded as requiring the most education, including professional; paraprofessional; technical; and executive, administrative, and managerial jobs, are expected to show a combined increase in percent of total employment from 24.1 percent in 1990 to 26.7 percent in 2005.[44]

According to research conducted through the 21st Century Jobs Initiative, a ten-month project funded through a grant from the U.S. Department of Energy, eight primary industries drive economic growth in the East Tennessee region. The 1995 project found that five of these eight economic engines are weakening. The eight economic engines identified by the initiative are: apparel, automotive, business services, food products, forest products, metals and materials, technology, and tourism.[45] Consultants working on the initiative identified technology, business services, and tourism as the areas where employment is on the rise.

DRI-McGraw Hill, one of the consultant groups, forecasts a decline in manufacturing jobs in the near future, with moderate growth in service jobs.[46] The resulting impact for the region will be slow growth in wage and salary income. In 1993, twenty-one percent of the jobs in the region were in the manufacturing sector and twenty-six percent in the service sector. DRI-McGraw Hill predicts that by 2004, only sixteen percent of the region's employment will be in manufacturing, while thirty-one percent will be in services. Thus, the study concludes, a greater share of the jobs in the region will be in lower-paying industries, unless measures are taken to change the direction of the region's economy.[47] Moreover, while many counties in the region are enjoying relatively stable employment, in some—Campbell and Cocke counties, for example—severe pockets of unemployment remain.[48]

One aspect of the 21st Century Jobs Initiative was to bring business and civic leaders together into working groups to identify the needs of industries. In a region dominated by DOE and TVA, two issues high on the list of critical needs were: 1) effective ways to transfer technology from the public to the private sector and 2) ways to assist businesses in converting this technology transfer to marketable products.[49] The study found that much of East Tennessee's economy relies on product development and conventional assembly, both of which are declining. Thus, the study concludes, East Tennessee needs to add more value and diversity to its economy, particularly in the areas of science and technology.[50]

From an environmental standpoint, little in the way of sustainability resulted from the initiative. "Overcoming opposition from environmentalists" was a common theme in at least two of the working groups. The forest-products working group advocated boosting the timber industry's image by educating the public (school children, in particular) about the "value" of timber-harvesting practices such as clearcutting.[51] The environment suffered from benign neglect through most of the process, with insightful comments surfacing from only one of the working groups. The tourist group cited the lack of a mass-transit system in the region as a deterrent to boosting the tourist economy. And it did recognize the need to protect the environment and quality of life in the region.[52] In this connection, it is worth mentioning that a recent survey of regional public and private sectors ranked "Environmental Services and Waste Management" as the most important emerging industry in the region.[53]

Government on the Downsize

One visible and highly publicized shift in regional employment is the loss of jobs through the downsizing of the Tennessee Valley Authority (TVA) and the Department of Energy (DOE). Overall in Tennessee, federal government jobs rank at the top of the list for declining employment. Between 1990 and 2005, federal government employment in the state is expected to decline by some 9,760 jobs, or 19.8 percent.[54]

The Tennessee Valley Authority, a significant employer and economic force since the 1930s, has seen its employment drop steadily over recent years while its debt mounts. In 1987, TVA had 32,731 employees; by November of 1996, that figure had fallen to 15,644—a reduction of more than half.[55] The sheer number of lost jobs has severely affected the regional economy, forcing family wage-earners to compete for a limited number of similar positions—particularly in high-paying managerial and technical fields—or leave the area to find employment elsewhere. Moreover, because of the importance of TVA facilities throughout the region, the "spin-off" effects have also been significant, as TVA contractors and local businesses feel the loss in service needs and thus declining business. TVA provides a number of non-power services, many of which have been or are being eliminated and will need to be taken on by other government or business agencies if they are to continue. Indeed, as this book goes to press, TVA board Chairman Craven Crowell is proposing the elimination of all federal funds for TVA, a move which could cost the region hundreds, if not thousands, of additional jobs—many in environmental fields.[56]

Approximately 18,565 East Tennesseeans were employed in DOE-related positions in 1994, with a payroll of more than $841 million.[57] Government cutbacks and the subsequent loss of high-paying jobs have plagued DOE strongholds in recent years, including the Oak Ridge facilities. There have been repeated calls in Congress to abolish the Department of Energy, and the debate is likely to continue as politicians look for ways to trim the federal budget. The Oak Ridge National Laboratory could suffer further losses in a restructuring of DOE. In the meantime, ORNL has been conducting its own "re-engineering" in order to improve its competitiveness with other national labs and private research facilities.[58] DOE announced in early December 1996 that 1,680 employees from the various Oak Ridge facilities would be losing their jobs.[59] Dr. Alvin Trivelpiece, director of ORNL, has remained guardedly optimistic because of recognition by the Clinton Administration and many in Congress of the value of science for the nation.[60] But, he says, ORNL is "...still in deep kudzu."[61] Deep indeed: these layoffs are a tragedy for science and for the future of our bioregion.

Sustainable Development

We have seen that the current economy, while growing steadily, is also in rapid and disruptive flux. Farmers and factory workers have become accountants, clerks, and waitresses, while TVA and DOE professionals compete for the rapidly declining jobs in their once-healthy fields of employment. Many workers still make their livings in industries—such as Tennessee Eastman; see Tables 1.1 and 2.1 in Chapters One and Two, respectively—that are among the worst-polluting in the nation. Such industries are likely to continue to pollute and certainly will consume natural resources, including land. While a service-oriented economy is in some ways less detrimental to the environment than heavy industry, it also means significantly lower incomes for the region's families, and it relies too heavily on unsustainable fossil-fuel-powered transportation (see Chapter Seven). All of this points to the need for new directions.

The goal of an economy that respects both ecological and social health is *sustainable development.* In 1987, the World Commission on Environment and Development published *Our Common Future*,[62] which contained what has become the most popularized and, perhaps, poetic definition of this concept: "Sustainable development is development that meets the needs of the present without compromising the ability of future generations to meet their own needs." [63]

Essential to the concept is the notion of "development," as opposed to "growth." To "grow" means to increase in size, while to "develop" means to make fuller or more mature or organized. While these terms can be, and often are, used synonymously, distinguishing between them allows us to emphasize economic improvements that are primarily qualitative, not quantitative.

The distinction is important for another reason as well. The ideal of "sustainable growth," often promoted by advocates of the current system, is a dangerous illusion.[64] Nothing grows forever. Healthy organisms or ecosystems eventually reach a state of maturity at which growth stops, though they usually continue to develop. A healthy human being, for example, stops growing after about two decades, but ideally continues to develop in knowledge, wisdom, and experience for many more. A healthy forest takes several centuries to reach maturity (a condition in which old trees die and new ones take their place at a more-or-less constant rate, so that the forest as a whole grows no taller) but, even after that, the forest changes and develops. Inability to stop growing is, in fact, a disease that eventually damages both the organism and its environment. The damage our economy is now inflicting on the mountains, rivers, valleys, and people of this bioregion is a sign that further growth would not be healthy; it is high time for that economy to stop growing and mature.

In a mature, sustainable economy, systems of production, distribution, and reuse are, like the mature systems of nature, organized cyclically, rather than linearly. They do not simply draw energy and raw materials from the environment, process these, and deposit them as unusable wastes back into the environment. Rather, the energy comes from renewable sources, such as sun, wind, or energy crops. "Wastes" generated by one operation become raw materials for others, circulating perpetually, like the biomass, water, and air of a mature forest. The aim of these cyclical processes is not ever-increasing wealth, but a special kind of dynamic equilibrium: health.

A sustainable economy would differ from the current economic system in a variety of ways. Rather than stimulating an endless sequence of frivolous and artificial desires, it would seek first to provide for long-term *needs*. Not that a sustainable economy would lack products, but its products would tend to be high-quality, low-input durable goods. Providing for long-term needs will, it is true, probably leave us with less to consume in the short run, but, in a healthy economy, the satisfaction currently gained through material consumption could be replaced by increased leisure, the enhancement of human relationships, and other nonmaterial goods. It is at least arguable that such nonmaterial goods are of greater ultimate importance than the continual accumulation stuff.

A sustainable economy would be largely bioregional, using local resources to supply local markets, and thus minimizing the environmental problems and energy waste that accompany long-distance transportation. It would, in particular, preserve and enhance regional forests and support a bioregional agriculture yielding a diversity of local food crops. This would produce local jobs and help to keep political power local, rather than dispersing it to big governments or multinational corporations, as the current economy does.

In a sustainable economy, repair, reuse, and recycling would take priority over replacement. There is, in the current economy, a distinct correlation between the manufacture and consumption of the most environmentally harmful products and the number of jobs associated with product manufacture. But this need not be so. Repairing products could create more jobs with fewer resources than would manufacturing new products, and energy conservation activities could generate more employment than investing in new power plants. It is already clear that recycling creates more jobs than incinerating or landfilling wastes.

A sustainable economy would also differentiate between physical goods and the services for which people purchase them. For example, more effective use of electronics can reduce our reliance on printed newspapers, magazines and telephone books. Housing, transportation, food, and many other aspects of our economy can be analyzed by differentiating service requirements ("the end") from physical commodities ("the means"). Simply implementing this idea with current technology could have a dramatic impact on our consumption of materials. Technologies already available today (materials-efficient architecture, for example, or the use of paper on both sides) could reduce the consumption of wood in the U.S. by half.[65]

A sustainable economy would preserve the value added to materials through processing, refining, and manufacturing (each of which has environmental costs). How well a product holds its value is indicative of its material efficiency. If, for example, a product becomes outmoded soon after its purchase because a better and cheaper model reaches the market, the resources, energy, and environmental expenses that went into designing and manufacturing the first product have been wasted. Products—particularly items like computers, whose technology changes rapidly—should instead be designed to be easily repaired or upgraded.

Looking at products as "service providers" encourages reuse or repair for additional years of service. Products can be leased, rather than sold outright, so that the manufacturer takes responsibility for ultimate disposal or reuse. This forces the manufacturer to think (in advance) about what to do with the product when it returns and to design the product so that it can be repaired and sent back to market or easily disassembled for recycling.

Industrial Ecology: A Recipe for Sustainability

We noted above that the plants and animals of natural ecosystems feed on each other and on each other's wastes, so that materials and energy circulate efficiently through the system, creating very little waste. The idea of an industrial system that operates on these same principles is termed "industrial ecology."

Producers in an industrial ecology seek to use as input the by-products from other manufacturing processes and, correlatively, take the responsibility of ensuring that their products and byproducts are efficiently used and reused.

We are far from that ideal today. The magnitude of solid waste disposal, by some estimates a twenty-billion-dollar-per-year business nationwide,[66] is an indication of the current inefficiency of materials use. Manufacturers can make any product that they think will sell, with virtually no regard for its ultimate disposal after its (one-time) useful life has ended.

Yet some industries have been pushed by regulation and growing public concerns toward closing the "industrial loop" and using materials and energy more efficiently. This is particularly true for hazardous wastes. Xerox, for example, has initiated the remanufacturing of toner cartridges and is designing more of its products to be "recycling friendly." Similarly, the 3M Corporation has begun using a formula that calculates the waste generated in the design and manufacturing of its products to help it increase efficiency and reduce waste.[67]

Some designers are beginning to view the industrial process as a closed cycle, with the manufacturer ultimately responsible for the entire loop—from input and manufacturing through the useful life of the product to its ensuing repair, recovery or disposal. By enlarging the scope of our thinking still further and considering the industrial system as a whole, we may find more complex and diverse opportunities to promote materials efficiency and reuse.

This vision is still lacking in most existing recycling programs. These typically concentrate on collecting materials from residences or businesses, which places all the responsibility on the residences or businesses and none on the manufacturers of the products they use. Many manufacturers claim that consumers prefer convenient products to products that are ecologically sound. However, in reality, most consumers want both. Shoppers do not want to think about the garbage or environmental harm that is produced from the product they buy; they simply want to buy it with a clear conscience.[68]

Many of the materials that are now landfilled or incinerated could be used as resources to revitalize declining industries. Abandoned facilities and workers who have been displaced by plant and mine closings could be employed in the reprocessing and recycling of these resources.[69]

One of the most outstanding examples of industrial ecology in our region is EcoGenics, Inc., in Sevierville, Tennessee. EcoGenics is the brainchild of Marc Cardoso, the former chairman of the Tennessee Gasohol Commission. The microproduction facility makes ethanol, which can be used as a substitute for gasoline to power cars and trucks. What is better, the ethanol is created from organic "waste" materials by a nonpolluting closed-loop process. Cardoso, a well-known advocate of alcohol fuels, engineered his own production facility and founded the associated Alternative Energy Coalition. For years, he has been researching, developing, and producing alcohols—experience that has captured the interest of media and garnered an annual invitation to Dollywood's Octoberfest events.

The EcoGenics facility produces not only alcohols, but fertilizer (comprised of high-protein, nutrient-rich slurry from the methane digester and spirulina algae that are used to process it) and food (tilapia fish that eat the algae). It can create fuel-grade alcohol at seventy-five cents per gallon, as well as organically-certified medicinal-grade alcohol. It also generates and collects methane gas, which can be used for fuel. All this is produced from what was heretofore considered "waste": agricultural spoilage, restaurant vegetable waste, organic landfill matter, and the like. Cardoso works with residents, community leaders, educators, and politicians to explore how his technologies might serve their needs, save them some money, and help preserve their environment.[70]

Another hopeful idea of industrial ecology is the eco-industrial park. In an eco-industrial park, businesses are located near others which can utilize their residuals or scrap materials in a symbiotic relationship: the by-product (or "waste") of one process becomes the raw material of the next. Such a system is currently in operation in the seaside Danish industrial town of Kalundborg, which has a population of about twenty thousand. Here a complex industrial symbiosis has developed over a period of about twenty-five years, as businesses have found inventive ways to use byproducts to reduce costs and comply with environmental regulations.[71] There are four enterprises involved: a power station, a plasterboard manufacturer, a pharmaceutical company, and an oil refinery.

The Asnaes Power Station, a coal-fired, 1,500-megawatt power plant, is the largest in Denmark. Typically, the efficiency of burning coal to generate electricity is limited to about forty percent, with more than half of the fuel's chemical energy going into the surrounding air and water as heat. By capturing this excess heat to generate enough steam to heat nearly all of the town's five thousand buildings, the power plant uses some ninety percent of the energy available in the coal.[72] An adjoining oil refinery (Statoil) receives twenty percent of its process steam from the power station, which it uses to heat oil tanks and pipelines.

Since groundwater is very scarce in the region, these enterprises (traditionally big water consumers) have tried to minimize water consumption. By using treated waste water for its cooling water, the power station has reduced its consumption of groundwater by ninety percent. A local trout farm also uses the warm cooling water from the power station.

The Statoil refinery, which manufactures a variety of petroleum products, also participates in this cyclical system. The refinery does not maintain a large eternal flame (a typical safety measure at refineries) to burn off ethane and methane. Instead, the flare has been reduced to a small "pilot light." GYPROC, a plasterboard manufacturer, and the power station use the surplus refinery gas as fuel. In this way, GYPROC has reduced its oil consumption by ninety to ninety-five percent, and the power station saves about two percent of its annual coal consumption.

The power station's scrubber, which reduces the amount of sulfur dioxide gas discharged into the air, generates nearly eighty-five thousand tons of calcium sulfate (industrial gypsum) per year as a by-product. The gypsum is then sold to GYPROC which uses it as a raw material, instead of importing natural gypsum (which would have to be mined elsewhere). The power plant also sells fly ash, the residue of coal burning, to be used in building roads and producing cement, thus eliminating the need to landfill or store the ash.[73] (TVA's coal-fired plants, incidentally, generate almost three million tons of fly ash and over two million tons of gypsum annually. But, though some of these wastes "may be marketed as by-products depending on their quality and market conditions," the rest, which may contain various levels of toxic contaminants, "are either disposed of or stored on the plant site in ash ponds or dry-stacked landfills."[74])

The Danish approach to environmental regulation contrasts markedly to the United States' "command and control" regulatory framework. Often in the U.S., pollution-reduction equipment is specified for use with each industrial process. While these measures have reduced emissions, the costs are high—about two to three percent of gross domestic product.[75] The Danish regulatory system, by contrast, is consultative, open, and flexible, encouraging businesses to invent their own ways to reduce their environmental impact.[76] Discussions between regulators and businesses are goal-driven and less confrontational. They use performance standards to establish the level of pollution reduction, rather than requiring a specific kind of equipment. This approach facilitates the kind of innovation exemplified by eco-industrial parks.

Eco-industrial parks have yet to become a reality in our bioregion, but there is talk of them in Chattanooga.[77]

The Example of Chattanooga

Chattanooga stands out as a hopeful example of what can be done simultaneously to improve the economy and the environment. Environmental problems came hard and early to the city; its air and water were badly polluted even before the Civil War. Coal mines, coke plants, railroads, foundries, and a federal ammunition plant may have contributed to economic growth, but they left the city veiled in smog, its waters fouled and ill-smelling. By the 1960s and 1970s, chemical plants and other industries had added dangerous new toxic chemicals to the mix, and Chattanooga's air was nearly the worst in the nation.[78] The early 1980s brought significant improvements, and the city finally met EPA ozone standards in 1991. However, the city still struggles with toxic waterways—especially Chattanooga Creek (see Chapters One and Six)—and an inadequate sewage system.[79]

Chattanooga Venture, a non-profit network of citizen groups, was formed in 1984 to foster involvement of Chattanooga's citizenry in charting the city's future. It instituted a public-participation process known as Vision 2000, which resulted in a set of forty goals for the city to attain by the year 2000. Among the most notable accomplishments of this process are an electric bus system, more extensive green spaces, the Tennessee Riverpark, and the Tennessee Aquarium.[80]

Building on the successes of Vision 2000, and again using the public/private partnership model, city leaders set out in 1993 to conduct another community-wide visioning process focused on the twin goals of economic development and becoming a "sustainable community." The result was another strategic plan, called "Target 1996/Chattanooga, The Environmental City." The Target 1996 plan includes ninety-four detailed recommendations, including steps toward a twenty-two-mile greenway system, an electric vehicle testing facility, a regional arts and cultural center, a national environmental executive conference center, and several other major programs. Curbside recycling and a continuing education program on environmental issues for teachers and other professionals are also parts of the plan.[81] Chattanooga is aiming, furthermore, to attract environmental businesses, reclaim brownfield sites in the inner city, and develop zero-emissions eco-industrial parks.[82] The city has also initiated two significant pollution-prevention programs. One is aimed in particular aimed at industries; it forces them to control the pollutants discharged into sewage-collection systems by requiring the pretreatment of industrial wastes.

Chattanooga has also embarked on the Global Action Plan, a campaign to encourage sustainable living among its citizens. The goal is to form a minimum of 640 "Household EcoTeams" comprised of representatives from six to eight households each, which meet to review household resource use, share ideas, and take actions which will lead to more sustainable lifestyles. A trained coach will provide assistance to each EcoTeam, and each team member will receive a workbook providing information on various aspects of more efficient lifestyles.

By 1998, the Plan calls for some five thousand households to be involved in an EcoTeam, with the ultimate goal of creating a mass of Chattanooga citizens knowledgeable of and committed to sustainable living. Results of the program will be tracked in order to verify increased efficiency in the use of resources and the resulting economic and environmental benefits to the greater Chattanooga region.

This household-by-household approach has been developed in twelve other countries, including Switzerland and the Netherlands. The Global Action Plan for the Earth, a U.S.-based non-profit organization, has partnered with the United Nations Environmental Programme and the President's Council for Sustainable Development to promote development of Household EcoTeams. Chattanooga was chosen by the President's Council on Sustainable Development as the first Global Action Plan community in the Southeast. Global Action Plan-Chattanooga is a community project of the Chamber Foundation and is partially funded by the City of Chattanooga Public Works Department. Additional funds and in-kind donations are being sought through foundations, business and industry and local and state governments.[83]

These are all remarkably forward-looking initiatives, and yet they must be viewed with caution. For one thing there are substantial obstacles: regulations regarding clean-up liability of brownfields make it safer to do nothing with these old industrial sites than to attempt to reclaim and reuse them. Moreover, traditional real-estate interests are uneasy with the idea of eco-industrial parks.[84] These obstacles will not be overcome easily.

Still more worrisome is the fact that the Chattanooga initiatives are based on a self-defeating assumption: they still aim, not for a stable economy, but for limitless growth.[85]

Obstacles to Sustainability

The transition to a genuinely sustainable economy will not be easy. There will be wholesale changes in industrial operations, shifts in jobs, and temporary dislocations of families and communities. The task is enormous and fraught with risks. It must be undertaken gradually, yet thoroughly. But the alternative of continuing the business-as-usual consumptive economy would be far worse, both for the ecological health of the region (as previous chapters have shown) and for its social health (since the current economy increasingly afflicts us with artificially-induced desires, longer working hours, and job insecurity).

One predictable consequence of the transition is that extractive and heavy industries will loose jobs and profit. Communities and regions whose economies are supported largely by primary materials production, such as logging and mining, and communities with a significant manufacturing base will initially experience losses as the economy shifts away from extraction and virgin-materials use. However, it is likely that far more jobs will be gained in energy efficiency, resource recovery, and public transportation than will be lost in these resource-intensive industries. Moreover, these new jobs and the economic benefits that accompany them will be more dispersed, not centrally located, as the extractive and energy industries are. Manufacturing that operates on recovered (recycled) resources, for example, will naturally locate near the local sources of these feedstocks, rather than importing them from far away.

One of the main deterrents to a sustainable economy is our current pricing structure, which fails to account for the full costs of the products we consume. We operate with what have been described as "nature-blind economic accounting systems."[86] Energy loss, extraction wastes, pollution, species extinction, the loss of virgin resources for future or alternative uses, waste disposal costs of packaging and products, and other forms of environmental degradation are considered "external" to the costs of production. While the costs of abating hazardous wastes associated with manufacturing are accounted for in the pricing of some products, consideration of these other external costs is minimal.

The short-term-payback requirements of businesses (and consumers) mean that products which are efficient in their use of materials and energy are often not considered because their initial cost is high, even though, over a few years, the savings could be substantial. This is true, for example, of solar-energy systems or compact fluorescent light bulbs (see Chapter Five).

The continued failure to deduct resource depletion in our accounting system inflates the net revenue of projects and thus overstates their rate of return. This in turn fosters misallocation of resources, especially overinvestment in the exploitation of nonrenewable resources.[87]

Overcoming our prejudices will also be difficult. People have become convinced that the global economy is the only way to sustain our high standard of living and raise the economic standards of other parts of the world. Since redistribution of existing wealth is impossible given the realities of current political power, many policymakers think a fivefold to tenfold expansion of the world economy is necessary in order to alleviate poverty and excessive disparities in income.[88]

But the world cannot grow its way to sustainability. The Earth is the source of all resources used to support the economic subsystem and the sink for all its wastes, and the Earth's ecological systems are stressed nearly to the breaking-point. It is possible that, in some respects, the world economy has already surpassed the sustainable limits. Thus, measures to expand on the current economy may eventually cause components of the global ecosystem to collapse.[89]

Public Remedies

Since the birth of our nation, government policies and programs have encouraged resource exploitation and the rapid expansion of mining and extractive industries through tax credits and depletion allowances, government support of research and development, exemptions from various environmental laws and regulations, and strategies to secure both material markets and supplies.[90] The assumption that these policies are necessary for economic growth or energy independence has been ingrained in our economic system. But a system we have constructed is a system we can modify, through the public process of democratic action.

The most effective way to reduce waste and increase the efficiency of materials use is to raise the cost of primary raw materials—especially fossil fuels—to account for all costs associated with materials extraction, processing, manufacturing, and disposal. The current tax structure encourages, and often subsidizes, resource extraction. Policies which affect pricing, especially tax policies, should be reviewed and modified where necessary. So should policies regarding timberlands, oil and coal depletion allowances, highway and hydroelectric dam construction, energy, solid waste, land use, transportation, government procurement, economic development, job training, health, defense, and foreign trade.

Preferential taxation, investment incentives, grants and other innovative means can be used to encourage or force manufacturers to design products that can be easily and safely reused or recycled. Consumers must at least have the option of buying products that are environmentally benign yet cost-competitive. Hence we must either require manufacturers, or give them incentives, to provide such choices. Similarly, we must ensure the viability of local farms and to lower the cost of locally grown, unprocessed food relative to prepared products imported from elsewhere.[91]

Sustainability can be encouraged by reducing income and payroll taxes and replacing them with taxes on virgin resource use, environmental degradation, and nonrenewable energy consumption. Since companies would be required to pay these "green taxes," the taxes would be included in the price paid for resources, products or services. This would induce companies to find new ways of manufacturing and distributing goods and services, while encouraging consumers to reconsider their consumption patterns.[92]

Existing subsidies on virgin resources should be phased out and tax credits for manufacturers that use recycled raw materials should be phased in, to give manu-facturers incentives to utilize recovered resources. A "primary materials con-sumption tax," similar to a value-added tax, might be placed on the use of virgin metals in industrial production, regardless of the origin of the ore.[93] It would be set at a level to compensate for the unrepaid environmental degradation caused by metals mining and would be dedicated to the cleanup of abandoned mines. Moreover, such a tax would encourage recycling and the use of recovered materials in manufacturing.

In short, raw-material production needs to be taxed, not subsidized. Moreover, it ought to be taxed differentially, depending upon its environmental impact. In many of our national forests, including some in our region, timber is currently sold below market cost, at a loss to the U.S. Treasury.[94] In a sustainable economy, this would not be so. All timber extraction would produce a net gain in public revenues. Moreover, timber logged from primary (virgin) forests would be taxed at a far greater rate than timber felled from secondary (previously cut) forests; timber cut using sustainable logging practices would be taxed still less. Real estate develop-ment, road building, and other practices that lead to deforestation would also be taxed according to their environmental impacts.

With regard to the national forests, federal laws encourage the U.S. Forest Service to promote extraction over recreational activities, because the agency is able to keep most of the revenues from timber sales. The Forest Service budget does not benefit from camping, hunting and other such activities, nor from the water, fish, and wildlife that depend on the forests. A system of user fees might help to foster these sustainable uses of forests. Forest managers who receive income from all forest users, including hikers and campers, will be less inclined to rely on extrac-tion of wood, minerals, and other commodities for revenues. Studies indicate that if the Forest Service charged as little as three dollars per day to visitors, it would generate more revenue than it does from timber sales.[95] This in turn could benefit many of the counties in our bioregion which have substantial tracts of public forests in their areas.

In all areas of the economy, green taxes would serve to internalize the environmental costs of production, encourage efficient use of materials, and discourage waste. They would give businesses financial incentives to find innovative ways to reduce pollution and meet (rather than fight) environmental regulations, while remaining competitive and efficient. European countries have already adopted many types of green fees, including deposits on automobiles that are given back when the car is taken to a scrap yard (which discourages illegal dumping) and taxes on wastewater effluent.

Green taxes could help to reverse the current trend in business to cut employment in order to improve the profit margin, forcing them instead to create new jobs in research and development as they search for innovative ways to avoid the green taxes. Moreover, incentives to improve energy efficiency and lower resource use may, in the long run, save businesses money and increase profits.

Such taxes must, of course, be phased in slowly to allow companies time to plan, invest in new equipment and innovate. Workers and consumers will also need time to adjust to changes in the workplace and new products.

Consumers will need to be informed about the extent of environmental damage caused by the production and consumption of the products they buy—from extraction and manufacturing to disposal. They will then have an opportunity (usually lacking today) to base their choices on a product's environmental impact. That much can be achieved by public action. But there is a further step that lies with each of us individually: we as consumers must take responsibility for the "stuff" we buy.

Small is Beautiful

We all have come (some of us generations ago) from rural roots. The traditional rural life is of necessity a life of frugality and moderation. We have also come from religious roots, and all the world's major religions—Christianity not least—condemn materialism. The current economic order is neither ancient nor permanent; only in this century have consumerism and materialism become central to our way of life. Thus, it is intriguing to consider that a return to family life, community, valued work, respect for skills, and enjoyment of nature—all of which many of us now miss—could result from greater economic self-sufficiency. Together, with local leadership and community action, we can begin immediately to create a sustainable economy. We thus end this chapter with a look at what a few people and communities in—or near—the bioregion are doing on a small scale to enhance sustainability.

The region has a long history of association with nature, through farming, hunting, and fishing. Traditions of bartering and trading of crafts, tools, and locally grown foods continue even today. Rural people throughout our bioregion have long augmented their income with a diversity of home-based or "back of the truck" businesses.[96] Garage sales, flea markets, crafts fairs, roadside stands still abound. More and more, however, communities have turned to big corporate employers in the scramble for economic growth. Often these companies are the pawns of huge and distant conglomerates, which care little about the traditions or the health of our region. Often, too, they produce goods through extraction of resources, either local or imported, at high environmental cost.

The alternative we envision is a bioregional economy that draws upon the resourcefulness of the people and the land. The human wealth of scientists and engineers who live here could be tapped to launch innovative ventures in environmental technologies (such as EcoGenics, discussed above). A sustainable bioregional economy would offer new opportunities for many nontraditional entrepreneurial efforts: materials reuse, sustainable lumbering, renewable-energy production, self-sustaining small-business networks, local organic agriculture, and cooperative marketing.[97]

One group that is working to promote these ideals is the Clinch-Powell Sustainable Development Forum, a regional consortium of community organizations, small businesses and public agencies working for sustainable, locally based development in the region. More than thirty-five participants from twenty different organizations have participated in the Forum, representing Hancock, Hawkins, Carter, Claiborne and Sullivan counties in Tennessee, and Lee, Wise, Scott, Dickenson and Russell counties in Virginia. Together they "affirm the need for development that is sustainable and beneficial for nature and people, for culture and community."[98]

The three development goals for the Forum are:[99]

1. *Create quality jobs through an economic life greatly diversified and locally controlled.*

2. *Create and support ecologically sensitive businesses.*

3. *Build skills and promote entrepreneurial innovation.*

Forum participants have outlined seven strategies, along with action plans for each, to reach these goals. The Forum welcomes local residents to participate in task forces to develop and expand these strategies for implementation.

The seven strategies are:[100]

Sustainable Wood Products: create and expand ecologically sustainable logging and value-added wood-products enterprises for Appalachian forest products.

Sustainable Home Construction: Create a network among interested businesses and develop markets for environmentally responsible construction and renovation.

Nature Tourism: Expand opportunities in ecologically sustainable and culturally sensitive recreation and tourism.

Regional Information Bank: Improve regional cooperation among Chambers of Commerce and provide support for sustainable enterprises by creating or enhancing regional information systems.

Sustainable Agriculture: Support diversified, sustainable growers and expand market opportunities for fruits and vegetables, locally processed foods, and specialty crops.

Land Resources: Perform a methodical inventory of land resources, natural resources, ownership patterns, economic resources, and land-use patterns to streamline sustainable and environmentally compatible economic development and form a private land trust.

Recycled Materials and Energy-Efficient Products: Establish a network of businesses to develop methods for reusing or recycling currently discarded products and create energy-efficient products.

More widely pursued, these goals would do much to promote sustainability. And there are other initiatives as well.

Hand-looming of garments was once a tradition throughout this country. While the skills of knitting and stitching remain popular, hand-looming as a form of economic subsistence was generally replaced by large textile factories that became a prominent industry throughout the South. Many of these textile operations have now fled to developing countries, in order to exploit the cheap labor.

In West Virginia, the nonprofit economic development organization Appalachian By Design (ABD) is helping to train rural women to set up their own home-based textile businesses. Women trained by ABD purchase or lease a $1,500 knitting machine and, working at their own pace, earn between $6.50 and ten dollars per hour.[101] Contracts are obtained through ABD with companies such as Aveda, Melcon Design, and others.

The women often care for their families or manage agricultural operations as they bring in extra income through their knitting contracts. ABD has also started marketing home furnishings and holiday-designed pillows and stockings.

According to the executive director of the Center for Economic Options (CEO) in Charleston, West Virginia, small businesses are becoming an important and growing sector in the economy of the Appalachian region. The Center cosponsored the first Appalachian Small Business Expo held in November 1996. The Expo was developed to assist small or micro-businesses in the region in developing new markets through a trade show and workshops. The Expo was also sponsored by the West Virginia Small Business Development Center. The Center for Economic Options has also assisted rural entrepreneurs with creating sustainable businesses through its Appalachian Flower Network and the Appalachian Knitwear Network. These networks promote group production and marketing for special niches.[102]

Another example is provided by Cocke County, forty percent of which lies within the Great Smoky Mountains National Park and the Cherokee National Forest. The county is classified by the state as one of nine counties in Tennessee that are economically depressed. One major reason is the pollution of the Pigeon River, which has hindered the county's ability to recruit industry and recreational tourism.[103] In response, Cocke County is formulating a marketing plan for the region based on "eco-tourism."[104] The county hired its first director of tourism, with the hope of promoting greater hiking, whitewater rafting, horseback-riding and similar activities—and not developing another Pigeon Forge.[105]

Yet another hopeful initiative is the Haymount community in Caroline County, Virginia. This 1,650-acre, environmentally responsible residential and commercial development will feature some four thousand residential units, retail and commercial space, a college, an inn, churches, schools, and community centers, all modeled after the traditional small-town setting. The community is laid out in a series of neighborhoods, each within a five-minute walk from the town center, civic greens, and other community gathering-places. It will employ a full-time environmental manager to administer environmental programs, including recycling and ecological education programs. Only thirty-four percent of the acreage in the community is planned for development, with the remainder of the land to stay in its natural state. An additional 50,000 trees and shrubs will be planted throughout the development. Construction began in May, 1996.

These initiatives point the way to a more hopeful economic future. The tenth, and final, chapter will provide some more personal examples of hope.

FIGURE 14: Solar panels provide all the electrical power needed in this rustic hermitage at Narrow Ridge Earth Literacy Center in Grainger County, Tennessee. Next to the photovoltaic panels is a greenhouse that provides passive solar energy to heat water and facilitate the breakdown of human wastes in a composting toilet.

Blessed of the Lord be this land, for the precious things of heaven, for the dew, and for the deep that coucheth beneath, And for the precious fruits brought forth by the sun, and for the precious things put forth by the moon, And for the chief things of the ancient mountains, and for the precious things of the lasting hills ...

— Deuteronomy 33:13-15

The Bankruptcy of Materialism

The ideology of incessant growth is thoroughly materialistic. Its aim is ever-increasing wealth, endless acquisition, production and consumption without limit. At its urging, we have defiled, disfigured, and degraded the once-beautiful mountains and valleys of Southern Appalachia until only tattered fragments remain. This materialism has, moreover, diminished us as people. Formerly relatively self-sufficient and independent, we have lately come to depend utterly on a vast, impersonal world economy—both for our needs, and for a host of artificial wants. Yet that economy is heartless—as many know who have lost community, farms, or neighborhoods to "development" or suffered the stress of accelerating competition. And it is also perilous; downsizing and the rapid and unpredictable fluctuations in markets and government budgets threaten everyone. Such injuries, both ecological and human, are a direct result of the supremacy we have granted in our public values to economic growth—a direct result, that is, of materialism.

But what we have wrought we can change, and there are signs that the wind is shifting. In 1995, the Merck Family Fund commissioned the Harwood Group, a public issues research firm, to study the views of Americans on consumption, materialism, and the environment. The study was based on a series of focus-group discussions and a national survey.

Here are its four main findings, quoted in full:

> *1. Americans believe our priorities are out of whack.* People of all backgrounds share certain fundamental concerns about the values they see driving our society. They believe materialism, greed, and selfishness increasingly dominate American life, crowding out a more meaningful set of values centered on family, responsibility, and community. People express a strong desire for a greater sense of balance in their lives—not to repudiate material gain, but to bring it more into proportion with the nonmaterial rewards of life.

2. Americans are alarmed about the future. People feel that the material side of the American Dream is spinning out of control, that the effort to keep up with the Joneses is increasingly unhealthy and destructive: "The Joneses is killing me," declared a man in one focus group. People are particularly concerned about the implications of our skewed priorities for children and future generations—they see worse trouble ahead if we fail to change course.

3. Americans are ambivalent about what to do. Most people express strong ambivalence about making changes in their own lives and in our society. They want to have financial security and live in material comfort, but their deepest aspirations are non-material ones. People also struggle to reconcile their condemnation of other Americans' choices on consumption with their core belief in the freedom to live as we choose. Thus, while people may want to act on their concerns, they are paralyzed by the tensions and contradictions embedded in their own beliefs. In turn, they shy away from examining too closely not only their own behavior, but that of others.

4. Americans see the environment as connected to these concerns—in general terms. People perceive a connection between the amount we buy and consume and their concerns about environmental damage, but their understanding of that link is somewhat vague and general. People have not thought deeply about the ecological implications of their own lifestyles; yet there is an intuitive sense that our propensity for "more, more, more" is unsustainable.[1]

In sum, this study documents a tendency in which we find hope: widespread disillusionment with materialism and a common yearning for a more meaningful and sustainable way of life.

What We Have Done

To the materialistic ideal of endless growth, we, the authors of this report, have opposed an ideal expressed by a cluster of words etymologically related to "health": healedness, haleness, wholesomeness, holiness, the harmony of the whole (see the Introduction).

An ecosystem that is healthy in this sense has sustainable integrity. It is robust and hale, beautiful and invigorating to the spirit. It preserves and constantly renews the original delight of Creation. It generates little or no waste. It is self-healing. It develops, but in a dynamic equilibrium, harmony, or balance. It does not impose its pattern on everything else. It does not grow without limit.

A healthy human society, in our view, exhibits the same sustainable integrity, the same absence of waste, the same delight, the same self-sustaining, self-healing dynamic balance, the same creative development, and the same sensitivity to the limits of growth. In a healthy society, the pursuit of material gain is subordinated to deeper and more wholesome values: the love of family, friends, and neighbors; responsibility to community; work that is meaningful, healthful, and beneficial to the whole; and respect for a Creation larger, more consequential, and more lasting than our material selves.

Our aim in this report has been to evaluate the state of the bioregion in the light of this ideal of health. The conclusion of that evaluation is now clear: the system of life that inhabits the watershed of the Upper Tennessee Valley is, in manifold and interconnected ways, unhealthy. The main symptoms are these:

Much of the water is polluted and burdened with trash or silt, much has been deprived of oxygen by the building of the dams. High in the mountains, the water is destructively and unnaturally acidic—as is the fog, snow, and rain. Much of our groundwater is contaminated. Many wetlands, nature's water purification systems, have been disabled or destroyed.

The air, though generally improving in quality, is still polluted with particulate matter, ozone, sulfurous haze, and a host of toxic chemicals. Indoor air is often more poisonous than the air outdoors. The noise of human activity is ubiquitous and inescapable. Our enormous emissions of greenhouse gases are gradually changing the climate—and perhaps contributing to increasingly violent weather. The deterioration of the stratospheric ozone layer is exposing most life-forms to increased ultraviolet-B radiation. We are slowly decreasing the oxygen content of the atmosphere.

Many native plants and animals are in decline or already extinct. The main causes of these losses are habitat destruction, pollution, and the introduction of invasive species. Multinational lumber and paper operations, converging on the region's forests as forests elsewhere are being rapidly felled, are likely to accelerate this loss of biodiversity. On a larger scale, we are witnessing the homogenization of nature; delicate, rare, and local species are increasingly being overwhelmed by tough, aggressive, "weedy," and globally-dominant species.

We can no longer, as a bioregion, feed ourselves. Our food is mostly grown far away. Many of the processes used in growing, processing, and transporting it are petroleum-intensive, soil-depleting, and unhealthy for both people and land. Our diet is unhealthy—not, generally, because of deficiencies, but because of the things we eat in excess: fats, meat, highly processed foods, artificial chemical additives, and pesticide residues.

The electricity we consume (often wastefully) is produced mainly by the burning of strip-mined coal. Coal-fired powerplants are largely responsible for the smog and haze that veil the mountains and valleys and turn the sky white in the hot summer months. They also contribute substantially to global warming. Much of the rest of our electricity is generated by nuclear fission, which creates long-lasting radioactive wastes and poses the small, but real, risk of a catastrophic nuclear accident. TVA's nuclear program has, moreover, accumulated an enormous debt, under the burden of which the agency has abdicated its leadership in energy conservation and begun to push for still more energy consumption.

We waste far too much. Litter pervades the landscape. Our landfills, already grown to the size of mountains, continue to grow. Mine waste, industrial waste, and nuclear waste contaminate large tracts of land.

Our transportation system runs on petroleum, which, though economically cheap, is socially and environmentally expensive. Roads and parking lots continually displace neighborhoods, farms, and forests. Driving deprives us of needed exercise, fouls the air, and makes us dependent on foreign oil. Excessive traffic frays nerves and increases stress. Accidents in the transportation system kill or injure thousands of people and millions of animals each year.

Population is growing rapidly in nearly all areas of our bioregion, compounding the problems mentioned above. Exceedingly rapid development is destroying or degrading agricultural land, shorelines, and the Great Smoky Mountains National Park.

Our current growth economy also exacerbates these problems. It is linear in structure, taking virgin materials as input and creating enormous quantities of waste as output, rather than cycling materials and minimizing waste, as a natural system does. Through advertising, it stimulates us to desire ever more, consume ever more, and waste ever more—hardly a prescription for health.

Some may object that this diagnosis is one-sidedly negative, ignoring much that is working well. It is true that we have not catalogued everything that is right with our bioregion, but that has not been our purpose. When a doctor diagnoses a patient, she does not enumerate all the respects in which the patient is healthy, but concentrates on the symptoms of harm. She does this not because she is cynical or negative, but because it is the injured systems, not the healthy ones, that need immediate treatment. Like the doctor, our intent is positive; we have examined the symptoms of dysfunction in our bioregion in the hope of motivating endeavors of protection and healing.

The New Environmentalism

Reflecting on the ills we have described, we see the need for a new environmentalism. Traditional environmentalism has had two main aims: to reduce industrial pollution and to set aside and preserve large natural areas. These aims remain important, but they are no longer paramount.

For one thing, current environmental damages are not primarily the result of toxic emissions by industry. Despite the recent congressional assault on environmental regulations, these regulations have worked—and worked well. Industry pollutes less, and, in some respects, the air and water are cleaner than they were several decades ago, despite rapid growth in population and productivity. Much still remains to be done (see Tables 1.1 and 2.1 in Chapters One and Two)—especially near the neighborhoods of the poor and disadvantaged—and vigilance is needed to insure that progress already achieved is not undone. But, on the whole, we have succeeded in reducing industrial pollution at the effluent pipe or smokestack. Further progress will involve increasing efficiency in materials and energy use and "closing the loop" to eliminate pollution and waste (see Chapter Nine).

The second traditional aim of environmentalism, preserving natural areas, is still critical, but it is no longer a question of setting aside large areas of wilderness. Wilderness no longer exists. What remains are a few large and many small outdoor museums that our predecessors had the foresight to preserve. It is now a matter of buffering these surviving natural areas from further degradation and of defending individual rivers, streams, mountains, wetlands, and farms from the development that threatens all the land.

The new environmentalism faces issues that are bigger, tougher, and more tangled in the heart of things than the traditional issues of reducing industrial pollution and preserving natural areas ever were. These more difficult issues are: excessive pop-

FIGURE 15: The mountains and forests of Southern Appalachia are a treasure worth defending.

ulation growth; extremely rapid, mindless, and unbridled development; and the unsustainable consumption of energy for transportation and power generation. Southern Appalachia and the Upper Tennessee Valley are being damaged more by the proliferation of roads, shopping malls, golf courses, strip developments, industrial parks, and subdivisions than they ever were by industrial pollution. This massive assault upon the land is inseparable from the problems of population growth and addiction to fossil fuels, and its consequences include virtually all the major problems documented in this report: loss of prime farmland, proliferation of waste, homogenization of nature, pollution of the air and water, and so on. The source of this drive to develop everything is our materialism. And the ills of materialism will not be cured until we find new ways to live.

In politics and economics, we must successfully resist what has so far been the irresistible momentum toward growth. Already this resistance has begun. Across the bioregion, small groups of citizens have organized to oppose road and development projects in their neighborhoods. These efforts, however selfishly motivated, represent legitimate human aspirations for open space and peace. We must organize to support them.

But opposition is not enough. We need a hopeful vision. Though we must resist *quantitative* growth, we can at the same time whole-heartedly pursue sustainable improvements in the quality of our lives. The chief obstacle to this pursuit, as the Merck Family Fund study demonstrates, is a widespread ambivalence. People are hesitant to address the quality of their lives (as distinct from the quantity of their things), because they are not acquainted with clear models of better ways to live. We contend that appropriate models exist, but they have remained largely hidden from public view. The next, and final, section of this report will describe a few of them.

Finally, we must recognize the mutual dependence of land and spirit. What we make of the land is a reflection of what we are, and the land in turn forms us. We have made of the land something confused, cacophonous, and ugly. The consequences—the resignation, cynicism, and silent despair—return to us, for we are not separate from the land. What we do to the land reflects back into our spirits ... and into the spirits of our children.

Protectors and Healers

It is not our aim to describe detailed solutions to the ills we have documented. We, the authors of this report, are a small group of volunteers working with limited resources. Our goals are, of necessity, correspondingly limited: to deepen understanding of the problems and motivate work toward solutions. The solutions themselves must be the product of many more hearts, minds, and hands than we can muster. Fortunately, many are already engaged in the work. In this final section, we describe some examples.

The single most effective *public* defender of land in our bioregion is the National Park Service. With the Park Service lies the stewardship of the Great Smoky Mountains National Park, a latter-day Noah's Ark, a last refuge of Creation in a roaring sea of traffic and development. The Park's founders were visionaries, some of whom foresaw this time of destruction and worked tirelessly to fortify the mountains against it. The National Park Service continues their work, standing at the forefront of efforts to preserve at least one small fragment of what once was here.

TVA, formerly much more active in conservation than it is today, also has an important role in protecting the land. Its River Action Teams have done much to improve water quality in some of the region's streams, and its Shoreline Management Initiative, though unpopular with developers and some shoreline landholders, is a brave attempt to stave off some of the worst aspects of the development that has begun to crowd the reservoirs. Unfortunately, much of TVA's good work, especially in energy conservation, has been crippled by budget cuts and by the agency's enormous nuclear debt. And, if current efforts to eliminate funding for TVA's non-power budget succeed, TVA's stewardship efforts will come to an end, much of its remaining public land will be sold to private developers, and the Tennessee Valley will have lost what was once one of the foremost conservation agencies in the world.

The National Park Service and TVA are only two of a host of public defenders and healers, from big federal organizations, like the Environmental Protection Agency and the Nuclear Regulatory Commission, to state or regional agencies, such as the Tennessee Department of Environment and Conservation, the Tennessee Wildlife Resources Agency, and the Southern Appalachian Man and the Biosphere Cooperative, down to local air pollution boards and solid waste task forces. None of these organizations is perfect. All are politically manipulable. But each makes, or can make, a significant positive contribution toward the health of the bioregion.

To the efforts of these public organizations must be added the vast number of citizen action groups which, in widely differing ways, help to defend the land. Here is a small (and very incomplete) sample: Clean Water Fund, Coalition for Jobs and the Environment, Dead Pigeon River Council, East Tennessee Vegetarian Society, Foothills Land Conservancy, Foundation for Global Sustainability, Friends of the Clinch and Powell Rivers, Great Smoky Mountains Regional Greenway Committee, Highlander Research and Education Center, Katuah Earth First!, Knox Greenways Coalition, Knoxville Interfaith Ecology Group, Narrow Ridge Earth Literacy Center, Save Our Cumberland Mountains, Sierra Club (various regional chapters), Tennessee Citizens for Wilderness Planning, Tennessee Environmental Council, Tennessee Valley Energy Reform Coalition, Tennesseans, Alabamans, and Georgians for Environmental Responsibility, Western North Carolina Alliance, Zero Population Growth ... and so on!

But mere defense is not enough; for, despite all the difficult stands being taken by these and other dedicated organizations, destruction is advancing on many fronts. And no victory is permanent. The forest we save from clearcutting this year may fall to roads and suburban development in a decade or two. Yet destruction is never permanent either. A forest will eventually rise again, even if it must force its way through concrete. If we are to witness such rebirths in our lifetimes, however, we will need practitioners of healing.

Hundreds of these practitioners are already at work, scattered here and there in the Upper Tennessee Valley and the Southern Appalachians. We can recognize them by their sense of individual responsibility; understanding of the interdependence of land and spirit; respect for physical work; defense of the heritage of neighborhood, community, and land; and recognition of the limits of growth. They are free spirits, living unconventionally, yet responsibly.

Living responsibly requires skill in perceiving and understanding the "hidden costs" of actions—the far-reaching effects of buying commercial supermarket produce, for example, or using utility electricity, or recruiting a new industry—and acting on that understanding to enhance the health of the whole. Though this is not easy, the difficulties are often exaggerated. Living responsibly does not, for example, mean living primitively, without hot water, adequate and reliable lighting, effective transportation, good food, or free time. Those who live responsibly can still enjoy all these things and one important benefit besides: peace of mind, the knowledge that one's living does not diminish the lives of others—neither humans, nor nonhumans, nor the land, neither now nor in times to come.

We do not make these claims groundlessly. The evidence lies in the accomplishments of those who have already embarked on the path of responsible living.

From hundreds of possible examples, we choose here to highlight a few:

Frances Lamberts, Jonesborough, Tennessee. Approached from the front, Lamberts' home seems typical of those in her neighborhood. But, from inside the gate, the charm and utility of her homestead become apparent. Lamberts, a psychologist by profession, has turned her lawns into gardens and natural habitats, reclaiming the productive potential of her land. She grows, harvests, and preserves nearly all her food, requiring only occasional trips to the market for items which cannot be grown or obtained at home. She accomplishes this feat of self-sufficiency with beautiful raised-bed organic gardens, a backyard orchard, small livestock areas, and continual composting of wastes. Like Lamberts, the many urban organic gardeners (who typically work away from their homes during the day) are providing more than crops; their efforts are modeling the methods of becoming more self-sufficient in food—while reducing the typical stream of curb-side garbage to an uncommon trickle.

Bob Grimac, Knoxville, Tennessee. Bob Grimac is the editor and publisher of *Tennessee Green,* a newspaper that offers timely coverage of socio-environmental issues not adequately covered by the traditional media. Distributed to some two hundred locations across the region, *Tennessee Green* brings new issues to light, provides alternative commentary, and facilitates communication of fair and factual information. Grimac himself walks his talk. He builds soil and manages wastes in the many compost piles and bins around his home, uses a bicycle for transportation (combined with mindful use of his car), and is a prime mover in such organizations as East Tennessee Vegetarian Society, the Knoxville Food Coop, and Community Shares. (WWW - http://www.korrnet.org/tngreen)

Watt and Jennifer Childress and Kathy Guthrie, Greenville, Tennessee. Dissatisfied with commercial food sources, and wary of the development and loss of regional farmlands, these small farmers produce weekly supplies of organically grown crops for approximately thirty families. Using horse-drawn plowing, rich farm-produced compost, and ecologically sound techniques for pest control and soil conditioning, they have successfully reintroduced traditional agricultural methods into a rural culture dominated by agribusiness. The Childresses and Guthrie operate a Community Supported Agriculture program (CSA; see Chapter Four) that provides families and individuals with locally produced, organically grown produce year-round.

Bill Nickle, Narrow Ridge Earth Literacy Center, Washburn, Tennessee. Nickle, a United Methodist minister, is the founder and Director of Narrow Ridge, a developing community of people who are creating homesteads that are energy-efficient, environmentally sound, appropriately scaled, resource-frugal, and aesthetically appealing. Whether built of straw bales, rammed earth, stone, wood, or even synthetic materials, these dwellings reflect a spirit of responsible, conscious living. From forty acres of private land and one man's dream in the late 1970s, Narrow Ridge, located about an hour northeast of Knoxville, has grown into several hundred acres of land trusts, a wilderness preserve, and a non-profit environmental education center that offers environmental programs, workshops, and retreat activities reflecting its commitments to community, sustainability, and spirituality.

Chuck Marsh, Earthaven Village, Black Mountain, North Carolina. The discipline that structures Earthaven Village is permaculture: the purposeful design and use of land, plants, animals, buildings, and infrastructures and the relationships between them to achieve balance, symbiosis, reciprocity, and sustainability.[2] Located about an hour north of Asheville, Earthaven is another excellent example of modern simple living. Marsh, and other residents of this developing community are working to reestablish and strengthen healthy relations with the land, their families, and colleagues. To prevent the degradation of soil and water commonly involved in the disposal of human sewage (see Chapter One), the residents of Earthaven use a centrally-located restroom facility equipped with composting toilets, instead of traditional bathroom facilities for each dwelling. This enables Earthaven to transform human wastes into safe organic fertilizer. Looking to local, natural ways of restoring holistic health, respecting ecosystems, and living within one's means, Marsh hopes to offer a model of alternative living that attends to both social and environmental responsibilities. (WWW - http://www.well.com/user/cmty/fic/cdir/list/Earthaven.html)

Avram and Jody Friedman of Friedman & Sun, Inc., Sylva, North Carolina. These entrepreneurs have created a sustainable business niche in a small town in western North Carolina by marketing environmentally responsible products and services. Low-toxic paints and finishes, eco-friendly personal health products, alternative building materials, recycled and tree-free paper products, and citrus- and veg-etable-based cleaning agents are but a few of their wares. Their many customers include local restaurants and businesses, evidence of the excellent performance of their eco-friendly products under demanding conditions. Their storefront sports a working prototype of a home power system that supports a television and electric lights. The Friedmans purchase, frame, and install solar panels for many applica-tions, and design and install solar water heaters. Best of all, they use what they sell, offering their customers not only value but first-hand experience. (WWW - http://www.digi-all.com/2316/friedman)

Anthony Flaccavento, Clinch-Powell Sustainable Development Initiative, Abingdon, Virginia. An outgrowth of the Coalition for Jobs and the Environment (CJE), the Clinch-Powell Sustainable Development Initiative aims to dispel the notion that employment is incompatible with environment. By creating new markets for locally produced, value-added products and services, sometimes with the help of micro-enterprise "seed money" loans, the initiative puts skilled people to work in ways that respect the Earth. Flaccavento is leading efforts to expand initiatives in sustainable forestry (involving horse-drawn logging methods and solar drying techniques), com-munity-supported agriculture, and eco-tourism.

Annie and Hector Black, Hidden Springs Nursery, Cookeville, Tennessee. Utilizing principles and methods of organic horticulture, the Blacks are raising and selling healthy fruit trees, ornamental shrubbery, and landscaping annuals and perennials. As part of their daily operations, the Blacks harness the power of the sun to light and heat their large greenhouse, which they built themselves years ago. Sunlight heats large water-filled barrels, which capture and store the heat, releasing it to the greenhouse after the sun goes down. Their operation demonstrates the efficacy of passive solar heating (the same principles can be used to heat a home) and enables the Blacks to grow year-round.

Leaf and Cielo Myczack, Broadened Horizons RiverKeeper Project, Chattanooga, Tennessee. Living aboard their twenty-two-foot ketch and traveling the Tennessee River, the Myczacks exemplify their motto, *"living simply, so that the River may simply live."* They are in the "business" of monitoring and protecting the health of the River and all its tributaries. Viewing the Tennessee River as the bioregion's lifeline, as well as their home, they challenge TVA, the U.S. Army Corps of Engineers, politicians, citizens, and communities to take responsibility for the life of the waters. Theirs is not an easy job; often they face angry opposition from those who regard abuse of the River as their right: polluters, developers, bureaucrats, and recreational (or, as Leaf would have it, "wreck-Creational") enthusiasts whose monster engines burn fossil fuel as if there were no tomorrow. But the Myczacks persevere. They also steadfastly oppose threats to the forests—most especially chip mills. By constantly watching, hearing, and (whether they want to or not) smelling the River, they have amassed a fascinating collection of lore and wisdom. If you see them, you will know it; theirs is the sailboat that travels slow, often with their kayak Feather trailing behind. If you meet them, be prepared to listen and learn; experts in their work, they are the most avid students of one of the biggest subjects in the bioregion.

Kathy Hogan and Bob Fairchild, BobKat Farm, Dreyfus, Kentucky; *Georgia Pomphrey and Tim Brown*, Blount County, Tennessee. Showing that the solar-powered homestead is viable and comfortable, these two couples exemplify honest-to-goodness "off-the-grid" living in both rural and semi-urban areas. Dismissing the notion that solar, wind, and micro-hydro alternative energies are impractical, they power their homes with environmentally sensitive and socially responsible technologies. Hogan and Fairchild have developed a homestead in rural southeast Kentucky that incorporates organic gardening and bee-keeping, solar and micro-hydro electric power generation, and on-site lumber milling. Surprisingly, with all this activity, they are not prisoners to their own design; they also work away from home and thus assume a lifestyle which, in many ways, is similar to that of "mainstream" America. Pomphrey and Brown's home is likewise powered completely by the sun. Using a bank of eight solar panels that feed a set of deep-cycle batteries, they harvest enough sunlight to provide more DC and AC power than they can use. Their well is equipped with a solar-powered pump, which provides not only drinking water but water for their vegetable gardens, carp pond, and fields of tiger lilies.

Albert Bates, Eco-village Training Center, The Farm, Summertown, Tennessee. For some thirty years, The Farm, a community of at least two hundred individuals in south-central Tennessee, has shown that conscious living can take place cooperatively. With an evolving vision of what a sustainable and just existence can be, The Farm has developed a social infrastructure that encompasses schools, health care services, communications, and entrepreneurial enterprises. The business ventures produce a range of goods from tofu and shitaki mushrooms to electronic equipment. Still, The Farm leaves plenty of room for woods and open fields, providing for the needs of wildlife as well as humans. The recent addition of the Eco-village Training Center, which is part of the Global Eco-village Network (GEN), compliments broader community efforts in sustainable living by offering workshops and programs that teach principles of permaculture, alternative energy, and related topics. In cooperation with other GEN officials and projects, Bates, the founder of the Eco-village Training Center and the GEN Secretariat of the Americas, has worked to produce a human-scale model of sustainable living that provides a high quality of life without taking more from the earth than it gives back. (WWW - http://www.gaia.org/farm)

These organizations and individuals, and hundreds of others like them—the protectors and healers of the land—are our sources of hope. They are working the cures for the ills we have documented and building the models of better ways to live.

Appendix 1: Definition of the Bioregion

This report takes a watershed approach to defining the Upper Tennessee Valley and Southern Appalachian bioregion. The bioregion, as we define it, consists of the seven watersheds which form the drainage basin of the upper Tennessee River: Clinch-Powell, Holston, French Broad, Watts Bar-Melton Hill-Fort Loudoun, Little Tennessee, Chickamauga-Nickajack, and Hiwassee. These occupy portions of four states: Tennessee, North Carolina, Virginia, and Georgia.

Though watershed boundaries do not correspond exactly to county lines, large portions of the following counties are included within the region covered by this study:

Tennessee: Anderson, Bledsoe, Blount, Bradley, Campbell, Carter, Claiborne, Cocke, Cumberland, Grainger, Greene, Hamblen, Hamilton, Hancock, Hawkins, Jefferson, Johnson, Knox, Loudon, Marion, McMinn, Meigs, Monroe, Morgan, Polk, Rhea, Roane, Sequatchie, Sevier, Sullivan, Unicoi, Union, Washington.

North Carolina: Avery, Buncombe, Cherokee, Clay, Graham, Haywood, Henderson, Jackson, Macon, Madison, Mitchell, Swain, Transylvania, Watauga, Yancey.

Virginia: Lee, Russell, Scott, Smyth, Tazewell, Washington, Wise.

Georgia: Catoosa, Dade, Fannin, Towns, Union, Walker.

The Great Smoky Mountains National Park is wholly included within the bioregion.

For comparison with the 1996 Southern Appalachian Assessment (SAA), it should be noted that the region covered by our report is only the central portion of the region covered by the SAA.

Since our definition of the bioregion does not precisely correspond with anyone else's definition, we have often had to make use of data for regions that only partially overlap our bioregion. For example, we make frequent use of data for the whole state of Tennessee, the state most central to the bioregion, or for the whole Tennessee Valley, or for the whole Southern Appalachian Assessment region. In such cases, we always specify the actual area covered; and, where we have further information, we note it, in an attempt to correct for inaccuracies that may be introduced by the geographic disparity.

The job could be better done. Limited volunteer time and research budget of zero dollars have prevented us from tailoring our statistics more precisely to the bioregion. We regret this, but find some consolation in the hope that what we have accomplished is better than nothing. Perfectly precise statistics are unavaible in any case, since bioregions, unlike political units, are fuzzy at the edges.

Appendix 2: About the Foundation for Global Sustainability, Narrow Ridge, and Earth Knows Publications

This report was researched and written by volunteers working for the Foundation for Global Sustainability's State of the Bioregion Program. The Foundation for Global Sustainability (FGS) is a nonprofit tax-exempt organization headquartered in Knoxville, whose aim is to promote environmental awareness and action. FGS supports five projects or programs in addition to the one that generated this book: the Oak Ridge Education Project, which from its Oak Ridge office monitors, publicizes, and influences Department of Energy activities on the Oak Ridge Reservation; the Southern Appalachian Biodiversity project, headquartered in Asheville, North Carolina, which works to protect and preserve biodiversity, especially in the National Forests adjacent to the Great Smoky Mountains National Park; the Energy Program, which, in conjunction with the Tennessee Valley Energy Reform Coalition, promotes environmentally responsible power generation and conservation; the Clean Water Program, which works to protect regional waters and wetlands; and the Sustainable Living Program, which through workshops, demonstation projects, and information exchange promotes models of sustainable living. For more information about FGS, call 423-524-4771 or visit our web page at http://www.korrnet.org/fgs.

The publisher of this book, Earth Knows Publications, is a project of Narrow Ridge Earth Literacy Center. Narrow Ridge, located in Washburn, Tennessee, is a nonprofit, tax-exempt organization dedicated to fostering a sustainable society—one in which human health and the health of Earth are seen as one. For further information on Narrow Ridge, see Chapter Ten. Narrow Ridge may be contacted at 423-497-2753 or by e-mail at narrowr@korrnet.org. An order form for books from Earth Knows Publications may be found on the last page of this book.

All proceeds from the sale of this book will be used to support the work of Narrow Ridge and FGS. Both organizations welcome private donations and bequests.

Introduction

1 Bartram 1988, pp. 276 ff.
2 Mooney 1900, pp. 1-2.
3 These words have a common etymology, a point whose significance is elegantly articulated in Berry 1995 and Berry 1977, pp. 102-4, 222.

Chapter 1

1 Johnson & Lindberg 1992.
2 NADP 1991.
3 Data communicated by Jim Renfro, Air Resource Specialist, Great Smoky Mountains National Park.
4 Johnson & Lindberg 1992.
5 Johnson & Lindberg 1992.
6 Stoddard 1994.
7 Johnson & Lindberg 1992.
8 Renfro 1996, p. 66.
9 Little 1995, p. 55.
10 Little 1995, Chapter 3.
11 Eager and Adams 1992, SAMAB 1996e, pp. 108-9.
12 Johnson & Lindberg 1992.
13 TVA 1995b, p. 5.
14 TDEC 1994, p. 51.
15 Dosser 1989.
16 Park 1992.
17 BHCWP 1992, p. 8, and observations by Riverkeepers Leaf and Cielo Myczack. Update in *Broadened Horizons* newsletter 40, March-April 1996, p. 5.
18 Davidson 1946, pp. 38-9.
19 Brune 1953, pp. 407-418.
20 Information on the dam comes from Mullican, *et al.*, 1960, pp. 1-2. The closure date is given in TVA 1983, p. 70.
21 Watson 1994.
22 Mermel 1958, p. 150, and TDEC 1994, p. 55.
23 TVA 1987b.
24 Amundsen 1994, p. 290.
25 Observation by Leaf Myczack.
26 Letter from A. David McKinney, state of Tennessee Department of Health and Environment, to Stan Stieff, Oak Ridge Operations, October 26, 1983.
27 OREP 1992, pp. 26-7.
28 Kornegay 1991, p. 147.
29 TVA 1995a, vol. 2 pp. T1.106.
30 McKinney and Schoch 1996, pp. 418-19.
31 Kauffman, 1988.
32 TVA 1995a, vol. 2, pp. T1.98-T1.100.
33 TVA 1995b, p 6.
34 TVA 1995b.
35 TVA 1995a, vol. 2, pp. T1.95-T1.96.

36 Source is EPA's 1994 Toxic Release Inventory.

37 TVA 1995a, vol. 2, vol. 1, p. T1.96.

38 TVA 1995b.

39 TDEC 1994, especially pp. 13-14. Some of the sources of the pollution listed here were obtained from the assessment section of this report.

40 TDEC 1994, p. 12.

41 "Robertshaw Controls Ordered to Stop Dumping Oil into Creek," 1989, p. 10A.

42 Information for the last three paragraphs was compiled from TVA 1995b, BHCWP 1992, and direct observation.

43 BHCWP 1992.

44 U.S. Army Corps of Engineers Public Notice #91-132, September 1991.

45 Tinker, et al. 1996.

46 *Broadened Horizons Clean Water Project Newsletter*, Fall 1991.

47 BHCWP 1992, TVA 1991, TVA 1995b.

48 TVA 1996

49 TVA 1995b.

50 TDEC 1994, p. 40.

51 NCDEM 1995, pp. vii - viii.

52 NCDEM 1995, pp. 4-16 to 4-17.

53 TVA 1995b, p. 2

54 John Nolt, personal observation.

55 TSPO 1994.

56 Murdock 1994.

57 TVA *et al.* 1993, p. 111.

58 Gwin and Kentula 1990.

59 Pearson 1994.

60 Moss 1993.

61 K/KCMPC 1994.

62 TDEC 1994. Our research has turned up widely varying estimates of this figure—from a high in excess of 64 percent (TVA 1995a, vol. 2, p. T1.97) for the entire TVA region, to a low of 9.3 percent for the North Carolina portion of the Southern Appalachian Region (Carl Bailey, North Carolina Department of Environment, Health, and Natural Resources). The discrepancies may be due to varying areas covered by the statistics.

63 Data supplied in correspondence by Jackye L. Bonds, Environmental Scientist, Ground Water Protection Branch, EPA Region 4. Assisting her in compiling the information were Carl Bailey, Ground Water Section, North Carolina Department of Environment, Health, and Natural Resources; Tom Moss, Ground Water Management Section, Tennessee Department of Environment and Conservation; and Mike Langreck, UST Program, Tennessee Department of Environment and Conservation. We gratefully acknowledge their help.

64 Raven, Berg and Johnson 1993, 404.

65 Statistics supplied by Dr. Richard Maas.

66 SOCM 1994

67 Raven, Berg and Johnson 1993, 472.

68 Information in this and the previous paragraph comes from OPEP 1992 and personal communication from Roger Clapp, Oak Ridge National Laboratory.

69 MMES 1995.

70 TDEC 1994, p. 15.

71   Alavanja, *et al.* 1978.

Chapter 2

1   Renfro 1996, pp. 2, 22, 67-8.
2   Renfro 1996, pp. 22, 67-8.
3   TVA 1995a, vol. 2, p. T1.32.
4   Cahill 1996.
5   TVA 1995a, vol. 2, pp. T1.19, T1.32-T1.33; Renfro 1996, p. 31; Malm 1992.
6   TVA data communicated to Jim Renfro, Air Resource Specialist, Great Smoky Mountains National Park.
7   TVA 1995a, vol. 2, pp. T1.32-T1.33, T1.40.
8   Interagency Monitoring of Protected Visual Environments 1988-94 data, communicated by Jim Renfro.
9   Interagency Monitoring of Protected Visual Environments 1988-94 data, communicated by Jim Renfro.
10   Interagency Monitoring of Protected Visual Environments 1988-94 data, communicated by Jim Renfro.
11   TVA 1995a, vol. 2, pp. T1.32-T1.33, T2.21-T2.22.
12   TVA 1995a, vol. 2, p. T1.32.
13   McKinney and Schoch 1996, ch. 17, especially p. 483.
14   Johnson and Lindberg 1992.
15   Renfro 1996, p. 69.
16   Fishman and Kalish 1990, p. 218.
17   Dosser 1991.
18   Renfro 1996, p. 69.
19   Peine, Randolph, & Presswood 1995, p. 519.
20   Krupa and Manning 1988.
21   Peine, Randolph, & Presswood 1995, p. 524.
22   EPA draft documents cited in TVA 1995a, vol. 2, p. T1.81.
23   McKinney and Schoch 1996, pp. 494-504.
24   Johnson 1993, p. 83.
25   EPA "Ozone Science," www.epa.gov/docs/ozone/science/marcomp.html, March 1995.
26   Bjorn, *et al.* 1993.
27   Flynn 1995.
28   McKinney and Schoch 1996, pp. 487-9, Shimek 1994.
29   "Study Links Smoking to Breast Cancer" 1996, p. B1.
30   McKinney and Schoch 1996, pp. 484-5.
31   Raven, Berg and Johnson 1993, pp. 435-9; McKinney and Schoch 1996, pp. 484-5.
32   McKinney and Schoch 1996, p. 484.
33   PA 1995b.
34   "You've Come a Long Way, BASF" 1995.
35   Selcraig 1996, p. 43.
36   Cheremisinoff, *et al.* 1994, p. 130.
37   Selcraig 1996, p. 41.
38   The toxic release figures listed in this table and in the preceding paragraphs are from the EPA's 1993 and 1994 Toxics Release Inventories. Summary data were obtained from EPA 1995b; details of specific chemical releases were obtained from EPA via the internet.

39   Savitz, *et al.* 1996, p. 7.

40   SOCM 1996.

41   TVA 1995a, vol. 2, p. T2.20.

42   TVA 1995a, vol. 2, pp. T1.66-T1.69.

43   Widner 1996.

44   Renfro 1996, pp. 33, 68.

45   TVA 1995a, vol. 2, p. T2.20; McKinney and Schoch 1996, pp. 504-15.

46   TVA 1995a, vol. 2, p. T1.70.

47   Information for this and preceding paragraphs is from McKinney and Schoch 1996, pp. 504-19, and from Hara, *et al.*, undated.

48   McKinney and Schoch 1996, p. 517.

49   McKinney and Schoch 1996, p. 507.

Chapter 3

1   This trend is documented in SAMAB 1996d, pp. 113-116.

2   For a discussion of this estimate for the sourcing area, see TVA *et al.* 1993, p. 53.

3   TVA *et al.* 1993, p. 212.

4   TVA *et al.* 1993.

5   October 5, 1991.

6   TVA *et al.* 1993, cover sheet.

7   Alligood 1995a.

8   Observation by Cielo Sand Myczack, Riverkeeper.

9   Doug Murray, personal communication.

10   Murray 1995.

11   TVA, *et al.* 1993, pp. 214-215.

12   SAMAB 1996d, p. 109.

13   Figures cited in TVA 1995a, vol. 2, p. T1.114, support this conclusion.

14   TVA *et al.* 1993, pp. 231-233.

15   TVA *et al.* 1993, p. 51.

16   Alligood, 1995b.

17   TVA *et al.* 1993, p. 51.

18   Likens, *et al.* 1978.

19   Boring, Swank, and Monk, 1987. See also TVA, *et al.* 1993, pp. 233-237.

20   TVA *et al.* 1993, p. 256.

21   Duffy and Meier 1992. For rebuttal and response, see Johnson, et. al 1993 and Duffy 1993. Matlack 1994 provides additional support for Duffey and Meier's conclusions.

22   SAMAB 1996d, p. 88.

23   Irwin 1996, p. 6.

24   Cornett, 1995.

25   Noss and Cooperrider 1994, pp. 192-197.

26   TVA 1983, p. 17.

27   Newman 1995.

28   Parker and Dixon 1980.

29   Amundsen 1994.

30   Sanders 1992.

31   TVA, *et al.* 1993, p. 55.

32 Dickens 1976, Introduction.
33 Hudson 1976, p. 41.
34 Mooney 1982, pp. 250-2; Hudson 1970; Hudson, 1976, pp. 158 and 346.
35 Hudson 1976, pp. 427-443.
36 Hudson 1976, p. 173.
37 Such thinking seems to have been common among Native American tribes elsewhere. See Martin, 1978.
38 Ross 1993a.
39 Ross 1993a.
40 Ross 1993b.
41 Noss and Cooperrider 1994, p. 204.
42 Morton 1994, p. 58.
43 Miller, *et al.*, 1992.
44 Leopold 1966, pp. 139-140.
45 Gittleman and Pimm 1991.
46 Ross 1993a.
47 McDade 1993 and NPS 1995, p. 6.
48 NPS 1996a, p. 6.
49 Ross 1993a.
50 Toops 1992.
51 Hatcher 1996, Ross 1993b.
52 Eager and Hatcher 1980, pp. C11-C12; TVA 1995a, vol. 2, pp. T1.132-T1.133.
53 Himebaugh 1993 and Richter, et.al.1993.
54 Hatcher 1996, Ross 1993b, Blackburn 1993, Campbell, *et al.* 1993.
55 Hatcher 1996, Ross 1993b.
56 Personal communication, Chuck Nicholson, TVA environmental scientist.
57 TVA 1994a, p. 3.
58 Ross 1993b.
59 Hatcher 1996.
60 Hatcher 1996.
61 Ross 1993a.
62 Quoted in Ehrlich, *et al.* 1988, p. 279.
63 Ehrlich, *et al.*, 1988, p. 279.
64 Terborgh 1992.
65 Quoted by Ross 1993a.
66 Ross 1993a.
67 Ehrlich, *et al.* 1988, pp. 275, 279.
68 Terborgh 1992.
69 McKinney and Schoch 1996, p. 321.
70 Terborgh 1992.
71 Terborgh 1992. See also Böhning-Gaese, *et al.* 1993 and Paton 1994.
72 Wilcove 1985.
73 Newman, *et al.* 1992, Parker and Dixon 1980, Eager and Hatcher 1980, together with personal communication from Chuck Nicholson.
74 Hatcher 1996.
75 SAMAB 1996e, pp. 66-67.

76 Parker and Dixon 1980, Eager and Hatcher 1980, Winfield 1993a, personal communication Chuck Nicholson.
77 Terborgh 1992.
78 Eager and Hatcher 1980.
79 Thackston, *et al.* 1991, SAMAB 1996a, p. 60.
80 Long, *et al.* 1995; Grant and Licht 1993.
81 NPS 1995.
82 Dodd [in preparation].
83 Petranka, *et al.* 1993. For a response and rebuttal, see Ash and Bruce 1994 and Petranka 1994.
84 Bennett, *et al.* 1980.
85 Mathews and Morgan 1982.
86 Dodd, in preparation.
87 Etnier and Starnes 1993, Eager and Hatcher 1980.
88 TVA 1996c, p. 4.
89 Etnier 1994, Eager and Hatcher 1980, pp. B101-B102.
90 David Etnier, personal communication.
91 Dinkins and Shute (in press).
92 Etnier 1994, Jenkins and Burkhead 1993.
93 Peggy Shute, personal communication.
94 Jenkins and Burkhead 1984. Unless otherwise noted, most of the information in the previous several paragraphs is from Etnier 1994 and Eager and Hatcher 1980.
95 Lennon and Parker 1959.
96 Peggy Shute, personal communication.
97 Etnier and Starnes 1993, pp. 587-590 and personal communication, Peggy Shute.
98 Etnier and Starnes 1993, pp. 161-163.
99 Etnier and Starnes 1993, pp. 350-352.
100 Renfro 1996.
101 Personal communication, David McKinney, Tennessee Wildlife Resources Agency.
102 Hatcher 1996.
103 McClure 1995.
104 Bates and Dennis 1985, pp. 48-61.
105 Parker and Dixon 1980, Bogan and Parmalee 1983.
106 TVA 1995a, vol. 2, pp. T1.136-T1.137 and SAMAB 1996b, pp. 38-39.
107 Hatcher 1996.
108 Our discussion of zebra mussels is compiled from many sources: Cathay 1992; Kuznik 1993; Ludanskiy, *et al.* 1993; McKinney and Schoch 1996, pp. 322-3; Ross 1994; TVA 1994a, p. 2; and Walker 1991.
109 McKinney and Schoch 1996, p. 72.
110 Opie 1981, p. 61.
111 NPS 1995, p. 7.
112 Bowen 1993, SAMAB 1996a, p. 71, SAMAB 1996e, p. 113.
113 NPS 1996b.
114 Searfoss 1995, SAMAB 1996e, pp. 109-111.
115 NPS 1996b.
116 SAMAB 1996e, pp. 111-113 and NPS 1996b.

117 Davis 1995, SAMAB 1996e, pp. 103-108.

118 Searfoss 1995, SAMAB 1996e, pp. 114-117.

119 NPS 1996b.

120 SAMAB 1996e, pp. 120-121.

121 Bowen 1993, SAMAB 1996e, pp 117-118.

122 NPS 1996b.

123 NPS 1995.

124 TVA 1995a, vol. 2, p. T1.129.

125 Allgood 1996, Loy 1996.

126 The sources for this table are TVA 1995a, vol. 2, pp. T1.132-T1.139, SAMAB 1996b, pp. 37-40, and SAMAB 1996e, pp. 150-158. Extinct or extirpated species are not included.

Chapter 4

1   Male 1984, p. 2.

2   Source: Agricultural Extension Service, University of Tennessee Institute of Agriculture.

3   Blakey, *et al.*, 1977, p.107.

4   These figures are from National Health and Nutrition Examination Survey III database for the state of Tennessee. We wish to thank Professors Betsy Haughton and Eugene Fitzhugh of the University of Tennessee, Knoxville, for accessing this database for us.

5   Census Bureau figures are inconsistent for the 1992 percentages. We have (conservatively) taken the higher figures. On some listings, there were only 75,076 farms in 1992, with a total of 11,169,086 acres.

6   Male 1984, p. 4, and personal observations of several East Tennessee vegetable growers.

7   Male 1984, pp. 4-5.

8   Male 1984, p. 5.

9   Blakey, *et al.*, p. 107.

10   USBC 1994.

11   McKinney and Schoch 1996, p. 423.

12   *Knoxville News-Sentinel*, August 6, 1996.

13   Austin 1994.

14   Austin 1994.

15   Fisher and Harnish 1981, p. 72.

16   Fisher and Harnish 1981, p. 71.

17   Hightower 1976, p. 167.

18   Dorman-Hickson 1994.

19   Berry 1977, pp. 45-6.

20   These recommendations are culled from Austin 1994 and Male 1984.

21   Reaganold 1989.

22   Jeavons 1991, pp. 70-97, 165-171.

23   Connie Whitehead, personal communication.

24   White, *et al.* 1981, p. 175.

25   TACD and TDA, undated.

26   SAMAB 1996b, p. 89.

27   TVA 1983, p. 111.

28   McKinney and Schoch, pp. 377-8.

29   Childress 1996.

30 Robbins 1987, pp. 148-305.

31 Robbins 1987, pp. 48-121.

32 McKinney and Schoch 1996, pp 356-357.

33 Whitehead 1995.

Chapter 5

1   Adapted from TVA 1995a, vol. 2, p. T5.16.

2   TVA 1995a, vol. 2, pp. T5.18-T5.19.

3   TVA 1992.

4   Working on-demand water heaters and passive solar water heaters may be seen at Narrow Ridge Earth Literacy Center. (See Appendix 2 for further information.)

5   Adapted from TVA 1995a, vol. 2, p. T5.13.

6   TVA 1995a, vol. 2, p. T5.13.

7   TVA 1995a, vol. 2, p. T5.13.

8   TVA 1995a, vol. 2, p. T5.14.

9   Various sources were used to complile this table. Most of it is from *Planning & Product Guide*, Sunelco, Inc., Hamilton, Montana.

10 TVA 1992.

11 McKinney and Schoch 1996, pp. 167-8.

12 TVA 1995a, vol. 2, p. T1.117.

13 *Powell Valley News*, October 18, 1994. See also TVA 1995a, vol. 2, p. T2.47.

14 Information supplied by Friends of the Clinch and Powell Rivers.

15 TVA 1995a, vol. 1, p. 1.4.

16 TVA 1995a, vol. 1, p. 1.3.

17 USGAO 1995a, p. 20.

18 TVA 1983, p. 46.

19 Williams 1996.

20 USGAO 1995a, p. 42.

21 USGAO 1995a, p. 26.

22 TVA 1995a, vol. 2, p. T3.1.

23 Dean 1996b.

24 USGAO 1995a, pp. 32-35.

25 USGAO 1995a, p. 58.

26 USGAO 1995a, pp. 60-62.

27 USGAO 1995a, p. 6.

28 USGAO 1995a, p. 7.

29 Grimac 1996.

30 TVA 1995a, vol. 1, p. G.2.

31 TVA 1995a, vol. 1, pp. 4.2-4.6.

32 TVA 1995a, vol. 2, p. T3.2.

33 TVA 1983, p. 70.

34 SOCM 1996, p. 8; see also SOCM Sentinel, November/December 1994, p. 8, and Dean 1996a.

35 TVA 1995a, vol. 2, pp. T1.21 and T3.4.

36 TVA 1995a, vol. 2, pp. T1.117 and T1.121.

37 Gabbard 1993.

38 TVA 1995a, vol. 2, p. T1.117.

39   Squillace 1990, p. 28.
40   Squillace 1990, pp. 19-20.
41   SOCM 1992a, p. 1.
42   Merrifield 1982.
43   Squillace 1990, pp. 28-34.
44   SOCM 1992a, pp. 19-30.
45   Hopps 1994.
46   Duffy and Meier 1992.
47   SOCM 1992b, p. 29; see also Carlson and Galloway 1988.
48   Watson 1984.
49   USGAO 1995, p. 21.
50   McKinney and Schoch 1996, p. 212-213; Raven, Berg and Johnson 1993, pp. 215-218
51   TVA 1995a, vol. 2, p. T1.121.
52   Matthiessen 1983.
53   TVA 1995a, vol. 2, pp. T1.121-T1.122.
54   TVA 1995a, vol. 2, p. T1.122.
55   Mansfield 1996.
56   TVA 1995a, vol. 2, pp. T1.123-T1.124.
57   McKinney and Schoch 1996, pp. 218-222.
58   TVA 1995a, vol. 2, pp. T3.7-T3.8.
59   TVA 1995a, vol. 2, pp. T8.24 and T8.30.
60   Blecker 1995.
61   TVA 1995a, vol. 2, p. T3.8.
62   TVA 1995a, vol. 2, pp. T6.6-T6.7 and T. 6.34.
63   McKinney and Schoch 1996, pp. 180-192.
64   USDOE 1995b.
65   McKinney and Schoch 1996, p. 507.
66   TVA 1995a, vol. 2, pp. T6.4-T6.5.
67   TVA 1995a, vol. 2, p. T6.31.

Chapter 6

1   "Cigarette Butts Highway Litter Leader," *Knoxville News-Sentinel*, August 11, 1996, p. B7.
2   Knox Solid Waste Planning Region 1994, pp. 8-1-8-2.
3   This information is from SOCM (Save Our Cumberland Mountains), which helped organize resistance at Shoat Lick Hollow.
4   SOCM 1995, p. 4 and *SOCM Sentinel*, January/February 1995.
5   EPA 1996a.
6   The lower figure is from Knox County Solid Waste Department [undated], the higher from TDEC 1996a, p. 9.
7   Knox Solid Waste Planning Region 1996, p. 2.
8   EPA 1996b, Executive Summary.
9   Locker 1991.
10   Knox Solid Waste Planning Region 1996, p. 2.
11   Mayor's Task Force 1991, p. 36.
12   TDEC 1996a, p. 9.
13   TDEC 1996b.

14 TDEC 1996b.

15 LeQuire, 1995.

16 National Recycling Coalition 1996, pp. 1 and 23.

17 McKinney and Schoch 1996, p. 540.

18 *Clearwater: Newsletter of the Friends of the Clinch & Powell Rivers*, June 1966.

19 National Recycling Coalition 1996, p. 11.

20 Personal communication, Karen Anderson, Knoxville Recycling Coalition.

21 Knox Solid Waste Planning Region 1996, p. 14.

22 McKinney and Schoch 1996, p. 532.

23 Zeller 1996.

24 EPA 1994 Toxic Release Inventory.

25 For a revealing account of the connections and practices of WMX, see Political Ecology Group, 1994.

26 OREP 1996, p. 3.

27 Oak Ridge Environmental Peace Alliance Newsletter, September 1994.

28 Munger 1996.

29 Material for most of this section was supplied in correspondence by Jackye L. Bonds, Environmental Scientist, Ground Water Protection Branch, EPA Region 4, and Carl Tenut, Mining Section, Tennessee Department of Environment and Conservation. We are grateful for their help.

30 Brill and Brill 1995, p. 46.

31 Tinker, *et al.*, 1996.

32 Powell 1995.

33 Beck 1985.

34 The name of the sender is illegible on copies provided to the Foundation, but the memo is on Nuclear Division stationery and references a letter by Alvin M. Weinberg dated March 24, 1969, which apparently also warns of the problem of sending plutonium to Witherspoon.

35 This memo, on Oak Ridge National Laboratory stationery, is from Julian R. Gissell to H. E. Seagren.

36 Beck 1985.

37 Beck 1985.

38 USDOE 1996b, p. 3-16.

39 These facts are drawn from the files on Witherspoon at the Tennessee Department of Conservation and Environment, Division of Superfund's Knoxville office and from USDOE 1996b.

40 USDOE 1996b, p. 4-27.

41 USDOE 1996a.

42 Unless otherwise noted, all material in this section is drawn from OREP 1992.

43 LeQuire 1996.

44 USGAO 1995b.

45 EPA 1994.

46 Durning 1993, p. 25.

Chapter 7

1 *Cf.* Smith 1993.

2 TDOT 1994, pp. VI-1-VI-5.

3   CBER 1994, p. 380.
4   Gordon 1991, p. 35.
5   TDOT 1994, p. VI-11.
6   TDOT 1994, pp. V-9-V12.
7   McKinney and Schoch 1996, p. 152.
8   TVA 1995a, p. T1.90.
9   All information and quotations in this paragraph are from Jaffe 1995.
10 Cheremisinoff, *et al.*, 1994, pp. 67-69.
11 Cheremisinoff, *et al.*, 1994, pp. 56-58.
12 Papacostas and Prevedouros 1993, p. 480; McKinney and Schoch 1996, p. 490.
13 Satterfield 1996.
14 Burbank 1995, p. 9.
15 Nadis and MacKenzie 1993, p. 52.
16 Nadis and MacKenzie 1993, p. 53.
17 Nadis and MacKenzie 1993, pp. ix, 12.
18 SAMAB 1996d, p. 177.
19 SAMAB 1996d, pp. 177-182.
20 Minutes of the May 23, 1995, Knoxville City Council meeting.
21 Cover letter, *Draft Environmental Impact Statement, Foothills Parkway, Section 8D*, November 1994.
22 Harmon, 1995.
23 Hahn and Pfeifer 1994, Nadis and MacKenzie 1993, p. 17.
24 Lutes, *et al.*, 1994, pp. 1-2 and 72-75; see Cheremisinoff, *et al.*, 1994, concerning carcinogenicity of the compounds mentioned.
25 TDOT 1994, p. VIII-9.
26 Tennessee Valley Authority and U.S. Dept. of the Army, Corps of Engineers, direct correspondence.
27 TDOT 1994, p. VIII-7.
28 ETDD 1995, p. 7
29 ETDD 1995, p. 7.
30 Welty 1993, p. 27.
31 ETDD 1995, p. 2.
32 ETDD 1995, p. 12.
33 TDOT 1994, p. I-3.
34 USBC 1992.

Chapter 8

1   Campbell 1960, p. 100.
2   Watts, p. 108.
3   Except as otherwise noted, all population figures in this section are from USBC 1992, SAMAB 1996d, and Greater Knoxville Chamber of Commerce [undated].
4   Tetzeli 1993, p. 14.
5   SAMAB 1996d, pp. 71-72.
6   SAMAB 1996d, p. 28.
7   SAMAB 1996d, p. 37, fig. 2.19.
8   SAMAB 1996d, p. 40, table 2.4.

9   SAMAB 1996d, p. 37, fig. 2.19.

10   SAMAB 1996d, p. 36.

11   Simmons 1995b, p. B2.

12   Simmons 1995b, pp. B2, B5.

13   SAMAB 1996d, p. 173.

14   SAMAB 1996d, Figure 2-16, pp. 32-3.

15   SAMAB 1996d, p. 55.

16   Ferguson 1991; SAMAB 1996d, p. 35.

17   SAMAB 1996d, pp. 40, 41.

18   AP 1996.

19   Paine 1996.

20   Leaf Myczack, personal communication.

21   TVA 1996a, p. 1.17.

22   TVA 1996a, pp. 1.18, 4.23.

23   TVA 1996a, pp. 3.19-3.20.

24   TVA 1996a, pp. 1.17, 1.18, 3.29, and 3.30.

25   Leaf Myczack, personal communication.

26   TVA 1996a, pp. 1.18, 4.27, 4.28.

27   Paine 1996.

28   TVA 1996a, pp. 1.1 and 2.27.

29   TVA 1996a, pp 2.11, 2.16; Paine 1996.

30   Powelson 1996.

31   SAMAB 1996d, p. 173.

32   Personal communication, Kay Powell, Pigeon Forge Chamber of Commerce, Department of Tourism.

33   Garland, 1996.

34   *Foothills News* 1996, pp. 2, 3.

35   Smith 1996, pp. 82-83.

36   Dean 1995.

37   Chatterjee, *et al.*, 1986.

38   Dean 1996c; the quotation from Stodola is originally from Tennessee Department of Environment and Conservation Office Correspondence addressed to Dan Eager, Natural Resources Section-NCO, December 11, 1995.

39   Smith and Associates 1996. This study, prepared for the developers, is excessively narrow in scope and fails to account for traffic increases due to nearby developments; nevertheless, it predicts a continued deterioration of the traffic situation in the area, even if Parkside Drive is built.

40   Hartley-McAndrew 1995, p. 2.

Chapter 9

1   Durning 1992, p. 45.

2   Durning 1992, p. 131.

3   Durning 1992, p. 106.

4   Durning 1992, p. 93.

5   Durning 1992, p. 50.

6   Haavelmo and Hansen 1992, pp. 39-40.

7 Haavelmo and Hansen 1992, p. 40.

8 Durning 1992, p. 51.

9 Durning 1992, p. 81.

10 Durning 1992, p. 82.

11 Durning 1992, pp. 82-83.

12 Lenssen and Roodman 1995, p. 95.

13 Lenssen and Roodman 1995, p. 97.

14 Durning 1992, p. 22.

15 Krugman 1996.

16 Krugman 1996.

17 See Austin 1995 and Clinch Powell Sustainable Development Forum 1994.

18 Goodstein 1989.

19 ALOTF 1983.

20 Although this study was completed in 1983, many of the study's findings are still relevant today. See Gaventa 1984 and Horton 1993 for a more thorough discusson of the research.

21 Quoted in Gaventa 1994, p. 10.

22 Park 1995c, p. D1.

23 TDES 1994, p. 13.

24 TDA 1994, pp. 31, 35.

25 Mundy 1995, p. 4.

26 Thomas 1996.

27 TDES 1994, p. 4.

28 AP 1995.

29 AP 1995.

30 Levinson 1995, p. 22.

31 TDES 1994, p. 6.

32 TDES 1994, p. 16.

33 TDES 1994, p. 16.

34 Park 1996c, p. A1.

35 Park 1996b, p. A1.

36 TDES 1994, p. 1.

37 TDES 1994, p. 1.

38 TDES 1994, pp. 1, 4.

39 TDES 1994, p. 4.

40 TDES 1994, p. 1.

41 TDES 1994, p. 2.

42 TDES 1994, p. 3.

43 TDES 1994, p. 4.

44 TDES 1994, p. 8.

45 Park 1995a, p. D4.

46 It should be noted that DRI-McGraw-Hill uses a somewhat more restrictive definition of service jobs that does the Tennessee Department of Employment Security, whose statistics were cited earlier.

47 DRI/McGraw-Hill & IC2 1996, p. 5

48 Geisel and Park 1995, p. D1.

49 Park 1995b, D1.

50   DRI/McGraw-Hill & IC2 1996, p. 11.

51   Park 1995c, p. D4.

52   McKinney 1995, p. D4.

53   Park 1996a.

54   TDES 1994, p. 4.

55   Statistics provided by TVA Human Resource Office.

56   Mansfield 1997.

57   Park 1995a, p. D1.

58   Munger 1996b.

59   Munger 1996b.

60   Munger 1996b.

61   Munger 1996b.

62   WCED 1987.

63   WCED 1987, p. 43

64   See Beder 1994.

65   Young and Sachs 1995, p. 84.

66   McMahon 1990, p. 18.

67   Frosch 1994, p. 64.

68   McMahon 1990, p. 20.

69   McMahon 1990, p. 18.

70   For more information on EcoGenics, consult their web page at http://www.ecogenics.com.

71   Gertler and Ehrenfeld 1996, p. 50. Parts of the discussion on the Kalundborg complex are derived from "Industrial Symbiosis: Exchange of Resources," a brochure distributed by the Kalunborg Center for Industrial Symbiosis.

72   Gertler and Ehrenfeld 1996, p. 50.

73   Gertler and Ehrenfeld 1996, p. 51.

74   TVA 1995a, vol. 2, pp. T1.117, T1.121.

75   Gertler and Ehrenfeld 1996, p. 50.

76   Gertler and Ehrenfeld 1996, p. 52.

77   Goldstein 1995, p. 8.

78   Summerlin 1995, p.15.

79   Summerlin 1995, p.15.

80   River Valley Partners, Inc., Development Packet.

81   Calthorpe Associates, *et al.* 1995.

82   RiverValley Partners 1995.

83   Information brochure on the Global Action Plan.

84   RiverValley Partners 1995.

85   River Valley Partners, Inc., Development Packet.

86   Durning 1992, p. 110.

87   Mikesell 1992, p. 82.

88   See Durning 1992.

89   Goodland *et al.* 1992, p. xiii.

90   Various goverment documents have addressed the issue of goverment subsidies and taxation, as have several publications from the World Watch Institute. See, for example, Young 1992 and Young and Sachs 1995.

91   Durning 1992, pp. 110-111.
92   Adapted from Hawken 1993, p. 171.
93   Hocker 1993, p. 5.
94   See USGAO 1995b, EPA 1994.
95   Durning 1993.
96   Clinch Powell Sustainable Development Forum 1994, p. 8.
97   Adapted from Clinch Powell Sustainable Development Forum 1994.
98   Clinch Powell Sustainable Development Forum 1994, p. 3.
99   Clinch Powell Sustainable Development Forum 1994, p. 6.
100 Clinch Powell Sustainable Development Forum 1994, pp. 6-7.
101 Goldstein 1996b.
102 Goldstein 1996a.
103 Simmons 1997.
104 Simmons 1995a, p. A1.
105 Simmons 1995a, p. A10.

Chapter 10

1   Merck Family Fund 1995, pp. 1-2, used with permission.
2   Mollison 1995, pp. 2-3.

Alligood, Leon [1995a], "Chipping Away Our Forests," *Nashville Banner*, September 5.

Alligood, Leon [1995b], "Doing Right by the Trees," *Nashville Banner*, September 8.

Alligood, Leon [1996], "Bee Deaths Stunt State Crops," *Nashville Banner*, July 10.

Alvanja, Michael, Inge Goldstein, and Mervyn Susser [1978], "A Case Control Study of Gastrointestinal and Urinary Tract Cancer Mortality and Drinking Water Chlorination," in *Water Chlorination: Environmental Impact and Health Effects*, Volume 2, Ann Arbor, Ann Arbor Science Publishers, Inc., pp. 395-409.

Amundsen, C.C. [1994], "Reservoir Riparian Zone Characteristics in the Upper Tennessee River Valley," *Water, Air and Soil Pollution* 77, 469-493.

AP (Associated Press) [1995], "Farmers Would Rather Switch than Fight," *The Tennessean*, November 2, 4B.

AP [1996], "State Says Dump Is Posing Threat to Groundwater," *The Knoxville News-Sentinel*, Nov. 28, A11.

Appalachia Land Ownership Task Force (ALOTF) [1983], *Who Owns Appalachia?*, Lexington, University Press of Kentucky.

Ash, Andrew N. and Richard C. Bruce [1994], "Impacts of Timber harvesting on Salamanders," *Conservation Biology* 8,1: 300-301.

Austin, Dick [1995], "Clinch Powell Sustainable Development Forum," a report given at the North American Regional Consultation on Sustainable Livelihoods, Washington D.C. January 13-15.

Austin, Richard Cartwright [1994], "The Spiritual Crisis of Modern Agriculture," *Christian Social Action*, October.

Bartlett, Richard A. [1995]. *Troubled Waters: Champion International and the Pigeon River Controversy*, Knoxville, University of Tennessee Press.

Bartram, William [1988] *Travels*, New York, Penguin Books (first published 1791).

Bates, John M. and Sally D. Dennis [1985], *Final Report, Mussel Resource Survey, State of Tennessee*, Knoxville, Tennessee Wildlife Resources Agency.

Beck, Randall [1985], "Woman's Cancer May Be Linked to Work in Radioactive Junkyard," *Knoxville Journal*, September 13, A1.

Beder, Susan [1994], "The Hidden Messages Within Sustainable Development," *Social Alternatives* 13,2: 8-12.

Bennett, D. H., J. W. Gibbons, and J. Glanville [1980], "Terrestrial Activity, Abundance, and Diversity of Amphibians in Differently Managed Forest Types," *American Midland Naturalist* 103, 412-416.

Benz, George W. and D.E. Collins [in preparation], *Aquatic Fauna in Peril: The Southeastern Perspective*, Decatur, GA, Lenz Design and Communications.

Berry, Wendell [1977], *The Unsettling of America: Culture and Agriculture*, San Francisco, Sierra Club Books.

Berry, Wendell [1995] "Health is Membership," *Plain* 7, Chesterhill, Ohio, Center for Plain Living.

BHCWP (Broadened Horizons Clean Water Project) [1992], *A Citizen's Guide to Pollution in the Tennessee River*, Whitwell, TN.

Bjorn, Lars O., Johan Moan, Wilhelm Nultsch, and Antony R. Young.,eds. [1993] *Environmental UV Photobiology*, New York, Plenum.

Blackburn, Norris [1993], "So That Eagles Can Soar Again," *The Tennessee Conservationist*, 59,5: 11-15.

Blakey, Robert C., et. al. [1977], *Food Consumption and Distribution in Knoxville*, Graduate School of Planning, University of Tennessee.

Blecker, David A. [1995], "Deadly Dollars: The Economic Fallout from TVA's Watts Bar Unit I," report prepared for Greenpeace by MSB Energy Associates, Inc.

Boepple, J. F. and R. E. Coker [1912], *Mussel Resources of the Holston and Clinch Rivers of Eastern Tennessee*, Washington: Government Printing Office.

Bogan, Arthur E. and Paul W. Parmalee [1983], *Tennessee's Rare Wildlife, Volume II: The Mollusks*, Tennessee Wildlife Resources Agency.

Böhning-Gaese, Katrin, Mark L. Taper, and James H. Brown [1993], "Are Declines in North American Insectivorous Songbirds Due to Causes on the Breeding Range?" *Conservation Biology* 7,1: 76-86.

Boring, L. R., W. T. Swank, and C. D. Monk [1987], "Dynamics of Early Successional Forest Structure and Processes in the Coweeta Basin," in Swank and Crossley 1987, 161-179.

Bowditch, Deborah J. {1992], "Tennessee Trash, Part III: Recycle, Reuse, Reduce, Refuse," *The Tennessee Conservationist* 58,1: 2-5.

Bowen, Brian [1993] "The Green Scourge: Invasive Alien Plants," *The Tennessee Conservationist*, 59,5: 29-32.

Boynton, A.C. [1994], "Wildlife Use of Southern Appalachian Wetlands in North Carolina," *Water, Air and Soil Pollution*, 77, 349-358.

Brede, Lawrence M. [1994], *Characterization and Analysis of Selected Water Quality Parameters of the Clinch and Powell River Basins in Northeast Tennessee*, Thesis, University of Tennessee, Knoxville.

Brill, Jack A. and Hal Brill [1995], "Company Spotlight: Molten Metal Technology," *In Business* 17,4 (July/August).

Brown, Lynn A. [1979], "Planning for Nonpoint Pollution Control in North Carolina," *Journal of Soil and Water Conservation* 34, 1979, 8-10.

Brune, G.M. [1953], "Trap Efficiency of Reservoirs," *Transactions of the American Geophysical Union*, 34, 407-418.

Burbank, Cynthia J. [1995], "ITS and the Environment," *Public Roads* , Spring, 9-11.

Busing, R.T. [1993], "Gradient Analysis of Spruce Fir Forests of the Great Smoky Mountains," *Canadian Journal of Botany*, 71, 7.

Busing, R.T. [1994], Mortality Trends in a Southern Appalachian Red Spruce Population," *Forest-Ecology and Management*, 64, 1.

Cahill, T. A. [1996], "Trends in Fine Particle Concentrations at Great Smoky Mountains National Park," presented at the Annual Meeting of the Air and Waste Management Association, Nashville, TN, June.

Calthorpe Associates and William McDonough Architects [1995], "A Comprehensive Revitalization Strategy: The South Central Business District Plan," report prepared for RiverValley Partners, Chattanooga.

Campbell, Anthony J., William R. Miller, Ruth Neff, Larry R. Richardson, and Edward L. Thackston [1993], "Tennessee Conservation League's 1993 Environmental Quality Index," *The Tennessee Conservationist* 59,6 (insert).

Campbell, Carlos C. [1960], *Birth of a National Park in the Great Smoky Mountains*, Knoxville, University of Tennessee Press.

Carson, Cathy and Thomas Galloway [1988], "SMCRA's Implementation is Flawed," *Forum for Applied Research and Public Policy* 3,1: 18-21.

Cathay, H. Joe [1992], "Zebras in Our Back Yard!" *The Tennessee Conservationist*, 58,5: 23-26.

Catholic Bishops of Appalachia [1995], *At Home in the Web of Life: A Pastoral Message on Sustainable Communities in Appalachia*, Webster Springs, West Virginia, Catholic Committee of Appalachia.

CBER (Center for Business and Economic Research) [1994], *Tennessee Statistical Abstract*, Knoxville, University of Tennessee.

Chatterjee, Arun, Richard A. Staley, and John R. Whaley III [1986], "Transportation Parks: A Promising Approach to Facilitate Urban Goods Movement," *Transportation Quarterly*, 40, 2 (April); 211-220.

Cheremisinoff, Nicholas P., John A. King, and Randi Boyko [1994], *Dangerous Properties of Industrial and Consumer Chemicals*, New York, Marcel Dekker.

Childress, Watt [1992], "Tennessee Trash, Part II: Individuals Are the Key to Solving Communities' Garbage Problems," *The Tennessee Conservationist*, 58,1: 18-20.

Childress, Watt [1996], "Eat Domestic Beef Raised Humanely," Knoxville, *Tennessee Green*, Spring, 19.

Clinch Powell Sustainable Development Forum [1994], "Sustainable Development for Northeast Tennessee and Southwest Virginia," Abingdon, Virginia.

Cook, R.B., et. al. [1994], "Acid-Base Chemistry of High Elevation Streams in the Great Smoky Mountains", *Water, Air and Soil Pollution* 72, 331-356.

Cornett, Zane J. [1995], "Birch Seeds, Leadership, and a Relationship with the Land," *Journal of Forestry* 93,9: 6-11.

Davidson, Donald [1946], *The Tennessee, Volume I: The Old River, Frontier to Secession*, New York, Reinhart & Company.

Davidson, Donald [1948], *The Tennessee, Volume II: The New River, Civil War to TVA*, New York, Reinhart & Company.

Davis, Marti [1995], "Fading Oak Population in Need of a Little Help," *Knoxville News-Sentinel*, October 30, B1.

Davis, Stacy C. and Patricia S. Hu [1991], *Transportation Energy Data Book*, 11th ed., Oak Ridge, January.

Dean, Jerry [1995], "Knox Waterfront Project Soon Will Take Shape," *Knoxville News-Sentinel*, Oct 30, A1, A3.

Dean, Jerry [1996a], "Feelings Run High on Pumped Storage at Sequatchie," *Knoxville News-Sentinel*, August 11, A1.

Dean, Jerry [1996b], "TVA's Debt Has Increased $9.2 Billion in Past Decade," *Knoxville News-Sentinel*, October 6, B1.

Dean, Jerry [1996c], "Wetlands, Commerce, Clash in West Knox," *Knoxville News-Sentinel*, March 31, A1, A7.

Dickens, Roy S., Jr. [1976], *Cherokee Prehistory: The Pisgah Phase in the Appalachian Summit Region*, Knoxville, University of Tennessee Press.

Dinkins, G. R. and P. W. Shute [in press], "Life Histories of *Noturus baileyi* and N. flavipinnis (Pisces: Ictaluridae), Two Rare Madtom Catfishes in Citico Creek, Monroe County, Tennessee, Bulletin of the Alabama Museum of Natural History.

Dodd, C. Kenneth [in preparation], "Imperiled Amphibians: A Historical Perspective," in Benz and Collins.

Dorman-Hickson, Nancy [1994], "The Mood of Agriculture 1994," *Progressive Farmer*, May, 16-19.

Dosser, Ralph [1989], "State Officials Probe Possible Waste Spill at Knox Firm," *Knoxville Journal*, March 24, 3A.

Dosser, Ralph [1991], "Knox Sees Harmful Ozone Levels," *Knoxville Journal*, January 8, p. 1.

DRI/McGraw-Hill & IC2 [1996], *21st Century Jobs Initiative: Building the Foundations for a 21st Century Economy*, Summary Final Report, February.

Duffy, David Cameron [1993], "Seeing the Forest for the Trees," *Conservation Biology* 7,2: 436-439.

Duffy, David Cameron and Meier, Albert J. [1992], "Do Appalachian Herbaceous Understories Ever Recover from Clearcutting?", *Conservation Biology* 6,2: 196-201.

Durning, Alan Thein [1992], *How Much is Enough? The Consumer Society and the Future of the Earth*, New York, W.W. Norton & Company.

Durning, Alan Thein [1993], *Saving the Forests: What Will It Take?*, World Watch Paper 117, Washington, D.C., Worldwatch Institute.

Dykeman, Wilma [1955], *The French Broad*, Knoxville, University of Tennessee Press.

Eager, Daniel C. and Robert M. Hatcher, eds. [1980], *Tennessee's Rare Wildlife, Volume I: The Vertibrates*, Tennessee Wildlife Resources Agency.

Eaher, C. and M.B. Adams [1992], *Ecology and Decline of Red Spruce in the Eastern United States*, New York, Springer-Verlag.

Emrich, Grover H. and Gary L. Merritt [1969], "Effects of Mine Drainage on Groundwater," *Groundwater* 7,3: 27-32.

EPA (Environmental Protection Agency) [1980], *Effects of Underground Coal Mining on Ground Water in the Eastern United States*, Cincinnati.

EPA [1994], *Federal Disincentives: A Study of Federal Tax Subsidies and Other Programs Affecting Virgin Industries and Recycling*, Office of Policy Analysis, (EPA 230-R-94-005).

EPA [1995a], *1993 Toxics Release Inventory: Public Data Release* (EPA 745-R-95-010).

EPA [1995b], *1993 Toxics Release Inventory: Public Data Release State Fact Sheets*, (EPA 745-F-95-002).

EPA [1995c], *National Air Pollution Emission Trends 1900-1994* (EPA-454/R-95-011).

EPA [1996a], *Environmental Fact Sheet: Recycling Municipal Solid Waste: 1995 Facts and Figures* (EPA530-F-96-034).

EPA [1996b], *Characterization of Municipal Solid Waste in the United States: 1995 Update*, March (EPA530-R-96-001).

Erlich, Paul R., David S. Dobkin, and Darryl Wheye [1988], *The Birder's Handbook*, New York, Simon & Schuster.

ETDD (East Tennessee Development District) [1995], *Evaluation and Update of the Transportation Plan*, Knoxville, May.

Etnier, David A. [1994], "Our Southeastern Fishes—What Have We Lost and What Are We Likely to Lose," *Southeastern Fishes Council Proceedings* 29, 5-9.

Etnier, David A. [in preparation], "Jeapordized Southeastern Fishes—A Search for Causes," in Benz and Collins.

Etnier, David A. and Wayne C. Starnes [1993], *The Fishes of Tennessee*, Knoxville, University of Tennessee Press.

Ferguson, Bruce K. [1991], "Urban Stream Reclamation,"*Journal of Soil and Water Conservation*, 46, 5: 324-328.

Fisher, Stephen L. and Mary Harnish [1981], "Losing a Bit of Ourselves: the Decline of the Small Farmer," *Proceedings of the 1980 Appalachian Studies Conference*, Appalachia Consortium Press, 68-88.

Fishman, Jack, and Robert Kalish [1990] *Global Alert: The Ozone Pollution Crisis*, New York, Plenum Press.

Flynn, John [1995], "Forest Death in Coal River Valley," *Earth Island Journal*, Fall 1995, 27.

Foothills News: The Newsletter of the Foothills Land Conservancy [1996], 4, 1 (Summer).

Frosch Robert [1994], "Industrial Ecology: Minimizing the Impact of Industrial Waste," *Physics Today* 47,11 (November): 63-68.

Gabbard, Alex [1993], "Coal Combustion: Nuclear Resource or Danger?" Oak Ridge, *Oak Ridge National Laboratory Review*, Number Three and Four.

Garland, Ken [1996], "Koella, TDOT Announce Funding for 16 Road Plans," *The Knoxville News-Sentinel*, July 19, A1, A6.

Gaventa, John [1984],. "Land Reform in Appalachia," in Charles Geisler and Frank Popper, eds., *Land Reform, American Style*, Totowa, New Jersey, Rowman and Allanheld, 233-244.

Gaventa, John [1994], "The Political Economy of Land Tenure: Appalachia and the Southeast," presented at *"Who Owns America? Land Tenure and Resource Tenure Issues in a Changing Environment,"* conference, Land Tenure Center, University of Wisconsin, Madison, June 21-24.

Geisel, Amy and Pam Park [1995], "Labor Shortage Cramps Firms' Expansion Plans," *Knoxville News-Sentinel*, June 25, D1.

Gertler, Nicholas and John R. Ehrenfeld [1996], "A Down-to-Earth Approach to Clean Production," *Technology Review* 99, 2 (February/March): 48-54.

Gittleman, J. L. and S. L. Pimm [1991], "Crying Wolf in North America," *Nature* 351, 524-525.

Goldstein, Jerome [1995], "Ecoindustrial Parks Based on Waste Reduction," *BioCycle* 36, 1 (January): 8.

Goldstein, Jerome, ed. [1996a], "Small Business in Appalachia," *In Business* 18, 4 (July/August), 6.

Goldstein, Jerome, ed. [1996b], "Training Artisans in Appalachia," *In Business* 18, 5 (September/October), 7.

Goodland, Robert, Herman Daly, and Salah El Serafy, eds. [1992], *Population, Technology and Lifestyle: The Transition to Sustainability*, Washington D.C., Island Press.

Goodstein, Eban [1989], "Landownership, Development, and Poverty in Southern Appalachia", *The Journal Of Developing Areas*, (July), 519-534.

Gordon, Deborah [1991], *Steering a New Course: Transportation, Energy, and the Environment*, Washington, Island Press.

Grant, K. P. and H. E. Licht [1993], "Effects of Ultraviolet Radiation on Life History Parameters of Frogs from Ontario, Canada," *Abstracts, Second World Congress of Herpetology, Adelaide, Australia*, 101.

Greater Knoxville Chamber of Commerce [undated], "Demographic Profile: Population Characteristics of Knoxville, Knox County, and the Knoxville MSA."

Grimac, Roberto [1996], "TVA Gets 'Lemon Award' for Worst Energy Ad in U.S.," *Tennessee Green*, Spring 1996, 7.

Gwin, S.E. and M.E. Kentula [1990], *Wetland Mitigation Effectiveness*, Corvalis, Oregon, U.S. EPA.

Haavelmo, Trygve and Stein Hansen [1992], "On the Strategy of Trying to Reduce Economic Inequality by Expanding the Scale of Human Activity," in Goodland, *et al.* 1992, 38-51.

Hahn, Hermann H. and Pfeifer, Rudiger [1994], "The Contribution of Parked Vehicle Emissions to the Pollution of Urban Run-Off," *Science Total Environment*, May 23.

Hara et. al. [undated], *Regional Assessment of Climate Change Impacts in the Southeast Summary of Workshop I - Vulnerable Resources and Predictive Capabilities*, Center for Global Environmental Studies and Environmental Science Division, Oak Ridge National Laboratory.

Harmon, John [1995], "Around the South, Creeping Development: 27-Mile Road Will Open to Tourists a Remote Area of North Carolina," *The Atlanta Journal* and *The Atlanta Constitution*, June 17.

Hartley-McAndrew, Deborah [1995], "FutureScapes of Pittman Center," *Scenic Tennessee*, Summer.

Hatcher, Bob [1996], "Endangered Species: We CAN Make a Difference," *Tennessee Wildlife* 19,6: 25-27.

Hawken, Paul [1993], *The Ecology of Commerce: A Declaration of Sustainability*, New York, Harper Collins.

Hightower, Jim [1976], *Eat Your Heart Out: Food Profiteering in America*, New York, Vintage Books.

Himebaugh, Glenn A. [1992], "Battling for Survival: Tennessee's Flying Mammals Face Long Odds," *The Tennessee Conservationist* 58,6: 23-28.

Hocker, Phillip M. [1993], "Mining and Materials Policy: A Micro-Introduction," Washington, D.C., Mineral Policy Center.

Hopps, Michael [1994], "Reforesting Appalachia's Coal Lands," *American Forests*, November/December, 40-45.

Horton, Billy D. [1993], "The Appalachia Land Ownership Study: Research and Citizen Action in Appalachia," in Park, et al., *Voices of Change,* Westport, Connecticut, Bergin and Garvey.

Hudson, Charles [1970], "The Cherokee Concept of Natural Balance," *The Indian Historian* 3, 51-54.

Hudson, Charles [1976], *The Southeastern Indians*, Knoxville, University of Tennessee Press.

Irwin, Hugh [1996], *Tennessee's Mountain Treasures: The Unprotected Wildlands of the Cherokee National Forest*, Washington, D.C., The Wilderness Society.

Jaffe, Mark [1995] "Study Shows 10 Percent of Cars Cause 50 Percent of Auto Pollution," *The Philadelphia Inquirer*, May 18.

Jeavons, John [1991], *How to Grow More Vegetables*, revised ed., Berkeley, Ten Speed Press.

Jenkins, R. E., and N. M. Birkhead [1984], "Description, Biology, and Distribution of the Spotfin Chub, Hybopsis monacha, a Threatened Cyprinid Fish of the Tennessee River Drainage, *Bulletin of the Alabama Museum of Natural History* 8: 1-30.

Jenkins, R. E., and N. M. Birkhead [1993], *Freshwater Fishes of Virginia*, Bethesda, Maryland, American Fisheries Society.

Johnson, A. Sydney, William M. Ford, and Philip E. Hale [1993], "The Effects of Clearcutting on Herbaceous Understories Are Still Not Fully Known," *Conservation Biology* 7,2: 433-435.

Johnson, D.W. and S.E. Lindberg [1992], *Atmospheric Deposition and Forest Nutrient Cycling: A Synthesis of the Integrated Forest Study*, New York, Springer Verlag.

Johnson, D.W. [1993], "Foliar Response of Red Spruce Saplings to Fertilization with Calcium and Magnesium in the Great Smoky Mountain National Park," *Canadian Journal of Forest Research*, 23,1.

Johnson, Rebecca L. [1993], *Investigating the Ozone Hole*, Minneapolis, Lerner.

Kauffman, Betsy [1988], "Ridge Scientists to Test Fish," *Knoxville News-Sentinel*, July 17, A2.

Kauffman, Betsy [1995a], "Long-Abused Knox Waterways Await Annual River Rescue, Years of Fixing," *Knoxville News-Sentinel*, March 26, A1.

Kauffman, Betsy [1995b], "Understanding Called Key to Improving Lakes," *Knoxville News-Sentinel*, March 26, A1.

Kauffman, Betsy [1995c], "State's Water Quality is Not Rising: Problems are Greatest in East Tennessee," *Knoxville News-Sentinel*, May 22, A1.

Keesler, William [1991], *The Appalachian Environment: Protecting Our Air, Land, and Water*, University of Kentucky and Berea College Brushy Fork Institute, Appalachian Civic Leadership Project.

K/KCMPC (Knoxville/Knox County Metropolitan Planning Commission) [1994], *Development Impacts on Drainage Basins*.

Kornegay, F.C., et. al. [1991], *Oak Ridge Reservation Environmental Report for 1990*, ES/ESH-18/V1, Department of Energy, Oak Ridge.

Knoepp, Jennifer Donaldson and Wayne T. Swank [1994], "Long-Term Soil Chemistry Changes in Aggrading Forest Ecosystems," *Soil Science Society of America Journal* 58,2: 325-331.

Knox County Solid Waste Department [undated], "Knox County Trash Truths & Trivia: A Pocket Primer," Knoxville.

Knox Solid Waste Planning Region [1994], "Municipal Solid Waste Regional Plan," Knoxville.

Knox Solid Waste Planning Region [1996], "Regional Solid Waste Plan Annual Progress Report (January 1, 1995, through December 31, 1995)," Knoxville.

Krugman, Paul [1996], "The Spiral of Inequality," *Mother Jones* (Nov/Dec), 44-49.

Krupa, S.V. and W.J. Manning [1988], "Atmospheric Ozone: Formation and Effects on Vegetation," *Environmental Pollution* 50, 101-137.

Kuznik, Frank [1993], "America's Aching Mussels," *National Wildlife*, October-November, 34-38.

LeBlanc, David C., N. S. Nicholas, and S. M. Zedaker [1992], "Prevalence of Individual-Tree Growth Decline in Red Spruce Populations of the Southern Appalachian Mountains," *Canadian Journal of Forest Research* 22,6: 905-914.

Lennon, R. E., and P. S. Parker [1959], *The Reclamation of Indian and Abrams Creeks, Great Smoky Mountains National Park*, U.S. Fish and Wildlife Service Special Scientific Report 306

Lenssen, Nicholas and David Malin Roodman [1995], "Making Better Buildings," in Lester Brown, et al., *State of the World 1995*, New York, W. W. Norton, 95-112.

Leopold, Aldo [1966], *A Sand County Almanac with Essays on Conservation from Round River*, New York, Ballentine Books.

LeQuire, Elise [1995], "Cookin' Up Compost: Knox, Blount Programs Reduce Organic Wastes Differently," *Tennessee Green*, Summer, 7.

LeQuire, Elise [1996], "Pay-As-You-Throw Pricing Relieves Burden on Landfills," *InSITES*, Knoxville, University of Tennessee Waste Management Research and Education Institute, 2.

Levinson, Richard A. [1995], "Smoke-Free America is Healthier America," *Forum for Applied Research and Public Policy* 10,3 (Fall).

Likens, G. E., F. H. Borman, R. S. Pierce, and W. A. Reiners [1978], "Recovery of a Deforested Ecosystem," *Science* 199, 492-495.

Lin, N.-H. and V.K. Saxena [1991], "In-Cloud Scavenging and Deposition of Sulfates and Nitrates: Case Studies and Parametrization", *Atmospheric Environment* 25a,10: 2301-2320.

Little, Charles E. [1992], "Report from Lucy's Woods," *American Forests*, March/April, 25 ff.

Little, Charles E. [1995],*The Dying of the Trees: The Pandemic in America's Forests*, New York, Viking.

Locker, Mary [1991], "Tennessee Trash: The State's New Solid Waste Management Plan," The Tennessee Conservationist, 57,6: 15-17.

Long, L. E., L. S. Saylor, and M. E. Soulé [1995], "A pH/UV-B Synergism in Amphibians," *Conservation Biology* 9, 1301-1303.

Loy, Wesley [1996], "Havoc in the Honeybee Hives," *Knoxville News-Sentinel*, June 30, p. A1.

Ludyanskiy, Michael L., Derek McDonald, and David MacNeill [1993], "Impact of the Zebra Mussel, a Bivalve Invader," *Bioscience*, September, 533-544.

Lutes, Christopher C., Raymond J. Thomas, and Renee Burnette [1994], *Evaluation of Emissions from Paving Asphalts*, EPA Office of Research and Development (EPA-600/R-94-135).

Male, Sue A. [1984], *The Tennessee Food System: Planning for Regeneration*, Emmaus, Pennsylvania, Rodale Press.

Malm, W. C. [1992], "Visibility and Acid Aerosols at Great Smoky Mountains National Park," in *Proceedings of the SAMAB Forum on Air Quality Management in the Southern Appalachian Class I Areas*, Air Quality Division, National Park Service, CIRA-Foothills Campus, Colorado State University, Fort Collins, Colorado.

Mansfield, Duncan [1996], "DOE Picks Watts Bar Plant for Tritium Testing," *Knoxville News-Sentinel*, August 11, B1.

Mansfield, Duncan [1997], "TVA's Crowell Tells Congress: Keep Your Money," *The Tennessean*, Nashville, January 22.

Martin, Calvin [1978], *Keepers of the Game: Indian-Animal Relationships and the Fur Trade*, Berkeley, University of California Press.

Mathews, R. C., Jr., and E. L. Morgan [1982], "Toxicity of Anakeesta Formation Leachates to Shovel-Nosed Salamander, Great Smoky Mountains National Park, *Journal of Environmental Quality* 11, 102-106.

Matlack, Glenn [1994], "Plant Demography, Land-Use History, and the Commercial Use of Forests," *Conservation Biology* 8,1: 298-299.

Matthiessen, Peter [1983], *In the Spirit of Crazy Horse*, New York, Viking.

Mayor's Solid Waste Task Force [1991], *Solid Waste Management for Knoxville*, Knoxville.

McClure, Alan D. [1995], "Zebras 'Mussel' Their Way into the Tennessee Valley," *EnviroLink*, Chattanooga, 9-10.

McDade, Arthur [1993], "Cry of the Red Wolf," *The Tennessee Conservationist* 59,2: 18-22.

McFadden, John, and John E. Sherman [1991], *Tennessee's Groundwater: A Resource at Risk*, Nashville, Tennessee Environmental Council.

McKinney, Melonee [1995], "Tourism Possibilities Debated," *Knoxville News-Sentinel*, June 25, D4.

McKinney, Michael and Robert M. Schoch [1996], *Environmental Science: Systems and Solutions*, Minneapolis, West Publishing Co.

McLaughlin, Samuel B., C. P. Anderson, P. J. Hanson, M. G. Tjoelker, and W.K. Roy [1991], "Increased Dark Respiration and Calcium Deficiency of Red Spruce in Relation to Acidic Deposition at High-Elevation Southern Appalachian Mountain Sites," *Canadian Journal of Forest Research* 21,8: 1234-1244.

McLaughlin, Samuel B., Mark G. Tjoelker, and W.K. Roy [1993], "Acid Deposition Alters Red Spruce Physiology: Laboratory Studies Support Field Observations," *Canadian Journal of Forest Research* 23.3: 380-386.

McLaughlin, S.B. [1994] "Two Hundred Year Variation of Southern Red Spruce Radial Growth as Estimated by Spectral Analysis," *Canadian Journal of Forest Research*, 24,11.

McMahon, James P. [1990], "Creating an Industrial Ecology," *Environmental Decisions* 2,4, (August): 18-21.

Merck Family Fund [1995], "Yearning for Balance, July 1995: Views of Americans on Consumption, Materialism, and the Environment," report prepared by the Harwood Group.

Mermel, T.W., ed. [1958], *Register of Dams in the United States*, New York, McGraw-Hill.

Merrifield, Juliet [1982], "Ailing in Appalachia," *Mine Talk* 12,9: 15-21.

Mikesell, Raymond [1992], "Project Evaluation and Sustainable Development" in Goodland *et al.* 1992, pp. 80-89.

Miller, S. G., S. P. Bratton, and J. Hadidian [1992], "Impacts of White-Tailed Deer on Endangered and Threatened Vascular Plants," *Natural Areas Journal* 12, 67-74.

MMES (Martin Marietta Energy Systems) [1995], *Environmental Update*, Spring Issue, Oak Ridge.

Mollison, B. [1995], *Introduction to Permaculture*, Tyalgum, Australia, Tagari Publishers.

Mooney, James [1900], "The Cherokee River Cult," *The Journal of American Folklore* 13, 1-10.

Mooney, James [1982], *Myths of the Cherokee and Sacred Formulas of the Cherokees*, Charles and Randy Booksellers.

Morton, Peter A. [1994], *The Living Landscape, Volume 5, Charting a New Course: National Forests in the Southern Appalachians*, Washington, D.C., The Wilderness Society.

Moss, Tom [1993], "Sinking Ground: Karst Topography is Mother Nature's Plumbing System," *The Tennessee Conservationist*, 59,1: 6-9.

Mullican, Harold N., Ralph M. Sinclair, and Billy G. Isom, [1960], "A Survey of Aquatic Biota of the Nolichucky River," Nashville, Tennessee Stream Pollution Control Board, Tennessee Department of Public Health.

Mundy, Darrell, M.D. [1995] "Tobacco Farmers Face Political, Economic Challenges," *Tennessee Farm Bureau News Supplement* 74, 9 (November).

Munger, Frank [1996], "Critics Fume Over Out-of-State Waste: Shipments to Ridge Called 'Outrageous'," *Knoxville News Sentinel*, November 11, A1.

Munger, Frank [1996b], "ORNL Director Warns Future of Lab is Uncertain," *The Knoxville News-Sentinel*, December 13, A6.

Murdock, Nora A. [1994], "Rare and Endangered Plants and Animals of Southern Appalachian Wetlands", *Water, Air and Soil Pollution* 77, 385-405.

Murray, Doug [1995], "Clear-cutting Begins in Campbell County," *Tennessee Green* 9, Summer.

Nadis, Steve and James J. MacKenzie [1993], *Car Trouble*, Boston, Beacon Press.

NADP (National Atmospheric Deposition Program) [1991], NADP/NTN Annual Data Summary, Precipitation Chemistry in the U.S. - 1990, Ft. Collins, CO, Natural Resource Ecology Laboratory.

NADP (National Atmospheric Deposition Program) [1993], NADP/NTN Annual Data Summary, Precipitation Chemistry in the U.S. - 1992, Ft. Collins, CO, Natural Resource Ecology Laboratory.

National Recycling Coalition [1996], "Recovery of Major Packaging Materials in MSW 1990-2000, A Briefing Paper from the National Recycling Coalition, Policy Research Committee, Economic Systems Subcommittee, Industry Core Team," 8/23/96.

NCDEM (North Carolina Division of Environmental Management) [1995], *French Broad River Basinwide Water Quality Management Plan* (Draft), Water Quality Section, Raleigh.

Neely, Jack [1994], "Where Dolly meets Dali: Pigeon Forge's Surrealism Was Painted in Commercial Hues," *Metro Pulse* 4,11 (June 3-17), Knoxville.

Neves, Richard J., Arthur E. Bogan, James D. Williams, Steven A. Ahlstedt, and Paul W. Harrfield [in preparation], "Status of Aquatic Mollusks in the Southeastern United States: A Downward Spiral of Diversity," in Benz and Collins.

Newman, Brownie, Hugh Irwin, Karen Lowe, Aimée Mostwill, Stephen Smith, and Jesse Jones [1992], "Southern Appalachians Wildlands Proposal," *Wild Earth Special Issue: Plotting a North American Wilderness Recovery Strategy*, 46-60.

Newman, Brownie [1995], "Biodiversity Project Hosts Forum on Mining; Miners Make Move on Chauga Gorge," Asheville, *Wild Mountain Times*, Spring/Summer, 7.

Nolt, John [1995], *Down to Earth: Toward a Philosophy of Nonviolent Living*, Washburn, Tennessee, Earth Knows Publications.

Noss, Reed F. and Allen Y. Cooperrider [1994], *Saving Nature's Legacy: Protecting and Restoring Biodiversity*, Washington, D.C., Island Press.

NPS (National Park Service) [1995], *Smokies Guide*, Gatlinburg, Tennessee, Summer issue.

NPS [1996a], *Smokies Guide*, Gatlinburg, Tennessee, Summer issue.

NPS [1996b], "Summary of Forest Insect and Disease Impacts, Great Smoky Mountains National Park, May 1, 1996."

Opie, John [1981], "Where American History Began: Appalachia and the Small Independent Family Farm," *Proceedings of the 1980 Appalachian Studies Conference*, Appalachia Consortium Press, 58-67.

OREP (Oak Ridge Education Project) [1992], "A Citizen's Guide to Oak Ridge," Knoxville, Foundation for Global Sustainability.

OREP [1996], "Local Groups Look at Incinerators," *Oak Ridge Environmental Peace Alliance Newsletter*, March, 3.

Paine, Anne [1996], "TVA Proposing Shoreline Growth," Nashville, *The Tennessean*, July 16, 1D.

Papacostas, C.S., and Prevedouros, P.D. [1993], *Transportation Engineering and Planning*, 2nd ed., Englewood Cliffs, Prentice-Hall.

Park, Pam [1992], "Knoxville Has Troubled Waters: Sewage, Trash, Oil Run High," *Knoxville News-Sentinel*, June 21, A1.

Park, Pam [1995a], "Jobs: A Plan for the Future," *Knoxville News-Sentinel*, May 28, D1, D4.

Park, Pam [1995b], "Getting High-tech on Track," *Knoxville News-Sentinel*, June 25, D1, D4.

Park, Pam [1995c], "Forest Group Aims to Polish Logging's Image," *Knoxville News-Sentinel*, June 25, D1, D4.

Park, Pam [1996a], "Survey Had Input from Regional Leaders," *Knoxville News-Sentinel*, February 11, D1, D5.

Park, Pam [1996d] "Philips Sells its Plants in Green County," *Knoxville News-Sentinel*, December 10, A1, A3.

Park, Pam [1996c], "Alpine to Employ 2,700 at its Green Facilities," *Knoxville News-Sentinel*, December 11, A1.

Parker, Warren and Laura Dixon [1980], *Endangered and Threatened Wildlife of Kentucky, North Carolina, South Carolina, and Tennessee*, North Carolina Agricultural Extension Service.

Paton, Peter W. C. [1994], "The Effect of Edge on Avian Nest Success: How Strong is the Evidence?" *Conservation Biology* 8,1: 17-26.

Pearson, Scott [1994], "Landscape-Level Processes and Wetland Conservation in the Southern Appalachian Mountains", *Water, Air and Soil Pollution* 77, 321-332.

Peck, Mike, Gary Cole and Carl Smith [1979], "Acid-Mine-Water Problems in Northern Appalachia," *Mountain State Geology*, December 1979, 16-19.

Peine, John D., J. C. Randolph, and James J. Presswood, Jr. [1995] "Evaluating the Effectiveness of Air Quality Management Within the Class I Area of Great Smoky Mountains National Park,." *Environmental Management* 19, 515-26.

Petranka, James W., Matthew E. Eldridge, and Katherine E. Haley [1993], "Effects of Timber Harvesting on Southern Appalachian Salamanders," *Conservation Biology* 7, 363-370.

Petranka, James W. [1994], "Response to Impact of Timber Harvesting on Salamanders," *Conservation Biology* 8, 302-304.

Platt, Brenda, Christine Doherty, Anne Claire Broughton, and David Morris [1991], *Beyond 40 Percent: Record-Setting Recycling and Composting Programs*, Washington, D.C., Institute for Local Self-Reliance.

Political Ecology Group [1994], *Toxic Empire: The WMX Corporation, Hazardous Waste, and Global Strategies for Environmental Justice*, Tides Foundation.

Powell, Robert [1995], "Tennessee Department of Environment and Conservation: Division of Superfund: Promulgated Sites as of August 1, 1995," Tennessee Department of Environment and Conservation, Nashville.

Powelson, Richard [1996], "Critics Hope to Capsize Shoreline Options," *Knoxville News-Sentinel*, July 19, A1, A6.

Raven, Peter H., Linda R. Berg, and George B. Johnson [1993], *Environment*, Fort Worth, Saunders College Publishing.

Ray, W.K. [1993] "Acid Deposition Alters Red Spruce Physiology," *Canadian Journal of Forest Research*, 23, 1.

Reganold, John [1989], "Farming's Organic Future," *New Scientist*, June 10, 49-52.

Renfro, James R. [1996], "Air Quality Monitoring and Research Program at Great Smoky Mountains National Park: An Overview of Results and Findings," Gatlinburg, TN, USDI-National Park Service, Great Smoky Mountains National Park, Division of Resource Management and Science.

Richter, Andreas R., Stephen R. Humphrey, James B. Cope, and Virgil Black, Jr. [1993], "Modified Cave Entrances: Thermal Effect on Body Mass and Resulting Decline in Endangered Indiana Bats (*Myotis solalis*)," Conservation Biology 7,2: 407-415.

RiverValley Partners [1995], "Eco-Industrial Park Initiative: A Model For Sustainable Development," status report to the Eco-Industrial Park Team of the President's Council on Sustainable Development, Chattanooga, February.

Robbins, John [1987], *Diet for a New America*, Walpole, New Hampshire, Stillpoint Press.

"Robertshaw Controls Ordered to Stop Dumping Oil into Creek" [1989]. *Knoxville News-Sentinel*, December 7, p. 10A.

Robichaud, P. R. and T. A. Waldrop [1994], "A Comparison of Surface Runoff and Sediment Yields from Low- and High-Severity Site Preparation Burns," *Water Resources Bulletin*, 30,1: 27-34.

Roosevelt, Theodore [1901], *Message from the President of the United States Transmitting a Report of the Secretary of Agriculture in Relation to the Forests, Rivers, and Mountains of the Southern Appalachian Region*, Washington, D.C., Government Printing Office.

Ross, Jack Winfield [1993a], "Tennessee Vanquished and Vanished Wildlife," *The Tennessee Conservationist*, 59,3: 8-11.

Ross, Jack Winfield [1993a], "Tennessee Wildlife on the Comeback Trail," *The Tennessee Conservationist*, 59,5: 24-28.

Ross, John [1994] "An Aquatic Invader is Running Amok in U.S. Waterways," *Smithsonian* February, 41-50.

SAMAB (Southern Appalachian Man and the Biosphere Cooperative) [1996a], *Southern Appalachian Assessment* Summary Report.

SAMAB [1996b], *Southern Appalachian Assessment Aquatic Technical Report.*

SAMAB [1996c], *Southern Appalachian Assessment Atmospheric Technical Report.*

SAMAB [1996d], *Southern Appalachian Assessment Social/Cultural/Economic Technical Report.*

SAMAB [1996e], *Southern Appalachian Assessment Terrestrial Technical Report.*

Sanders, Gregory [1992], *The Role of Fire in the Regeneration of Table Mountain Pine in the Southern Appalachian Mountains*, unpublished master's thesis, University of Tennessee, Knoxville.

Satterfield, Jamie [1996], "Tightening Competition Urges Big Rigs to Speed," *Knoxville News-Sentinel*, November 18, A1.

Savits, Jacqueline D., Christopher Campbell, Richard Wiles, and Carolyn Hartmann [1996], *Dishonorable Discharge: Toxic Pollution of Tennessee Waters*, Washington, D.C., Environmental Working Group.

Searfoss, Deborah [1995], "Mountains Mourning: Pest Invaders Threaten Tennessee's Trees," *Tennessee Green* 9, Summer.

Selcraig, Bruce [1996]. "What You Don't Know Can Hurt You," *Sierra* 82,1: 38-43 and 94-95.

Shimek, Susie [1994], "Your Home May Hide a Silent Killer," *The Tennessee Conservationist* 60,1: 15-22.

Silsbee, D.G. and G.L. Larson [1982], "Water Quality of Streams in the Great Smoky Mountains National Park," *Hyrdobiologia* 89, 97-115.

Simmons, Morgan [1995a], "Eco-Tourism: Cocke County Foresees its Future Based on Luring New Kind of Tourist," *Knoxville News-Sentinel*, September 17, A-1, A10.

Simmons, Morgan [1995d], "Beavers' Spread in E. Tennessee Triggers a Flap," *Knoxville News-Sentinel*, October 22, B2, B5.

Simmons, Morgan [1997], "Pollution Hurts Cocke Economy, Official Says," *Knoxville News-Sentinel*, January 18, A1, A3.

Smith, Arthur [1993], "Current Transportation Policies Threaten Our Future," *Oikos: Newsletter of the Sierra Club's Southern Appalachian Highlands Region*, 1,4: 14-15.

Smith, Kelly D [1996], "Knoxville is Heavenly; The Big Apple Is Hellish," *Money*, January.

Smith, Wilbur, and Associates [1996], "Roadway Network Analysis and Traffic Impact Study: Lovell Road/Campbell Station Road Environs, Knox County, Tennessee," report prepared for Turkey Creek Land Partners LLC and Farragut Land Partners LLC.

Snodgrass, W. R. [1996], *Tennessee's Trash in the 1990's*, Nashville, Comptroller of the Treasury, Office of Research.

SOCM (Save Our Cumberland Mountains) [1992a], *Does Reclamation Work?: A Study of Water Quality at Reclaimed Stripmine Sites in the Sewanee Coal Seam of Tennessee*, Lake City, Tennessee.

SOCM [1992b], *Stripmining in Tennessee after Seven Tears of Federal Enforcement: A Review of the Enforcement Record of the Office of Surface Mining Reclamation and Enforcement*, Lake City, Tennessee.

SOCM [1994], "Hamblen County Residents Win Water after 15 Month Fight," *The SOCM Sentinel*, November/December.

SOCM [1995], *1994 SOCM Annual Report*, Lake City, Tennessee.

SOCM [1996], *1995 SOCM Annual Report*, Lake City, Tennessee.

Squillace, Mark [1990], *Strip Mining Handbook*, Environmental Policy Institute and Friends of the Earth.

Stoddard, J. [1994], "Long-Term Changes in Watershed Retention of Nitrogen: Its Causes and Aquatic Consequences," in L. A. Baker, ed., *Environmental Chemistry of Lakes and Reservoirs*, Advances in Chemistry Series Number 237, Washington, D.C., American Chemical Society.

"Study Links Smoking to Breast Cancer" [1996], *Knoxville News-Sentinel*, June 3, p. B1.

Summerlin, Vernon [1995], "Chattanooga: Becoming 'The Environmental City'," *The Tennessee Conservationist* 58,5 (September/October): 14-17.

Swank, Wayne T. and D.A. Crossley, Jr., eds. [1987], *Forest Hydrology and Ecology at Coweeta*, New York, Springer-Verlag.

TACD (Tennessee Association of Conservation Districts) and TDA (Tennessee Department of Agriculture) [undated], *A Matter of Natural Resources* (pamphlet).

TDA (Tennessee Department of Agriculture) [1994], *Tennessee Agriculture 1994*, Nashville, July.

TDEC (Tennessee Department of Environment and Conservation) [1990], *Tennessee Erosion & Sediment Control Handbook*, Nashville.

TDEC [1994], *The Status of Water Quality in Tennessee: 1994 305(b) Report*, Division of Water Pollution Control, Nashville.

TDEC [1996a], *Tennessee's Environment: 25 Years of Progress*, Nashville.

TDEC [1996b], *Report on the 25% Waste Reduction Goal*, Nashville, Tennessee Department of Environment and Conservation, Division of Solid Waste Assistance.

TDES (Tennessee Department of Employment Security) [1994], *Tennessee Employment Projections 2005 Summary*, Occupational Employment Statistics Unit, Research and Statistics Division, Nashville, January.

TDOT (Tennessee Department of Transportation) [1994], *State Transportation Plan*, Nashville.

Terborgh, John [1992], "Why American Songbirds are Vanishing," *Scientific American*, May, 98-104.

Tetzeli, Rick [1993], "The New Promised Land: Tennessee?", *Fortune*, Feb 22.

Thackston, Edward L., William R. Miller, Daryl Durham [1991], "Checking our Progress: Tennessee Conservation League Tennessee Environmental Quality Index—1991," *The Tennessee Conservationist*, 57:7 (insert).

Thomas, Lois Reagan [1996], "Burley Demand Strong; '96 Crop Price Likely to Be High," *Knoxville News-Sentinel*, November 19, C1, C2.

Tinker, Tim, Georgia Moore, and Cynthia Lewis-Younger [1996], "Chattanooga Creek," *The Tennessee Conservationist* 62,1: 14-18.

Toops, Connie [1992], "Baiting the Bears," *National Parks*, November/December, 39-42.

Trimble, S. W. [1974], *Man-Induced Soil Erosion in the Southern Piedmont, 1700-1970*: Ankeny, Iowa, Soil Conservation Society of America.

TSPO (Tennessee State Planning Office) [1994], *Tennessee State Wetlands Conservation Strategy*.

TVA (Tennessee Valley Authority) [1963], *Nature's Constant Gift: A Report on the Water Resource of the Tennessee Valley*.

TVA [1983], *The First Fifty Years: Changed Land, Changed Lives*.

TVA [1987a], *Results of Fish Tissue Screening Studies from Sites in the Tennessee and Cumberland Rivers*, Chattanooga.

TVA [1987b], *TVA Handbook*, Mills, Debra D., ed., TVA/OCS/PS-87/8.

TVA [1989], *PCB Studies on Fish from Watts Bar, Fort Loudoun, Tellico, and Chilhowee Reservoirs—1987*, Chattanooga.

TVA [1991], *Reservoir Monitoring—1990 Summary of Vital Signs and Use Impairment Monitoring on Tennessee Valley Reservoirs*.

TVA [1992], *TVA Fiscal Year 1992 Statistical Report*, TVA document number 229051.

TVA [1994a], *RiverPulse: A Report on the Condition of the Tennessee River and Its Tributaries in 1993*.

TVA [1994b], *Tennessee Valley Authority 1994 Annual Report*.

TVA [1995a], *Energy Vision 2020: Integrated Resource Plan Environmental Impact Statement*, 3 vols.

TVA [1995b], *RiverPulse: A Report on the Condition of the Tennessee River and Its Tributaries in 1994*.

TVA [1996a], *Shoreline Management Initiative Draft Environmental Impact Statement*.

TVA [1996b], *Lake and Stream Conditions in the Clinch-Powell Watershed*.

TVA [1996c], *TVA River Neighbors*, Resource Group, September.

TVA, U. S. Army Corps of Engineers, and U.S. Fish and Wildlife Service [1993], *Final Environmental Impact Statement: Chip Mill Terminals on the Tennessee River*, vol 1.

UCAR (University Corporation for Atmospheric Research) [1991], *Southern Oxidants Study*, Georgia Tech. University.

USBC (U.S. Bureau of the Census) [1975], *Historical Statistics of the United States: Colonial Times to 1970*, Bicentennial Edition, Part I, Washington, D.C.

USBC [1984], *Statistical Abstracts of the United States*, 105th ed., Washington, D.C.

USBC [1992], *Census of Population and Housing, 1990*, County Demographic Data for Georgia, North Carolina, Tennessee, Virginia; Summary Tape File on CD-ROM, Washington, D.C.

USBC [1994], *1992 Census of Agriculture*, Vol. I., Part 42, Tennessee State and County Data, Washington, D.C.

USBC [1995], *Statistical Abstracts of the U.S.*, 115th ed., Washington, D.C.

USDOE (U.S. Department of Energy) [1993a], *Environmental Restoration and Waste Management Plan: Fiscal Years 1994-1998*, Government Printing Office, Washington, D.C.

USDOE [1993b], *Electricity from Biomass: Renewable Energy Today and Tomorrow*, Washington, D.C., Solar Thermal and Biomass Power Division, Office of Solar Energy Conversion.

USDOE [1996a], "Technical Evaluation Summary of the In Situ Vitrification Melt Expulsion at the Oak Ridge National Laboratory on April 21, 1996, Oak Ridge, Tennessee," Office of Environmental Management, Oak Ridge National Laboratory, ORNL/ER-374.

USDOE [1996b], *Remedial Investigation/Feasibility Study for the David Witherspoon, Inc., 901 Site, Knoxville, Tennessee*, Vol. I., Office of Environmental Restoration and Waste Management, Oak Ridge, DOE/OR/02-1503/V1&D1.

USGAO (United States General Accounting Office) [1995a] *Tennessee Valley Authority: Financial Problems Raise Questions About Long-term Viability*, Washington, DC. GAO/AIMD/RCED-95-134.

USGAO [1995b], "Fact Sheet for the Ranking Minority Member, Subcommittee on Interior and Related Agencies, Committee on Appropriations, House of Representatives, on the Forest Service, Distribution of Timber Sales Receipts, Fiscal Years 1992-1994," Washington, D.C., GAO/RCED-95-237FS.

Vubtila, Peter [1995], "Can We Overcome Automobile Dependence? Physical Planning in an Age of Urban Cynicism," *Cities*, February.

Walker, Tim [1991], "Dreissena Disaster: Scientists Battle an Invasion of Zebra Mussels." *Science News*, May 4, 282-284.

Watson, Aubrey [1994], "The Greening of Copper Basin," *The Tennessee Conservationist* 60,3: 21-26.

Watson, A. P. [1984], "Energy Analysis of the Coal Fuel Cycle in an Appalachian Coal County," *Human Ecology* 12,1: 65-86.

Watts, Ann DeWitt [1981], "Cities and Their Place in Southern Appalachia," *Appalachian Journal*, 8,2 (Winter): 105-118.

WCED (World Commission on Environment and Development) [1987], *Our Common Future*, Oxford, Oxford University Press.

Welty, Gus [1993], "Railroads and the Environment," *Railway Age* 194,2: 27-30.

White, Fred C., James R. Hairston, Wesley N. Musser, H.F. Perkins, and J.F. Reed [1980], "Relationship between Increased Crop Acreage and Nonpoint-Source Pollution, *Journal of Soil and Water Conservation* 36.3: 172-180.

Whitehead, Connie [1995], *The Perpetual Garden Calendar*, Planted Earth Press, Strawberry Plains, Tennessee.

Widner, Tim [1996], "First Results in Assessment of Iodine-131 Emissions," *Oak Ridge Health Studies Bulletin*, 5,2 (Fall).

Wigley, T. Bentley and Thomas H. Roberts [1994], "Forest Management and Wildlife in Forested Wetlands of the Southern Appalachians", *Water, Air and Soil Pollution* 77, 445-456.

Wilcove, David [1985], "Nest Predation in Forest Tracts and the Decline of Migratory Songbirds," *Ecology* 66, 1211-14.

Wilhelm, Gene, Jr. [1981], "Appalachia and the Third World: Eco-Development as an Alternative in the New Economic Order," *Proceedings of the 1980 Appalachian Studies Conference*, Appalachia Consortium Press, 34-43.

Williams, Michelle [1996], "Watts Bar Plant May Get NRC Go-Ahead Soon," *Chattanooga Free Press*, January 22, B2.

Wilson, A. D. and D. J. Shure [1993], "Plant Competition and Nutrient Limitation during Early Succession in the Southern Appalachian Mountains," *The American Midland Naturalist* 129, 1-9.

Yeakley, J.A., J.L. Meyer, and W.T. Swank [1994], "Hillslope Nutrient Flux During Near-Stream Vegetation Removal I. A Multi-Scaled Modeling Design", *Water, Air and Soil Pollution* 77, 33-50.

Young, John E. [1992], "Mining the Earth," Worldwatch Paper No. 109, Washington, D.C., Worldwatch Institute.

Young, John E. and Aaron Sachs [1995], "Creating a Sustainable Materials Economy," in Lester Brown, *et al.*, *State of the World 1995*, New York, W. W. Norton, 76-94.

"You've Come a Long Way, BASF" [1995], *EnviroLink*, September 1995, Chattanooga, Mary Walker & Associates.

Zeller, Janet Marsh [1996], "Champion's Pollution Game—Now You See It, Now You Don't!" *Wild Mountain Times*, Late Summer.